AGING AND PUBLIC HEALTH

AGING AND PUBLIC HEALTH

Technology and Demography: Parallel Evolutions

GARI LESNOFF-CARAVAGLIA, Ph.D., Editor

CHARLES C THOMAS · PUBLISHER, LTD.
Springfield · Illinois · U.S.A.

Published and Distributed Throughout the World by

CHARLES C THOMAS • PUBLISHER, LTD.
2600 South First Street
Springfield, Illinois 62704

©2001 by CHARLES C THOMAS • PUBLISHER, LTD.

ISBN 0-398-07214-0 (hard)
ISBN 0-398-07215-9 (paper)

Library of Congress Catalog Card Number: 2001027977

Printed in the United States of America
SR-R-3

Library of Congress Cataloging-in-Publication Data

Aging and public health : technology and demography-parallel evolutions / edited by Gari
Lesnoff-Caravaglia.
    p. cm.
  Includes bibliographical references and index.
  ISBN 0-398-07214-0 – ISBN 0-398-07215-9 (pbk.)
    1. Aged–Health and hygiene–United States. 2. Aged–United States–Social conditions.
3. Aged–Services for. 4. Aging–Psychological aspects. I. Lesnoff-Caravaglia, Gari.

RA564.8 .A397126 2001
362.1'9897'00973–dc21
                                                  2001027977

CONTRIBUTORS

Thomas A. Arcury, Ph.D., Associate Professor, Department of Family and Community Medicine, Wake Forest University School of Medicine, Winston-Salem, NC.

Laurence G. Branch, Ph.D., Professor, Center for the Study of Aging; Director, Long Term Care Research Program, Duke University Medical Center, Durham, NC.

Bob G. Knight, Ph.D., Merle H. Bansinger Professor, Andrus Gerontology Center, University of Southern California, Los Angeles, CA.

Gari Lesnoff-Caravaglia, Ph.D., Professor, School of Health Sciences, Ohio University, Athens, OH.

Michele L. Maines, NIA Predoctoral Trainee, Andrus Gerontology Center, University of Southern California, Los Angeles, CA.

Michele Morrone, Ph.D., R.S., Assistant Professor, School of Health Sciences, Ohio University, Athens, OH.

Sara A. Quandt, Ph.D., Professor, Section on Epidemiology, Department of Public Health Sciences, Wake Forest University School of Medicine, Winston-Salem, NC.

Ann Rathbun, Ph.D., Assistant Professor, School of Health Sciences, Ohio University, Athens, OH.

Timothy J. Ryan, Ph.D., CIH, CSP, Assistant Professor, School of Health Sciences, Ohio University, Athens, OH.

Katherine E. W. Will, Ph.D., L.N.H.A., R.D.H., Assistant Professor, School of Health Sciences, Ohio University, Athens, OH.

Namvar Zohoori, M.D., Ph.D., Senior Lecturer, Tropical Medicine Research Institute, University of the West Indies, Mona, Jamaica, and Department of Nutrition, Schools of Public Health and Medicine, and Carolina Population Center, University of North Carolina, Chapel Hill, NC.

PREFACE

The presence of an increasing older population occasions the need to reevaluate the meaning of life, death, and the lived experience. Aging does not occur in isolation but is a process that reflects societal attitudes and their practical outcomes. Since such practical responses are principally the purview of public health, this provides the inevitable link between the fields of aging and public health.

As the population continues to age, traditional concerns must expand from physical and biological concerns to incorporate social and behavioral perspectives. Professionals in the fields of aging and public health need to assess the nature of the increased panoply of services that must, perforce, be developed to match the requisites of such a population in a humane and cost-effective manner. Such considerations must take into account not only individual and generational differences, but the diversity resulting from particular groups and subgroups within the aging population. Such heterogeneity represents such factors as geography, disease, disability, and ethnicity.

Provision for persons ranging in ages from 70 to 125 is the challenge that confronts the aging world. Assistance through social and health programming must develop from an underlying understanding of the older population as consisting of individuals with long personal histories, whose needs continue to evolve in the face of the changing circumstances of their lives. Individuals age at differing rates, and their aging may be accommodated, made burdensome, or hastened depending upon the felt obligations and capabilities of a society to assume such responsibilities on their behalf. How one ages, when one ages, and why one ages are reflections of the societal milieu in which the process occurs.

The wide span of biological, psychosocial, environmental, and social influences that impinge on the aging process have particular relevance for a public health perspective on health and social issues in late adult life. In this book, there is systematically developed a significant link between such concerns and a perspective that unites these two fields. Their joint concerns are presented within the context of an examination of the contemporary situation, current needs, and future trends.

The book is further divided into seven sections, each dealing with a particular focus. The sections are preceded by an introductory chapter that provides a broad view of the demographic, mortality, and morbidity trends in an aging world. The manner in which lifestyle and the quality of life are interrelated is given particular attention. The effect of behavioral, social, and environmental risk factors on the morbidity and mortality of older populations lays the groundwork for the chapters that follow.

Section II addresses the biological aspects of aging and public health. Chapter 2 focuses on the life span and life expectancy, normal aging, premature aging, diseases in old age, and sensory loss. It covers the biological and disease aspects of aging and outlines the relationship between normal aging and premature aging brought on by heredity, disease, and environment. Health-risk factors, such as behavioral, social, psychological, and socioenvironmental, are highlighted. The relationship between technological advances and their influences upon lifestyle, life expectancy, and health care are also addressed. Chapter 3 discusses nutrition and older adults by examining food and nutrition recommendations, the physiological and psychological influences on nutritional status, and the socioeconomic and environmental influences on diet. Nutrition is also examined in light of the diversity among older groups and its effects upon health status and the prevalence of disability and disease.

Section III examines the psychosocial aspects of aging and public health. Chapter 4 covers the psychosocial parameters of aging and includes societal attitudes toward aging, the heterogeneity of the aging experience, and behavior and lifestyle as determinants of health. Chapter 5 deals specifically with mental health issues and the aging population covering such factors as gender and sex differences, death and bereavement, and suicide and life-threatening behavior.

Special population groups and public health concerns are the focus in Section IV. Chapter 6 describes the invisible elderly, persons who often fall outside the purview of health providers. Included in these special population groups are victims of family violence and self-neglect, as well as the single-room occupants or persons who withdraw from the mainstream of life and become passive observers of the world. Chapter 7 covers the problems presented by an increasing older prison population. The prison environment as a setting for aging is described, as well as special issues, such as the occurrence of suicide. The special needs and interest of the rural elderly provide the focus for Chapter 8. The access to services for an increasingly diverse, older population presents an additional challenge as does the greater geographic distribution of the older population across urban, suburban, and rural environments.

The prevention that occurs before the onset of disease can be instituted by controlling those environmental and behavioral factors associated with disease conditions. Serious physical injuries can also be controlled by specific prevention strategies. The environment as a significant factor that provides the background for aging is developed in Section V with Chapter 9 focusing on the environment itself, including air quality, communicable-disease control, infections, toxic agents, and food safety. The significant effects of air and water pollution on the older population are clearly delineated. The safety of the older adult population in the community is the theme of Chapter 10. Prevention strategies related to injuries resulting from a variety of sources, such as falls, automobile use, fire, and domestic mishaps, are described.

In Section VI, Chapter 11 examines the linkage between technology and the burgeoning presence of older adults. Attention is given to the potential alteration of environmental conditions, health care, and social services through technological applications. The security issues faced by an aging population are the focus of Chapter 12, including crimes perpetuated against the older population. Social problems that impinge upon the security of the elderly are also highlighted.

The market forces that have changed the structure and character of health care settings during the last decade or so have stimulated the initiation or expansion of a variety of services, including outpatient health services, services specifically for the chronically ill and aged, rehabilitation centers, and long-term-care and terminal-care services. Increased attention is being given to prevention as well as intervention with health-promotion centers established within communities and work sites. In Section VII, Chapter 13 covers the wide array of health services available to the older adult. Although the problems of an aging population are currently being addressed, the approach has been fragmented, inefficient, and uncoordinated. Many older persons still lack adequate care. The responses of public and private agencies to health services for the elderly is delineated, and attention is given to health care planning and the older population. It is patently clear there are methods to mitigate, delay, modify, or even prevent some of the disability associated with aging. The combined effects of interventions by all levels of government, private, and voluntary programs has had both positive and negative effects on the older population and health policies serving the elderly. Attention is also brought to bear on the fact that a public health approach to the study of aging requires an understanding of health and illness in later years, as well as appreciating the fact that the quality of life is an important measure of health status. Particular emphasis is given to the fact that many of the new efforts to address the health needs of an aging society will be based on political and fiscal considerations. The need for a national, public health agenda is accentuated due to the increasing numbers of older persons, as well as to the increasing diversity among the elderly and broad range of health conditions and disabilities.

The emphasis throughout this book is on the importance of an integration of both public health and aging to foster expanded services to deal with chronic disease and disability, secondary and tertiary prevention, a community orientation, and appropriate interventions for older persons. The health of the general population is now seen as a public concern and is no longer purely a private matter. Such resulting changes in perception derive from the growth of medical sciences and technology, the growing expectations and demands of the public, the escalating costs of health care, and the need to reduce the wide spectrum of barriers to care.

This book is designed to aid professionals and students in understanding the multiple forces that impinge on the health and social status of aging populations. This book is also an invaluable tool for policy makers, researchers, and practitioners in related fields who are interested in the well-being of the elderly.

GARI LESNOFF-CARAVAGLIA, PH.D.

CONTENTS

I. Introduction: Altering Perspectives on Aging and Public Health

II. Biological Aspects of Aging and Public Health

III. Psychosocial Aspects of Aging and Public Health

IV. Special Population Groups and Public Health

V. Environmental Aspects of Aging and Public Health

VI. Technology and Aging

VII. Health Services and the Older Adult

AGING AND PUBLIC HEALTH

I. INTRODUCTION: ALTERING PERSPECTIVES ON AGING AND PUBLIC HEALTH

Chapter 1

THE AGING WORLD

LAURENCE G. BRANCH

THE WORLD WAS MARKEDLY DIFFERENT at the turn of the twenty-first century from what it was at the turn of the twentieth century. It is estimated that one-half all the people in the history of the world who have reached age sixty-five are alive today. There are myriad reasons for the advances in longevity: improvements in sanitation, an understanding of infectious diseases and germ theory, the discovery of penicillin and the subsequent development of other pharmaceuticals, technological advances in health care delivery in general and the modern hospital in particular, and, more recently, the attention on health promotion and disease prevention.

Let us consider some of the major trends and events of the twentieth century that have markedly influenced the older population as it enters the twenty-first century. An examination of the factors that have shaped society's collective history may provide an understanding of the present and permit predicting the future with greater confidence, if not with increased accuracy.

MAJOR TRENDS IN THE UNITED STATES DURING THE TWENTIETH CENTURY

1900

It was the dawn of the twentieth century. In Europe, Germany was well on its way to implementing industrialization in the work place. Manufactured goods were going to be mass produced. Otto von Bismarck, the Chancellor of Germany during the early era of industrialization, was faced with a new challenge, one never before experienced in the history of the world. Germany was operating at perceived maximum efficiency, but there were younger workers trying to get into the workforce, and there were no more jobs for them. The solution recommended by von Bismarck's economic advisors was indeed radical. The recommendation was to furlough some older workers permanently, to provide them with a lifelong pension and to hire the new younger workers to replace them. Age sixty-five was recommended as the cutoff for furloughing workers because the economy could afford to provide lifelong pensions to that number of workers, and that number of workers would release enough jobs to allow for the employment of younger workers. It appeared to be an ideal solution. This was the birth of the concept of retirement of able-bodied workers based on age rather than functional ability.

In the preceding millennia, societies of hunters, gatherers, farmers, and guildsmen did not have a parallel for providing pensions to otherwise able workers. In all the previous societies, the hunters, the gatherers, the farmers, the trades workers all worked as long as they could and at the rate or pace that their physical capacities would allow. Their societies did support those unable to work or those whose work was exemplary, but general societal support for those able to work was previously unheard of. Individuals could choose to cease contributing to the production of goods and services in their own society if they so wished (often for reasons of sufficient wealth), but society generally did not provide them a pension.

While Chancellor von Bismark's successors were implementing this new concept of retirement in Germany, in the United States, a White girl infant born in 1900 could expect to live 48.7 years. A White boy infant could expect to live 46.6 years. If the infant was not White, life expectancy was only 33 years. If a woman celebrated a sixty-fifth birthday in 1900, she could expect to live another 12.2 years; men could expect another 11.5 years. In total, there were about 3 million people aged sixty-five and over, representing about 4 percent of the total population.

Most people were not living to a ripe old age but rather were dying from a myriad of preventable diseases. The top three causes of death, accounting for nearly one of three deaths, were infectious diseases, such as pneumonia and influenza (11.7%), tuberculosis (11.3%), and diarrhea and enteritis (8.3%). Only 8.0 percent were dying of heart diseases, and only 3.7 percent were dying of cancers in 1900. Infant mortality was high; childbirth had considerable risk.

1920s–1940s

The success of industrialization in Germany was not wasted on industrialists in the United States. Along with the growth of industrialization came the growth of labor unions. The unions sought among other things to protect the rights of workers, to maximize their wages, to make their working environments safe, to provide them with health insurance, and to provide them with retirement benefits that often included both pensions and retirement health insurance. These benefits came from private sources—employers and employees—unlike the German governmental model.

1930s

A component of the early American dream was shattered. The Great Depression of 1929 provided a lesson to many people that self-reliance on their own resources for a rainy day was insufficient during a deluge. The tragedy of the depression and images of men, women, and children standing in bread lines was seared in the American consciousness. By 1935, the federal government had passed the Social Security Act that signaled the beginning of an era in which the federal government would become involved in social issues and income-transfer programs. The Social Security Act of 1935 established the federal government as the institution providing for unemployment insurance, for disability insurance, and for retirement pensions.

The school teachers in Dallas, Texas, were pleased with the agreement their union forged in 1929 with Baylor Hospital to provide inpatient care to any of its teachers; each teacher paid fifty cents a month for this coverage. This arrangement was the beginning of the Blue Cross & Blue Shield hospital and health insurance system that became a stalwart of health care financing during the latter half of the twentieth century.

1940s and 1950s

The end of the Second World War began another chapter of the American dream. Large numbers of people went to college under the G.I. bill; large numbers of people were able to afford their own homes; large numbers of people bought automobiles for their own use; and large numbers of couples had babies. The Baby Boom that affected so many aspects of American life during the second half of the twentieth century–school systems, labor markets, housing prices–will have an even greater impact during the twenty-first century when all the Baby Boomers retire.

1950s and 1960s

A new problem faced the American dream. Retirees were facing personal bankruptcy because of the costs of hospital care. At the same time, other industrialized societies were deciding that health care was a right of citizenship and began to provide central government funding for health care. Some countries even went so far as to develop central government provision as well as financing of health services. Although there were many debates about national health insurance in the United States, government financing of health care for all citizens was not part of the political consensus. However,

solving the hospital-cost problem for older people was, and the Medicare program was passed in 1965 as an addition to the Social Security Act. The federal government would pay for hospital costs under a single program. Medicare, however, was established to solve only the problem of hospital costs for older people, not to provide full health care that included prevention services, ambulatory care, inpatient care, and long-term care. Political consensus in 1965 also produced the Medicaid program as an addition to the Social Security Act intended to finance full health care as just defined to poor people in federal–state partnerships. The year 1965 also saw the passage of the Older Americans Act (OAA) that provided federal financial support to a broad array of community services to older people, including Senior Centers that now dot the nation.

1970s–1990s

Since the implementation of Medicare and Medicaid in 1966, the federal government's share of payments for health care costs more than tripled from 8 percent in 1965 to 27 percent in 1975. In 1980, 1985, and 1990, the federal government's share of health care costs was constant at 29 percent. By 1995, that share had jumped again to 35 percent. The factors contributing to that jump in federal expenditures for health care during the early 1990s were likely the same factors that prompted the then new-President Clinton to attempt a sweeping health care reform during the first year of his term in office. Clinton's health care reform was not passed, and no substantial overhaul of health care delivery or health care financing came from the federal government.

The year 1975 saw the passage of another addition to the Social Security Act, the Home and Community Based Services Act, or often more simply just Title XX. This program was important because it facilitated a rash of new policies fostering alternative forms of long-term care to augment the nursing home and the substitution of home and community services for institutional care.

The 1980s and 1990s saw repeated attempts to control health care costs. One strategy was to turn away from paying bills at the usual and customary rates of submitters, and to turn toward composite or bundled services. One of the first of these approaches was to pay all Medicare-participating hospitals essentially the same fee for the same services (with some adjustments based on regions and other factors) regardless of the length of time in the hospital. Another was the renewed interest in managed care, in which the provider of health care agreed to provide all necessary care for the agreed-upon annual amount of payment for the beneficiary. Accepting this payment, also called the annual capitation rate, has the effect of relieving the payer of the responsibility of paying all bills by shifting the responsibility to the provider to provide all care within the capitation amounts.

2000

It is now the twenty-first century, a new millennium. Life expectancy in the United States for a newborn girl is 79.4 years and for a newborn boy is 73.6 years (based on 1997 data presented in the *Health and Aging Chartbook: Health, United States, 1999;* Kramarow, Lentzner, Rooks, Weeks, & Saydah, 1999). Life expectancy for a man just turning sixty-five years of age is 15.9 years; for a woman 19.2 additional years. There are approximately 35 million people past their sixty-fifth birthdays, representing approximately 13 percent of the population. Women are 58 percent of the population aged sixty-five and older and 70 percent of the population aged eighty-five and older. In 1998, about 41 percent of older women were living alone, com-

pared with 17 percent of older men. The current generation of older people has substantially more formal education than previous generations, and the trend will continue. In 1998, approximately one in ten (11%) of older women and one in five (20%) of older men graduated from college. The economic well-being of the older population at the start of the twenty-first century was markedly improved relative to prior generations. In 1959, about 35 percent of the older people lived below the established federal poverty level, whereas in 1998 this was true of only about 11 percent (Federal Interagency Forum on Aging-Related Statistics [FIFAS], 2000).

The causes of death have changed markedly during the twentieth century as well. At the turn of the twenty-first century, deaths caused by infectious diseases had been reduced considerably to 5 percent of all deaths, with pneumonia and influenza accounting for fewer than 4 percent of the deaths and Acquired Immunodeficiency Syndrome (AIDS) fewer than 2 percent. Diseases of the heart account for nearly one of three deaths at 32 percent. Malignant neoplasms (or cancers) account for nearly one in four deaths (23%). Cerebrovascular diseases (notably stroke) account for another 7 percent, and chronic obstructive pulmonary (or lung) diseases account for nearly another 5 percent. Maternal mortality resulting from complications of pregnancy, childbirth, or the puerperium decreased from 83.3 per 100,000 live births in 1950 to 7.1 in 1995.

THE FUNCTIONAL STATUS OF OLDER PEOPLE IN THE UNITED STATES

In addition to these broad and dramatic societal movements and public policy developments of the last century, a myriad of mysteries continue to cloud society's understanding of the individual older person. For example, why are there two to three older people (we will use the convention of sixty-five years and older for this chapter) living in their homes and communities with the same profile of diseases and disabilities as those living in nursing homes? What leads the one to enter the nursing home and the other two or three to stay in the community? At present, there are no definitive answers to these questions.

Some things about older people are known definitively. At the turn of the twenty-first century, there were approximately 1.6 million nursing home residents in 17,000 nursing homes occupying the 1.8 million licensed nursing home beds available in the United States, compared to 1.1 million licensed hospital beds in 6,000 hospitals. On any given day, there are approximately 5 percent of those aged sixty-five and over in nursing homes, but the rate varies dramatically by age. Only about 1 to 2 percent of those aged 65 to 74 years reside in a nursing home; about 4 to 5 percent of those aged 75 to 84; and about 19 to 20 percent of those aged eighty-five and older. Furthermore, nearly one-half of those aged sixty-five will enter a nursing home sometime during their life (FIFAS, 2000).

Over one-half of the current nursing home residents are eighty-five years of age or older, and three of four are female. In terms of the basic activities of daily living (ADLs) that define the daily components of personal care (bathing, dressing, toileting, transferring from bed to chair, and eating), 8 percent are independent in all five activities, 8 percent are dependent in one, 9 percent dependent in two, 5 percent dependent in three, 24 percent dependent in 4, and 46 percent dependent in all five (Cowles, 1997). About one in five (21%) are able to walk on their own; another 7 percent are bedfast. Nearly one-half (45%) are taking at least one type of psychoactive medication, with one in four (25%) taking an antidepressant (Cowles, 1997).

These older people who are residents of nursing homes and who share these characteristics represent about 5 percent of the population aged sixty-five and older. The characteristics of the community-dwelling older population present a different configuration. Based on the 1995 Medicare Current Beneficiary Survey (Olin, Liu, & Merriman, 1999), 14 percent have three or more ADL limitations, an additional 22 percent have one or two ADL limitations, and over one-half (53%) report difficulty walking that coexists with an ADL or an IADL limitation. (IADL refers to Instrumental Activities of Daily Living: the activities that most people need to do to live independently in the community, such as shopping, food preparation, housekeeping, using the telephone, taking medications, or managing money.)

Some interesting facts emerge from reviewing the circumstances related to the support received by frail elders living in the communities. According to the National Academy on an Aging Society (NAAS, 2000), much of the support is provided by spouses (28% among White elders and 15% among African American elders), but adult children provide the most support (41% among White elders and 42% among African American elders). Adult grandchildren also provide primary informal support (4% among White elders and 10% among African American elders). Other sources of care, which include paid and unpaid caregivers in the home, account for 27 percent of the care for White elders and 33 percent of the care for African American elders. It is also interesting to note that this same report estimated that unpaid caregivers provided care worth an estimated $196 billion in 1992; payments to nursing homes amounted to about one-third that amount (NAAS, 2000).

LIFESTYLES AND QUALITY OF LIFE

In 1990, the Surgeon General of the United States published health objectives for the nation (Healthy People 2000: National Health Promotion and Disease Prevention Objectives, 1990) for the year 2000. The report emphasized those domains most important for enhancing the quality of life of older people, namely, enhanced physical function; avoidance of motor vehicle crashes, fires, falls, fall-related injuries, fractures, and pneumonia-influenza; and attention to dental, hearing, and vision statuses. Notably absent from these domains was cognitive function, not due to lack of importance but rather to a lack of consensus as to how to state a measurable goal. The means to maximizing those domains listed included exercise, immunizations, and access to health services.

The *Healthy People 2000 Objectives* of older people are summarized next. For those aged sixty-five and older, the major overarching objective was the following:

> Reduce to no more than 90 per 1,000 people the proportion of all people aged 65 and older who have difficulty in performing two or more personal care activities, thereby preserving independence. (Baseline in 1984–85 was 111 per 1,000.) (p. 587)

In addition, there were these twelve other key health status objectives targeting older adults:

1. Reduce suicides among White men aged sixty-five and older to no more than 39.2 per 100,000. (Age-adjusted baseline in 1987 was 46.1 per 100,000.)
2. Reduce deaths among people aged seventy and older caused by motor vehicle crashes to no more than 20 per 100,000. (Baseline in 1987 was 22.6 per 100,000.)
3. Reduce deaths among people aged sixty-five through eighty-four from falls and fall-related injuries to no more than 14.4 per 100,000. (Baseline in 1987 was 18 per 100,000.)
4. Reduce deaths among people aged eighty-five and older from falls and fall-related injuries to no more than 105 per 100,000. (Baseline in 1987 was 131.2 per 100,000.)
5. Reduce residential fire deaths among people aged eighty-five and older to no more than 3.3 per 100,000. (Baseline in 1987 was 4.4 per 100,000.)
6. Reduce hip fractures among people aged sixty-five and older so that hospitalizations for this condition are no more than 607 per 100,000. (Baseline in 1987 was 714 per 100,000.)
7. Reduce to no more than 20 percent the proportion of people aged sixty-five and older who have lost all of their natural teeth. (Baseline in 1986 was 36%.)
8. Increase years of healthy life expectancy to at least fourteen years among those aged sixty-five. (Baseline in 1980 was twelve years.)
9. Reduce significant hearing impairment among people aged forty-five and older to a prevalence of no more than 180 per 1,000. (Baseline from 1986–88 was 203 per 1,000.)
10. Reduce significant visual impairment among people aged sixty-five and older to a prevalence of no more than 70 per 1,000. (Baseline from 1986–88 was 87.1 per 1,000.)
11. Reduce epidemic-related pneumonia and influenza deaths among people aged sixty-five and older to no more than 7.3 per 100,000. (Baseline from 1980–87 was 9.1 per 100,000.)

12. Reduce pneumonia-related days of restricted activity among people aged
sixty-five and older to thirty-eight
days per 100 people. (Baseline in 1987
was forty-eight days.) (p. 125)

In addition, there were four other key
risk reduction objectives targeted for the
older population:

1. Increase to at least 30 percent among
people aged sixty-five and older the
proportion who engage regularly,
preferable daily, in light to moderate
physical activity for at least thirty minutes per day.
2. Reduce to no more than 22 percent
among people aged sixty-five and
older the proportion who engage in
no leisure-time physical activity.
3. Increase both pneumococcal pneumonia and influenza immunizations
among people aged sixty-five and
older to at least 80 percent.
4. Increase to at least 40 percent the proportion of people aged sixty-five and
older who have received as a minimum all the screening and immunization services and at least one of the
counseling services appropriate for
their age and gender as recommended
by the U.S. Preventive Services Task
Force. (p. 125)

There were no precise baseline rates available at the time the risk-reduction goals were
established.

In the near future, the federal government plans to announce the nation's rate of
success in meeting the overall objective, the
health status objectives, and risk reduction
objectives among those aged sixty-five and
older. The quality of life for older people in
the twenty-first century may be directly pro-
portional to the success in reaching and exceeding these Year 2000 objectives.

However, some preliminary information
is available. Concerning the overarching objective, according to data from the 1994
National Long-Term Care Survey, approximately 111 per 1,000 were dependent in three
or more ADLs (their measure included a
sixth ADL–walking around inside–added to
the original five, and hence this rate reflects
dependencies in three of six rather than in
two of five as stated in the original objective).
Furthermore, this 1994 rate of 111 per 1,000
includes 51 per 1,000 who reside in nursing
homes. Apparently, there was very little
movement during the first several years after
the objective was offered because this 1994
rate of 111 per 1,000 was identical to the
1984–85 baseline rate.

Concerning risk-reduction objective two,
in 1995 about one-third (34.4%) of older people in the United States reported a sedentary
lifestyle defined as no leisure-time physical
activity in the previous two-week interval.
This rate is far short of the goal of no more
than 22 percent.

Concerning risk-reduction objective three,
the three-year average between 1993–95 for
report of ever having a pneumococcal vaccination was 30.4 percent for older men and
28.5 percent for older women (once in a lifetime is sufficient). The three-year average between 1993–95 for an annual flu shot was 56.2
percent for men and 53.5 percent for women.
Clearly, the 1993–95 rates were considerably
short of the national objective of 80 percent.

These are only preliminary assessments
taken relatively early during the initiative.
There is reason to expect that the rates of
compliance with the year 2000 objectives for
the older population in the United States will
be much closer to the stated targets. The quality of their lives may well depend on it.

REFERENCES

Cowles, C. M. (1997). *Nursing home statistical yearbook, 1997.* Anacortes, VA: Johns Hopkins University Press and Cowles Research Group.

Federal Interagency Forum on Aging-Related Statistics. (2000). *Older Americans 2000: Key indications of well-being.* Washington, DC: U.S. Government Printing Office.

Healthy People 2000, National Health Promotion and Disease Prevention Objectives. DHHS Publication No. (PHS) 91-50212. James O. Mason, Asst. Secretary for Health 1990.

Kramarow, E., Lentzner, H., Rooks, R., Weeks, J., & Saydah, S. (1999). *Health and Aging Chartbook. Health, United States, 1999* DHHS Publication No (PHS) 99-1232-1. Hyattsville, MD. National Center for Health Statistics.

National Academy on an Aging Society. (2000). *Caregiving: Helping the elderly with activity limitations. Challenges for the 21st century: Chronic and disabling conditions (No. 7).* Washington, DC: The Gerontological Society of America.

Olin, G. L., Liu, H., & Merriman, B. (1999). *Health & health care of the medicare population: Data from the 1995 medicare current beneficiary survey.* Rockville, MD: Westat.

II. BIOLOGICAL ASPECTS OF AGING
AND PUBLIC HEALTH

Chapter 2

HEALTH AND AGING

Gari Lesnoff-Caravaglia

Two major changes that have altered contemporary society are the presence of a large number of older persons throughout the world and the rapid advances in modern technology. Such changes reflect potentially both positive and negative aspects as they affect individuals, society, the notion of community, public health, and lifestyles, in terms of opportunities and responsibilities.

In the United States, the nation's older population is expected to more than double by the year 2050. The composition of that population will be more racially and ethnically diverse than generations before them, thus intensifying the need for flexible and sensitive provision of services at all levels.

At the turn of the twentieth century, life expectancy was approximately forty-nine years, and the median age was 22.9. At the initiation of the twenty-first century, people live a quarter of a century longer, with the life expectancy for women now reaching eighty-three and for men seventy-eight. The number of years persons lived as postparental years in 1940 was seventeen years; it is currently thirty-three years. Married women can expect to live twenty to thirty years with a spouse, whereas in 1800, the expectation was twelve years. Sixty-eight percent of all women are widows at age seventy-five. Women, also, make up two-thirds of the population over the age of seventy-five, and it is likely that such age disparity between the sexes will continue (Lesnoff-Caravaglia, 2000).

Older persons play significant roles in all areas of human experiencing, in the work place, in the home, and as prominent experts in a wide range of professional fields. Many persons, although advanced in age, do not internalize a different self-image, nor do they regard themselves as "old" in the sense of being antiquated or superceded by younger persons with respect to acumen or capabilities. As the population continues to age, older persons are found to be involved in all aspects of life—both the positive and the negative. Prominent world figures of venerable age have included the Pope, heads of state, heads of the mafia and other criminal organizations, and Justices of the U.S. Supreme Court.

PROFILE OF THE ELDERLY

The older population is made up principally of women, most of whom live alone. They remain in the community setting for as

15

long as possible. Most are unemployed, and many live under reduced economic circumstances. Some suffer from two or more debilitating chronic illnesses. Despite societal changes, the lives of such older persons continue unchanged, and, as they continue to age, their only expectation is eventual institutionalization or death.

The general apathy toward the aging process and older persons leads to premature aging, wherein persons become more prone to exhibit behavior patterns and disease symptoms that are generally characteristic of much older persons. Persons of 70 appear 90; those 90 appear 110 or older. There is a concomitant lack of fit between the person and the environment. The environment, unadapted to the physiological and psychological needs and concerns of older persons, is antiquated, and thus provides little accommodation of older adults. Such lack of environmental accommodation causes older persons to assume stereotypical postures and behaviors. Older persons are not encouraged to develop skills to deal with the environment, and the rigidity of the environment promotes the onset and growth of disease (Klerk, Huijsman, & McDonnell, 1997).

Freedom and independence have been promised through the adaptation of technologies to offset the debilities of age and are yet to be forthcoming. The home environment of many persons has changed little from the post-World War II era. The SMARTHOUSE that has long been promised that would incorporate various facets of modern technology permitting older persons to remain in their own homes and within the community setting indefinitely has not even enabled older persons to change a light bulb safely (Lesnoff-Caravaglia, 1999). The SMART nursing home has not gone beyond the incorporation of bathroom grab bars. SMART hospitals are nonexistent in terms of daily patient care (McConnel & Murphy, 1990), and the care mar-

shaled out to patients is best characterized as "reluctant care."

UNDERSTANDING AGING

Although it is recognized that biological changes are inevitable as part of the aging process, it is not clear why such changes occur. The process of aging, in and of itself, is poorly understood. An ancient belief held that there was a magic elixir or potion that could halt aging or retard its progress. The explorer Ponce de León was sent to the New World by Queen Isabella of Spain to find the "fountain of youth." His mission was inspired by the fact that the Queen's husband, King Ferdinand, reported to be several years her junior, would lose interest in her as she grew older. Ponce de León did not find the fountain of youth, but he discovered Florida. The Florida that, curiously enough, became the haven of the elderly of today.

It is not unusual to see an old human being, but aged animals exist only in captivity. Wild animals do not usually reach extreme old age or even what in humans is referred to as middle age. Wild animals thus resemble ancient or prehistoric human beings who rarely, if ever, saw an old person. Of the 300 Neanderthals found, only one may have been a postmenopausal woman (Hayflick, 1994).

There is extensive documentation that not only physical vigor, but also less obvious powers, such as the ability to resist disease and the physiological capacity of many major organs, peak and then decrease in human beings and other animals following sexual maturation. Some of the more obvious normal age changes include loss of strength and stamina, farsightedness, new hair growth in ears and nostrils, decline in short-term memory, balding, loss of bone mass, decrease in height, hearing loss, and menopause. Although most of these changes can be viewed externally, they have their origins at levels not readily perceived by the senses (Hayflick, 1994).

Normal age changes make humans more vulnerable to diseases that in youth would be more easily repulsed. As the immune system ages, it becomes less efficient in defending the body and more likely to make errors in defense. It may mistake normal proteins in the body for foreign proteins, thus producing antibodies against its own cells and result in an autoimmune disease (Ross, 1995).

The diseases associated with old age are not part of the normal aging process. Cancer, heart disease, Alzheimer's disease, and strokes become more prevalent as persons age because of the reduced capacity to repel them. Often their long maturation permits them to manifest themselves in old age, although they are initiated at much younger ages. Some diseases, such as herpes and tuberculosis, can be dormant for years and become reactivated in old age (Lesnoff-Caravaglia, 1988). This increase in vulnerability results from the normal aging process.

The improper understanding of the aging process leads to the physiological losses experienced in old age and, ultimately, death. Unless more attention is paid to the fundamental processes of aging, the fate of everyone fortunate enough to become old will be death on or around his or her 100th birthday. The true causes of those deaths will probably be unknown because of lack of basic research that would increase the knowledge of the fundamental aging process and insights into how to reduce human vulnerability to the current causes of death (Hayflick, 1994).

Contemporary theories of aging cannot account for the reasons why people age. One theory, the wear-and-tear theory, maintains that the body simply wears out over time. Other theories deal with the changes within the cells themselves, while still others state that aging is programmed and is regulated by an aging clock located in the hypothalamus. The gene theory maintains that there are certain genes that contribute to bodily dysfunctions, and that these genes appear to become activated as persons grow older. In addition, there is the cellular-garbage theory that claims there are certain deposits (such as lipofuscin) that accumulate in cells to create dysfunctions that lead to aging and, ultimately, death.

The autoimmune theory is gradually commanding the greatest attention. According to this theory, the immune system gradually breaks down and, thus, permits certain diseases to be activated in old age or causes diseases of long maturation to manifest themselves in old age. This results because the immune system in older persons appears to function less efficiently.

No theory adequately explains why people age, or how they age. Some hypotheses promulgated to help retard the aging process include: lowering the caloric intake, sleeping in colder environments, or developing special diets. The ideal appears to be to keep people young for as long as possible, and to avoid old age altogether.

Aging occurs within the body at the cellular level, as well as outwardly. Yet, it is the outward signs that are referred to when commonly describing aging, such as the graying of the hair, wrinkled skin, loss of hair, stooped posture, or other alterations in appearance. In some older persons, the posture is so bent that the person appears to be facing the ground. Such postural changes probably provided the basis for the old proverb that the grave beckons the old.

CHRONOLOGICAL AGE

Chronological age refers to the number of years a person has lived or an individual's birthday age. There is also the term *physiological age* or the physical age of the person. An individual may be ninety years old, but have the health status that is equivalent to a fifty-year-old. A person at age sixty suffering from a heart ailment may have a heart that can be equated to that of an eighty-year-old. Even within one individual, organs age at different rates. A person's kidneys may be one age, the heart another, and the liver still another.

One overarching change linked to the aging of an individual is that the individual responds less well to stress. More time is required to recover from stress. There is also an inherent vulnerability that accompanies the aging process (Oram, 1997). Persons who appear hale and hearty prior to a stressful event, such as experiencing a fall, may have great difficulty, physically and psychologically, in overcoming resultant trauma or stress.

BIOLOGICAL AGING

There are a number of older persons who function very well into advanced old age, and because of better lifestyle choices and increased income, educational level, and accessibility of new medical technologies, their number will continue to grow. Those who are well-endowed with respect to genetic structure and have experienced the advantages of good health throughout their lifespan will very likely enjoy a healthy old age (Andrews, 1998).

There are inevitable biological changes that occur as an individual becomes older. Such changes, however, are not the result of disease but are more aptly attributed to the aging process known as *senescence*. Senescence refers to the bodily changes that occur, and the limitations that such changes may engender. This term is not to be confused with the word *senile* which is often used as a

pejorative term to describe older persons who may be suffering from physical or mental dysfunctions.

There are some diseases that are more likely to occur as a person continues to age. This does not mean that persons will necessarily suffer from such diseases. Diseases that may have had their onset in early periods of life manifest themselves as persons live to reach advanced old age. Such diseases can be the result of individual unhealthful lifestyles for a number of years. Cancers and diseases of the circulatory system are among those that manifest themselves in old age. The use of a number of medications to treat the multiple chronic diseases sometimes suffered by older persons can also lead to additional health problems (Stolley & Buckwalter, 1991). Drug dosages and uses in older persons have not been sufficiently studied.

The prevalence of health-risk factors increases as persons age. Some individuals are at risk for chronic conditions because of factors that cannot be modified, such as genetic predisposition, gender, and age. Risk factors related to health behaviors, however, can be modified. The majority of adults have risk factors for chronic conditions because of their health-related behaviors. Individuals who modify their health-related behaviors can reduce the risk of developing chronic conditions and enhance the quality of their lives. Such modifications include weight reduction, physical activity, lowering cholesterol levels and alcohol consumption, and not smoking.

Many modifiable risk factors are associated with chronic diseases, such as hypertension, heart disease, diabetes, cancer, and stroke. There is a close association between excess weight and an increased risk of dying from heart disease or cancer. Obesity and smoking are the leading causes of preventable death (Calle, Thun, Petrelli, Rodriguez, & Health, 1999). Adults at risk for chronic conditions are much more limited in their ADLs, such as bathing, dressing, eating, toileting, and walking. The elderly have a higher rate of heart disease than any other age group. A healthy lifestyle can significantly reduce the risk of heart disease. Coronary heart disease is the leading cause of premature, permanent disability in older persons.

Arthritis is common in old age, and approximately one-half of the elderly population suffer from this chronic condition. Arthritis, or joint inflammation, affects a larger proportion of older women. Many need assistance to accomplish activities associated with daily living. Use of a social worker, adult day care, rehabilitations, transportation, chronic pain-management programs and Meals-on-Wheels is significantly higher for the elderly who have arthritis. People with arthritis are more likely to have Medicaid coverage, and participation in the Supplemental Security Income (SSI) Program is higher for those who have arthritis.

The incidence of hip fractures is rising in many countries as the population continues to age. For example, the number of hip fractures in elderly Finnish men and women is increasing at a rate that cannot be explained merely by demographic changes. The precise reasons for this are unknown, but deterioration in age-adjusted bone-mineral density and strength, with accompanying increase in the age-adjusted incidence of injurious falls of the elderly, could partly account for the development (Kannus et al., 1999).

preference. After the age of eighty, the health status of individuals appears to reach a plateau, and few serious disabilities occur for at least another decade.

Since the elderly will have followed healthier lifestyles, their physical condition will be superior to that of the older population of today. Older persons today exhibit what can be termed as "premature aging," brought on by stress, improper diet, unhealthful living conditions and habits, and unsound work patterns. An amelioration of the total environment will not only prolong life but can add immeasurably to the maintaining of youthfulness. In some cultures, long-living men who have led healthful lifestyles are found to possess viable sperm at the age of 100. Women in such environments menstruate until the age of sixty or later (Lesnoff-Caravaglia & Klys, 1987). With the more recent advances in conception and the added possibilities of "rent a womb," there is now the possibility for women at ages much older than had been thought possible to give birth and to nurture children. Through uterus replacement, there is the potential to eliminate menopause altogether.

The sex life of the future may be characterized as being "age independent" and, once sexual maturity is reached, not tied by function to any particular period of chronological age. The enjoyment of family and intimacy may take on entirely new configurations. Romance until death may well be the norm.

SEX AND AGING

The elderly of the future will have considerably more time to devote to interpersonal relationships, and there, no doubt, will be an increased interest in personal appearance. Cosmetic surgery offers opportunities to maintain a personal image based on personal

BIOLOGICAL SYSTEMS

Although the systems within the body are frequently described as separate systems, they do not operate independently but often share or complement bodily functions and are intimately interconnected. They are treated as separate systems to understand their functioning for didactic purposes. For example, alterations in the respiratory system can affect the cardiovascular system, which, in turn, can affect the general balance of the organism or the homeostasis of the body.

In addition, diseased conditions of one part of the body can seriously compromise several other systems. When oral health is compromised due to the presence of periodontal disease, one of every four persons will lose all of one's teeth by the age of sixty. Oral bacteria also may be linked to stroke, heart attack, respiratory illness, gastrointestinal problems, and severe systemic infections because poor oral health becomes more common as persons age.

Older persons suffering from high levels of stress are especially prone to Alzheimer's disease and depression, both of which severely affect memory. While the types of stress differ among individuals, well-known causes often include illness, financial concerns, the death of loved ones, and resonating fears with regard to one's own health.

to live another ten to thirty years. This variability is not trivial to the understanding of age changes. It is not surprising, for example, that older persons have nutritional needs and metabolic characteristics that are different and more limiting than those of their youth. If there is no particular value in these functions lasting in optimal form beyond the reproductive period of life, then some may deteriorate as aging occurs, while others randomly persist (Evers, Townsend, & Thompson, 1994). Gerontologists, who study all aspects of aging, and geriatricians, the biomedical group interested in the health of the aged, must look at the variable physiological characteristics of the aged and develop new understandings.

The study of aging must be multidisciplinary, drawing substantially from fields of study such as sociology, psychology, biology, genetics, and biochemistry. Physiology remains central in considering the mechanisms of the body and the processes by which they are carried out.

INCREASED LONGEVITY

Advances in medical knowledge, combined with better dietary and sanitary measures, have led to an increase in life expectancy. This increase in the number of elderly people is accompanied by a greater incidence of the health disorders of the aged. The aging of the population is a universal change and has kindled increased interest in the study of population changes or demography.

A conspicuous feature of an aged population is the range, or variability, of function seen in any given age group. An individual, age seventy, who is near death and has many systems failing to maintain homeostasis, provides a notable contrast with those of the same age and in good health who may expect

LIFE EXPECTANCY AND LIFE SPAN

Life expectancy varies and changes, and since the 1880s, there has been a gradual increase in life expectancy. If an individual had reached the age of fifty in early 1900s, this individual was considered to be old. People of that age were regarded in the same light as are people today who are 125 years of age. They were considered to be the very old persons in the society.

There were a number of reasons to account for the shorter life expectancy: The standard of living was lower, there were more environmental dangers, and women died in childbirth more often. Currently, health concerns have been more successfully resolved due, in part, to the presence of advanced technologies allowing people to experience new health care interventions. Health care intervention has changed, along with the educational levels of the population. Some persons currently in their eighties and nineties did not progress beyond the sixth grade. It was unusual in their age cohort for an individual to have graduated from high school. It was not until after World War II that many people who were not affluent had the opportunity to attend institutions of higher learning. This was largely due to the G.I. Bill that permitted people who had served in the armed services an opportunity to advance their educations.

With the expansion of educational opportunities, people became more sophisticated with respect to caring for their health and to their expectations of health and social services. They have also become aware of the relationship between political astuteness and the ability to seek services through active political participation. People increasingly take an entrepreneurial attitude toward their own health care and want to participate in the decision-making process that intimately affects them. This attitude has brought about changes in the doctor–patient relationship (Rowe & Kahn, 1996). People have also become aware of the relationship between more healthful lifestyles and better health care and personal longevity. They also realize that better education, better jobs, and higher incomes all lead to increases in life expectancy.

Better sanitary systems, the control of pests, and improved plumbing have helped to further increases in life expectancy. Such environmental alterations have led to the absence of plagues, such as the bubonic plague or the black plague that in prior times obliterated large sections of the world and caused entire cities to disappear from the face of the earth.

There are, also, gender differences with respect to life expectancy. Life expectancy in most industrialized societies for women is approximately six to ten years greater than it is for men. Environmental factors for women are different from those of men. Men are more prone to experience industrial accidents, to become exposed to toxic substances, to be involved in greater numbers in automobile accidents, to participate in greater numbers in suicidal and homicidal deaths, and to engage in unhealthful lifestyles that include the abuse of alcohol and tobacco. All of these factors significantly reduce life expectancy.

Some population groups experience shorter life expectancies. For example, Native Americans have very short life expectancies compared to White Americans due, in part, to poor nutrition, poor health facilities, and abuse of alcohol and tobacco. The life expectancy for a male Native American is approximately forty-five years of age, while the life expectancy for the average White American male is approximately seventy-eight years of age.

Formerly, it was common for persons to enter custodial-care settings, such as nursing homes, when they were approximately sixty-two years of age. Now, it is more common for persons to enter nursing homes at an age closer to ninety; the average age is eighty-six.

Mandatory retirement age for many years was placed at sixty-five years of age. Persons had to leave their positions, their jobs, and their professional associations. Mandatory retirement has been effectively abolished, primarily because it became meaningless and irrelevant. People became healthier and were able to continue in their work activities. Concomitantly, there was a change in demography, resulting in changes within the population structure. There was no longer the presence of large groups of young people. The knowledge and expertise of older workers was needed and led to the abandonment of mandatory retirement allowing persons to remain longer in the work-force. The increase in numbers of older women who lived below the poverty level helped to focus attention on the need to re-cruit more women in the workforce and on their participation in pension and investment plans to offset their financial reliance on pub-lic funding. Economic constraints, more than feminist movements, fueled such occupation-al change.

The establishment of age sixty-five as a retirement age was an arbitrary one. It was not based on biological or psychological aging, or serious studies of the detriments of maintaining the older worker. Age sixty-five had been established in Germany by Chan-cellor von Bismarck who determined that persons who had worked long and hard to establish the current society should be re-warded by an acknowledgement of this con-tribution to the welfare of the state by a pension plan. The plan was to go into effect when persons reached the age of sixty-five. He picked that age because in that time peri-od few people lived long enough to reach this age, and, consequently, since the numbers of person who could claim such pension benefits would be small, the burden on state coffers would be light. No one, of course, could pre-dict that life expectancy would increase dra-matically, and that people in the future who reached age 65 would not be regarded as old.

Nonetheless, age sixty-five was seized upon by the rest of the world as a chronolog-ical marker with respect to age. After age sixty-five, people were to be retired from work and were, in general, to be regarded as the older portion of the population. Age sixty-five thus took on a negative connota-tion, and, since much attention is paid to in-dividuals' ages, to say one was sixty-five years old was tantamount to admitting to being old and nonproductive. Lying about one's age probably increased in momentum due to the negative stereotyping of older individuals.

There was the growth of ageism, a negative way of regarding older persons much as is sexism or racism.

In the United States, the Social Security Act was instituted in the mid-1930s to princi-pally assist persons with little or no income to subsist in old age. The intention originally was to provide some assistance, but not to provide totally for an individual's needs. This notion changed over the years, and many people do, in fact, have only Social Security benefits to support them in their old age.

There is nothing biologically, sociologi-cally, or psychologically, that determined that age sixty-five was an appropriate age to limit persons' work activity. Older women, in particular, suffered from the negative stereo-typing associated with growing older. Women not only suffered from ageism, but, if they be-longed to a minority group, they suffered racism, and, being women, they also faced sexism. Such prejudice is heightened by the fact that approximately 50 percent of the older women, as compared to older men, live below the poverty level.

Life span, by contrast, is species deter-mined. There are mice that live six months and insects that live only hours. The average life span for the cat is approximately 25 years, the dog 30 years, the horse 30 years, some turtles 200 years, and some birds 100 years. The life span for the human species for some time had been considered as 100 years, but the figure now accepted is 125 years.

Everything ages; not only human beings, but material things as well. Wood, furniture, buildings, cities, sections of cities, trees, ore deep in the ground–everything goes through the aging process. At the time of conception, the individual begins the process of aging. People age over time, and their aging is man-ifest in their appearance, interests, and life ex-periences. Changes are more rapid at certain periods of life, such as infancy, but changes continue to occur, perhaps more subtly in later stages of development. Some changes are viewed with joy and anticipated, others at other stages of life appear depressing, and there may be the wish to conceal or to hide such changes.

In the Western world, most cultures are future oriented. People plan their lives in terms of future expected events and pay little heed to the past or its influence. Such future orientation created a problem for the older population because such an emphasis diminished the importance of past events and lives already lived. When individuals reached age sixty-five, they felt apprehensive about their lives, depressed that there was little to look forward to as they had been asked to retire from their jobs. Death was the only future life event. The denial of aging and death resulted from the emphasis on a future orientation. Life was not perceived as a progression from birth to death, but rather birth to retirement. Those who continued to live beyond age sixty-five were hard pressed to give life meaning. Some engaged in reminiscence, some became ill, while others fought against the established norms that gave rise to such groups as the Gray Panthers.

Reminiscence was heralded as a positive life review. Such a hanging on to significant events of the past was regarded as probably the only way that older persons could maintain their personal integrity. What was overlooked was that reminiscence was more symptomatic of the unsympathetic climate in which aging was experienced, rather than a healthy looking back at one's life and trying to provide it with meaning and coherence. As a result, many older persons were guilty of repeatedly recounting past experiences they felt were significant that only succeeded in boring their relatives. For example, one grandmother repeatedly related in great detail how she came to the United States in the hold of a ship, barefoot, and alone. The reason for such repetition is that the older person does not have new experiences, or interesting current events to relate, and, thus, to appear interesting, focuses on past dramatic episodes. This also partially explains the sick role played by older persons to gain the attention of children. The sick role is acceptable, whereas the role of older person is fraught with ambiguity.

The chronological age of sixty-five as the hallmark of aging also meant that older persons were categorically regarded as ill or prone to soon become so, and health care providers were reluctant to spend time on older patients. They were regarded as already doomed, and intervention was seen as futile. The ignoring of health care needs of older persons still finds its reverberation today in the lack of support for research on the diseases that primarily affect the elderly. This also, in part, accounts for the lack of adequate mental health care.

A further negative aspect of the emphasis upon chronological age is that aging became associated with death. At the turn of the century, death was more common among children. Family plots in older cemeteries include as many as thirteen children, many of whom lived less than six months. Because of better standards of living and health care, the infant mortality rate has been reduced, and death now occurs more frequently among older persons. Along with increases in life expectancy, older persons live longer, and the age group eighty-five and older continues to expand.

Old age, in and of itself, is not a disease. It is not a sickness that gradually overwhelms persons if they live long enough. Rather, aging is a process that occurs over time and is initiated at conception and continues until the organism expires. Aging is experienced at different rates by individuals and is affected by a wide variety of factors including heredity, lifestyle, economics, and the environment.

The older client in visiting the physician is often presented with the question: "What do you expect at your age?" Older persons expect answers and diagnoses of their conditions in the same way as do younger individuals.

Older persons are probably more different one from the other, than any other age group. They differ more than do adolescents who certainly have major differences among them. One of the reasons why older persons differ so much from one another is that they have all had differing life experiences. Such differences include their social experience, health history, experience of life events, education, and personal history. When the medical history is taken of an older person, much of this personal equation must be included. This is why geriatrics, the study of the diseases of aging, a medical specialty, must focus on the individual, not just the disease process. Geriatrics was not seriously studied until the end of World War II. Another area of study, gerontology, focuses on the processes of aging from a multidisciplinary perspective. Some hospitals may have a gerontology unit that assists in the evaluation and placement of individuals in long-term care settings.

RELIGION AND WARS

The two important factors that affect society in terms of health care and its provision are religion and wars. Religion has played a significant role in the development of health care and the development of health care institutions. Early hospitals were constructed in the shape of a cross, and the religious concept of caring for others further fostered the presence of religion in health care. The first nurses were monks, but, subsequently, there were many orders of nuns that specialized in nursing care.

Wars helped to spread medical information, and soldiers often returned from distant lands with new knowledge in health care and new interventions. This was particularly true of the Crusades that, although a religious war, resulted in bringing significant medical knowledge from the East and North Africa to the European continent. This was a significant avenue for the exchange of information between differing cultures. The American Civil War was also a time for new medical discoveries. Anesthetics, surgery, embalming (preparing dead soldiers to send back to their families) and rehabilitation including prosthetic devices and artificial limbs were all results of treating the injured with greater effectiveness.

World War II revolutionized health care. The Mobile and Surgical Hospital (MASH) units of World War II were largely responsible for the introduction of radical surgeries and treatment modalities into the health care field. Current emergency-room service was significantly altered following World War II. Prior to that time, patients were picked up in a hearse, not in an ambulance. Providing care with minimal medical assistance or medications called for extensive innovation. Having to make do with just what was available proved to be a remarkable lesson for many health care units. In emergency situations, they dared the impossible and often succeeded. This daring spirit is what sparked the burgeoning of advanced health care technologies following World War II.

INCREASING LIFE EXPECTANCY

Lifestyle is probably a major determinant as to an individual's life expectancy. How one lives one's life will determine its length. The analogy of the machine is a pertinent one. An automobile that is properly maintained, is regularly checked, and furnished with the best fuel, will last much longer than will a machine that is neglected or maltreated. The same is true of the human organism. Proper nutrition, exercise, intellectual growth, the avoidance of such harmful practices as the use of tobacco products or drugs, or abuse of alcohol, appropriate health care, and living in a healthful environment are factors that contribute to longevity or long life.

There are basically two ways of increasing life expectancy. The first is through health promotion and disease prevention. The second is through broader and intensified research efforts, including the findings of molecular and cellular biology. It is probably more helpful to the older population to apply existing information, and to educate them of its beneficial effects. It is abundantly evident that exercise through aerobic activity and resistance training reduces physical frailty, but there is a reluctance on the part of older persons to engage in physical activity. Listed among the top ten causes of death are pneumonia and its complications, but the majority of persons over the age of sixty-five do not receive the pneumococcal vaccine. Although many older persons die of the flu in an epidemic, approximately one-half of the persons aged sixty-five and over get a flu shot in the fall. Cancer of the lung has surpassed breast cancer in women, but smoking among women continues to increase, particularly among younger age groups. Diseases related to tobacco use and alcohol abuse continue to be the primary factors in premature death involving heart disease and cancer. In addition, older Americans continue to consume high-fat diets, even though such foods have been clearly demonstrated to increase the incidence of heart disease and cancer.

The delay of dysfunction means reduction both in the length and the amount of dependency. The redundancy of various bodily systems and their capability to repair themselves are underlying factors for the biological basis of the mechanism of delay. Caloric re-striction has shown to delay dysfunction and to even ward off death. Gene regulation is key to controlling a wide panorama of potential dysfunction. Stress reduction is increasingly associated with treatments for brain disorders, including Alzheimer's disease.

AGE CATEGORIES

As the population continues to age, there is the realization that the elderly have been too globally perceived and that demarcations as to age groups are exceedingly important if this group is to be served appropriately. Unfortunately, a number of euphemisms continue to be employed in describing the older population, and researchers have used terms that, in some cases, have bordered on the esoteric.

Language directly affects behaviors. If persons are referred to in negative ways, there is a tendency to ignore such individuals and to provide less well for them. This, unfortunately, is also true of aging. The disparaging terms used to describe this age group include such terms as "golden agers," "senior citizens," "old fogies," "old geezers," and "crocks." Such labeling, by and large negative, has hampered society's ability to deal effectively with the older population both conceptually and scientifically.

Researchers have confounded their studies by dividing older persons into amorphous categories, such as the "young old," "old old," "oldest old," "frail elderly," "well elderly," and "long-living." Others have facetiously referred to older age groups as the "slow go," "no-go," and the "go-go," or simply "the risky" and "the frisky."

Unfortunately, such stereotyping of older persons persists in spite of dictionary terms that have been available to adequately describe older age groups. Most people until they reach age seventy are not markedly different from other age groups. A proper terminology would include the following:

Septuagenarians	70–79
Octogenarians	80–89
Nonagenarians	90–99
Centenarians	100–109
Centedecinarians	110–119
Centeventenarians	120–129
Centetrentenarians	130–139

The last three appellations are neologisms coined to meet modern exigencies to properly define older age groups. A further advantage to the use of such nomenclature is that these terms have a Latin base and allow for international comprehension of their use to describe particular age groups.

It is clear that such terms as "the elderly" do not sufficiently distinguish between the age groups, particularly since there is a vast difference between the health, physical functioning, and health or social services required by septuagenarians and centenarians which spans a thirty-year interval. This is tantamount to regarding a one-year-old as being equivalent to a thirty-year-old. Unfortunately, for too long, everyone over the age of sixty-five has been labeled elderly, and it is only now patently clear that such a distinction is practically meaningless.

Appropriate terminology is important in scientific investigations, in the clinical study of geriatrics, in assessing the needs of persons, and in ascribing clarity to specifically what group of persons is under discussion.

garding many of the diseases that people suffer in old age. Lack of interest in the diseases of the elderly has long prevailed. Until fairly recently, autopsies were not routinely performed on older patients. The disinterest in the elderly extended to a disinterest in knowing of what they had died. Death certificates frequently listed as the cause of death "old age." Research on aging was not seriously undertaken until after World War II.

The increase in the aging of the population led to the realization that as people lived longer, they also used more health care services due to the increased incidence of disease and disability. From a purely economic standpoint, the importance of scientific research to uncover preventive measures spurred the establishment of centers for the study of aging.

The principal study conducted in the United States is the Baltimore Longitudinal Study conducted by the National Institute of Health on the male population. The study of women, despite the fact that women have historically lived longer than men, was instituted much later.

Much of the information available on aging has been derived from animal studies. Such information, however valuable, has its limitations. There is a danger in extrapolating information based on animal studies and applying it to the human species. The shorter life expectancy of many animals makes them easier to study because they can be followed from birth to death, and, also, scientific experimentation on animals is permissible.

RESEARCH ON OLD AGE

There is yet to develop a level of scientific information requisite to an appropriate study of aging and the processes of aging. There is currently a lack of information re-

DEMOGRAPHY

A proper assessment of population growth and change is vital to proper planning for the needs and concerns of society. Demography is the study of such population changes and their effect on the broader society. Such studies are particularly significant when such changes affect the nature of human experiences because of age changes and population shifts and the provision of services to match such population changes.

One such change that has decided ramifications for health care services is that the sector of the population aged eighty-five and older is growing at a rapid rate. This population group also suffers from multiple health problems and occasions greater costs in terms of health expenditures. Research on maintaining health in old age is also of economic interest to offset costs of hospitalization and long-term care. Whereas long-term care had been characterized by various levels, its principal focus now is on the provision of skilled care in skilled nursing facilities. People admitted to skilled nursing facilities are in their eighties or older and generally require total care. The development of retirement centers, home health care, and the general overall improvement of health in older persons has led to such changes (Haug, 1994).

CONCLUSION

The chronic, nonfatal disorders of longevity destroy the quality of life and drain society's resources. A full 80 percent of all deaths occur after age sixty-five. People over the age of eighty-five are now the fastest growing segment of the population. Dementia, arthritis, diminished hearing and visual acuity, incontinence, and hip fractures all continue to occur at the same age as they did in the past. Through appropriate prevention and intervention strategies, it is possible to defer disease and to minimize dysfunction (Butler & Brody, 1995).

Aging research at all levels is essential to lower disability rates and to lengthen life. Ad-

ditional years of life spent bedfast or in an institutional setting are not the anticipated rewards of long life. While it is accepted that aging contributes to increased vulnerability to disease and disability, it is vital to understand what precedes or leads to particular types of dysfunction. The three major precursors to disease that can be significantly altered through extensive research efforts include genetics, aging, and the environment. To postpone dysfunction may, in the case of aging, carry greater significance than the possibility for cure (Fries, 1980).

REFERENCES

Andrews, G. R. (Ed). (1998). Ageing beyond 2000: One world one future. *Australian Journal on Aging, 17* (1), Supplement.

Butler, R. N., & Brody, J. A. (Eds.). (1995). *Delaying the onset of late-life dysfunction*. New York: Springer.

Calle, E., Thun, M., Petrelli, J., Rodriguez, C., & Health, C. (1999). Body-mass index and mortality in a prospective cohort of U.S. adults. *The New England Journal of Medicine, 341* (15), 1097–1105.

Evers, M., Townsend, C., & Thompson, J. (1994). Organ physiology of aging. *Surgical Clinics of North America, 74* (1), 23–39.

Fries, J. F. (1980). Aging, natural death, and the compression of morbidity. *New England Journal of Medicine, 303*, 125–130.

Haug, M. R. (1994). Elderly patients, caregivers, and physicians: Theory and research on health care triads. *Journal of Health and Social Behavior, 35*, 1–12.

Hayflick, L. (1994). *How and why we age*. New York: Ballantine.

Kannus, P., Niemi, S., Parkkari, J., Palvanen, M., Vuori, I., & Jaumlrvinen, M. (1999). Hip fractures in Finland between 1970 and 1997 and predictors for the future. *Lancet, 353* (9155), 802–805.

Klerk, M., Huijsman, R., & McDonnell, J. (1997). The use of technical aids by elderly persons in the Netherlands: An application of the Andersen and Newman Model. *The Gerontologist, 37* (3), 365–373.

Lesnoff-Caravaglia, G. (Ed.). (1988). *Handbook of applied gerontology.* New York: Human Sciences Press.

——. (1999). Ethical issues in a high-tech society. In T. Fusco Johnson (Ed.), *Handbook on ethical issues in aging* (pp. 271–288). Westport, CT: Greenwood Press.

——. (2000). *Health aspects of aging.* Springfield, IL: Charles C Thomas Publishers.

Lesnoff-Caravaglia, G., & Klys, M. (1987). Lifestyle and longevity. In G. Lesnoff-Caravaglia (Ed.), *Realistic expectations for long life* (pp. 35–48). New York: Human Sciences Press.

Oram, J. J. (1997). *Caring for the fourth age.* London: Armelle.

McConnel, E., & Murphy, E. (1990). Nurses' use of technology: An international concern. *International Nursing Review, 37,* (5), 331–334.

Ross, I. K. (1995). *Aging of cells, humans & societies.* Dubuque, IA: Wm. C. Brown Publishers.

Rowe, J. W., & Kahn, R. (1996). *Successful aging.* New York: Pantheon.

Stolley, J., & Buckwalter, K. (1991). Iatrogenesis in the elderly. *Journal of Gerontological Nursing, 17* (9), 30–34.

Chapter 3

NUTRITION AND OLDER ADULTS

Namvar Zohoori

INTRODUCTION

THE CONCEPT OF SUCCESSFUL AGING is gaining increased prominence as an important factor in aging research. There is increasing awareness and debate that morbidity, functional disability, and senescence need not be inevitable consequences of aging. While there is as yet no generally accepted theory of cellular aging, it is believed that longevity and morbidity are affected by a mix of environmental and genetic factors. In the absence of such a theory on aging, and in view of the fact that the role of nutritional factors in the development and exacerbation of chronic diseases, as well as in the development of age-related changes, is being increasingly recognized, there is a growing interest, among both health care providers and consumers, in the field of nutrition and its relationship to changes with age.

It is important, therefore, for public health professionals, to be familiar with key nutrition facts as they relate to older populations, particularly recommendations, assessment, and factors that can affect diet and nutritional status, as well as availability of nu-

trition services for older adults. Every older adult is more of a distinct individual than every younger adult. The myriad injuries, diseases, and experiences that a body is subjected to throughout life, as well as the varying states of health, multiple medication use, and nutritional status, combine to produce a much more heterogeneous population as the age of the older population rises. The major implications of this process are that it is more difficult to generalize research findings about the elderly; notwithstanding, for the public health practitioner, it is necessary to have a certain basic and general understanding of the nutritional factors affecting older adults.

FOOD AND NUTRITION RECOMMENDATIONS

Getting adequate nutrients is particularly challenging for many older adults. On the one hand, due to a combination of reduced physical activity and altered sensory acuity, including satiety and taste (see section on Physiological, Psychological and Other Influ-

29

ences on the Nutritional Status of Older Americans), food and energy intake are reduced significantly with age (Elahi et al., 1983; McGandy et al., 1966). On the other hand, however, micronutrient requirements do not decrease significantly with age, and, in fact, in some cases, increase. Consequently, it becomes more difficult for older adults to obtain recommended levels of many nutrients on a daily basis. The development of dietary guidelines and nutrient recommendations for older adults continues to be much debated and has been a challenging area in public health nutrition.

Nutrient Recommendations

Recommended dietary allowances (RDAs), which have been in use since 1941 and are familiar to most Americans, were intended to provide an estimate of the nutrient needs of all healthy people (Institute of Medicine [IOM], 1989). However, for many years, the RDAs, the latest revision of which was published in 1989, were criticized for a number of shortcomings, particularly as they relate to older adults. First, these official recommendations for nutrient intakes of adults have included older adults as a single category of fifty-one years and over, a practice that is now recognized by many in the field of nutrition and aging to be unrealistic (Russel & Suter, 1993; Schneider, Vining, Hadley, & Farnham, 1986; Wood, Suter, & Russell, 1995). Second, the RDAs, as originally formulated, consist of a single value for each nutrient that were primarily intended for the prevention of deficiency diseases among otherwise healthy populations. With the increasing understanding of the importance of nutrition in the maintenance of health and the prevention of chronic diseases, and the concomitant need for a set of recommendations that can be used to these ends, the RDAs have been deemed inadequate.

Partly as a result of these limitations, in 1997, the Food and Nutrition Board, Institute of Medicine, released the first set of Dietary Reference Intakes (DRIs) (IOM, 1997). One relevant advantage of the DRIs is that nutrient values are provided for two groups of older adults—fifty-one to seventy years old, and seventy-one years and older. Another advantage is that for each age-gender group, and for each nutrient, the DRIs provide a range of values contained in four indices (IOM, 1999):

1. *The Estimated Average Requirement (EAR)* is the nutrient intake value estimated to meet the requirement in 50 percent of the individuals in a life stage and gender group. The EAR is expressed as a daily value averaged over time, at least one week for most nutrients, and it includes an adjustment for an assumed bioavailability of the nutrient. The EAR is used in setting the RDA and may be used as one factor for assessing the adequacy of intake of groups and for planning adequate intakes by groups.

2. *The Recommended Dietary Allowance (RDA)* is the average daily dietary intake level that is sufficient to meet the nutrient requirements of nearly all (97% to 98%) individuals in a life stage and gender group. The RDA applies to individuals, not to groups. If data are insufficient for a specific life-stage group to set an EAR, then no RDA will be set. An AI will be developed based on the data available (see next). The RDA for a nutrient is a value to be used as a goal for dietary intake by healthy individuals. It is not intended to be used for assessing the diets of either individuals or groups or to plan diets for groups.

3. *The Adequate Intake (AI)* is set instead of an RDA if sufficient scientific evidence is not available to calculate an EAR.

The AI is based on observed or experimentally determined estimates of average nutrient intake by a group (or groups) of healthy people. The main intended use of the AI is as a goal for the nutrient intake of individuals.

4. *The Tolerable Upper Intake Level (UL)* is the highest level of daily nutrient intake that is likely to pose no risks of adverse health effects to almost all individuals in the general population. As intake increases above the UL, the risk of adverse effects increases. The UL is not intended to be a recommended level of intake. There is no established benefit for healthy individuals associated with nutrient intakes above the RDA or AI. (p. 4)

The various components of the DRI can be used for both assessment and planning purposes, for both individuals and groups. The suggested uses of the various components are shown in Table 3.1. It is important to note that this new scheme underscores the fact that the use of the RDA itself is limited to planning purposes for individuals as an intake level toward which to aim.

DRIs for all nutrients are not yet available. Several committees of the Food and Nutrition Board are studying available scientific data and working on developing DRIs for related groups of nutrients. To date, DRIs have been released for three sets of nutrients: Calcium and related nutrients (Phosphorus, Magnesium, vitamin D, and Fluoride) (IOM, 1997), B vitamins (Thiamin, Riboflavin, Niacin, vitamin B6, Folate, vitamin B12, Pantothenic Acid, Biotin, and Choline) (IOM, 1998), and antioxidants (vitamin C, vitamin E, Selenium, Beta-Carotene, and other carotenoids) (IOM, 2000). Table 3.2 presents the most recent official recommendations. For all other nutrients, the RDAs from the 1989 edition are currently used as of this printing. It should be noted, however, that some of the

1989 values are now considered by many not to be the most appropriate. For example, the current official recommendation for protein of 0.8 g/kg body weight is strongly felt to be inadequate for many older adults. More recent studies indicate the protein requirement for older adults to be at least 1 g of high-quality protein per kg body weight, and many practitioners use this higher value.

Food Recommendations

It is obviously difficult for most people to think in terms of nutrients when considering their personal diet. Guidelines expressed in terms of foods are more intuitive and easier to convey in educational campaigns and one-on-one counseling. For this reason, the U.S. Department of Agriculture (USDA) and the U.S. Department of Health and Human Services (DHHS) have periodically published "Dietary Guidelines for Americans." The latest (fifth) edition of the guidelines was published in 2000 (USDA & DHHS, 2000) and the main sections are summarized in Table 3.3. A companion document, "The Food Guide Pyramid," has also been published for educational purposes and to make food choices easier (USDA, 1992).

In these publications, very little attention has been paid to the special needs of the elderly. As mentioned earlier, energy needs decrease with advancing age, thus necessitating decreased food intake. Thus, when dealing with older adults, it is important to highlight foods that offer a high-nutrient density (high ratio of micronutrients to energy). Partly because of these concerns, suggestions have been made for modification of the Food Guide Pyramid for people over seventy years of age (Russell, Rasmussen, & Lichtenstein, 1999). While still based on the principles of the Dietary Guidelines and emphasizing variety, diets high in grain products, vegetables, and fruits, and low in saturated fatty acids,

TABLE 3.1
Uses of Dietary References Intakes for Healthy Individuals and Groups

Type of Use	For the Individual	For a Group
Assessment	**EAR**: use to examine the possibility if inadequacy of reported intake. **AI**: intakes at this level have a low probability of inadequacy. **UL**: intake above this level has a risk of adverse effects.	**EAR**: use to estimate the prevalence of inadequate intakes within a group. **AI**: mean intake at this level implies a low prevalence of inadequate intakes. **UL**: use to estimate the prevalence of intakes that may be at risk of adverse effects.
Planning	**RDA**: aim for this intake **AI**: aim for this intake **UL**: use as a guide to limit intake; chronic intake of higher amounts may increase risk of adverse effects.	**EAR**: use in conjunction with a measure of variability of the group's intake to set goals for the median intake of a specific population.

Note: Compiled from Institute of Medicine (IOM), 1998, 1999.

cholesterol, sugar, salt, and alcohol, this modified Food Guide Pyramid also emphasizes the lower energy requirement of the elderly as well as the need for particular attention to intakes of water, fiber, calcium, vitamin D, and vitamin B-12.

COMMUNITY NUTRITION ASSESSMENT

Generally, community nutrition assessment has as its aim the identification of nutritional needs and problems within a defined community, as opposed to individuals. The ultimate goal of such assessment is the development of policies, programs, and services for the improvement and prevention of nutritional and health problems in the population being assessed. Based on a number of studies, simple protein-energy malnutrition among the elderly is a common occurrence in a variety of clinical situations, but is rarely recognized or treated (Miller, Morley, Rubenstein, Pietruszka, & Strone, 1990; Mowe & Bohmer, 1991). This, and most other common nutritional problems of the elderly are multifactorial in origin, thus making their prevention and treatment particularly challenging and underlining the need for comprehensive nutrition assessments.

While particular assessment activities may have very specific goals, in general, there are a number of important issues common to older populations that will have to be addressed in most community-based assessments, and for which data are needed. For a comprehensive assessment, a number of types of data are useful. Table 3.4 outlines the main types of data and possible general sources. While very project- and population-specific data need to be collected locally, a number of large-scale surveys provide information at national and regional levels. The applicability of these data to, and their coverage of, older populations has been uneven, although recent improvements have been

TABLE 3.2
**Recommended Dietary Allowances (RDA's) and Dietary Reference Intakes (DRI's)
for older Americans**

| | RDA's | | DRI's | | | |
| | 51+ years | | 51–70 years | | >70 years | |
Nutrient	Male	Female	Male	Female	Male	Female
Protein (g)	63	50				
Vitamin A (µg)	1,000	800				
Vitamin E (mg)	10	8				
Vitamin K (µg)	80	65				
Vitamin C (mg)	60	60				
Iron (mg)	10	10				
Zinc (mg)	15	12				
Iodine (mg)	150	150				
Selenium (µg)	70	55				
Calcium (mg/day)			1,200	1,200	1,200	1,200
Phosphorus (mg/day)			700	700	700	700
Magnesium (mg/day)			420	320	420	320
Vitamin D (µg/day)			10	10	15	15
Fluoride (mg/day)			4	3	4	3
Thiamin (mg/day)			1.2	1.1	1.2	1.1
Riboflavin (mg/day)			1.3	1.1	1.3	1.1
Niacin (mg/day)			16	14	16	14
Vitamin B_6 (mg/day)			1.7	1.5	1.7	1.5
Folate (µg/day)			400	400	400	400
Vitamin B_{12} (µg/day)			2.4	2.4	2.4	2.4
Panthotenic acid (mg/day)			5	5	5	5
Biotin (µg/day)			30	30	30	30
Choline (mg/day)			550	425	550	425

Note: Compiled from data from IOM, 1989, 1997, 1998.

TABLE 3.3
Dietary Guidelines for Americans

AIM FOR FITNESS . . .
    Aim for a healthy weight.
    Be physically active each day.
BUILD A HEALTHY BASE . . .
    Let the Pyramid guide your food choices.
    Choose a variety of grains daily, especially whole grains.
    Choose a variety of fruits and vegetables daily.
    Keep food safe to eat.
CHOOSE SENSIBLY . . .
    Choose a diet that is low in saturated fat and cholesterol and moderate in total fat.
    Choose beverages and foods to moderate your intake of sugars.
    Choose and prepare foods with less salt.
    If you drink alcoholic beverages, do so in moderation.

Note: Adapted from USDA & DHHS, 2000.

made. For example, the first two waves of the National Health and Nutrition Examination Surveys (NHANES) had an upper age limit that excluded the elderly from the sample of participants. However, NHANES III, conducted between 1988 and 1994, had no upper age limit and included a deliberate oversampling of older citizens, thus making it particularly useful for studies of nutrition among the elderly. Among other information, NHANES III included data on food intake, dietary habits, food security, anthropometry, blood levels of various nutrients, and dental examinations, and bone-mineral-density measurements (National Center for Health Statistics [NCHS], 1991). Similarly, the latest wave of the Continuing Survey of Food Intake by Individuals (CSFII), conducted in 1994–96, which is based on a nationally representative sample of U.S. noninstitutionalized individuals, included an oversampling of both low-income and elderly populations with no upper age limit (Life Sciences Research Office [LSRO], 1995). The Nationwide Food Consumption Survey, conducted decennially since 1935, also provides information on national trends in food consumption of households and individuals.

These national datasets notwithstanding, community-nutrition assessments of elderly populations, to be most useful and depending on their purpose, will probably need to be conducted at a more local level, identifying specific populations at risk. A number of instruments have recently been developed and validated for nutritional assessment of older persons. Many of these instruments were developed in response to the need for quick yet sensitive tools for early identification of nutritional problems among older populations and for targeting preventive and curative resources to those at greatest risk. Table 3.5 summarizes the components of the major instruments suitable for use in community settings, such as senior citizens' and adult day care centers, congregate meal sites, and as part of a home-delivered-meals program.

The Nutrition Screening Initiative (NSI) was developed in 1990 as a collaborative effort of the American Dietetic Association, the National Council on Aging, and the American Academy of Family Physicians as a tool for identifying older individuals at risk, as well as an educational tool. The NSI is administered at three levels (an initial checklist, a level I screen, and a level II screen), each level designed for more in-depth assessment than the previous one. Older adults who score poorly at each level are then assessed using the subsequent screening tool. The simple checklist can be self-administered or by a public health or community health worker. The level I screen, which goes into more detail regarding diet, nutritional and functional status, is usually administered by a health care worker in either a community or inpatient setting. A high score on this screen points to high nutritional risk and indicates the need for a level II screen. The latter is designed for use by physicians and other health professionals and is accompanied by a physical exam and more in-depth biochemical and clinical tests. The NSI has been adopted and initiated by Departments of Aging in a majority of states (Barrocas et al., 1995) and has been shown to be an effective and useful tool for identifying older individuals at greater risk of malnutrition (Herndon, 1995; Melnik, Helferd, Firmery, & Wales, 1994; Spangler & Eigenbrod, 1995).

The Nutrition Risk Index (NRI) is a simpler instrument consisting of sixteen questions that can be administered in a variety of community settings. Areas covered by the NRI include health conditions, oral and gastrointestinal health, medication use, smoking, diet, and recent weight change. A score of seven or more is indicative of greater risk of malnutrition. The NRI has been validated against a number of biochemical and clinical indicators of nutritional status (Wolisnky et al., 1990).

TABLE 3.4
Types of Data Needed for General Community-Level Nutrition Assessment

Data	Examples (not exhaustive)	Possible Source(s)
Objective data on nutritional status of community	• Levels of dietary intakes of specific nutrients • Anthropometric data (weight, height, skinfold thicknesses and circumferences) • Prevalence of specific nutritional problems (obesity, underweight, nutrient deficiencies, etc.)	Primary data: Collected by researchers themselves, based on specific perceived problems being investigated; Secondary data: Use of data available through various other national and local, public and private sources
Objective data on socioeconomic and environmental factors	• Income levels within the community, particularly among the elderly • Size of community and areas to be served • Demographic data about the population • Types and numbers of facilities where population resides	• Federal, state and local databases • Published literature
Objective data on available community resources	• Current nutrition programs and their levels, e.g., Congregate meals sites, home-delivered meals, Food Stamp, etc. • Public transportation facilities and their accessibility to the elderly • Levels of available state and federal funding	• Federal, state and local databases • Local service providers, companies and agencies • Volunteer organizations
Subjective data on perceived problems	• Specific subgroups at risk • Unusual or population-specific problems, eg migrants, minorities and cultural issues affecting nutrition and health	• Community leaders • Samples of population being assessed • Mangers and operators of current nutrition programs serving the elderly • Community residents • Health, nutrition and social workers serving the population • Senior citizen centers • Religious organizations

Note: Based on information in Bayerl (2000).

Similarly, the Mini Nutrition Assessment (MNA) has been validated among a wide range of older populations in a number of countries (Guigoz, Vellas, & Garry, 1994). The MNA is composed of simple measurements and of rapid questions to be performed in less than ten minutes. The broad areas covered in the MNA are the following:

1. anthropometric measurements (weight, height and weight loss),
2. dietary questionnaire (eight questions related to number of meals, food, and fluid intake and autonomy of feeding),
3. global assessment (six questions related to lifestyle, medications, and mobility), and
4. subjective assessment (self-perceptions of health and nutrition).

In addition, if necessary, a set of biological markers (biochemical indices such as albumin, cholesterol, and white cell count) can be added, taking a estimated additional ten minutes. The scoring of each part allows elderly persons to be categorized as normal (adequate nutrition), borderline (at risk of malnutrition), or frankly undernourished (Guigoz et al., 1994)

Physiological, Psychological and Other Influences on the Nutritional Status of Older Adults

Physiological change is an inevitable part of the aging process. This change can either be a result of underlying diseases, or part of "normal" aging, meaning not associated with any disease process. While it is important to differentiate these two, it is not always easy. In a healthy older adult normal daily body processes should be no different than those of a healthy younger adult. However, one of the hallmarks of aging is a decreased ability to respond to changes in the environment and to increased demand in times of stress. Under such conditions, the body can either fail to make the necessary homeostatic adjustments to deal with the insult, or once the insult has occurred, it can take a longer time to recover.

In general, almost all organ systems within the body undergo losses in reserve capacity. Such reserve capacity for maximal performance, which is usually severalfold the average daily demand under usual circumstances, allows most older individuals to function normally in their day-to-day activities. The rate and degree of loss in any one individual determines that person's level of ability to remain active and to cope with stress and disease. According to data from the Baltimore Longitudinal Study of Aging, which has been ongoing since 1958, the range of loss can vary greatly between various organ systems and between individuals (U.S. Department of Health and Human Services, 1984). Between the ages of thirty and eighty, loss in maximum breathing capacity can be as much as 60 percent, and loss in maximum work capacity as much as 70 percent. Resting cardiac output can decrease by 30 percent (U.S. Department of Health and Human Services, 1984). These changes in work, cardiac, and respiratory capacity have direct effects on the activity levels of many older individuals, which, in turn, can affect their energy output and intake. This is one of the main nutritional problems of the elderly with many nutritional consequences.

Table 3.6 provides a summary of the major physiological and other changes that can affect nutritional status in the elderly. Worthy of note is that most nutritional deficiencies in the elderly are multifactorial in origin, resulting from a combination of biological, socioeconomic, and psychological factors. In fact, as mentioned earlier, under normal circumstances, with adequate social, economic, and psychological support in an otherwise healthy older individual, physiological factors alone should not lead to major malnutrition. The active elderly population does not differ nutritionally from younger groups (Vellas, 1992). It is often a combination of the other factors that begin the cycle of downward nutritional status. A nutritional risk factor has been defined by White, Ham, Lip-

TABLE 3.5
Nutrition Assessment Instruments for Older Adults

Indicators measured	Checklist	Level 1 Screen	Level 2 Screen	NRI	MNA
Anthropometric					
Height		X	X		X
Weight		X	X		X
BMI		X	X		X
Weight change	X	X	X	X	X
Circumferences			X		X
Skinfolds			X		
Biochemical					
Albumin			X		
Cholesterol			X		
Clinical					
Clinical signs			X	X	
Functional status	X	X	X		X
Oral status	X	X	X	X	
Mental status			X		X
Drug use			X	X	X
Dietary					
Food group intake	X	X	X		X
Nonalcoholic fluid intake					X
Alcoholic beverage intake	X	X	X		
Change in food intake	X		X	X	X
Eating alone	X		X		
Food insecurity	X	X	X		
Appetite		X	X	X	
Special diet		X	X	X	
Other					
Living environment		X	X		X
Smoking				X	
Self-assessed nutritional and health status				X	X
Target Population					
Free-living	X	X		X	X
Adult day-care center	X	X		X	X
Congregate meal site	X	X		X	X
Home-delivered meal program	X	X			
Long-term care facility			X		X
Medical office			X		X
Hospital			X		X

NRI: Nutritional Risk Index
MNA: Mini Nutritional Assessment
BMI: Body Mass Index
Adapted from Schlenker (1998).

schutz, Dwyer, and Wellman (1991) as: ". . . a characteristic or occurrence that increases the likelihood that an individual has or will have problems with nutritional status" (p. 783). Among the most commonly cited major risk factors are oral status, depressive symptoms, multiple medication usage, and social isolation (Browne et al., 1997; Davies & Knutson, 1991; White, 1991; White et al., 1991).

Loss of loved ones, changing life circumstances, and loss of autonomy are important contributors to depression in old age. Among the U.S. civilian noninstitutional elderly population, there is an increasing prevalence of symptoms of depression with increasing age (Federal Interagency Forum on Aging-Related Statistics [FIFAS], 2000). Approximately 15 percent of persons ages sixty-five to seventy-nine have severe symptoms of depression, increasing to 21 percent of persons ages eighty to eighty-four, and 23 percent of persons aged eighty-five and older (FIFAS, 2000). Depressive symptoms are significantly associated with higher rates of physical illness, functional disability, and poor nutritional status (Kritchevsky et al., 1999; Payette, Gray-Donald, & Boutier, 1995; Wells et al., 1989).

Polypharmacy, or the use of multiple drugs, is recognized as an important risk factor for poor nutritional status among the elderly. Partly as a result of multiple chronic diseases and lack of well-coordinated medical care, and partly due to self-prescribed, over-the-counter (OTC) medications and supplements, a great number of older individuals are on multiple medications at any one time. The use of multiple prescription and OTC medications places older adults at risk for drug–nutrient interaction, drug–drug interaction, and increased risk for poor nutrition (Dwyer, 1994; Golden et al., 1999; Lassila et al., 1996; Schrader et al., 1996; Stoehr, Ganguli, Seaberg, Echement, & Belle, 1997; Wallsten et al., 1995; White, 1991; White et al.,

1991). Additionally, indiscriminate dietary-supplement use may also be of concern in the elderly because of the following:

1. adverse effects due to enhanced potential for toxicity;
2. interactions among nutrients, which may mean that large supplemental intakes of one nutrient could result in deficiencies of another;
3. the risk of supplement interference with drug absorption;
4. substantial expenditure on supplements, reducing the money available for food; and
5. reliance on dietary supplements being associated with an artificial sense of security about nutrient adequacy, thus potentially impairing the adequacy of food intake (Horwath, 1991).

Related to these concerns is the problem of self-imposed and deliberately altered dietary intakes. These alterations can potentially have serious effects on the nutritional and disease status of the elderly, particularly when superimposed on the already-low diet quality of the majority of the elderly. According to data from the *Continuing Survey of Food Intakes by Individuals,* 13 percent of individuals sixty-five years and older had diets rated as "poor" based on the Healthy Eating Index (Bowman, Lindo, & Gerior, 1998), and the diet of another 67 percent needed improvement, while older persons living in poverty were more likely to report a poor diet (21%) than were older persons living above the poverty level (11%) (FIFAS, 2000).

Probably the most manifest outcome of the various factors affecting nutritional status in the elderly is a derangement in energy balance. As a result of the combination of physiological, psychological, and socioeconomic factors, energy intake is reduced in the elderly, resulting in weight loss (Berkman, Foster, & Campion, 1989; Braun, Wynkle, & Cowl-

TABLE 3.6
Major Age-Related Physiological and Other Changes of Nutritional Significance

Musculoskeletal system	↓ bone mass and stature
	↓ lean body mass
	↑ body fat
	↓ body water
Gastrointestinal system	↓ digestive function
	↓ absorptive function
	↓ bowel function (resulting in constipation and diverticulosis)
Hepatic/Renal system	↓ liver size and function
	↓ renal capacity
Cardiopulmonary system	↑ blood pressure
	↓ lung capacity
	↓ adaptation to physical exertion
Oral cavity	↓ gum and dental health
	↓ saliva production
	↓ esophageal and other muscle tone
	↑ swallowing difficulties
Sensory changes	↓ taste, smell, vision and hearing
Psychological factors	↑ risk for bereavement
	↑ risk for depression
	↑ risk for dementia
Socioeconomic factors	↑ risk for social isolation
	↑ problems with transportation and housing
	↓ income
	↓ independence and autonomy
Functional abilities	↓ in diet related functional abilities (shopping, cooking, feeding skills)
Chronic diseases	↑ risk for major chronic diseases
	↑ risk for multiple medications (both medically prescribed and self-administered)

Note: Adapted from: Bartlett, Marian, Taren, & Muramoto, 1998.

ing, 1988; Elahi et al., 1983; McGandy et al., 1966). This weight loss is often composed of both lean and fat mass. In addition, relative physical inactivity leads to further loss of muscle mass, and possible losses in functional status. Loss of lean tissue, in turn, leads to lower basal metabolic rates, and the latter, combined with lower activity levels, reduces energy requirements, leading to lower dietary intakes. The cycle thus created can lead to a number of undesirable consequences, such as anorexia of aging, failure to thrive, sarcopenia (further loss of muscle mass), and micronutrient deficiencies (Berkman et al., 1989; Duffy, Backstrand, & Ferris, 1995).

FOOD AND NUTRITION SERVICES FOR OLDER ADULTS

From the foregoing, it is clear that the elderly are at particular risk of nutritional problems. In 1998, approximately 1.6 million to 2 million elderly households experienced problems in obtaining a sufficient amount or quality of food (General Accounting Office [GAO], 2000). Of these, about 1 million to 1.2 million, or 60 percent, were low income, and approximately 500,000 to 660,000 reduced their food intake to the point that they experienced hunger. Therefore, special attention needs to be paid to nutritional support of the elderly in all settings. Mainly as a result of this recognition, many government agencies and professional agencies have developed guidelines and recommendations for nutritional services targeted at older citizens. In response to these recommendations, several federally mandated programs now exist to provide elderly-nutrition support.

The Elderly Nutrition Program

The Elderly Nutrition Program (ENP) is a program of the Administration on Aging (AOA) mandated by Titles III and VI of the Older Americans Act. It is the largest U.S. community-nutrition program for older persons. The ENP, which is intended to improve the dietary intake of, and provide social support for, older Americans, provides grants, through Title III, to State Units on Aging, and their Area Agencies on Aging, and through Title VI, to Tribal Organizations throughout the country. These funds provide for congregate and home-delivered meals, at least once a day, and five or more times per week, in a variety of settings. In addition, a range of related services are provided by some of the aging network's nutrition-service providers. These include nutrition screening, assessment, education, and counseling. Together, these services provide not only meals, but also a range of services aimed at helping older participants to identify their general and special nutrition needs, to learn to shop for or to plan and prepare meals that are economical and healthy, and to provide positive social contacts with other older adults at group meal sites. Meals provided through ENP support are required to provide at least one-third of daily RDAs for nutrients.

There are two main components to the ENP (Figure 3.1). On the one hand, a large number of participants receive their meals at congregate meal sites. These may include senior centers, religious facilities, schools, public or low-income housing, or residential-care facilities. Under this scheme, social and other health and nutrition services are also provided at the site. On the other hand, for those elderly who are homebound, meals are delivered to homes by a number of local agencies and volunteers. These volunteers are encouraged to spend some time with the elderly. The volunteers also offer an important opportunity to check on the welfare of the homebound elderly and are encouraged to report any health or other problems that they may note during their visits.

There are no specific-means tests for participation in the ENP, and basically any person sixty years and older is eligible. Generally, the program is targeted at older people with low income and greater social need. In addition, other specific criteria include the following:

1. a spouse of any age,
2. disabled persons under age sixty who reside in housing facilities occupied primarily by the elderly where congregate meals are served,
3. disabled persons who reside at home and accompany older persons to meals,
4. and nutrition service volunteers.

In 1998, the AOA estimated that about 244 million meals were served as part of the ENP, with about 53 percent being home delivered (GAO, 2000). This represents an 11-percent increase in home-delivered meals compared to 1990. In this same period, the number of congregate meals decreased by about 20 percent. The average cost of an ENP meal, including the value of donated labor and supplies, was estimated at $5.17 for congregate meals and $5.31 for home-delivered meals under Title III in 1996. The comparable costs for Title VI are $6.19 and $7.18, respectively (Posza, Ohls, & Millen, 1996). It is, however, felt that federal dollars spent on the ENP are cost-effective, because they are highly leveraged by state, tribal, local, and other federal funding and services and are also augmented by donations from participants. Typically, $1.00 of Title III funds spent on congregate services is supplemented by an additional $1.70 from other sources, and $1.00 of Title III funds spent on home-delivered services is supplemented by an additional $3.35 from other sources (Posza et al., 1996). Leverage of Title VI funds are significantly lower.

Over the years, a number of studies have been conducted to evaluate the effectiveness of the ENP in meeting its objectives and the needs of the elderly citizens that it serves (Posza, Ohls, & Millen, 1994). Although the majority of these studies have methodological flaws, such as small, local, and unrepresentative samples, together they have pointed to a number of important features of the program. There seems to be agreement that, overall, participants have higher nutrient intakes and greater levels of socialization. Also a number of programs provide services above and beyond that required by the ENP mandate. These include important links to other needed supportive in-home and community-based services, such as homemaker-home health aide services, transportation, fitness programs, and even home-repair and home-modification programs, as well as breakfast, weekend and evening meals, ethnic meals, food pantries, and therapeutic diets (Balsam & Rogers, 1989).

The largest and most comprehensive recent evaluation of the ENP was mandated by the Congress itself. This report, released in 1996, was aimed, among other things, at evaluating the program's effects on participants' nutritional status and socialization, and evaluating who is using the program and how effectively the program serves targeted groups (U.S. Department of Health and Human Services, 1996). The study was based on a national sample of fifty-five state units on aging and a random sample of program participants, nonparticipants, and agencies. This study showed that the average age of participants is higher than the general U.S. population sixty years and older; about 70 percent are females, compared to 58 percent in the general elderly population; about 26 percent are of minority ethnic–racial origin, compared to 14 percent in the general older population; between 80 and 90 percent of participants have incomes below 200 percent of the poverty level, which is twice the rate for the overall U.S. elderly population; more than twice as many Title III participants live alone, compared with the overall elderly population; about two-thirds of participants are either over- or underweight, placing them at increased risk for nutrition and health problems; and Title III home-delivered participants have more than twice as many physical impairments, compared with the overall elderly population. Furthermore, the study confirmed that the ENP has succeeded in accomplishing its mission of improving the nutritional intakes of the elderly, as well as in decreasing their social isolation. ENP meals provide approximately 40 to 50 percent of participants' daily intakes of most nutrients, and those who receive ENP meals have higher daily intakes of key nutrients than similar nonparticipants. Participants have more social contacts per month than similar nonparticipants, and most participants are satisfied with the services the ENP provides (HHS, 1996).

However, the study also points to shortcomings of the ENP. Chief among these is

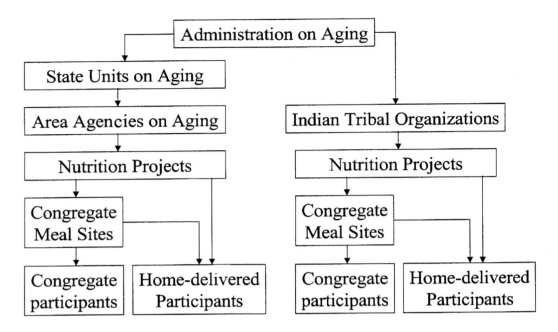

Figure 3.1. Structure of the elderly nutrition program

that, based on funding level, many agencies are already at their maximum capacity for serving meals to the elderly population. Forty-one percent of Title III ENP service providers have waiting lists for home-delivered meals, and another 9 percent have waiting lists for group meal programs, suggesting a significant unmet need for these meals (HHS, 1996). These figures are, in fact, likely to be underestimates, since many nutrition programs with unmet needs do not maintain waiting lists (GAO, 2000).

Food Stamp Program

The Food Stamp Program (FSP) administered by the Food and Nutrition Service (FNS) and run by state public-assistance agencies through their local offices, is the largest federal program serving older adults in both the number of participants and cost.

In 1998, FSP had an average monthly participation of 1.5 million elderly households, spending about $1 billion in benefits for these households (GAO, 2000).

Eligibility and amounts of benefit are dependent on the type and amount of income, as well as household size and other expenses. For elderly households, certain special concessions apply. For example, while general recipients must meet both gross- and net-income limits, elderly households are only required to meet the net-income limit, thus meeting eligibility at higher gross incomes. Based on household size, the maximum food stamp allotment is set annually at the cost of the U.S. Department of Agriculture's Thrifty Food Plan and indexed annually for food-price inflation. Food stamp allotments are based on the maximum allotment, adjusted for household size, less 30 percent of monthly net income. The FSP, therefore, is not intended to provide a complete food budget, and most households must spend a portion of their own cash along with the food stamps in order to buy adequate amounts of food.

According to FNS quality-control data for 1998, FSP older participants have an average age of sixty-six years, are 73 percent female (compared to 58% in the general U.S. population sixty years and over), have gross and net monthly incomes of $589 and $334, respectively, and are three times more likely to be from minority groups compared to the general U.S. population sixty years and over (42% vs. 14%, respectively). Compared to the ENP, therefore, FSP participants are a population more vulnerable to malnutrition (more economically disadvantaged, older, more likely to live alone, more rural, with a greater proportion from minority groups).

Studies that evaluate the effectiveness of the FSP in improving the nutritional status of the elderly are few, and whether the FSP is effective in improving the nutritional status of older participants remains questionable. Akin, Guilkey, and Popkin (1985) reported higher levels of nutrient intake among participant elderly persons than among nonparticipants. However, in the same year, Butler, Ohls, and Posner (1985) found no significant differences in nutrient intakes of otherwise similar participant and nonparticipant older individuals. Data from NHANES I and II have also shown that for the poor elderly, food stamp use was not consistently associated with differences in energy status, as indicated by weight, skinfold, and energy intake (Lopez & Habicht, 1987a) or with better iron nutrition (Lopez & Habicht, 1987b). These studies seem to indicate that, although there may be an improvement in the nutrient intake of older Food Stamp participants, these increases are not necessarily translating into better nutritional status. Further evaluation of the effectiveness of the FSP among the elderly and the reason for these discrepancies is needed.

Other Programs

Two other programs that provide for elderly nutrition are worthy of mention. The Commodity Supplemental Food Program (CSFP), authorized under section 4(a) of the Agriculture and Consumer Protection Act of 1973, currently operates in twenty-two states and the District of Columbia, and in most of these states, the program operates only in parts of the state. Although the CSFP has a relatively small and fluctuating budget ($88.3 million in fiscal year 2000), about 71 percent of the enrolled participants are elderly (270,000 of 382,000 people) (GAO, 2000). Other eligible participants, who actually get preference over the elderly, are low-income infants, children, and pregnant, postpartum, and lactating women. Older persons must meet state-residency requirements and have household incomes below 130 percent of the federal poverty level to qualify. Under this program, participants receive, at no cost, boxed and canned goods generally distributed once a month through distribution centers in locations generally accessible to low-income citizens, such as churches and community centers. The program also provides nutrition education through these centers. There are no comprehensive data on the evaluation of this program, or regarding the characteristics of the older population served.

Older Americans over sixty years old who attend nonresidential day care facilities are also eligible for meals at these facilities through the Child and Adult Care Food Program (CACFP). Under this program, the USDA provides partial-meal reimbursements to licensed day care facilities, and meals are provided either free (for those from families with an income below 130% of the poverty level), or at a reduced price (for those with a family income between 130% and 185% of the poverty level). Meals served must meet certain minimum-nutritional requirements, and each participant can receive either two meals and one snack or one meal and two snacks per day. Adult participation in CACFP has increased every year since 1993, from an average daily attendance of 36,000 to about 63,000 in 1999, while the number of participating facilities has increased from 1,222 to 1,855 (GAO, 2000). During this same period, federal reimbursement to adult day care centers for meals has more than doubled to about $36.5 million in 1999. Although the USDA does not maintain a separate database for the adult participants in the CACFP, the latest available information indicates that 84 percent of the participants have incomes below 130 percent of the poverty level, 40 percent are not married and live alone, and the majority also participate in Medicaid, SSI, and Food Stamp programs (USDA, 1993).

The trends in participation rates and funding levels, and the characteristics of participants in these programs, underscore the increasing need for nutritional services and support aimed at older individuals. At the same time, the federal government has recognized that many older individuals who are eligible for, and could benefit from these programs, are not participating in them. According to a federal report released in August 2000 (General Accounting Office [GAO], 2000), a number of reasons account for older persons' nonparticipation in federal nutrition-assistance programs. Some reasons cut across programs, such as lack of awareness regarding the existence of the programs or the application process, or the belief by some older individuals that accepting food assistance would compromise their independence; and the constraints on funding, which contribute to waiting lists for ENP home-delivered meals or limit the range of CSFP services. Other reasons are associated with a particular program, such as the perceived burdensome application procedure for food stamps, or a shortage of licensed adult care facilities participating in CACFP (GAO, 2000).

Public health practitioners and those working with older individuals, agencies, and organizations can have a direct role in improving coverage and participation rates in these programs. Activities in this area can range from public education and advocacy campaigns, to individual counseling with older persons and their families and care providers.

CONCLUSION

Older individuals are a nutritionally vulnerable segment of the population. Many nutritional problems in the elderly go undetected by health care providers and public health workers, mainly due to a lack of awareness of the existence of the problem and its manifestations. In addition, the elderly, their family members, and caretakers need to be educated regarding issues of nutrition and diet among older persons. Several government programs have been instituted in support of nutrition among the elderly. However, there are a number of unmet needs in this area, and these are likely to increase as the older segment of society increase in size and proportion over the next few decades.

REFERENCES

Akin, J. S., Guilkey, D. K., & Popkin, B. M. (1985). The impact of federal transfer programs on the nutrient intake of elderly individuals. *Journal of Human Resources, 20,* 382–404.

Balsam, A. L., & Rogers, B. L. (1989). Food service trends in the elderly nutrition program. *Journal of Nutrition for the Elderly, 9,* 19–26.

Bartlett, S., Marian, M., Taren, D., & Muramoto, M. L. (1998). *Geriatric nutrition handbook.* New York: Chapman and Hall.

Barrocas, A., Bistrian, B. R., Blackburn, G. L., Chernoff, R., Lipschitz, D. A., Cohen, D., Dwyer, J., Rosenberg, I. H., Ham, R. J., & Keller, G. C. (1995). Appropriate and effective use of the NSI checklist and screens. *Journal of the American Dietetics Association, 95,* 647–648.

Bayerl, C. T. (2000). Nutrition in the community. In L. K. Mahan & S. Escott-Stump (Eds.). *Krause's food, nutrition and diet therapy.* Philadelphia: W.B. Saunders Company.

Berkman, B., Foster, L. W., & Campion, E. (1989). Failure to thrive: paradigm for the frail elder. *Gerontologist, 29,* 654–659.

Bowman, S. A., Lindo, M., & Gerior, S. A. (1998). *The healthy eating index 1994–96.* Hyattsville, MD: Human Nutrition Information Service. CNPP-5.

Braun, J. V., Wykle, M. H., & Cowling, W. R. III. (1988). Failure to thrive in older persons: A concept derived. *Gerontologist, 28,* 809–812.

Browne, J. P., O'Doherty, V. A., McGee, H. M., McLaughlin, B., O'Boyle, C. A., & Fuller, R. (1997). General practitioner and public health nurse views of nutritional risk factors in the elderly. *Irish Journal of Medical Science, 166,* 23–25.

Butler, J. S., Ohls, J. C., & Posner, B. M. (1985). The effect of the food stamp program on the nutrient intake of the eligible elderly. *Journal of Human Resources, 20,* 405–419.

Davies, L., & Knutson, K. C. (1991). Warning signals for malnutrition in the elderly. *Journal of the American Dietetics Association, 91,* 1413–1417.

Duffy, V. B., Backstrand, J. R., & Ferris, A. M. (1995). Olfactory dysfunction and related nutritional risk in free-living, elderly women. *Journal of the American Dietetic Association, 95,* 879–884.

Dwyer, J. (1994). Nutritional problems of elderly minorities. *Nutrition Reviews, 52,* S24–S27.

Elahi, V. K., Elahi, D., Andres, R., Tobin, J. D., Butler, M. G., & Norris, A. H. (1983). A longitudinal study of nutritional intake in men. *Journal of Gerontology, 38,* 162–180.

Federal Interagency Forum on Aging-related Statistics (FIFAS). (2000). *Older Americans 2000: Key indicators of well-being.* Hyattsville, MD: Author.

General Accounting Office (GAO). (2000). *Food assistance: Options for improving nutrition for older Americans.* Washington, DC: Author.

Golden, A. G., Preston, R. A., Barnett, S. D., Llorente, M., Hamdan, K., & Silverman, M. A. (1999). Inappropriate medication prescribing in homebound older adults. *Journal of the American Geriatrics Society, 47,* 948–953.

Guigoz, Y., Vellas, B., & Garry, P. J. (1994). Mini nutritional assessment: A practical assessment tool for grading the nutritional state of elderly patients. *Facts and Research in Gerontology, Suppl. 2,* 15–60.

Herndon, A. S. (1995). Using the Nutrition Screening Initiative to survey the nutritional status of clients participating in the home-delivered meals program. *Journal of Nutrition in the Elderly, 14,* 15–29.

Horwath, C. C. (1991). Nutrition goals for older adults: A review. *The Gerontologist, 31,* 811–821.

Institute of Medicine (IOM). (1989). *Recommended dietary allowances: 10th edition.* Subcommittee on the Tenth Edition of the Recommended Dietary Allowances, National Research Council. Food and Nutrition Board. Washington, DC: National Academy Press.

——. (1997). *Dietary reference intakes for Calcium, Phosphorus, Magnesium, vitamin D, and Fluoride.* A report of the Standing Committee on the Scientific Evaluation of Dietary Reference Intakes and its Panel on Calcium and Related Nutrients and Subcommittee on Upper Reference Levels of Nutrients, Food and Nutrition Board. Washington, DC: National Academy Press.

——. (1998). *Dietary reference intakes for Thiamin, Riboflavin, Niacin, vitamin B6, Folate, vitamin B12, Pantothenic Acid, Biotin, and Choline.* A Report of the Standing Committee on the Scientific Evaluation of Dietary Reference Intakes and its Panel on Folate, Other B Vitamins, and Choline and Subcommittee on Upper Reference Levels of Nutrients. Food and Nutrition Board. Washington, DC: National Academy Press.

——. (1999). *Dietary reference intakes: A risk assessment model for establishing upper intake levels for nutrients*. Food and Nutrition Board. Washington, DC: National Academy Press.

———. (2000). *Dietary reference intakes for vitamin C, vitamin E, Selenium, and Carotenoids*. A Report of the Panel on Dietary Antioxidants and Related Compounds, Subcommittees on Upper Reference Levels of Nutrients and Interpretation and Uses of DRIs, Standing Committee on the Scientific Evaluation of Dietary Reference Intakes. Food and Nutrition Board. Washington, DC: National Academy Press.

Kritchevsky, S., Satterfield, S., Rubin, S., Wing, R., Tylavsky, F., & Harriss, T. (1999). Patterns and correlates of self-reported short-term weight loss. *The Gerontologist, 39,* 192.

Lassila, H. C., Stoehr, M., Seaberg, E. C., Gilby, J. E., Belle, S. H., & Echement, D. A. (1996). Use of prescription medications in an elderly rural population: The MoVIES Project. *Annals of Pharmacotherapy, 30,* 589–95.

Lopez, L. M., & Habicht, J. P. (1987a). Food stamps and the energy status of the U.S. elderly poor. *Journal of the American Dietetic Association, 87,* 1020–1024.

———. (1987b). Food stamps and the iron status of the U.S. elderly poor. *Journal of the American Dietetic Association, 87,* 598–603.

Life Sciences Research Office (LSRO). (1995). *Third report on nutrition monitoring in the United States, Vol. 1.* Federation of American Societies for Experimental Biology. Washington, DC: U.S. Government Printing Office.

McGandy, R. B., Barrows, C. H., Spanias, A., Meredith, A., Stone, J. L., & Norris, A. H. (1966). Nutrient intakes and energy expenditure in men of different ages. *Journal of Gerontology, 21,* 581–587.

Melnik, T. A., Helferd, S. J., Firmery, L. A., & Wales, K. R. (1994). Screening elderly in the community: The relationship between dietary adequacy and nutritional risk. *Journal of the American Dietetics Association, 94,* 1425–1427.

Miller, D. K., Morley, J. E., Rubenstein, L. Z., Pietruszka, F. M., & Strome, L. S. (1990). Formal geriatric assessment instruments and the care of older general medical outpatients. *Journal of the American Geriatrics Society, 38,* 645–651.

Mowe, M., & Bohmer, T. (1991). The prevalence of undiagnosed protein-calorie undernutrition in a population of hospitalized elderly patients. *Journal of the American Geriatrics Society, 39,* 1089–1092.

National Center for Health Statistics (NCHS). (1990). *National health and nutrition examination survey (NHANES III) data collection forms.* Hyattsville, MD: U.S. Department of Health and Human Services. NTIS No. PB90-236738INZ.

Payette, H., Gray-Donald, K., Cyr, R., & Boutier, V. (1995). Predictors of dietary intake in a functionally dependent elderly population in the community. *American Journal of Public Health, 85,* 677–683.

Posza, M., Ohls, J. C., & Millen, B. E. (1994). *Elderly nutrition program evaluation literature review.* Princeton, NJ: Mathematica Policy Research, Inc.

———. (1996). *Serving elders at risk: The Older American Act nutrition programs. National evaluation of the elderly nutrition program, 1993–1995.* Washington, DC: Office of the Assistant Secretary for Planning and Evaluation. Office of the Assistant Secretary for Aging, U.S. Department of Health and Human Services. NTIS No. PB97-106769.

Russell, R. M., & Suter, P. M. (1993). Vitamin requirements of elderly people: an update. *American Journal of Clinical Nutrition, 58,* 4–16.

Russell, R. M., Rasmussen, H. M., & Lichtenstein, A. H. (1999). The Food Guide Pyramid for people over seventy years of age. *Journal of Nutrition, 129,* 751–753.

Schlenker, E. D. (1998). *Nutrition in aging.* Boston, MA: McGraw-Hill.

Schneider, E. L., Vining, E. M., Hadley, E. C., & Farnham, S. A. (1986). Recommended dietary allowances and the health of the elderly. *New England Journal of Medicine, 314,* 157–160.

Schrader, S. L., Dressing, B., Blue, R., Jensen, G., Miller, D., & Zawada, E. T. (1996). The Medication Reduction Project: Combating polypharmacy in South Dakota elders through community-based interventions. *South Dakota Journal of Medicine,* 441–448.

Spangler, A. A., & Eigenbrod, J. S. (1995). Field trial affirms value of DETERMINE-ing nutrition-related problems of free-living elderly. *Journal of the American Dietetics Association, 95,* 489–90.

Stoehr, G. P., Ganguli, M., Seaberg, E. C., Echement, D. A., & Belle S. (1997). Over-the-counter medication use in an older rural community: The MoVIES Project. *Journal of the American Geriatrics Society, 45,* 158–165.

U.S. Department of Agriculture, Human Nutrition Information Service. (1992). The Food Guide Pyramid. *Home and Garden Bulletin,* No. 252. Washington, DC: Superintendent of Documents.

U.S. Department of Agriculture (USDA). (1993). National study of the adult component of the child and adult care food program (CACFP): Final report. Princeton, NJ: Mathematica Policy Research.

U.S. Department of Agriculture and Department of Health and Human Services. (2000). *Dietary guidelines for Americans, 5th ed. Home and Garden Bulletin,* No. 232. Washington, DC: Superintendent of Documents.

U.S. Department of Health and Human Services (USDHHS). (1984). *The Baltimore longitudinal study of aging.* (NIH Publication No. 84-2450.) Washington, DC: U.S. Government Printing Office.

——. (1996). *Serving elders at risk: The Older Americans Act nutrition programs–national evaluation of the Elderly Nutrition Program 1993–1995.* Washington, DC: Administration on Aging.

Vellas, B. (1992). Effects of the aging process on the nutritional status of elderly persons. In H. Munro & G. Schlierf (Eds.), *Nutrition of the elderly.* Nestle Nutrition Workshop Series, Vol. 29 (pp. 75–78). New York: Vevey/Raven Press.

Wallsten, S. M., Sullivan, R. J., Hanlon, J. T., Blazer, D. G., Tyrey, M. J., & Westlund, R. (1995). Medication taking behaviors in the high- and low-functioning elderly: MacArthur Field Studies of Successful Aging. *Annals of Pharmacotherapy, 29,* 359–64.

Wells, K. B., Stewart, A., Hays, R. D., Burnam, M.A., Rogers, W., Daniels, M., Berry, S., Greenfield, S., & Ware, J. (1989). The functioning and well-being of depressed patients. Results from the Medical Outcomes Study. *Journal of the American Medical Association, 262,* 914–919.

White, J. (1991). Risk factors for poor nutritional status in older Americans. *American Family Physician, 44,* 2087–2097.

White, J., Ham, R., Lipschitz, D., Dwyer, J., & Wellman, N. (1991). Consensus of the Nutrition Screening Initiative: Risk factors and indicators of poor nutritional status in older Americans. *Journal of the American Dietetics Association, 91,* 783–787.

Wolinsky, F. D., Coe, R. M., McIntosh, W. A., Kubena, K. S., Prendergast, J. M., Chavez, M. N., Miller, D. K., Romeis, J. C., & Landmann, W. A. (1990). Progress in the development of a nutritional risk index. *Journal of Nutrition, 120,* 1549–1553.

Wood, R. J., Suter, P. M., & Russell, R. M. (1995). Mineral requirements of elderly people. *American Journal of Clinical Nutrition, 62,* 493–505.

III. PSYCHOSOCIAL ASPECTS OF AGING AND PUBLIC HEALTH

Chapter 4

PSYCHOSOCIAL PARAMETERS OF AGING

ANN RATHBUN

SOCIETAL ATTITUDES TOWARD AGING

Social Theories of Aging and Old Age

AMERICAN SOCIETY IS BASED on a youthful stereotype that glorifies looking, feeling, and being young. Part of the social reality in the United States is that one is not "right" if one is wrinkled, one's face is lined, or if one does not have the body of a "supermodel." These images, fueled by the media, are pervasive in society. Such images do not allow for the representation in the media of the majority of individuals who make up society.

Moreover, the pervasiveness of these images is detrimental to many facets of society, principally the elderly. To watch television and to rarely see images of elders is more evidence that older Americans are not as highly valued, interesting, or entertaining as is the "younger generation." Even when older Americans are seen on the small (or big) screen, they are often portrayed as lifeless, boring, demented, ill, or disabled. Of the top ten television shows of the 1990s, none had older individuals as a main character. In addition, the top movies of the 90s did not depict older Americans as a lead character. According to Schobeloch (2000), the images of older Americans in prime time television seem to be negative. In one scene of a popular television show, it was consistently asked of an older character, "Is he still alive?" This character was playing a security guard at a school, and the younger characters repeated this question during the thirty-minute episode of this sitcom. There is socialized shame about growing old. One is socialized to lie about one's age, to cover lines on one's face, and to think that surgery is the solution to not looking older. There are few other "conditions" that share the same stigma as aging; however, gerontophobia can carry as much stigma as disability, racism, classism, or homophobia. A phobia is defined as "an irrational or intense fear" of something. In American society, there is an irrational or intense fear of growing old.

It is important to note that implications for ageism and gerontophobia are manifested in the medicalization of aging. There are many health care dollars spent in the last years of one's life, and there are many at-

51

tempts made to "fix" aging bodies and minds. There is a wide array of medications marketed to older individuals. These pharmaceuticals include drugs to fix sexual dysfunction and bladder incontinence. Physicians are anxious to oblige the aging person in an individual quest to feel better, to feel normal, and to perform in an accustomed manner.

There are a number of factors that contribute to this irrational and intense fear of growing older. Ageism, as discussed here, is one. A fear of dying and facing one's own mortality is another.

Public health professionals and other health care practitioners need to be educated with respect to what constitutes "normal" aging and what alterations disease and dysfunction render as one ages. Public health professionals and other health care practitioners have a responsibility to dispel the myths surrounding aging.

Silverman and Maxwell (1978) devised a system for measuring the degree of esteem granted to those who are aged. The system is titled the "deference index." There are seven types of deference that an individual may enjoy. They include the following:

1. *Spatial deference:* being given special places to sit, park, or other physical places of honor in the society (e.g., Japan's public transportation system has "Silver Seats" which are given to seniors on buses).
2. *Victual deference:* receiving special foods (particularly reserved for the elder), or being served before others.
3. *Linguistic deference:* being addressed with a special title based on the age of the individual. Being referred to as Señora or Señor in Latino–Mexican American cultures, or being referred to as "grandfather" as members of certain West African or Native American tribes (regardless of whether one is a blood relative or not).

4. *Presentational deference:* gestures such as bowing honor those in the society who are older.
5. *Service deference:* work or service performed for the elder (not specifically due to the physical or mental status of the individual).
6. *Prestative (gift-giving) deference:* gifts are given out of respect with no expectation for reciprocation.
7. *Celebrative deference:* ceremonies, plays, or other productions are held to honor the elders in a society.

Deferential treatment also extends to behaving in an unusually respectful manner toward elders in social situations. Respect is also demonstrated through the seeking of advice from older family or community members or by naming children after an elder in the family or community.

As one grasps a deeper understanding of societal views of aging, it is important to understand the theories that accompany such views. Theories provide public health professionals with a foundation for understanding the "changing phenomenon of aging" (Brown, 1990, p. 57).

Although aging theories continue to evolve, there are some warnings given by Lomranz (1998) with regard to stereotyping older Americans based on particular studies (and their subsequent theories). Lomranz (1998) is highly critical of developmental theories as they relate to aging and contends that the "impact of society is inadequately discussed" (p. 220). Lomranz further states that by failing to look at social and cultural "dynamics," the social reality of older individuals is not brought to light in some (developmental) theories of aging. It seems that the "culture of aging" is transformed into the dominant culture's experience of aging in many of the theories of aging. This will be discussed in more detail later in this chapter.

Concern for the isolation and potential lack of worth felt by elderly individuals in contemporary society led to the development of the field of social gerontology in the 1950s. A series of theories of aging soon followed that eventually provided the basis for current attitudes on aging.

One of the earliest theories was entitled the *disengagement theory* (Cumming & Henry, 1961). The theory assumed that social and psychological disengagement was a normal part of aging and that the elderly were naturally supposed to stop being active and to withdraw from the mainstream of life. The theory implied that this disengagement was universal, and that it applied to all elderly. Furthermore, the theory excused the phenomenon of social isolation and mental health issues for the elderly as perfectly natural; therefore, there was nothing that could or should be done to alleviate these "problems" in the older population.

One other popular theory developed by social gerontologists was the *activity theory*. The theory assumed that the needs or interests of older adults were similar to those of younger adults. The theory did not take into consideration cultural differences. Problems inherent in the activity theory included not fully recognizing the aging process, why older persons become inactive, whether or not older persons were choosing to be inactive or whether inactivity was "forced" on them by lack of choices. Other problems included questions regarding meaningfulness of activity in older versus younger populations. To start a theoretical base for the discipline was important, and the activity theory was, indeed, a starting point.

Social gerontologists began to combine theories in the 1960s to focus on the understanding of older persons as individuals. Such combinations resulted in ways of thinking that were related to loss of major life roles, and the effect that loss was having on older individuals. In this new approach, loss of roles was responsible for disengagement and lack of activity. Individuals were thought to be dissatisfied with life, and their level of activity was primarily indicated by the roles that had once been theirs and now were lost. These roles provided older persons with a sense of purpose, gave them personal identity, and furnished meaning to their lives.

One of the main losses and a source for dissatisfaction was the loss of a formal work life. Even women, who were not typically working outside the home during the early 1960s, were thought to experience some of the same losses due to the return of the men to the household or to children leaving the home (empty nest). Work is so central to this society that, as soon as one is not able to (or willing to) "contribute" to society, that person may be regarded as less valuable than those who are still in the workforce. There are built-in rewards for working. Rewards could include being given auxiliary roles in the civic and religious society by being elected as leaders, contributors and/or members. When one is no longer working, the built-in rewards of work are also "lost." The idea of "loss" began to touch on some of the attitudes that are still pervasive in society today. Losses experienced by older individuals in our society have very little to do with conscious social withdrawal or role loss by this group. The losses felt may have more to do with the way in which our "busy" productivity-oriented society views older Americans. The views of mainstream society often picture older people as less productive and taking more from the system than they give (back). Normal losses (whether they be physical, familial, or peer loss through death) and a lack of alternatives make adjustments more difficult for elders as they lack psychosocial support from society at large.

This concept seems rather classist in nature, in that, not all Americans were fortunate enough to work (some due to disability, geographic restraints, or extreme poverty). Another pervasive theme is heterosexism. Not all women were married to men (or vice versa) and had children, making this concept seemingly unrelated to some segments of the population.

The *continuity theory* maintains that elders behave, later in life, exactly as they did in the early stages of their lives. For example, if individuals were socially active and engaged in life, then they would be socially active and engaged in later life. An overriding theme of this theory was to allow society to accept the aged individual in the context of that individual's life (personality and long-standing behavior) and not really from the perspective of accepting social responsibility for this group. This theory did not enjoy wide acceptance by either social theorists or gerontologists.

The *socially disruptive events theory* brought together the work of Tallman and Kutner (1970) and Brown (1974). Both projects discovered that social disengagement was due to the number of events (death of a spouse, retirement, and loss of physical capacities), and the timing of these events was the most important predictors of disengagement. If an individual were to experience grief complicated by physical incapacity, that individual would be likely to disengage socially and probably find it difficult to reengage without great difficulty. Disengagement was found to be undesirable, but inevitable after events of such severity and of such lengthy duration.

All the theories that had been constructed from the 1950s through the 1970s had their basis in a negative view of older individuals. The *reconstruction theory* (Kuypers & Bengtson, 1973) has at its base the idea that older individuals accept the negative labels, stereotypes, and societal view of them as weak and dependent. According to this theory, older individuals tend to incorporate society's definitions and viewpoints, resulting in behavior that reinforces the stereotypes. This cycle was thought to be vicious and unbreakable unless some sort of intervention (social services, teaching self-confidence, redefining roles) were to occur.

In the early 1980s, there was a new, positive focus on the elderly. There was evidence that older individuals were changing roles rather than losing them, and that there were untapped resources (wisdom, skills, self-healing) in the elder community that needed to be recognized. This capacity building is still a pervasive theme among professionals who seek to build positive, healthy communities. This new point of view also heralded the advocacy of rights for residents in institutions.

The infusion of sociological principles (those of race, gender, power, and privilege) in gerontology led to an understanding that age was also to be considered in issues of inequality in our society.

The *age stratification theory* (Riley, 1971) helped to explain how age was making some individuals in society "different" simply by the natural process of aging. The phenomenon of aging coupled with class differences were discovered to be the two most stratifying forces in the culture. The theory states that age stratification depends on two factors (basically internal and external). The first factor is that of internal change: physical and mental changes. The second factor is what external events (historical) occur as an individual ages. This theory appears to be culturally appropriate in that factors are both individually and culturally driven.

The *modernization theory* (Cowgill & Holmes, 1972) looked at the loss of status as one aged. The loss of social status was not peculiar to Western societies alone. Cowgill and Holmes discovered that loss is a universal experience in all cultures regardless of economic, religious, political, or social traditions. Social losses can occur following the modernization of the society. The study (Cowgill

& Holmes, 1972) and resulting theory examined fifteen societies and described four of the most common aspects of aging in modern societies. The commonalities were:

1. an increased life span due to technological advances,
2. loss of job role and a loss of expertise in the aging populations due to modernization (economic development and advanced economies),
3. separation of work from home and separation of old from young due to urbanization, and
4. formalized education that leaves the elderly literally and educationally disadvantaged.

There are some exceptions to the commonalities found in societies that hold their elderly in high esteem and have advanced rapidly economically and technologically.

Future trends in social gerontology research need to focus on an evolution in aging research (that drives policymaking in public health and governmental programs) that provides qualitative and quantitative work that intersects aging research at gender, race, and class. Dressel, Minkler, and Yen (1997) are concerned with the intersections of gender, race, class, and age. They state that focusing on intersections of race, class and gender in research on aging is critical to how aging is experienced. In doing so, Dressel et al. suggest that only then can the field of aging "move beyond . . . established and limited ways of thinking" (p. 596).

HETEROGENEITY OF THE AGING EXPERIENCE

The United States is often referred to as a "melting pot." This terminology infers that once persons of different cultures come to the United States and "melt" into one large society, a new heterogeneous culture is created. The term "melting pot" incorporates an ethnocentric viewpoint that maintains that all members of society should look, act, and think alike.

The problem of the melting pot analogy falls short in the face of the dominant culture of the United States. Dominant culture can be defined as the "recognizable, predictable way of life" that is "associated with the values of middle-class America" (Holmes & Holmes, 1995, p. 169). The dominant culture in the United States sets the cultural norm for education, entertainment, social services, government, and economy. This way of life is imposed primarily by those who have historically been in power—white, middle-class males. Furthermore, this presupposes that those who are white, of the upper and middle class, married, able bodied, and employed in white-collar positions have the "right" values. The dominant culture then projects its values on all individuals in the country regardless of race, marital status, sexual orientation, ability, or class. Characteristics of the dominant culture include a high value on self-reliance and independence, youth orientation (association of beauty with youth), future time orientation (and time driven), a wasteful "throw away" mentality, competitiveness, and a view that the universe is at the mercy (slave) of humans (the masters) (Holmes & Holmes, 1995). This set of values is quite different from that of other cultures. For example, in Eastern cultures there is an emphasis on not filling every waking second with activity. The practice of contemplation is highly valued. In some Latin cultures, individuals take time to rest each day after lunch and to reopen shops or return to work as soon as the "siesta" is over. If one is inactive and quiet or rests during the middle of the day in Western culture, that individual is viewed as lazy and unproductive.

An appreciation of the pervasiveness of the dominant culture is requisite to understanding the changing face of the United States and how it affects the aging population. It will be a great challenge, in this century, to serve the wide variety of older individuals who are now living in the United States. In the following sections, a variety of underserved groups and their experience of aging will be described. These descriptions are intended to assist public health professionals to adequately meet the needs of different groups in the twenty-first century and beyond.

GENDER DIFFERENCES

More older women live alone in this country due to two phenomena: a longer life expectancy, and the age disparity that is the result of marrying men older than themselves (Barer, 1994). These phenomena are the foundations for many gender differences in aging individuals.

Men who live beyond the age of eighty-five are more likely to be in better health than are women who survive into their mid-eighties. Men remain functional and independent longer, yet, they are more prone to acute and fatal disease than women. This translates into having interests outside of the home, maintaining hobbies and property, and fulfilling community-service obligations.

Women are more prone to disabling chronic conditions and have been found to be more impaired in their abilities to perform activities of daily living. Due to gender roles and social norms, women have better adaptability and help-seeking behavior than do men. Women are more likely to sustain social relationships and their sense of well-being, although not significantly more than men (Barer, 1994).

Women may experience more "role continuity" than do men. That is to say, women who are aged may find themselves homebound much as they were when raising a family and running a household. They also have less role adjustment to caregiving due to role continuity.

ECONOMIC DISPARITIES IN OLD AGE

Just under one-half of all women over the age of eighty-five, which accounts for over 70 percent of the population over eighty-five, are living in poverty or near poverty. These women live alone and may not have the economic means to provide for a healthy and enriching lifestyle. Approximately 76 percent of elderly African American women live alone and live in poverty. Women make up 60 percent of the older population. It is estimated that 45 percent of all African American elderly and 34 percent of all Hispanic elderly live in poverty or live just above the poverty level (Greenberg & Motenko, 1995).

The link between gender, marital status, and income is a significant factor to understanding how poverty affects older Americans. Because of company pensions, social security payments, and other social advantages for men, women are more likely to live in poverty in old age. Women are left alone with a fixed income after the spouse dies. If that spouse was ill or in a long-term care facility, the couple may have had to "spend down" their savings to cover health care expenditures. These factors increase a woman's susceptibility for living in poverty as she approaches old age. Male partners may also have to spend down if the spouse is institutionalized.

Illness and poverty, unfortunately, often go hand in hand. Disease and illness can play a part in the psychosocial health of the elderly. As one's ability to carry out activities of daily living, to be mobile, and to attend social events decreases due to illness or disability, one is particularly at risk for psychological and social isolation. The overall health (psychological, spiritual, mental, emotional, and social) of an individual may be related to an initial physical illness or disability. In the case of the poor elderly, such restrictions may compromise their overall capacity to combat and to recover from disability or disease.

As the female caregiver experiences loss of her spouse and moves into widowhood, she may become susceptible to emotional and economic issues that will affect her health (Grau, 1988). For both men and women (especially women who have been in the workforce), retirement may mean loss of income and a decrease in quality of life. Social security benefits are fixed, and there are no adjustments made for geographic location, cost of living, inflation, or health care costs. The higher cost of technologically advanced health care may not benefit those who are at the highest risk of becoming ill. In that case, access can be named as an agent contributing to illness.

HISPANIC ELDERLY

One cannot label all persons of Hispanic origin as Mexican or Latino/Latina because not all individuals who are Hispanic originate from Mexico or Latin America. The Hispanics in America have their roots in Mexico, South and Central America, Spain, and Cuba (see Chart 4.1). Hispanics from Mexico (Mexican Americans) comprise 60 percent of the Hispanic population in the United States, while 83 percent of Mexican Americans are geographically clustered in the Southwest with approximately three-fourths living in Texas and California (O'Hare, 1992). Puerto Rican Americans, who have settled primarily in the Northeast (especially New York state) make up about 12 percent of the Hispanic population in the United States. Cuban Americans make up 5 percent of the Hispanic population. A disproportionate number of Cuban Americans reside in southern states (70%); the majority of Cuban Americans who reside in the South live in Florida. The remaining 23 percent of Hispanics in the United States are descendants from Spain, Central America, or South America. Within these groups, there is no evidence of the type of clustering that is so obvious among the other Hispanic groups living in this country.

According to O'Hare (1992), the numbers of Mexican Americans grew rapidly through the 1980s and 1990s; however, those Hispanics of Spanish, Central, or South American descent were the fastest growing group of immigrants.

Immigrants from Mexico have the lowest educational attainment level (less than 5% have four years of college) (Waldrop, 1992). Based on educational status, Mexican immigrants are more likely to be at risk for health problems based on ability to pay and on environmental factors relating to the type of jobs that are performed by this group (i.e., manual labor, seasonal or migrant field work). There is evidence that approximately 30 percent of Mexican Americans are uninsured (Trevino, Trevino, Medina, Ramirez, & Ramirez, 1996).

Characteristics of Aging Hispanics

There are four basic tenets or values of the Hispanic–Chicano culture that are important in considering the aging Hispanic in American culture (Maldonado, 1979). These tenets help explain the role of aging Hispan-

Aging and Public Health

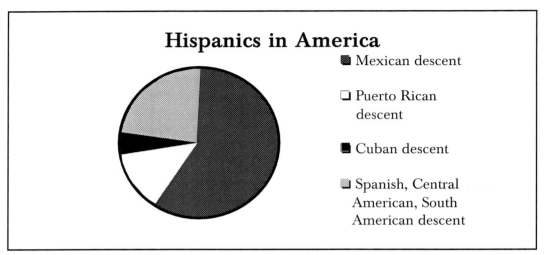

Chart 4.1. Hispanics in America.

ics in their own family unit as well as in the community at large.

1. *Familism:* This concept is best explained by feeling that the family is the most important element in one's life and that family interest always come first. The wealth, health, and welfare of the family are placed above that of the individual. The family, then, is called on to care for its older members and to meet all of their needs. At times, such expectations of care could be detrimental to the caregiver and the elderly person, particularly, when such demands exceed caring and coping capabilities. Familial concern may be expressed through the presence of a Hispanic family in the waiting room or examination room to show support and concern for the individual who is ill. There may also be language gaps, and a family member may act as an interpreter for another family member. Health services need to accommodate such needs

and to remain sensitive to such cultural characteristics.

2. *Age hierarchy:* The eldest persons in the family are to be respected and obeyed. This extends to older siblings who give younger brothers and sisters advice and (sometimes) protection. "As an individual matures, he/she increases in status" (Maldonado, 1979, p. 179). Grandchildren revere their grandparents and great-grandparents and often gather around them to support them as they age.

3. *Male leadership:* Males make the major decisions in the household. Their role is to act as the family representative in the family and in the community. It is important for public health professionals to understand the role of the male in the decision-making process.

4. *Mutual aid and support:* The family can and should supply all of an individual's needs as the individual ages. This is crucial in caregiving. There are few Hispanics who are institutionalized due to this value. Several studies show that

Hispanics seek assistance from their families before anyone else. It is a given in this culture that one does whatever one can for family members to support and to aid them in times of need. There is also an expectation that the best of everything is reserved for the older members of the culture. This attitude incorporates expectations regarding governmental support and support given by those outside the family.

5. *Folk medicine:* It is particularly important for health practitioners to honor the traditional medicine of Hispanics. This includes (but is not limited to) the use of herbal medicine, strong spirituality, and attention to the spirit world in health and healing. It is necessary for the public health professional to understand and to honor the cultural differences of Hispanics so that individuals to be served feel that the professional is not insulting their culture, lifestyle, or background. Such an attitude will also help ensure that the patient or consumer is being treated with dignity and respect.

ASIAN ELDERLY

As with Hispanic groups, it is an error to regard all persons of Asian descent as Asians. There are many different groups that make up the Asian population living in the United States. The groups that make up the Asian population in the United States are Hmong, Laotian, Cambodian, Vietnamese, Korean, Thai, Hawaiian, Filipino, Chinese, Japanese, and (Asian) Indian individuals (Fujiwara, 1998). This list is, by no means, exhaustive.

According to the 1990 U.S. Census, the elder members of these groups consume almost one-third of all public assistance funds.

More foreign-born females depend on public assistance than do their counterparts (Fujiwara, 1998).

Like Hispanics, Asian immigrants and refugees tend to cluster in urban areas. Most Asians (45%) tend to live in the western United States. A large percentage of Hmong, Japanese, and Filipino immigrants and refugees live in California. Some 70 percent of Asian immigrants enter the United States through three ports: San Francisco, Los Angeles, or New York–Newark (Edmondson, 1997). When Asians from India cluster, they normally choose to reside in the Northeast (one-third live in the Northeast). Although there is great diversity in the Asian population in the United States, this chapter will focus on the two groups that make up the majority of Asian population, specifically aging Japanese and Chinese Americans.

Characteristics of Aging Japanese Americans

There is a national holiday in Japan to honor their elders called "Respect-the-Aged" day. The presence of this celebration underscores the importance and respect afforded older Japanese. Elders are also considered to be the keepers of tradition and are, therefore, sought out for guidance and wisdom.

It is the duty of children in Japanese society to be caregivers to their aging parents. As parents age, they move in with their eldest son (traditionally). The daughter-in-law becomes somewhat subservient to her husband's mother. The son's mother has great latitude with how the household is run (Holmes & Holmes, 1995).

Socioeconomics play a part in how Japanese individuals age and what they are able to enjoy. The upper class *(samurai)* follow strict Confucian law and tradition. That is, the upper class has the privilege to follow the strict philosophies regarding treatment of older members of the group. Confucian philosophy dictates that elders be treated with utmost respect and dignity, that they be given a wide berth to enjoy their status, and that they are to be "indulged by their juniors" (Keifer, 1974, p. 171). Those in lower socioeconomic classes do not have this luxury and are more focused on keeping the family business alive and well and on the survival of the members of the family. There is some evidence that authority in the family is based on economic support and that an individual's status is tied to his or her capacity to contribute economically.

As individuals become frail, and possibly demented, they may "ready" themselves to die by praying at specially erected temples. The prayer is often to die a speedy, painless death. There have been some cultural myths regarding the abandonment of elders in Japanese society; however, there is no evidence for this phenomenon (Holmes & Holmes, 1995).

Characteristics of Aging Chinese Americans

There are some beliefs related to aging in China. Endurance, independence, frugality, and faith are the tenets that appear to make up a large part of the coping strategies of Chinese Americans. The individuals seem to be able to survive on the reduced incomes of retirement by exercising frugality and by being independent. Part of the "endurance" ethic deals with the tie to work and the endurance that it takes to accept their aging status as reality and to endure it (Holmes & Holmes, 1995). The faith ethic is another coping strategy that allows Chinese American elders to have "strength to cope with many (of the) problems" (Wu, 1975, p. 274) of aging.

According to Holmes and Holmes (1995), elderly Chinese Americans feel iso-

lated partly as a function of the inability to adequately communicate. Holmes & Holmes go on to further state that if the Chinese would have stayed in China they would be enjoying a life of leisure, full of joy and respect. As a result, some Chinese Americans may feel isolated and lonely in the latter part of their lives in America. There is some evidence that Chinese American elders do find support from the community, friends, friendship clubs, and family (Cheng, 1978). These resources are helpful in supplying a sense of identity to older Chinese Americans.

African American Elderly

There have been many studies relating to the differences in the aging experience of African American as compared to Whites in the United States. The studies concentrated on identifying "model differences between black and white senior citizens' lifestyles" (Holmes & Holmes, 1995, p. 188). The model differences provide public health professionals with a foundation for better understanding of the aging African American population; although to compare this population to Whites is another example of ethnocentricity.

African Americans view old age as a reward, are proud of their age, and are less likely to lie about their age. African Americans have less anxiety about aging than do Whites. This leads to higher morale in old age. African Americans are much less likely to commit suicide in old age. This is in direct opposition to older White males who have the highest suicide rate for any population.

African Americans have a lower life expectancy and are in poorer health than their White counterparts. However, once African Americans reach the age of seventy-five, they are more likely to live longer than Whites. Overall, access to health care is a significant issue in lower life expectancies. Later detection (rather than early detection) of fatal diseases, transportation, and economics are some access issues that play a part in racial disparities in life expectancy for populations in the United States.

African Americans remain close to their families as they age. The elder will also continue in roles that are seen as useful and acceptable by younger members of the family. Because of these two facts, older African American individuals are highly respected and well-treated. Even as some peculiarities arise with aging, these are tolerated more readily than are behaviors of aging Whites. African American elders may tap into mutual assistance and feel supported by friends, neighbors, and the community. Older African American individuals are less likely to feel integrated into the broader society.

African Americans are more likely to be religious and remain so throughout their life span. The elders are less likely to be involved in political and economic matters, although they often feel that their votes can make a difference (Brown & Barnes-Nacoste, 1993).

NATIVE AMERICAN ELDERLY

Native Americans are probably one of the most heterogeneous racial groups in the United States; there are 307 official tribes that speak more than 125 languages. Due to the diversity in the makeup of this population, the aging experience varies greatly. There are, however, some commonalities as described by Connelly (1980) to set a firm foundation for understanding general characteristics of Native American groups. They can be characterized to some extent by a certain "cautious" set of values and characteristics.

Native American groups show an appreciation for the earth, nature, and all living things. Respect for the land is a way for Native American groups to give thanks for the

gifts that the earth offers them. As individuals, Native Americans seek autonomy and individual freedom. As a member of a group there is little focus on a hierarchical system of governance, rather groups tend to value consensus. Native American groups operate from a perspective of family, tribal, and individual pride; consequently, an overriding theme for individuals is to "avoid bringing shame to oneself, family, clan or tribe" (Connelly, 1980, p. VI-19). Native American groups are very respectful and willingly share the gifts of hospitality. Native American groups believe in a supreme being and are deeply spiritual and believe in life after death.

Aging in Native American culture is as varied as is their language. There is some evidence that suggests that the behavior toward older persons can range from strangulation of elders and other forms of hastening death to providing elders with deferential treatment.

According to Baldridge (1996), traditionally, elders were respected, valued for their wisdom, regarded as reinforcers of the culture and lore, given opportunities to contribute to the community (were asked to tend fields, tend children, do light housekeeping tasks), and were nurtured by their extended families. Currently, however, older persons are forced to work for a living, act as caregivers (instead of being cared for), and to live in poverty (partially resulting from the lack of educational opportunity), substandard housing, and isolation.

Spirituality (not necessarily religion) seems to be the only tradition that Native American elders have been able to preserve. It is the belief of Native American Elders (as they are referred to) that "the Indian people will endure well beyond present society" (Baldridge, 1996, p. 187).

Aging individuals living on reservations continue to have some of the same problems that have faced them throughout their lifetimes. Concerns that continue to plague Native American elderly are poverty (more than one-half of all Native American Elders live 200 percent below the poverty line), isolation (living on reservations that are far from health centers, long-term-care facilities, and sometimes family), and chronic health problems (alcoholism and diabetes). Other problems that keep Native American Elders from aging well are due to access. Access issues may include not being able to gain access to Social Security benefits, access to health care centers to treat chronic disease, the cost of health care (as the Indian Health Service may have to contract with managed-care organizations to deliver health care), confusion regarding how to pay for services, and cultural issues in service delivery.

The Indian Health Service's (IHS) Elder Care Initiative has designed a program "to promote the development of high-quality care for American Indian and Alaska Native Elders" (Indian Health Services [IHS], 1999, p. 1). The Initiative works to act "as a consultation and liaison resource (between) for (sic) IHS, tribal, and urban Indian health programs" (IHS, 1999, p. 2) The initiative is based on the fact that there are more Native American Elders than ever, especially those individuals who are considered the oldest individuals in particular service areas. The IHS recognizes Native American Elders as a valuable resource and stresses that the Elders are deserving of respect and honor. The initiative also recognizes that Native American Elders need an expansion of services. The expansion of services to be offered by the IHS is considered a "high priority" by the Elder Care Initiative. "The core activities of the Elder Care Initiative are in information and referral, technical assistance and education, and advocacy" (IHS, 1999, p. 2). The initiative includes creating interdisciplinary teams to educate, to provide (appropriate) services, and to develop current resources. The initiative also focuses on end-of-life issues for El-

ders, addressing the holistic health of Elders (an assessment tool is being developed), and addressing Elder needs inside a public health framework (IHS, 1999). Future plans by the IHS Elder Care Initiative are directed at collaboration, conference planning, and needs assessment.

BEHAVIOR AND LIFESTYLE AS DETERMINANTS OF HEALTH

American society tends to focus on treatment rather than prevention. If greater attention were paid to prevention, society would benefit through an improvement in health status and a reduction in health care expenses. Prevention might include controlling stress more effectively, getting adequate sleep, understanding prescription medications, exercising regularly, eating a well-balanced diet, and taking in moderate amounts of alcohol. It is a difficult undertaking to break long-held beliefs and values, and habits (such as only seeking medical care when one is ill). Changes in beliefs and behaviors would naturally assist all members of society to age better and to engage in more effective management and treatment of chronic illness. Unfortunately, many Americans postpone seeking medical advice until there is a health crisis. If one were to change one's health behavior before the onset of a crisis, one would very likely age more successfully.

According to Green, Krueter, Deeds, and Partridge (1980), health promotion is "any combination of health education and related organizational, political, and economic changes conducive to health" (p. 7). Health-promotion theories recognize the importance of the whole individual, including one's social support, knowledge, attitudes, beliefs, environment, self-efficacy, and motivation. It is critical that the health care system, beginning with individual responsibility, recognize the whole person when working with issues of health promotion. Practitioners need to examine the differences between prevention and health promotion. Are the two synonymous? If practitioners promote healthy behaviors and provide programs and education, would that (promotion) also act as a prevention tool? Promotion and prevention are not synonymous with regard to the treatment of chronic illness. Rather, health promotion assists an individual in knowing how to manage the illness or condition more effectively. However, for the individual who has advanced to old age without a chronic illness or disability, health promotion may be synonymous with prevention.

Health Behavior and Health Outcomes

There appears to be an increase in the quality of an individual's life (mobility, sociability, attitude, independence) with an increase in health-seeking behaviors and behavior change. Illness, by contrast, causes a decrease in an individual's quality of life. The physical impact of disease and disability in older individuals has an economic dimension as well. The economic issues on an individual level may include more out-of-pocket expenses for those with disease or disability. Nationally, and globally, more health care dollars are spent by individuals in the last years of their lives putting additional strain on the health care system. Personal economics may be effected as well. Poor health may result in loss of independent lifestyle.

Self-Efficacy in Health Promotion

Self-efficacy is self-confidence or belief in oneself (Bandura, 1977). Bandura (1991) identifies four sources of self efficacy:

1. past and present experience of performance (comparing current physical ability to past abilities),
2. observing others perform,
3. social influence (verbal persuasion/ urging by others), and,
4. psychological arousal (considering whether or not one is ready to take on new behavior).

Self-efficacy decreases over the life span, specifically, when chronic illness is present. As one ages and presents with chronic illness, it is particularly important for the individual to remain active. Increased activity levels are associated with fending off chronic illness and decreasing depression. Conversely, lack of activity has been associated with onset of chronic illness (or at least hastening onset) and depression in older adults. Once a pattern of activity can be established, it will lead to a more positive health trend for older adults. If a pattern does not establish itself, there is the risk that individuals will not have the confidence or perception that they can profit from increased activity. A vicious cycle, then, manifests itself.

Behavior Change

It is never too late to begin a health-promotion program regardless of age. Malmgren, Koepsell, Martin, Diehr, & LaCroix (1999) state that "Older adults have not passed the point that positive health behavior changes are effective in reducing mortality" (p. 57). In his work, Fries (1980, 1992; Fries, Green, & Levine, 1989) presents similar results. Fries's studies show that morbidity close to the end of life, and possibly mortality, can be "compressed" by adhering to health-promoting behaviors late in life. Based on her meta-analysis of health-promotion literature, Heidrich (1998) found that, in longitudinal studies of health behaviors and health outcomes, "Older adults are as likely or more likely to engage in positive health practices as young or middle-aged adults" (p. 178). Heidrich also states that most studies found that gender (being female), income (higher levels of income), and (higher) education were positively correlated with health-promotion activities. Nigg et al. (1999) report that public health personnel should be keenly aware that losing weight and exercise are behaviors in which older adults were in the precontemplation stage regarding behavior change. Therefore, it is paramount for professionals to assess individual needs, create programs, and evaluate outcomes in the areas of weight loss and exercise.

Durham et al. (1991) and Watkins & Kligman (1993) examined barriers to involvement. Both studies examined health-promotion programs set up for the elderly. Results from both indicate that those individuals with multiple, chronic health problems and those who were socially isolated were less likely to attend formal health-promotion programs than their peers.

There may be those, both young and old, who believe that learning new habits may be too difficult for older individuals and that "you can't teach an old dog new tricks." This is an ageist perspective and perpetuates the myth that older individuals cannot adopt new learning late in life. Older individuals can be highly adaptive to whatever their situations might be, whether it is widowhood, disability, changes in living situations, or loss of role(s). Older individuals may be more adaptive to new situations than younger individuals.

Lifestyle

Smoking, diet, and exercise are lifestyle factors that play a role in determining the health and wellness in all individuals. There are a few longitudinal studies that have helped professionals learn more about the effects of lifestyle on disease, morbidity, and mortality. The Framingham Heart Study is one such study. The Framingham study has followed a representative sample of 5,209 adult residents in Framingham, Massachusetts, since 1948. The main objective of the study has been to study the epidemiology of cardiovascular diseases. Health officials have learned the circumstances under which cardiovascular diseases arise, evolve, and cause death in particular populations. The Framingham Study is designed to find out how individuals who develop cardiovascular diseases differ from those individuals who remain disease free (American Heart Association, 2000). According to Yen (1999), "Framingham has linked obesity, smoking and inactivity to increased rates of heart disease and stroke" (p. 223). Yen also indicates that weight loss and a lower incidence of disease are direct benefits of exercise; furthermore, weight loss is helpful in increasing mobility. Weight loss or maintenance of a healthy weight level has direct, positive benefits for an individual with respect to blood cholesterol, blood pressure, and blood sugar.

According to the National Institute on Aging (NIA, 1998), "Older people become sick or disabled more often from not exercising than from exercising" (p. 3). The NIA also indicates that the numbers of disabled persons over the age of sixty-five has been steadily declining. The NIA infers that this trend may be due, in part, to "increased physical and better diets" (1998, p. 3).

There is clear evidence to indicate that health promotion in old age can be beneficial to older adults. Practitioners should pay attention to reaching those with chronic illness, and those who are socially isolated. Support from family and friends has been shown to be significant in motivating older individuals to participate in (particularly) physical-activity programs (Chogahara, Cousins, & Wankel,

1998). Hence, health-promotion programs need to be accessible to individuals regardless of age, and should be sensitive to cultural and social differences.

Coping and Adaptive Behavior

Coping is defined as "consistently changing cognitive and behavioral efforts to manage specific external and/or internal demands that are appraised as taxing or exceeding the resources of the person" (Lazarus & Folkman, 1984, p. 141). There seem to be some common themes of coping behaviors. These themes are "demands, appraisal, resources, and mastering life strains" (Ruth & Coleman, 1996, p. 309). These themes refer to coping in older age as a part of adult development. Lazarus (1998) warns that to view coping as a part of the developmental process is to deny that individuals are not wholly acceptable as individuals; that is, individuals are more than just the emotions, behaviors, and processes of coping. Individual coping cannot be separated by type (problem focused vs. emotion focused), nor can they be separated from their person (denying differences in environment, beliefs, and resources). Finally, according to Lazarus (1998), individual coping cannot be separated from emotions of coping. This does not appear to be a cause–effect relationship.

Atchley (1991) defines adaptation as "the process of adjusting to fit a situation or environment" (p. 259). General adaptation to life change has three stages (Atchley, 1991):

1. *continuity:* keeping a sense of oneself even though circumstances may change,
2. *anticipation:* taking action to avoid negative consequences, and
3. *compensation:* action that allows for loss of function; physical, psychological, and/or social losses.

Specific adaptation can be linked to changes that are especially unique to aging individuals and can be either sudden or gradual. Sudden changes in the life of an aging individual require increased levels of coping and social support. Gradual changes require routine coping. Sudden changes could be acute illness or acute onset of disability, death of a loved one, or change in environment (relocation of primary residence due to a move, retirement, or necessity due to health). Gradual changes might include loss of functionality in physical capabilities due to normal aging.

According to Bee (1996), external resources helpful for coping are good health and vitality, a stable income, having hope or belief in someone or something (a deity, a person, a program), good social skills, and the ability to form close, personal relationships. Holahan and Moos (1987) include higher education and its set of occupational skills (and all of its benefits) as an external resource for better coping in old age. With the benefits of higher education (better jobs that may provide an income stream and health benefits), individuals may have access to resources that someone who has not had the benefit of getting a higher education would not normally have.

Internal resources include internal locus of control ("I control me" thinking), hardiness (personal commitment, control, and challenge), and self-efficacy (self-confidence or belief in oneself). These internal resources also lead to an individual's ability to cope better with the stresses of aging.

Coping strategies can be categorized as either approach strategies or avoidance strategies. Individuals who exercise avoidance tend to have more depression and physical illness than those who use approach strategies to cope (Holahan & Moos, 1986, 1987, 1990). Schwartz, Peng, Lester, Daltroy, & Goldberger (1998) state that younger individuals have "higher levels of self-reported coping variability than do chronically ill individuals or the elderly" (p. 41).

Lazarus (1993) states that coping is situational. Along those same lines, according to Billings & Moos, one needs to employ a variety of action, thinking, and feeling mechanisms for an individual to remain healthy (Billings & Moos, 1981; Moos & Billings, 1982). Moos & Billings (1982) describe action-based coping as being problem focused. That is, one sees the problem and takes direct action to cope. Furthermore, they go on to define thinking-based coping as being appraisal focused: one thinks about the problem and internalizes ways to cope. Finally, Moos and Billings (1982) describe feeling-based coping as being emotion focused: one adapts an emotional stance to cope with the situation. Gross et al. (1997) contend that the emotional realm expands as one ages. Older individuals have the ability to heighten good emotional experiences, and to "dampen" emotions such as sadness, anger, and fear. Older subjects in their study reported more control over their emotions than younger subjects.

As mentioned previously, managing stressful situations through a variety of interventions help an individual to age more successfully. Stressful situations in older age may stem from a variety of experiences determined from societal attitudes, incongruities in the aging experience of different ethnic groups, poor health, a health care system that is not equipped to view the individual in a holistic manner (social, mental, psychological, physical, and spiritual).

CONCLUSION

It is important that the public health professional be familiar with the factors that affect the health of the population they are serving. Ageism, cultural tradition, health-seeking behaviors, and coping are all factors

that lead to the overall psychosocial health of aged individuals. Recognizing and evaluating the bearing of psychosocial parameters is an integral part in serving aging populations sensitively and appropriately.

REFERENCES

American Heart Association. (2000). Framingham heart disease epidemiology study. Retrieved 06/24/01 from the World Wide Web: www.americanheart.org/Heart_and_Stroke_ A_Z_Guide/fram.html

Atchley, R. (1991). *Social forces and aging: An introduction to social gerontology.* Belmont, CA: Wadsworth.

Baldridge, D. (1994). Native America in the 20th century. In M. Davis, J. Berman, M. Graham, & L. Mitten (Eds.), *Native America in the twentieth century: An encyclopedia.* New York: Garland.

Bandura, A. (1977). Self-efficacy: Toward a unifying theory of behavioral change. *Psychological Review, 84,* 191–215.

——. (1991). Self-efficacy mechanism in physiological activation and health promoting behavior. In J. Madden IV, S. Mathysse, & J. Barchas (Eds.), *Neurobiology of learning, emotion and affect* (pp. 229–270). New York: Raven Press.

Barer, B. (1994). Men and women age differently. *International Journal of Aging and Human Development, 38* (1), 29–40.

Bee, H. (1996). *The Journey of Adulthood* (3rd ed.). Upper Saddle River, NJ: Prentice Hall.

Billings, A., & Moos, R. (1981). The role of coping responses and social resources in attenuating the stress of life events. *Journal of Behavioral Medicine, 4,* 139–157.

Brown, A. (1974). Satisfying relationships for the elderly and their patterns of disengagement. *The Gerontologist, 14* (3), 258–262.

Brown, A. (1990). *The social processes of aging and old age.* Englewood Cliffs, NJ: Prentice Hall.

Brown, R., & Barnes-Nacoste, R. (1993). Group consciousness and political behavior. In J. S. Jackson, L. M. Chatters, & R. J. Taylor (Eds.),

Aging in Black America (pp. 217–232). Newbury Park, CA: Sage.

Cheng, E. (1978). *The elder Chinese.* San Diego: Campanile.

Chogahara, M., Cousins, S., & Wankel, L. (1998). Social influences on physical activity in older adults: A review. *Journal of Aging and Physical Activity, 6,* 1–17.

Connelly, J. (1980). An expanded outline and resource for teaching a course on the Native American. In G. A. Sherman (ed.), *Curriculum guidelines in minority aging* (vol. 6, pp. 1–66). Washington, DC: National Center on Black Aged, Inc.

Cowgill, D. & Holmes, L. (1972). *Aging and modernization.* New York: Appleton-Century Crofts.

Cumming, E., & Henry, W. (1961). *Growing old: The process of disengagement.* New York: Basic Books.

Dressel, P., Minkler, M., & Yen, I. (1997). Gender, race, class and aging: Advances and opportunities. *International Journal of Health Services, 27* (4), 579–600.

Durham, M., Beresford, S., Diehr, P., Grembowski, D., Hecht, J., & Patrick, D. (1991). Participation of higher users in a randomized trial of Medicare reimbursement for preventive services. *Gerontologist, 31* (5), 603–606.

Edmondson, B. (1997). New frontiers: Asian Americans in 2001. *American Demographics, 19* (2), 16–17.

Freidenberg, J. N. (1995). Growing old in Spanish Harlem: A multimedia, bilingual exhibition. *Migration World, 23* (1–2), 34–38.

Fries, J. (1980). Aging, natural death and the compression of morbidity. *New England Journal of Medicine, 303,* 130–155.

———. (1992). Strategies for reduction of morbidity. *American Journal of Clinical Nutrition, 55,* 1257S–1262S.

Fries, J., Green, L., & Levine, S. (1989). Health promotion and compression of morbidity. *Lancet, 1,* 481–483.

Fujiwara, L. H. (1998). The impact of welfare reform on Asian immigrant communities. *Social Justice, 25* (1), 82–104.

Grau, L. (1988). Illness-engendered poverty among the elderly. In C. Perales, & L. Young

(Eds.), *Women, health and poverty* (pp. 1103–118). New York: Plenum Press.

Green, L., Kreuter, M., Deeds, S., & Partridge, K. (1980). *Health education planning: A diagnostic approach.* Palo Alto, CA: Mayfield.

Greenberg, S., & Motenko, A. K. (1995). Reframing dependence in old age: A positive transition for families. *Social Work, 40* (3), 382–390.

Gross, J., Carstensen, L., Pasupathi, M., Tsai, J., Skorpen, C., & Hsu, A. (1997). Emotion and aging: Experience, expression, and control. *Psychology and Aging, 12* (4), 590–599.

Heidrich, S. (1998). Health promotion in old age. *Annual Review of Nursing Research, 16,* 173–195.

Holahan, C., & Moos, R. (1986). Personality, coping, and family resources in stress resistance: A longitudinal analysis. *Journal of Personality and Social Psychology, 51,* 389–395.

———. (1987). Risk, resistance, and psychological distress: A longitudinal analysis with adults and children. *Journal of Abnormal Psychology, 98,* 3–13.

———. (1990). Life stressors, resistance, factors, and improved psychological functioning: An extension of the stress resistance paradigm. *Journal of Personality and Social Psychology, 58,* 909–917.

Holmes, E., & Holmes, L. (1995). *Other cultures, elder years.* Thousand Oaks, CA: Sage.

———. (1995). *Other cultures, elder years: An introduction to cultural gerontology.* Thousand Oaks, CA: Sage.

Indian Health Service. (1999). Elder care initiative: Promoting quality care for American Indians and Alaskan Natives Elders. Retrieved 06-24-01 from the World Wide Web: www.ihs.gov/MedicalPrograms/ElderCare/about.asp.

Keifer, C. W. (1974). *Changing cultures, changing lives.* San Francisco: Josey-Bass.

Keifer, C. W. (1990). The elderly in modern Japan: Elite, victims, or plural players? In J. Sodolovsky (Ed.), *The cultural context of aging: World perspectives* (pp. 181–195). New York: Bergin and Garvey.

Kuypers, J., & Bengtson, V. (1973). Social breakdown and competence: A model of normal aging. *Human Development, 16,* 181–202.

Lazarus, R. (1993). Coping theory and research: Past, present and future. *Psychosomatic Medicine, 55,* 234–247.

———. (1998). Coping with aging. In I. Nordhus, G. VandenBos, S. Berg, & P. Fromholt (Eds.), *Clinical geropsychology* (pp. 109–127).Washington, DC: American Psychological Association.

Lazarus, R., & Folkman, S. (1984). *Stress, appraisal and coping.* New York: Springer.

Lomranz, J. (1998). An image of aging and the concept of integration: Coping and mental health implications. In J. Lomranz (Ed.), *Handbook of aging and mental health* (pp. 217–250). New York: Plenum Press.

Malmgren, J., Koepsell, T., Martin, D., Diehr, P., & LaCroix, A. (1999). Mortality, health services use, and health behavior in a cohort of well older adults. *Journal of the American Geriatric Society, 47,* 51–59.

Malonado, D. (1979). Aging in the Chicano context. In D. E. Gelfand & A. J. Kutzik (Eds.), *Ethnicity and aging* (pp. 175–183). New York: Springer.

Moos, R., & Billings, A. (1982). Conceptualizing and measuring coping resources an processes. In L. Goldberger & S. Breznitz (Eds.), *Handbook of stress. Theoretical and clinical aspects* (pp. 212–230). New York: Free Press.

National Institute on Aging. (1998). *Exercise: A guide from the National Institute on Aging* (Pub. no. 98-4258). Bethesda, MD: Author.

Nigg, C., Burbank, P., Padula, C., Dufresne, R., Rossi, J., Velicer, W., Laforge, R., & Prochaska, J. (1999). Stages of change across the health risk behaviors for older adults. *The Gerontologist, 39* (4), 473–482.

O'Hare, W. (1992). America's minorities–The demographics of diversity. *Population Bulletin, 47* (4), 2–47.

———. (1996). A new look at poverty in America. *Population Bulletin, 51* (2), 2–48.

Riley, M. (1971). Social gerontology and the age stratification of society. *Gerontologist, 11* (2), 79–87.

Ruth, J., & Coleman, P. (1996). Personality and aging: Coping and management of the self in later life. In J. Birren & K. Schaie (Eds.), *Handbook of the Psychology of Aging* (pp. 308–322). San Diego, CA: Academic Press.

Schobeloch, J. (2000). [Ageism and the Media]. Unpublished raw data.

Schwartz, C., Peng, C., Lester, N., Daltroy, L., & Goldberger, A. (1998). Self-reported coping behavior in health and disease: Assessment with a card sort game. *Behavioral Medicine, 24,* 41–44.

Silverman, P., & Maxwell, R. (1978). How do I respect thee? Let me count the ways: Deference towards elderly men and women. *Behavior Science Research, 13* (2), 91–108.

Tallman, M., & Kutner, B. (1970). Disengagement and morale. *The Gerontologist, 10* (4), 317–320.

Trevino, R., Trevino, F., Medina, R., Ramirez, G., & Ramirez, R. (1996). Health care access among Mexican Americans with different health insurance coverage. *Journal of Health Care for the Poor and Underserved, 7* (2), 112–121.

Waldrop, J. (1992). Seasons: The Mexican way. *American Demographics, 14* (5), 4.

Watkins, A., & Kligman, E. (1993). Attendance patterns of older adults in a health promotion program. *Public Health Reports, 108* (1), 86–90.

Webster's New Collegiate Dictionary. (1973). Springfield MA: Merriam Company.

Wilmoth, J. M., DeJong, G. F., & Himes, C. L. (1997). Immigrant and non-immigrant living arrangements among America's white, hispanic, and Asian elderly population. *The International Journal of Sociology and Social Policy, 1997,* 17 (9–10), 57–82.

Wu, F. Y. (1975). Mandarin-speaking aged Chinese in the Los Angeles area. *The Gerontologist, 15,* 271–275.

Yen, P. (1999). Diet lessons learned from aging hearts. *Geriatric Nursing, 20* (4), 223–224.

Chapter 5

MENTAL DISORDERS AND MENTAL HEALTH SERVICES IN LATE LIFE: ISSUES FOR PUBLIC HEALTH AND PUBLIC POLICY

BOB G. KNIGHT AND MICHELE L. MAINES

INTRODUCTION

MENTAL DISORDERS ARE a major public health problem facing older adults and the persons who care for them, both family members and the professional community. However, mental disorders and mental health programs and policy are often neglected in discussions about health policy and in discussions about aging policy. A failure to address these issues directly has implications for the optimal care of older adults with mental disorders and also indirectly affects their health care, since mental disorders influence health and the adherence to health care plans.

This chapter explores the public health and public policy issues related to the common mental disorders of late life and the development of the systems of care that provide mental health services to older adults. The framework used is that of the multisystem, multilevel, and diagnosis-specific conceptualization of the mental health systems of care that has been developed in earlier work on managed care issues in mental health and aging (Knight & Kaskie, 1995) and in comparing the systems of care for older adults with mental disorders in the United States and the United Kingdom (Knight, Kaskie, Woods, & Phibbs, 1998). For the sake of simplicity, this framework hereafter is referred to as the multisystems model.

Rather than the traditional argument that there is a system of care for older adults that has gaps in it, the multisystems model argues that several distinct systems of care (health, mental health, social services, and an evolving system of dementia care services) have developed for specific purposes and fail to articulate with one another for a variety of reasons including economic and political pressures as well as distinct and sometimes unreconcilable worldviews and organizational cultures. This model also maintains that it is nearly meaningless to talk of mental disorders in the aggregate, but rather that broad diagnostic classes have very explicit needs, policy issues, and often different treatment systems that require separate consideration:

dementias, serious mental illness (SMI; e.g., schizophrenia, paranoid states, and bipolar disorder), acute mental disorders (depression and anxiety), and substance-abuse disorders.

In the following sections, the prevalence and specific prevention, intervention, and policy issues for each diagnosis are explored. This is followed by an examination of the systems-level issues regarding the development of mental health services in the United States, the undoing of that development, and apparent current and future trends in mental health policy that can be expected to shape the mental health service delivery mechanisms of the twenty-first century.

PREVALENCE AND TREATMENT OF MENTAL ILLNESS IN THE ELDERLY

Mental disorders are a significant health problem among the elderly. Gatz, Kasl-Godley, and Karel (1996) estimate that about 22 percent of older adults meet the criteria for some mental disorder. The combined prevalence for all mental disorders is thus similar to that among younger adults, but the relative prevalence of specific disorders differs. Dementias, cognitive impairments based on changes to the brain, are more common in later life, whereas the so-called functional disorders are less common in older as compared to younger adults. As in any age group, there are several mental illnesses that affect older adults. Some of these, such as schizophrenia, typically have an early onset; while others, dementia for example, usually have a later onset. There are yet others, such as depression or alcoholism, that can begin to affect a person either early or late in the life course. The mental illnesses most frequently experienced by older adults are reviewed in the following sections.

Dementia

Dementia describes a class of brain disorders characterized by irreversible declines in cognitive abilities that interfere with social and occupational functioning (American Psychiatric Association, DSM-IV, 1994). Although most individuals can expect some cognitive change with age, in a number of individuals the decline "goes beyond what may be considered 'normal' and [is] relentlessly progressive, robbing them of their memories, intellect, and eventually their abilities to recognize spouses or children, maintain basic personal hygiene, or even utter comprehensible speech" (Crook et al., 1986). Severe dementia affects about 6 percent of those over age sixty-five, with mild dementias affecting another 10 to 15 percent. Risk is strongly related to age and doubles with every five years of age past sixty-five (Zarit & Zarit, 1998). About one-half of individuals in nursing homes and large proportions of those in residential care facilities and community-based long-term care have dementia (Knight & Kaskie, 1995). Dementia strikes more women than men; however, this may be partly due to the fact that women live longer.

Dementia can be caused by one of a variety of diseases, but the main hallmarks for diagnosis are (1) memory impairment, (2) cognitive disturbances in one or more other areas of functioning (such as disturbances of language, motor function, recognition, and executive functioning), and (3) interference with social or occupational functioning (DSM-IV, 1994). Many of the behaviors common among those with dementia, such as wandering and lashing out at others, can make provision of care difficult and cause severe stress in caregivers. When attempting to diagnose dementia (as with any mental illness), it is important to determine that cognitive symptoms are due to dementia and not to another cause that might be reversible (e.g., physical illness, treatment, delirium, or depression). According to Zarit and Zarit (1998), there are over fifty causes of dementia; however, vascular dementia and Alzheimer's disease (AD) account for nearly 90 percent of all cases. Other causes of dementia include Huntington's disease, Pick's disease, Acquired Immunodeficiency Syndrome (AIDS), and Parkinson's disease.

Vascular dementia is caused by neuron loss as the result of small infarcts, or strokes. Thus, it is also known as multi-infarct dementia. It is estimated to cause between 5 and 20 percent of all dementias (Zarit & Zarit, 1998), and it is not uncommon for individuals to have both AD and vascular dementia. Unlike AD, where the deterioration is progressively global, the symptoms of vascular dementia reflect the locations of the infarcts. Vascular dementia is also distinguished from AD through brain scans (e.g., MRI and PET) that reveal the infarcts.

Alzheimer's disease is the most common cause of dementia (about 50% of cases) (Zarit & Zarit, 1998). AD is a neurodegenerative illness of unknown origin that causes neuron death and slow, continuous deterioration of functioning, usually beginning with impairments in memory and learning and leading to inability to carry out basic tasks of everyday life. It is diagnosed through a series of tests to rule out other causes. There are medications, such as Aricept®, which can slow the progression of symptoms in AD early on, but there is little else that can be done medically. Other treatments include environmental interventions and behavior management (see review of empirically validated treatments for behavioral, mood and memory problems in dementia patients by Gatz et al., 1998). Interventions aimed at caregivers can alleviate some of the burden they face, improving the mental health of the caregiver and the quality of care they can provide for their loved ones with dementia. A number of different caregiver interventions have been found to be effective in reducing depression and perceived burden among caregivers (Gatz et al., 1998).

Although research on the dementias, and especially on AD, has been a key priority of the National Institute on Aging and a focus of research by other institutes and state agencies, little is known about the prevention and treatment of the dementias. Presumably, declining prevalence of heart disease and stroke (e.g., American Heart Association, 2000; Reynolds, Crimmins, & Saito, 1998) will lead to lower rates of vascular dementia in future cohorts of older adults, although the number of cases may increase due to population aging. Smyer (1995) states that although the progression of decline in AD is fairly well understood, there is little known about preventive measures. He lists the strategies suggested by Nolan and Blass (1992) (nutrition, education, prevention of vascular disease and prompt care for infections), but states that there had been no systematic investigation of these recommendations.

Behavior management techniques appear to be quite effective (Gatz et al., 1998) and offer an alternative to the use of psychoactive medications, which have a history of overuse and abuse with this population. Birkett (1991) summarizes a number of survey studies suggesting high rates of use of antipsychotics, sedatives, and hypnotics with one study (Burns & Kamerow, 1988) showing no documentation of the need for the medication in one-third of cases reported. Psychotropic medications are prone to produce side effects and paradoxical effects with an elderly and cognitively frail patient population. Greater reliance on behavioral strategies could reduce the need for chemical restraint in long-term care settings.

At present, the primary issues for mental health treatment of the dementias involve the management of problem behaviors in both the home care setting and in institutional care settings. The majority of care for dementia patients takes place in the family home, with much of the remainder in nursing homes. Programs exist to assist family caregivers (e.g., federal and state tax breaks, or a low "wage" or reimbursement for time and money spent providing care in some states). Medicare covers limited hospital and post hospitalization institutional and in-home care, but patients needing around-the-clock skilled nursing facility care must rely on private long-term care insurance or spend down to qualify for Medicaid, which covers more nursing home expenses. Furthermore, the positioning of dementia care within the medical and long-term care systems tends to erect barriers to the integration of psychological and psychiatric expertise into dementia care.

Moreover, dementia is often considered a physical health issue, and patients may not be considered mental health care clients. It is difficult to integrate behavioral technology into dementia-care settings, and it requires extensive training and ongoing monitoring and reinforcement of staff to do this effectively (Lichtenberg, 1994; Smyer, Cohn, & Brannon, 1988; Stevens et al., 1998). These barriers are also exacerbated by payment structures under Medicare and Medicaid, which tend to require that expert consultation on behavioral problems be taken out of the day-rate reimbursement to the facility. Since most facilities feel that the rate for a day's care is already quite low, the practical effect of this policy is to discourage consultation by mental health professionals for dementia care.

Serious Mental Illness

The severely mentally ill elderly include older adults with schizophrenic and paranoid disorders as well as bipolar disorder and some severe or chronic cases of major depressive disorder. Schizophrenia is a severe and persistent mental illness that affects about one percent of the population and severely compromises most aspects of functioning and daily living. Hallmarks of the illness are disordered perceptions, thinking, and behaviors. Onset is usually between ages sixteen and thirty with only 23 percent of cases occurring after age forty (Smyer & Qualls, 1999). About 12 percent of cases have an onset after age sixty-four. These late-onset paranoid disorders often follow a lifelong history of marginal adjustment or a recent sensory loss (Zarit & Zarit, 1998).

Thus, most elderly individuals with schizophrenia have been living with the illness all their lives. Unfortunately, not much is currently known about course and treatment in late life. Women tend to have a slightly later onset than men and often have better social support networks as they are more likely to have married and had children prior to onset. In some older adults, there is a trend for gradual improvement with age and at times complete remission (Smyer & Qualls, 1999; Zarit & Zarit, 1998). At younger ages, schizophrenia is also highly associated with substance abuse and suicide. Available treatments usually include medications (which can have severe side effects) and psychosocial interventions (Schneider, 1995).

Bipolar disorder is marked by mood swings that alternate between severe depression and periods of mania (which is characterized by euphoric mood, hyperactivity, and delusions of grandeur). The elderly with bipolar disorder comprise about 5 to 10 percent of those who are referred for treatment of affective disorders (Smyer & Qualls, 1999), and the illness is present in about 0.1 percent of the elderly population (Fiske, Kasl-Godley & Gatz, 1998). Onset can be early or late (in which case, it usually follows many years of severe depression). Similar to schizophrenia, there are pharmaceutical and psychosocial treatment options available.

The elderly with SMI comprise a sizable proportion of institutionalized elderly. Historically, older persons have tended to be overrepresented in inpatient psychiatric units (Redick & Taube, 1980) and still account for about 16 percent of all psychiatric inpatients (Stiles, 1994). These facts have typically been attributed to the rising prevalence of the dementias in the later years of life. However, Knight and Carter (1990) reported that most older adults admitted to the inpatient unit in their study (Ventura County, California) suffered from psychosis or affective disorders. The elderly with SMI are also present in long-term care settings; it is estimated that 30 percent of residents of nursing homes have a chronic mental disorder, excluding dementia (Shadish, 1989).

Older persons with SMI have tended to be neglected by all systems of care that might have responsibility for them. The long-term-care system has discouraged explicit recognition of the presence of patients with SMI by adopting policies that explicitly encourage their treatment elsewhere, without addressing the question of where else they would go. They often are present in long-term care, but without special programs to meet their needs. They also get some services in residential care for the elderly and in community programs for older adults, but again without explicit recognition of their needs, and they are often ejected from such programs when their needs become acute (e.g., during psychotic episodes).

The mental health system has tended to ignore the fact that schizophrenic persons age, as does the rest of the population. The working image of the population with SMI that guides program and policy development, as well as advocacy by groups like the National Alliance for the Mentally Ill, has been of a younger- to middle-aged adult with psychosis. At times, this image (along with the focus of much of the mental health and aging community on depression and dementia), has created a sense of competition between aging programs and SMI programs.

In other instances, persons with SMI have been reclassified for dementia programs as they have become older. Some older persons with SMI will have cognitive impairment, either because of the coincidental comorbidity of a dementing illness or because of the iatrogenic effects of psychiatric treatment of the psychosis over several decades (long-term use of neuroleptic medications, extensive use of electroconvulsive therapy in past decades, and psychosurgery in past decades). However, the moves are generally rationalized in terms of matching the older patient with SMI with a more age-congruent patient population. Matching persons to programs based on age rather than diagnosis is not likely to result in effective treatment.

While this population is receiving increasing attention in general treatments of mental health and aging (e.g., Smyer & Qualls, 1999; Zarit & Zarit, 1998), specific programs and policies for them are still lacking. The coming years will bring a new cohort of elderly with SMI into long-term care and aging programs: those that have lived their lives in community programs and have endured the presumably benign neglect of the deinstitutionalization policies that emptied state hospitals between approximately 1955 and 1975. These new cohorts are likely to pose new challenges as older persons with SMI with histories of limited treatment, sporadic treatment, and no treatment are introduced into community-based services for the elderly and into the long-term care system.

Acute Mental Disorders (Depression, Anxiety)

Depression and anxiety are examples of two acute mental illnesses that commonly affect the elderly. Depression is one of the most prevalent mental illnesses among older adults. Depression is characterized by depressed mood and the presence of other symptoms, such as psychomotor agitation or retardation, appetite and sleep disturbances, fatigue, sense of worthlessness, and ideations of death or suicide (*DSM-IV,* 1994). Symptoms differ between age groups with lower levels of dysphoria, guilt, and self-blame among older depressed people (Fiske et al., 1998) and can interfere with detection and proper treatment. Like dementia, depression is more common in women than in men, but this trend reverses in extreme old age (Fiske et al., 1998).

Several different subtypes of depression have been identified that differ by the number of symptoms present as well as their duration. According to the American Psychiatric Association, a diagnosis of major depressive disorder (MDD) is given to individuals who experience five or more of the previously listed symptoms (with one being depressed mood or loss of interest or pleasure) over a two-week period, as well as disruption of social or occupational functioning (*DSM-IV,* 1994). About one-half of those who experience one MDD episode experience another at some time in their life. Dysthymic disorder occurs when one experiences two or more symptoms on and off for at least two years. Minor, or subsyndromal depression, is a newer experimental diagnostic category that is similar to MDD but requires fewer symptoms.

In their review of the prevalence literature, Fiske et al. (1998) found that in elderly samples prevalence of MDD varied from 0.9 to 5.7 percent (with some of the variance attributable to differences in criteria and cut-off scores for diagnosis of depression). Dysthmia was found in 1 to 2 percent of participants and minor depression in 2.7 to 12.9 percent. Studies also showed that significant depressive symptomatology was much more pervasive, affecting 9 to 16.9 percent of elderly community samples. Depression is also common in hospital settings. In a sample of 130 consecutive hospital patients aged seventy years and older, Koenig, Meador, Cohen, and Blazer (1988) detected major depression in 11.5 percent and other depressive disorders in 23 percent. Thus it appears overall that rates of depressive symptoms are quite high among older adults, but a clinical diagnosis is much less common. It is important to note, however, that rates of depressive disorders among the elderly are lower than those for other age groups, especially those aged 25 to 44 (Rabins, 1992).

There are several treatments available to older adults with depression. A variety of medications have been found to be effective (Zarit & Zarit, 1998). However, when prescribing antidepressant medications to this population, it is important to keep in mind possible interactions with medications the patient is already taking for other health problems as well as the lower body mass and decreased metabolism of older adults that can lead to an increased risk for side effects. Also available are effective psychotherapeutic treatments, such as behavioral, cognitive behavioral, and psychodynamic therapies (again see Gatz et al., 1998, for review of empirically validated psychological treatments for depression). It has been found that long-term treatment is the most effective (Schneider, 1995), and research has shown that a combination of pharmaceutical and psychological therapies can have the most long-lasting effects (Zarit & Zarit, 1998). Finally, electroconvulsive therapy is used in older patients who do not respond to other treatments. It is effective in 50 to 70 percent of these patients (Agency for Health Care Policy & Research [AHCPR], 1999).

Due to the structure of the health care system, the first professional many older depressed patients see is their primary care physician where their depression is less likely to be detected, and patients are less likely to be prescribed or referred to the most appropriate treatments.

Anxiety is believed to be the most common functional mental disorder in the elderly. Estimates of prevalence vary from 6 to 30 percent, and it is more common among women (Wetherell, 1998). The Epidemiological Catchment Area (ECA) study first brought attention to the prevalence of anxiety disorders among older adults (Rabins, 1988) where they were found to be more pervasive than depression. Despite these high rates, anxiety disorders, like depression, are more common at younger ages, and there are high rates of older adults with anxiety symptoms but comparably low rates of diagnosis for actual anxiety disorders. It is also understudied in comparison to other mental disorders, and especially with regard to older adults.

Anxiety disorders come in many forms (Smyer & Qualls, 1999). The most common are phobias, or persistent fears of particular objects or situations (e.g., spiders or heights). Generalized anxiety disorder is a generalized experience of excessive or unrealistic anxiety that persists for more than six months. An individual with obsessive–compulsive disorder experiences recurring obsessive thoughts and/or compulsive behaviors in response to obsessive thoughts. Panic disorder is characterized by bouts of severe anxiety, called panic attacks, that can occur in response to a particular situation or for no reason at all. Finally, post-traumatic stress disorder can occur after a traumatic event and results in re-experiencing the event in intrusive ways.

In her review of the anxiety literature, Wetherell (1998) found that most anxious older adults do not seek help due to beliefs that it is an inevitable part of aging, or it just related to another illness. As with depression, the first line of treatment for anxiety is through the primary care physician, who in most cases treats symptoms with medications. As a result, Wetherell (1998) points out, older adults are the chief consumers of anti-anxiety medications. Mellinger, Balter, and Uhlenhuth (1984) found in their probability sample of 3,161 adults in the general population, that of the 11 percent who used antianxiety medications, 52 percent were fifty to seventy-nine years old. Furthermore, 69 percent of those who used anxiolytics daily for at least four months during the previous year fell into that same age group.

A variety of psychological treatments, such as cognitive-behavioral therapy, relaxation training, and life review, are effective in the treatment of anxiety symptoms in older adult clients (see Gatz et al., 1998).

Prevention of depression and anxiety has been the focus of research efforts, and a number of effective methods have been identified. In their review of the literature on prevention of mental illness in older adults, Gatz and colleagues (in press) found empirical support for the use of various means to reduce the risk of developing affective disorders in old age including relaxation training, stress-management training, life review, and support groups for lonely and bereaved individuals as well as caregivers. The results of existing studies provide strong support for the use of such prevention measures in older adults, yet the use of scientifically strong research designs in this area of research points to a need for further investigation of these types of activities.

Key questions and policy issues for the acutely mentally ill population include the likelihood that future cohorts of older persons (e.g., the Boomers as they age) will have both higher prevalence rates of depression and anxiety and a higher demand for services than earlier-born cohorts (Koenig, George, & Schneider, 1994). Greater attention to the treatment of anxiety in later life, given its high prevalence among older adults, is urgently needed. If future editions of the *DSM* system recognize minor depression as a legitimate disorder (as the International Classification on Diseases [ICD]-10 does), then the prevalence of depressive-spectrum disorders among older adults will increase. Primary service issues include parity between mental health and physical health coverage under Medicare (which covers longer inpatient hospital stays for medical problems than for mental health needs, and covers 80 percent of outpatient medical services, but only 50 percent of mental health services), Medigap, and Medicaid programs and the question of whether managed care programs should have different treatment limits for older adults, especially for the octogenarians and nonagenarians (Knight, 1988).

Substance Abuse

Although they are less likely to misuse illegal narcotics than younger adults, alcohol and substance abuse is a serious problem in the elderly, and, in fact, is the third most common mental disorder in this age group (Smyer & Qualls, 1999). The ECA study established that alcohol abuse was one of the four most common mental health problems among older men (Curtis, Geller, Stokes, Levine, & Moore, 1989). In their review of the prevalence literature, Atkinson, Ganzini and Bernstein (1992) found that between 6 and 24 percent of community-dwelling men reported that they drank heavily, and 1 to 12 percent had drinking problems that adversely affected their health, behavior, and social life. For women, these figures were 1 to 2 percent and 0.01 to 1 percent, respectively. Rates of alcohol abuse are higher in hospital and psychiatric patients, as well as in retirement communities (Zarit & Zarit, 1998). It appears that (like the other nondementing disorders) alcohol abuse is less common among older

persons than among younger adults, but remains a serious concern (Bucholz, Sheline, & Helzer, 1995; Knight & Satre, 1999).

About one-third of elderly alcoholics have a late onset, while the rest are lifelong problem drinkers (Smyer & Qualls, 1999). Prescription drug abuse is also an area of concern for the elderly, especially given that this population is prescribed more drugs and purchases more over-the-counter medications than younger age groups. Substance abuse is related to other mental illnesses, particularly schizophrenia and depression. Addiction to tranquilizers appears to be a serious problem among depressed elderly (Zarit & Zarit, 1998).

There appear to be a variety of programs that show promise of being effective with older adults, and age-specific programs appear to work better with alcohol abuse (Knight & Satre, 1999). Again like the other diagnoses, the effects of alcohol and drug abuse on physical health and the complications of treating substance abuse in physically-frail older adults are issues specific to later life and complicate interventions with older adults who have substance abuse problems. Gatz and colleagues (1998) found in their review that (1) age-segregated treatment settings, (2) a focus on reminiscence of good times when the patient had not been drinking, and (3) a supportive environment (as opposed to one in which the emphasis is on challenging denial) were elements of successful treatment programs for older drinkers. Education of physicians to recognize substance abuse in older adults and to emphasize treatment of co-existing problems (e.g., pain) are suggested by Zarit and Zarit (1998).

Historically, substance abuse programs have often been separate from both mental health and physical health care systems. Also, the role of self-help groups (e.g., Alcoholics Anonymous and other twelve-step programs) has been especially salient in interventions with substance abusers. Up to the present, neither the professional substance-abuse system nor the self-help programs seem to be integrated with the aging services network or with mental health programs for older adults. It seems likely that the Boomers and other later-born cohorts of older adults will have higher rates of substance abuse disorders than the cohorts that are currently older adults.

Suicide

The suicide rate is the highest among those aged sixty-five and over compared to all other age groups. According to the National Center for Health Statistics (NCHS), one in five suicides is committed by an elderly person (Peters, Kochanek, & Murphy, 1998). Thus, although the elderly comprise 12 percent of the population, they represent about 20 percent of all suicides. The suicide rate for the nation as a whole in 1996 was 11.6 deaths per 100,000 population. Among those aged sixty-five and over, the rate was 17.3. The rate of elderly suicide has been greater than that of the population as a whole since official statistics were first recorded in the 1930s (McIntosh, Santos, Hubbard, & Overholser, 1994). There are concerns that the rate and absolute number of elderly suicides could increase even more in the future when the Baby Boomer cohort reaches old age (Haas & Hendin, 1983). Younger cohorts are currently committing suicide at higher rates than previous cohorts did at their age, and it is projected that the suicide rate, in addition to the absolute number of elderly suicides, will increase over coming decades (Blazer, Bachar, & Manton, 1986).

To prevent suicide, researchers have sought to identify risk factors by examining coroner's records or using psychological autopsy methods. In addition to increasing age, gender is also a strong risk factor; at all ages, men commit suicide at much greater rates than women, about five times more often (Peters et al., 1998). Rates among White men in the United States peak between ages twenty and thirty and then decline slightly through age sixty and increase greatly through old age. Among women, rates increase through middle age and then decline through old age.

Typically, Whites have the highest rates, and Hispanics have the lowest. Whites and Asians tend to have greater suicide rates in old age whereas African Americans and Hispanics peak in the twenties and thirties and then decline with age (Peters et al., 1998). Regardless of age and sex, suicide rates are lowest among married people. Divorced individuals have the highest rates, followed by widowers (Charatan, 1979; McIntosh et al., 1994). Divorce particularly affects women, while widowhood increases the risk more for men. A link has also been found between suicide risk and family conflict, loss, and stressors. Stressful life events have been found to be precursors for suicide. These include disrupted family environment, divorce, bereavement, violence, loss of employment, and imprisonment (Moscicki, 1995). Among the elderly, there is a strong relationship between suicide and the desire to not be a financial or time burden on the family (McIntosh et al., 1994).

Isolation can lead to loneliness and increased hopelessness and depression. Of all living situations, living alone is most highly associated with suicide (McIntosh et al., 1994). Childlessness can also increase risk of suicide (Charatan, 1979). The elderly who do not see friends or relatives regularly are more liable to attempt suicide.

Finally, among the elderly, one of the most important risk factors for suicide is physical health. Research has found that certain illnesses increase risk for suicide, such as stroke, renal disease, certain forms of cancer (e.g., lung, upper airways, gastrointestinal tract, central nervous system, lymphorecticular system, pancreas, and kidney), AIDS, multiple sclerosis, epilepsy, and chronic respiratory problems (Harris & Barraclough, 1994), as well as urinary disorders (Light & Lebowitz, 1994), and chronic pain (Fishbain, Cutler, Rosomoff, & Rosomoff, 1997). Suicide risk is higher among those with psychological illness, most commonly depression, substance abuse, and schizophrenic disorders.

Beyond the identification of risk factors, some research has also examined the effectiveness of various prevention and intervention strategies, although very little of this research has focused on elder suicide. Family support and social support are particularly critical positive factors for suicide prevention among the bereaved (Farberow, Gallagher-Thompson, Gilewski, & Thompson, 1992). In their review of the literature, Fiske and Arbore (2000–2001) conclude that psychotherapeutic and psychopharmacological treatments for depression may be effective in suicidal older adults, although they have not yet been widely tested. Community agencies with specialized programs for older adults also show promise. Another potential opportunity for intervention stems from the fact that many elderly suicides see their physician before taking their own lives. Conwell, Olsen, Caine, and Flannery (1991) found that one week before death, 39 percent of older suicides saw a doctor and 75 percent a month before death. However, the implications of these data for targeting suicide-prevention efforts on physician visits may be limited by the fact that older adults visit ambulatory medical care services about 6.0 to 7.5 times per year on the average (Schappert, 1999), raising questions as to whether persons contemplating suicide visit more frequently than the base rates.

Although researchers can identify risk factors, putting this information to good use is a separate challenge. Efforts are being made to educate those who work with the elderly to recognize the risk factors for suicidality and to address problems in an effective manner. One example of this is the Prevention of Suicide in Primary Care Elderly Collaborative Trial (PROSPECT), a study sponsored by the National Institute of Mental Health (NIMH). The aim of this multisite study is to test the effectiveness of improving recognition of suicidality and depression in primary care practices.

Suicide rates among the elderly have been a major public health issue for a long time, but there has been little focus on intervention and prevention efforts among policy makers. The current U.S. Surgeon General, David Satcher, has made suicide prevention one of his main causes. With the help of the other agencies including the NIMH and the Substance Abuse and Mental Health Services Agency (SAMHSA), the Surgeon General's office released a *Call to Action to Prevent Suicide* in July, 2000. The plan lists a series of goals that various government agencies are to work on, including dissemination of information to the public and improving education on suicide risk among physicians (U.S. Public Health Service, 1999).

Physical Health

Older adults often have one or more chronic conditions; psychological problems can be secondary to these conditions. As described earlier, physical conditions can lead to mental health problems, such as depression or anxiety, and in extreme cases to suicide. Moreover, many medications and treatments (e.g., mood-affecting medications or a difficult treatment, such as dialysis) can lead to delirium, anxiety, or depression (Zarit & Zarit, 1998).

Mental disorders can also have indirect consequences on physical health by influencing symptom presentation, recovery from physical illness, and adherence to medical treatments (Haley, 1996; Kemp, 1990). The distinction between physical health and mental health problems is not always clear at any age and is often less clear among the elderly who are more likely to have comorbid physical and mental health problems and also present both medical and psychological disorders in atypical ways (e.g., Knight, 1996). Some physical and mental conditions have overlapping symptoms (e.g., fatigue or appetite changes are common in depression but also occur in many physical health problems as well) that complicate diagnosis and identification of appropriate treatments. As a result, psychological symptoms go undetected and untreated. Separate measures of psychological symptomatology are being developed that allow the identification of mental illnesses, such as depression, in physically ill individuals who may have overlapping symptoms (see Miller et al., 1992 for an example). Also, the *DSM-IV* (American Psychiatric Association, 1994) has, in fact, designated a separate diagnosis for depression related to physical health problems.

The problem of detection runs in the other direction as well. Cohen and colleagues (2000) pointed out that many patients with SMI suffer from physical illnesses that their doctors fail to detect. They reported that nonpsychiatrist physicians miss one-third, and psychiatrists miss one-half of their psychiatric patients' comorbid illnesses, including Parkinson's disease, ulcers, epilepsy, asthma, cancer, and rheumatoid arthritis (Cohen et al., 2000).

The problem of distinguishing between the two domains at times becomes a policy issue in itself, with the dementing illnesses sometimes being considered primarily a physical health issue (as a neurological disorder) and, at other times, being considered as a mental health issue. For example, Medicare will cover outpatient visits to diagnose and treat AD at the medical rate (80%), but treatment of depression or behavioral problems in a person with AD will be reimbursed at 50 percent, if reimbursed at all.

Summary

The purpose of this section has been to describe the prevalence, course, treatment and prevention–intervention issues of the most common mental disorders affecting older adults. It is clear that the interactions between physical and mental health are of particular importance in this age group. Treatments are available for most disorders, but relatively little is known about primary prevention (Gatz et al., in press), and the available treatments are not widely accessible to older adults who suffer with these disorders. With the rapid growth of the aging population, it seems imperative that research on the course, prevention, and treatment of mental disorders become a high priority in the twenty-first century. The distinctive symptoms, courses, and treatments for these disorders suggest a need to develop policies and programs for each disorder, rather than a global policy on mental health among the elderly. It makes no more sense to have a uniform policy or program for mental disorders than it would to have a uniform policy to cover heart disease, cancers, arthritis, and diabetes, for example. The next section explores the development, current status, and future prospects for the systems of care for mental disorders among the elderly in the United States.

DEVELOPMENT OF MULTISYSTEM MENTAL HEALTH CARE IN THE UNITED STATES

The current system of mental health care in the United States is a collection of distinct care systems that evolved at different times under the influence of specific historical and economic pressures. Knight and Kaskie

(1995) described this complex web as multisystem, multilevel, and diagnosis-specific. Multisystem refers to the many distinct networks of care provision that exist. These include the systems for medical care, long-term care, mental health care, aging network, dementia care, and substance abuse services. Given the complexity of the problems of later life and the frequent co-occurrence of problems from more than one of these domains, older adults with psychological problems may surface in any of these systems (Knight, 1996).

To better understand why the multisystem structure of mental health care exists in the United States, it is important to examine the history of its development. It can be seen that over the decades, the different systems evolved in response to historical demands and continue to develop to this day as a product of economic and political pressures. Thus, rather than being the product of poor planning within a unified system, mental health care in the United States is the result of multilayered growth and change. In the following sections, the history of mental health care systems in the United States will be explored and the future considered.

As described by Knight et al. (1998), the state hospital system for psychiatric care in the United States started in the late nineteenth century and, in contrast to the United Kingdom and other European countries, replaced no care for the mentally ill, rather than an earlier institutional system. Prior to this, most mentally ill were cared for by their families, or they lived in overcrowded almshouses and prisons (Rosen, Pancake, & Rickards, 1995). In the late nineteenth century, Dorthea Dix led a movement to replace almshouses and prisons with more humane settings. The primary public response to mental disorders—a mix of SMI, depressive disorders, and dementias—was a state and locally funded and operated inpatient system that remained until the late 1950s.

Following World War II, the federal government became more involved in mental health issues with the passage of the National Mental Health Act in 1946, which created the National Institute of Mental Health. In 1955, The Mental Health Study Act was passed with appropriations for the Joint Commission on Mental Illness and Health that was to provide an analysis and reevaluation of the human and economic problems of mental health.

A combination of concerns about overcrowded state hospitals, the expense of building more hospitals, and the advent of effective psychoactive medications led to large-scale deinstitutionalization of some patients and "transinstitutionalization" of others, especially the elderly. During the early 1960s, the Kennedy administration encouraged the enactment of the Community Mental Health Centers Act of 1963 that financed development of comprehensive mental health centers (CMHCs) to provide services to deinstitutionalized mentally ill individuals and those needing intermittent care (Knight et al., 1998). It was not until 1975 that Congress mandated that CMHCs provide specialty care to older adults. Even then, very little emphasis was placed on services for older adults.

About the same time in the 1960s, the enactment of Medicare and Medicaid led to the expansion of long-term care for the elderly. This was primarily a physical-medicine program, and long-term care facilities were largely intended to move long-stay, physically frail older adults out of acute care medical-surgical hospitals. However, many of the deinstitutionalized older adults who moved out of the state hospital system moved into long-term care facilities, usually with primary diagnoses that were physical rather than psychiatric, so as not to violate the cap on psychiatric admissions to long-term care facilities.

In the early 1970s, the Nixon administration started what became a long-term trend of moving the federal government back out of service provision and into a coordination and technical advice role. In contrast, the Carter Administration in the late 1970s made older adults a priority target population for the CMHCs. The 1977 Presidential Commission on Mental Health emphasized a need for improved community-based services, and the Commission's 1980 Mental Health Systems Act provided for special staffing and grants for CMHCs with aging programs.

Unfortunately for the development of mental health services for older adults, the Reagan Administration of the 1980s sharply curtailed the role of the federal government in mental health and started a program of devolution of responsibility and funding for mental health programs back to the state level. President Reagan signed the Omnibus Budget Reconciliation Act (OBRA) of 1981 which repealed the Mental Health Systems Act and consolidated mental health treatment and substance-abuse-rehabilitation service programs into a single block grant that enabled each state to administer its allocated funds. The implementation of this policy included an initial 25 percent reduction in federal funding, with further reductions in following years. With the repeal of the community mental health legislation and the establishment of block grants, the federal role in services to the mentally ill became one of providing technical assistance to increase the capacity of state and local providers of mental health services (National Institute of Mental Health, 2000).

The post-Reagan landscape of public services for the mentally ill, especially for the population with SMI, appeared to be very nearly a return to the pre-Dorthea Dix days of family-provided care, prison-based care for those who broke laws and were jailed, and a variable patchwork of public and private clinic services for those who could find them.

The U.S. federal government responded to the relocation of the elderly mentally ill into long-term care facilities with the Nursing Home Act of 1987. This Act recognized that older adults with psychiatric conditions were overrepresented in nursing homes and stipulated that nursing homes must screen patients for psychiatric illness. If a patient was diagnosed with a mental illness, then the nursing home was required to (1) provide appropriate psychiatric care or (2) deny admission to the individual and/or transfer the individual to a more appropriate facility (Smyer, 1989). Reports suggest sharp increases in mental health service provision in nursing homes after the passage of this law (Knight & Kaskie, 1995; Office of Inspector General, 1996), rather than discharges of patients with mental health problems. However, there are concerns about service standards and about fraud: approximately 24 percent of Medicare billings in 1993 for mental health services to nursing home residents were estimated to be medically unnecessary (Office of Inspector General, 1996). Two-fifths of the insurance carriers for the Medicare program considered part of the problem to be "excessive entrepreneurialism" on the part of mental health professionals (Office of Inspector General, 1996, p. 13).

The outpatient sector of mental health services has also changed dramatically since the 1980s. Services have been privatized in the sense that there has been a move from organized clinics like the community mental health centers to outpatient care by private practitioners, reimbursed by Medicare in one form or another. This change followed both the decline of public sector CMHCs under the devolution doctrines of the Reagan years and also the liberalization of mental health coverage (relative to prior standards) under Medicare in the 1989 OBRA changes that brought increases in coverage of private practice outpatient visits, and also increases in coverage of private sector inpatient, and partial hospitalization visits.

At the same time, managed care became a major part of the health and mental health systems, both under Medicare and in the private sector. In 1982, managed care programs began to enroll Medicare patients and to receive a set, monthly per capita payment from the government to pay for services. Funds that are not spent on services can be kept by the managed care organizations, and thus there are economic incentives for managed care organizations to find ways to cut costs, and, possibly, to limit access to care. In many regions of the country, the shift from fee-for-service to managed care reimbursement of health and mental health care resulted in Medicare's becoming a more competitive payment source for private practice mental health professionals in that Medicare rates stayed roughly stable while other rates of pay declined to (or below) the Medicare reimbursement level, sometimes with even more review and bureaucratic complexity than the government program. As noted by Knight and Kaskie (1995), this could have had positive implications for mental health services for older adults in that managed care could coordinate health and mental health services and tends to encourage outpatient over inpatient care.

Unfortunately, as noted by Kiesler (2000), managed care to date has been generally characterized by "carve-outs" for mental health treatment, and typically separate carve-outs for substance-abuse treatment. Carve-outs are contracted services that provide separate organizational management and a separate risk pool for these services, often viewed as mysterious or particularly risky by health care organizations without specialty care experience. Thus, the organizational culture of the health and mental health systems have tended to block the coordination necessary for truly integrated serv-

ices, even under managed-care systems. Kiesler (2000) argued that, for all ages, mental health and substance-abuse services will change in the future to "carve-ins," a step that would be essential in his view to realizing any savings in health care costs due to mental health and substance abuse services. He also argued that the growing number of older adults in managed care plans, with the concomitant increase in management of chronic health and mental health conditions, will necessitate greater coordination of services (Kiesler, 2000).

Neither the private sector outpatient services nor the long-term care services (also increasingly offered by managed care groups) emphasize expertise in geriatrics and gerontology among their providers. Here, as in other areas of managed care, the focus is on using generalists rather than (presumably more expensive) specialists. In aging and mental health, this presents potentially serious problems since it requires expert knowledge to distinguish among mental disorders in older adults (Zarit & Zarit, 1998) and among health, mental health, and social services problems in potential older clients (Knight, 1996). Furthermore, older adults and those around them (family, primary care physicians, aging network services workers) tend not to identify or to refer for mental health problems. Active case finding has been a key element of all model programs for delivering mental health services to older adults (Knight, Rickards, Rabins, Buckwalter, & Smith, 1995).

CURRENT STATUS OF THE SYSTEMS OF CARE FOR MENTAL HEALTH AND AGING

In terms of changes in service delivery, there appears to be a mélange of good and bad news. The old public sector systems, both of state hospital care and of community mental health centers, have declined dramatically. In their place is greatly increased attention to older adults on the part of private-sector services at the inpatient, day treatment, and outpatient levels and in long-term care settings. Some of this activity is operated by managed care groups and most is paid for by public funds (through Medicare and Medicaid) although operated by private, often for-profit, providers. However, little or no information is available on who receives services, for what problems, and from what type of professionals (Kaskie, Linkins, & Estes, 2000).

The devolution of services and policy from the federal government to the states from the Nixon through the Reagan years has returned mental health policy to the individual states, where it rested for most of the history of mental health policy in the United States, except for the brief period starting with the Kennedy administration. Kaskie et al. (2000a) described the history of dementia-care policy and noted that the states were the first (starting in the 1930s) and are currently the principal movers in dementia policy. State policies are, of course, highly variable. This variability can be positive if it reflects responsiveness to local needs and desires, or negative if it reflects chaotic variation due to the vagaries of personal interest in the topic on the part of individual legislators and executive branch members and other political factors unrelated to public need for services.

In short, these trends could be summarized by saying the old systems of care emphasizing public sector services based in state psychiatric hospitals and later in CMHCs have largely been terminated. The replacements for these older systems have involved shifting mental health patients into long-term care and into the medical care system, the privatization of mental health services paid

for by federal funds, a current reliance on managed-care payment and organizational options, and a return to state-level responsibility for mental health policy and programming that is not handled by private providers.

SYSTEM CHANGES AND THEIR IMPACT ON OLDER ADULTS WITH MENTAL DISORDERS

The impact of these policy changes has probably been different for each diagnostic group among the elderly. In general, one would expect that persons with acute conditions that can be treated within managed care (and fee-for-service) Medicare session limits will do better and may now have improved access to services: persons with depression, anxiety, and possibly substance abuse. In principle, services should improve to persons whose psychological problems affect their medical condition and, in fact, some integrated managed care organizations have programs to identify depression in older patients coming to primary care medical settings.

In contrast, schizophrenics and persons with dementia are likely to do worse than in the past. Both conditions are chronic and tend to be managed rather than treated. This poses problems for any Medicare-funded service. Medicare is intended for active medical treatment rather than for habilitative care, by Congressional mandate. The economic incentives of managed care tend to further undermine the likelihood that persons with these chronic conditions will receive care under the current rules. Both of these groups need extensive services, and it is not feasible to turn a profit while providing good care for them under controlled-payment systems. (Caring for wealthy schizophrenics and persons with dementia is likely profitable, but that is not the focus of concern here.) In the following sections, the impact of these changes on older adults in each category is explored.

Dementia

There has clearly been increasing emphasis on dementia over the last few decades, with increases in both state and federal policy making and in programs within many of the states (Kaskie et al., 2000a). The historical impetus for these changes is generally attributed to the Alzheimer's Association and the National Institute on Aging (e.g., Fox, 1989), but empirical analysis suggests that state activity has been shaped by a combination of state-level advocacy by Alzheimer's Association chapters, the presence of legislative advocates in state legislatures, and consumer demand (as indexed by dementia special care unit beds, Kaskie, Knight, & Liebig, 2000b). A key policy issue in the area of dementia care vis-a-vis mental health policy is whether dementia should be considered a mental health issue or a health issue. Historically, the dementias were typically included in psychiatric care, and much of the treatment and management of persons with dementia relies upon psychoactive drugs and behavior management principles. However, the presence of large numbers of persons with dementia in long-term care settings for the elderly, the identification of dementia with aging services more generally, and the desire of advocacy groups like the Alzheimer's Association to avoid the perceived stigma of designation as a mental disorder and the associated discounting of coverage under Medicare for mental health treatment (50% coverage as opposed to 80%) have combined to form a trend to see dementia as part of health policy or long-term-care policy rather than mental health policy per se. At least in the 1980s and 1990s, the program trends appeared to be toward separate services for persons with dementia, although the effectiveness of dementia-specific services has remained a topic of considerable debate (Kutner, Mistretta, Barnhart, & Belodoff, 1999; Phillips et al., 1997).

It is likely that the trend toward viewing dementia as a health care issue and toward the development of a separate dementia-service system will continue into the early twenty-first century. To the extent that some dementia care requires mental health expertise in diagnosis and cognitive function assessment, in psychopharmacology, and in behavior management, this shift in focus will be successful only to the extent that the dementia care system and related policy include a mental health component as well as health and social service components. Attention particularly is needed in defining the essential mental health components of dementia care within the long-term care industry. Since dementia care is by definition care for persons with a chronic and progressive disorder, it is likely to require Congressional action to clarify what the role of Medicare should be in funding such services.

Serious Mental Illness

As noted previously, there has been little specific attention to older adults within the SMI category. The trends in mental health policy in recent decades have tended to undermine care to the older adults with SMI in general. Deinstitutionalization is generally considered to have failed this population on the national scale. In spite of the development of good model programs in specific locales, large numbers of persons with SMI were moved from hospital care to no care or substandard care in the community. The focus on managed care more recently has tended to change the target population of even public sector programs to persons whose mental health treatment can be expected to result in health care cost savings, usually enrollees with acute mental disorders affecting medical treatment and persons with substance abuse disorders. In short, the general movement in policy has been toward decreasing services for the population with SMI in general, at a time when the needs of the older population with SMI were just beginning to be recognized. In the absence of organized advocacy for the older population with SMI, we are pessimistic about the likelihood of focused public policy attention to this group in the foreseeable future.

Acute Mental Disorders: Depression and Anxiety Disorders

This grouping of acute, functional mental disorders has received the most consistent attention as explicit mental health and aging topics over the years. They seem to have been the most favored over the course of the development of the mental health system and of mental health policy. In the latter half of the twentieth century, the locus of care has moved from state psychiatric hospitals to the community to privatization of care, to managed care schemes for organizing private care. The increase in service provision is a positive trend and augurs well for future policy developments to include greater acceptance of home visit delivery of mental health services (Knight, 1994), parity of mental health coverage with medical coverage under Medicare, Medigap, and Medicaid policies, and the integration of mental health services with medical services under managed care, without equating mental health services with psychopharmacology.

Much of the mental health service provision in long-term care settings is rationalized in terms of treatment of depression and anxiety (Parmalee, Katz, & Lawton, 1992) and is discussed in greater detail next. This points to a tricky policy issue in its own right. There can be no doubt that there are rather high levels of depression and anxiety in long-term care facilities. Parmalee et al. (1992) found in a sample of 868 elderly long-term facility residents that 15.7 percent suffered from possible MDD and another 16.5 percent presented minor depressive symptomatology. These same researchers also found in a sample of 451 elderly residents of long-term care facilities that 3.5 percent suffered from anxiety or panic disorders and another 13.2 percent reported milder symptoms (Parmalee et al., 1992).

When the depression is comorbid with a dementia, regulatory bodies and Medicare intermediaries often argue that there is no point to the treatment and do not approve services. Expert care providers would counter that, at least for many demented residents in long-term care, depression and other functional disorders can represent a complicating factor or source of excess disability in the person with dementia (e.g., Rovner & Katz, 1993). This decision likely needs to be made at a higher and more centralized level than the day-to-day negotiation between providers and Medicare intermediaries.

A "wild card" regarding future service delivery in this domain is the prospects for managed care itself as part of the Medicare program; currently (Summer, 2000), newspapers are filled with stories about managed care groups pulling out of the Medicare program while advocacy groups for consumers lobby for greater consumer protections. It seems likely that the twenty-first century will bring a restructuring of health care for older adults once again, with mental health services likely being reorganized in the process in its historical status as a footnote to health care reforms (Kiesler, 1992).

Substance Abuse Services

As is true of most mental health-related services, there has been relatively little attention to older adults in service programs for substance abuse. The roots of much of the substance abuse services system in employer-driven programs (e.g., employee assistance programs) leads to older adults who are post-retirement being left out of the scope of policies and programs. To the extent that substance abuse treatment is often initiated by demands for sobriety from family and from employers, older adults may be less subject to such external pressures. In fact, much of the motivation for seeking substance abuse treatment among older adults seems to come from health concerns (Finlayson, Hurt, Davis, & Morse, 1988).

With the Boomers and future cohorts of older adults, it seems likely that the need and the demand for substance abuse interventions in older populations will increase in the future. It is likely that cost savings in health care programs could be realized by the treatment of alcohol abuse, prescription drug abuse, and (especially in future cohorts) of illegal drug abuse.

CONCLUSION

In the twenty-first century, mental health policy for older adults would appear to be entering a new phase. Service delivery is largely privatized, with little federal or state oversight. Mental health services for older persons with acute mental disorders and substance abuse diagnoses are being delivered in long-term care and in medical settings, and in managed care organizations specializing in mental health carve-out contracting. Older adults with acute mental disorders and those in nursing homes would seem to be receiving more attention than ever, but virtually nothing is known about the targeting or the effectiveness of the services delivered.

The fifty states are largely going their own way in developing mental health policies and often are competing with the private sector for federal monies. The introduction of managed care principles, the expectation of showing cost savings, and other economic pressures tend to deflect program resources away from the elderly with SMI and other traditional targets of public mental health services in favor of acute disorders, substance abuse, and psychological problems affecting physical conditions. These trends mean that the elderly with SMI are receiving fewer services and less appropriate services than in the past.

A separate dementia care service network has been developing since about 1980 in response to political and economic incentives and without much input from program evaluation regarding the effectiveness of dementia-specific services. While separating programs for persons with dementia from those for persons with SMI is a sensible response to their differing symptom profiles and service needs, to date that separation has also severely limited the accessibility of psychiatric and psychological expertise within dementia network programs.

A rational and empirically based mental health policy for older adults would need to take into account the distinctiveness of the different classes of disorders, the variety of social contexts in which older adults with mental disorders appear, and accumulating knowledge about the disorders and what works in their treatment and prevention. The multiple systems that enact those policies in front-line programming need to be carefully examined and retooled to meet the specific mental health needs of today's older adults and of today's middle-aged adults who will be tomorrow's elderly in need of services.

REFERENCES

Agency for Health Care Policy & Research. (1999). *Depression in primary care: Volume 2, Treatment of major depression, clinical practice guideline, Number 5.* (AHCPR Publication No. 93-0551.)

American Heart Association. (2000, October). *Cardiovascular disease and strokes.* Retrieved 10-18-2000 from the World Wide Web: http://www.americanheart.org/catalog/Scientific_catpage70.html

American Psychiatric Association. (1994). *Diagnostic and statistical manual of mental disorders* (4th ed.). Washington DC: Author.

Atkinson, R. M., Ganzini, L., & Bernstein, M. J. (1992). Alcohol and substance-use disorders in the elderly. In J. E. Birren, R. B. Sloane, & G. D. Cohen (Eds.), *Handbook of Mental Health and Aging* (2nd ed., pp. 516–545). San Diego, CA: Academic Press.

Birkett, D. P. (1991). *Psychiatry in the nursing home: Assessment, evaluation, and intervention.* New York: Haworth Press.

Blazer, D. G., Bachar, J. R., & Manton, K. G. (1986). Suicide in later life: Review and commentary. *Journal of the American Geriatrics Society, 34,* 519–525.

Bucholz, K. K., Sheline, Y. I., & Helzer, J. E. (1995). The epidemiology of alcohol use, problems and dependence in elders: A review. In T. Beresford & E. Gomberg (Eds.), *Alcohol and aging* (pp. 19–41). New York: Oxford University Press.

Burns, B. J., & Kamerow, D. B. (1988). Psychotropic drug prescriptions for nursing home residents. *Journal of Family Practice 26,* 155–160.

Charatan, F. B. (1979). The aged. In L. D. Hankoff (Ed.), *Suicide: Theory and clinical aspects* (pp. 253–262). Littleton, MA: PSG Publishing Company.

Cohen, C. I., Cohen, G. D., Blank, K., Gaitz, C., Katz, I. R., Leuchter, A., Maletta, G., Meyers, B., Sakauye, K., & Shamoian C. (2000). Schizophrenia and older adults: An overview: Directions for research and policy. *American Journal of Geriatric Psychiatry, 8,* 19–28.

Conwell, Y., Olsen, K., Caine, E. D., & Flannery, C. (1991). Suicide in later life: Psychological autopsy findings. *International Psychogeriatrics, 3,* 59–66.

Crook, T., Bartus, R. T., Ferris, S. H., Whitehouse, P., Cohen, G.D., & Gershon, S. (1986). Age-associated memory impairment: Proposed diagnostic criteria and measures of clinical change. Report of National Institute of Mental Health Work Group. *Developmental Neuropsychology, 2,* 261–276.

Curtis, J. R., Geller, G., Stokes, E. J., Levine, D. M., & Moore, R. D. (1989). Characteristics, diagnosis and treatment of alcoholism in elderly patients. *Journal of the American Geriatrics Society, 37,* 310–316.

Farberow, N. L., Gallagher-Thompson, D., Gilewski, M., & Thompson, L. (1992). The role of social supports in the bereavement process of surviving spouses of suicide and natural deaths. *Suicide and Life-Threatening Behavior, 22,* 107–124.

Finlayson, R. E., Hurt, R. D., Davis, L. J., & Morse, R. M. (1988). Alcoholism in elderly persons: A study of the psychiatric and psychosocial features of 216 inpatients. *Mayo Clinic Proceedings, 63,* 761–768.

Fishbain, D. A., Cutler, R., Rosomoff, H. L., & Rosomoff, R. S. (1997). Chronic pain-associated depression: Antecedent or consequence of chronic pain? A review. *Clinical Journal of Pain, 13,* 116–137.

Fiske, A., & Arbore, P. (2000–2001). Future directions in late life suicide prevention. *Omega, 42,* 37–53.

Fiske, A., Kasl-Godley, J. E., & Gatz, M. (1998). Mood disorders in late life. In A. S. Bellack & M. Hersen (Eds.), *Comprehensive Clinical Psychology, Vol. 7: Clinical Geropsychology* (pp. 193–229). Oxford: Pergamon.

Fox, P. (1989). From senility to Alzheimer's disease: The rise of the Alzheimer's disease movement. *The Milbank Quarterly, 67,* 58–102.

Gatz, M., Crowe, M., Fiske, A., Fung, W., Kelly, C., Levy, B., Maines, M., Robinson, G., Satre, D. D., Serrano Selva, J. P., Suthers, K., Watari, K., & Wetherell, J. L. (in press). Promoting mental health in later life: A review of the evidence. In D. Glenwick, & L. Jason (Eds.), *In-*

novative strategies for preventing psychological problems. New York: Springer Publishing Company.

Gatz, M., Fiske, A., Fox, L. S., Kaskie, F., Kasl-Godley, J. E., McCallum, T. J., & Wetherell, J. L. (1998). Empirically-validated psychological treatments for older adults. *Journal of Mental Health and Aging, 4,* 9–46.

Gatz, M., Kasl-Godley, J. E., & Karel, M. J. (1996). Aging and mental disorders. In J. E. Birren & K. W. Schaie (Eds.), *Handbook of the psychology of aging* (4th ed., pp. 365–382). San Diego: Academic Press.

Haas, A. P., & Hendin, H. (1983). Suicide among older people: Projections for the future. *Suicide and Life-Threatening Behavior, 13,* 147–154.

Haley, W. E. (1996). The medical context of psychotherapy with the elderly. In S. H. Zarit, & B. G. Knight (Eds.), *A guide to psychotherapy and aging: Effective interventions in a life stage context* (pp 221–240). Washington, DC: American Psychological Association.

Harris, E. D., & Barraclough, B. M. (1994). Suicide as an outcome for medical disorders. *Medicine, 73,* 281–296.

Kaskie, B., Knight, B. G., & Liebig, P. S. (in press, a). Dementia policy revisited: An analysis of the state laws targeted toward individuals with dementia. *Journal of Aging and Social Policy.*

——. (in press, b). State legislation concerning individuals with dementia: A comparison of three theoretical models of policy formation. *Gerontologist.*

Kaskie, B., Linkins, K., & Estes, C. (2000). *The provision of mental health services to older adults: A resource database of state Medicaid programs, state mental health administrations and state units on aging.* Washington, DC: Substance Abuse and Mental Health Services Administration.

Kemp, B. (1990). The psychosocial context of geriatric rehabilitation. In B. Kemp, K. Brummel-Smith, & J. W. Ramsdell (Eds.), *Geriatric rehabilitation* (pp. 41–60). Boston: College Hill Press.

Kiesler, C. A. (1992). U.S. mental health policy: Doomed to fail. *American Psychologist, 47,* 416–421.

——. (2000). The next wave of change for psychology and mental health in the health care revolution. *American Psychologist, 55,* 481–487.

Knight, B. G. (1988). Factors influencing therapist-rated change in older adults. *Journal of Gerontology, 43,* 111–112.

——. (1994). Editorial: Home delivered mental health services: An idea whose time has come? *Gerontologist, 34,* 149.

——. (1996). *Psychotherapy with older adults, 2nd edition.* Thousand Oaks, CA: Sage Publications.

Knight, B., & Carter, P. M. (1990). Reduction of psychiatric inpatient stay for older adults by intensive case management. *Gerontologist, 30,* 510–515.

Knight, B. G., & Kaskie, B. (1995) Models for mental health service delivery to older adults. In M. Gatz (Ed.), *Emerging issues in mental health and aging* (pp. 231–255). Washington, DC: American Psychological Association.

Knight, B. G., Kaskie, B., Woods, R. T., & Phibbs, E. (1998). Community mental health services in the United States and the United Kingdom: A comparative systems approach. In A. S. Bellack, & M. Hersen (Series Eds.), & B. Edelstein (Vol. Ed.) *Comprehensive clinical psychology: Vol. 7. Clinical geropsychology* (pp. 455–475). Oxford: Elsevier Science.

Knight, B. G., Rickards, L., Rabins, P., Buckwalter, K., & Smith, M. (1995). Community-based services for mentally ill elderly. In B. Knight, L. Teri, J. Santos, & P. Wohlford (Eds.), *Applying geropsychology to services for older adults: Implications for training and practice* (pp. 212–230). Washington, DC: American Psychological Association.

Knight, B. G., & Satre, D. D. (1999). Cognitive behavioral psychotherapy with older adults. *Clinical Psychology: Science and Practice, 6,* 188–203.

Koenig, H. G., George, L. K., & Schneider, R. (1994). Mental health care for older adults in the year 2020: A dangerous and avoided topic. *Gerontologist, 34,* 674–679.

Koenig, H. G., Meader, K. G., Cohen, H. J., & Blazer, D. G. (1988). Depression in elderly hospitalized patients with medical illness. *Archives of Internal Medicine, 148,* 1929–1936.

Kutner, N. G., Mistretta, E. F., Barnhart, H. X., & Belodoff, B. F. (1999). Family members' perceptions of quality of life change in dementia SCU residents. *Journal of Applied Gerontology, 18*, 423–439.

Lichtenberg, P. A. (1994). *A guide to psychological practice in geriatric long-term care.* New York: Haworth Press.

Light E., & Lebowitz B. D. (1994). Psychological factors in urinary disorders. In P. D. O'Donnell (Ed.) *Geriatric urology* (pp. 469–477). Boston: Little, Brown.

McIntosh, J. L., Santos, J. F., Hubbard, R. W., & Overholser, J. C. (1994). *Elder suicide: Research, theory, and treatment.* Washington, DC: American Psychological Association.

Mellinger, G. D., Balter, M. B., & Uhlenhuth, E. H. (1984). Anti-anxiety agents: Duration of use and characteristics of users in the U.S.A. *Current Medical Research and Opinion, 8* (Suppl. 4), 21–36.

Miller, M. D., Paradis, C. F., Houck, P. R., Mazumdar, S., Stack, J. A., Rifai, A. H., Mulsant, B., & Reynolds, C. F. (1992). Rating chronic medical illness burden in geropsychiatric practice and research: Application of the Cumulative Illness Rating Scale. *Psychiatry Research, 41*, 237–248.

Moscicki, E. K. (1995). North American perspectives: Epidemiology of suicide. *International Psychogeriatrics, 6*, 355–361.

National Institute of Mental Health. (2000). *National Institute of Mental Health: Important events in NIMH history.* Retrieved 10-18-2000 from the World Wide Web: http://www.nih.gov/about/almanac/organization/nimh/history.html.

Nolan, K. A., & Blass, J. P. (1992). Preventing cognitive decline. *Clinics in Geriatric Medicine 8*, 19–34.

Office of Inspector General, Department of Health and Human Services. (1996). *Mental health services in nursing homes.* (OEI Publication No. 02-91-00860). New York: Author.

Parmalee, P. A., Katz, I. R., & Lawton, M. P. (1992). Incidence of depression in long term care settings. *Journal of Gerontology, 47*, M189–196.

Peters, K. D., Kochanek, K. D., & Murphy, S. L. (1998). Deaths: Final data for 1996. *National Vital Statistics Report, 47*(9). DHHS Publication No. (PHS) 99-1120. Hyattsville, MD: National Center for Health Statistics.

Phillips, C. D., Sloane, P. D., Hawes, C., Koch, G., Han, J., Spry, K., Dunteman, G., & Williams, R. L. (1997). Effects of residence in Alzheimer disease special care units on functional outcomes. *JAMA, 278*, 1340–1344.

Rabins, P. V. (1992). Prevention of mental disorder in the elderly: Current perspectives and future prospects. *Journal of the American Geriatrics Society, 40*, 727–733.

Redick, R. A., & Taube, C. A. (1980). Demography and mental health care of the aged. In J. E. Birren, & R. B. Sloane (Eds.), *Handbook of mental health and aging* (pp. 57–74). Englewood Cliffs, NJ: Prentice Hall.

Regier, D. A., Boyd, J. H., Burke, J. D., Rae, D. S., Myers, J. K., Kramer, M., Robins, L. N., George, L. K., Karno, M., & Locke, B. Z. (1988). One-month prevalence of mental disorders in the United States. *Archives of General Psychiatry, 45*, 977–986.

Reynolds, S. L., Crimmins, E. M., & Saito, Y. (1998). Cohort differences in disability and disease presence. *Gerontologist 38*, 578–590.

Rosen, A. L., Pancake, J. A., & Rickards, L. (1995). Mental health policy and older Americans: Historical and current perspectives. In M. Gatz (Ed.), *Emerging issues in mental health and aging* (pp. 1–18). Washington, DC: American Psychological Association.

Rovner, B. W., & Katz, J. R. (1993). Psychiatric disorders in the nursing home: A selective review of studies related to clinical care. [Special issue.] *International Journal of Geriatric Psychiatry, 8*, 75–87.

Schappert, S. M. (1999). Ambulatory care visits to physician offices, hospital outpatient departments, and emergency departments: United States, 1997. *Vital & Health Statistics—Series 13 Data From the National Health Survey 143*, 1–39.

Schneider, L. (1995). Efficacy for clinical treatment of mental disorders among older persons. In M. Gatz (Ed.), *Emerging issues in mental health and aging* (pp. 19–71). Washington DC: American Psychological Association.

Shadish, W. R. (1989). Private sector care for chronically mentally ill individuals: The more things change, the more they stay the same. *American Psychologist, 44,* 1142–1147.

Smyer, M.A. (1989). Nursing homes as a setting for psychological practice: Public policy perspectives. *American Psychologist, 44,* 1307–1314.

——. (1995). Prevention and early intervention for mental disorders of the elderly. In M. Gatz (Ed.), *Emerging issues in mental health and aging* (pp. 163–182). Washington, DC: American Psychological Association.

Smyer, M. A., Cohn, M. D., & Brannon, D. (1988). *Mental health consultation in nursing homes.* New York: New York University Press.

Smyer, M. A., & Qualls, S. H. (1999). *Aging and mental health.* Malden, MA: Blackwell Publishers.

Stevens, A. B., Burgio, L. D., Bailey, E., Burgio, K. L., Paul, P., Capilouto, E., Nicovich, P., & Hale, G. (1998). Teaching and maintaining behavior management skills with nursing assistants in a nursing home. *Gerontologist, 38,* 379–384.

Stiles, P. G. (1994, November). *Utilization of ambulatory mental health services by the elderly: A preliminary report on the effects of recent Medicare reimbursement changes.* Paper presented at the meeting of the Gerontological Society of America, Atlanta, GA.

U.S. Public Health Service. (1999). *The Surgeon General's call to action to prevent suicide.* Washington, DC: Author.

Wetherell, J. L. (1998). Treatment of anxiety in older adults. *Psychotherapy, 35,* 444–458.

Zarit, S. H., & Zarit, J. M. (1998). *Mental disorders in older adults.* New York: The Guilford Press.

IV. SPECIAL POPULATION GROUPS
AND PUBLIC HEALTH

Chapter 6

THE INVISIBLE ELDERLY

Gari Lesnoff-Caravaglia

GENERAL CHARACTERIZATIONS of the older population assume fairly standard profiles with respect to lifestyle, marital status, economic situation, health care, and life history. While such commonalities serve to describe a large portion of the population, they also provide a screen that obliterates the fact that many older persons do not easily fit within such an all-embracing clustering.

Another unfortunate aspect of such global descriptions is that they serve to ostracize those groups that present a problem of "fit," and hence exclude them from public health policy considerations. While it is true that many of these marginal groups do not seek services, the reasons for such lack of appeal remain obscure, and, consequently, services that may be of benefit may not be introduced or may appear in guises unacceptable to particular older-aged groups.

Diversity in the older population is not due only to cultural, racial, economic, or social distinctions, but is caused by lifestyle conditions–physical, emotional and psychological–that precede old age and may well have their roots in infancy and childhood. The maturation of an older person is as de-pendent on these variables, as is every other stage of life in human development.

THE ELDERLY SINGLE-ROOM OCCUPANTS

The elderly single-room occupants (SROs) choose a lifestyle characterized as "alone" by living in "single-room only" hotel accommodations and rooming houses located in inner cities or downtown commercial areas with buildings that are usually deteriorating or are in the process of being destroyed. They select a lifestyle that deliberately excludes other persons and minimizes social contact. Although, there is a determined effort to remain aloof, the elderly SRO is not essentially an isolated person. The preferred form of social involvement is that of an observer.

SROs prefer the independence, the anonymity, and the convenience of a hotel. Hotel living enables people to keep up whatever life they can afford, answers their social needs, and allows them to become a part of a built-in community. It functions well for persons who could not or do not want to set up housekeeping. However, in cheaper hotels, the conditions can be quite unpleasant, and, in some instances, unsafe. There is little supervision and security, and owners provide a minimal number of toilet or bathing facilities. Heating and ventilation is also often inadequate. Although these facilities answer a need, they commonly develop into what is known as "skid row."

By the nature of these lifestyles, it is quite clear that housing is more than just a building and the patterns of use within it. The location of hotel and rooming-house districts within the city, such as San Francisco, is closely tied to the proximity of other businesses and services on which hotel residents depend, and that, in fact, are seen as extensions of their homes. This is particularly true for persons whose living quarters do not include laundry facilities or a kitchen. Such components of "home" are scattered up and down one's street by way of lunch counters and launderettes.

Department stores are used as places for entertainment and diversion. Many older persons sit in the shoe departments or in the lounges and restrooms. Again, the desire to observe at a distance and not to interact is paramount. Both the downtown environment and the hotels that accept and frequently nourish the SRO population provide the needed resources and allow for its lone pattern of living.

The gradual destruction of the old hotel sections of some cities is partly prompted by the belief that the SRO lifestyle contributes to alcohol and drug abuse, sexual promiscuity, and an irresponsible withdrawal from society. Life within a family unit and the maintenance a family home has long been considered a primary civilizing force. The hotel residents, in comparison, are seen as outside of the mainstream of society. The hotel lifestyle continues to persist in spite of the fact that SRO housing is less widely available and is constantly threatened. Such housing may be the last remaining alternative before turning to living on the street.

For the elderly who establish roots in the downtown section of the city, who depend on hotels as a major source of shelter, cities planning renewal operations pose a dilemma. The loss of downtown hotels that have provided residences for aged persons creates a critical condition of enforced displacement. The elderly manage to stay just one step ahead of what is described as the "headache ball" by going from one hotel to another as their current living structures become dilapidated and slated for redevelopment. With their limited incomes, they find fewer and fewer housing and service options. Downtown renewals have meant the obliteration of their environments.

The preferred housing of the SRO is a room with a view of a busy street in a downtown location. A view that includes around-the-clock constant activity is considered choice. Rooms that overlook fire stations, train stations, or police stations are much sought after.

The major activity of the SRO is to sit by the window and to observe life at a distance. It is not unusual to have the window as the focus within the room, not the television set. In front of the window stands a table for food preparation and consumption. A toaster, a coffeemaker, jars of condiments, and snack foods cover the tabletop and are stacked on a nearby chair or under the table. An easy chair, such as an ancient upholstered chair or chair bolstered with cushions, stands next the table facing the window.

In the event that a street activity occurs that occasions an upward glance to search for witnesses, the SRO withdraws from the window. There is no response to knocks at the door and the ringing of the doorbell. Even when a telephone is affordable, many relinquish this service.

The halls of buildings inhabited by elderly SROs are oddly quiet, with an occasional outburst from a drunken tenant. The cleaning service is randomly attended to, and the complex has an unlived-in quality. Doors are opened and shut swiftly and quietly. If upon opening a door, a person is sighted, the door is immediately shut. If greeted in the hall, the response is reluctant and often hardly audible. Those who know one another from long association do not speak.

The problems of tenant isolation and loneliness are due to family relationships that are either nonexistent or not substantial, and friendship patterns that do not develop easily. Feelings of depression and powerlessness may have contributed to low self-esteem and a disinclination to care for or about oneself. SROs tend to avoid the existing medical and social agencies that could assist them. Those who insist on assisting them have to go to the tenants to offer their services.

For those who seek involvement, even at a minimal level, it is easily obtainable in a SRO hotel. No matter what the time of day or night, there is activity in the lobby of an SRO hotel. People are about and awake to talk to, to stand next to, to argue with, or to have a drink with. Such human availability can serve to reassure those who need it of a place among the living.

Many of these hotels do not provide such formal supportive services as meals, recreation programs, or other hotel activities. In some hotels, few of the rooms are equipped with telephones. Many SROs have lived in the downtown area for as long as two to thirty years; others may have moved downtown as recently as a few years ago.

Regardless of years of residence downtown, few appear to have close friends. "Visiting" and "friendship" have different connotations for the SROs who interpret the terms as casual lobby, neighborhood bar, or restaurant relationships and conversations. Visiting or entertaining in their room is simply not an accepted part of their lifestyle. Few use downtown senior centers when they are available. The health care pattern consists of the general avoidance of all health care facilities.

The percentage of older persons who choose the SRO lifestyle is difficult to determine. However, there are some 50,000 people living in approximately 300 SRO hotels in New York City. Twenty percent of the population of San Francisco is over the age of sixty. Of the population over the age of sixty, 38 percent live alone, and 19 percent live on a poverty-level income. Twenty-five percent of the older population belongs to minority groups, primarily Chinese, African American, Spanish speaking, and Filipino. In San Francisco, the elderly SRO equivalents, those who share the same lifestyle but live dispersed throughout the city and who live on a poverty-level income, far outnumber the SROs.

The typical SRO lacks most, or all, of the relationships that satisfy the basic human needs. A one-legged man, helpless without his crutches, slept with a hatchet over his bed so he had some protection if his door was broken down (National Council on the Aging, 1976).

There appears to be a distinct SRO personality type and lifestyle built on a pattern of existence detached from other people and social systems. The housing of choice is the downtown "single-room only" residence, and the preference is for a particular lifestyle. A strong interrelationship between SRO personality and environmental factors serves to strengthen the preference.

The SRO psychological profile indicates people who disclose very little of themselves. Their form of life adjustment requires a withdrawal from strong personal or communal investment. SROs appear psychologically adjusted in spite of minimal social interaction or lack of close friends. They could be characterized as not reaching out to people and not caring for or about other people.

This pattern of low interaction is strengthened as downtown residence and age increase without the development of significant relationships. The length of time spent living downtown does not increase the number of friends or the level of visiting. There is a purposeful distance between persons living in proximity.

Tenants become suspicious should anyone inquire about their families, social life, or lifestyle. Such information might lead to requests for loans of money that would not be repaid, or the stealing of possessions from the room. They do not wish to become vulnerable to such actions and thus prefer to maintain a distance from others.

The pattern of aloneness is further determined through the low usage or an involvement in community systems or resources. Maintaining good health is a social and psychological necessity for SROs; it furthers an individualistic lifestyle within a hotel environment. Nonetheless, there is a low usage of health care facilities and a tendency to put off seeking health care. They call the desk clerk in case of emergency, but, otherwise, would not contact any secondary support system for help. They may have little working knowledge of the social system and how to receive helpful benefits. The failure of elderly SROs to use available services points to a narrow, routinized social lifestyle.

Whether male or female, they exhibit certain characteristics. They have always been alone. Some may have tried marriage and failed. Many may have been problem drinkers. Their working lives were spent at the bottom end of the scale, and as old persons they receive Social Security checks too small to support them. If they have families, they do not acknowledge this fact.

As a result, the role of the hotel desk clerk increases in importance. Although the hotel owner may serve as father, mother, counselor, and sometimes general factotum for tenants, the hotel owner also operates for profit. Often, it is the desk clerk who assumes such significant roles.

Desk clerks read and write their letters, help them with their shopping, lend money when needed, make doctors' appointments, arrange ambulance service when necessary, and provide them with food when they are unable to obtain their own. They might even cash their monthly checks, and, in some cases, dole out money a bit at a time. Although some SROs are perfectly capable of caring for themselves; others may require all manner of help. They all have unchanging habits. If a guest does not appear at 10:00 A.M. according to habit, the desk clerk immediately checks that guest's room. Because of financial problems, some do not eat properly, do not see a physician, and wear shabby clothes. The financial problems inevitably lead to health problems because the only thing that they can cut down on is food. The provision of preventive medicine, along with hot, well-balanced meals, is a necessity rarely met.

The people living in hotels like it; they have always lived in them or rooming houses. They like having someone to take care of their needs. They do not know what it means to take care of an apartment. They could not or would not clean or cook. Although they may not realize it, perhaps, many do need help.

Society functions on the assumption that anyone who is really ill will seek some type of medical assistance, but with the elderly SRO who are frightened of agencies and often too infirm to get to a doctor or clinic, the assumption is a fallacy. Without telephones, they cannot call for assistance, and, fearful of their neighbors, they sometimes never seek help.

The hotel life is the chosen way of life for these people. It is convenient. The tenants have no place to go once the hotels are torn down; there are simply not enough old hotels to house them. It is not that SROs do not want to live better, but that they do not want to move to another neighborhood.

They know their neighbors, but not their names. They are not friends as people commonly recognize the term. For example, they always eat in the same place; their relationship with the waiter or waitress is important to them. It is a relationship of a particular stamp.

Many of the men have never married or have been left by divorce, or by their own desertion, with no knowledge of the whereabouts of their now middle-aged children. When visited by a son unexpectedly, whom he had not seen for some twenty years, one old man was annoyed that his son's visit coincided with a baseball game he had planned to watch on television.

Hidden from view, in the country's most viable communities, live unknown, unseen, and unserved people of all ages, particularly the older poor. Pride, independence, fear, and reluctance to relate to other people are an intermix in the personalities of these individuals who comprise what may be the most vulnerable segment of the aging population. Many adopted their singular lifestyle long ago; many became isolated only as they grew older. Some were victims of child abuse and neglect. There are more similarities than differences in the SRO population. Most, characteristically, are alone and deprived, victims of the barriers they have erected to protect themselves from intrusion by the outside world. Fear generated by crime and hostility reinforces the pattern of the isolated, increasing their already-high vulnerability to exploitation.

Urban nonfamily poor are generally people living on fixed incomes derived primarily from Social Security, small pensions, and disability insurance. All receive some form of government assistance, veterans pension, Social Security, or Supplemental Security Income. They exist just over or in proximity to the poverty line. They can generally meet the minimum requirements for shelter, clothing, and food but rarely have funds for anything else.

Elderly SROs are found in all ethnic groups throughout the country. The SRO population is a varied one, including men and women, employed and nonworking, well and disabled, stable and socially deviant. A small portion are the aged poor left behind in the aftermath of urban change. They encounter problems of isolation and often of mental and physical illness, aggravated by societal disinterest, avoidance, apathy, and neglect.

Elderly SROs are ignored and rejected in urban-development plans and forced to relocate from one area to another according to fluctuating real estate markets. Urban-renewal programs spell death to the way of life of the SRO elderly.

As urban renewal mushrooms, it eliminates the only housing in which SRO feel some security. Rentals remain higher in SRO hotels than for small apartments in other sections of the city. Even with the destruction of hotels, residents stay in the area, moving from one hotel to another. The fact that the downtown environment allows for preservation of individuality may compensate for the higher rents and higher costs of groceries and other items secured at convenience stores. As the length of residence in the hotel increases, the desire to move decreases. Since the downtown commercial area provides both goods and services within a framework of low social interaction, this area is the choice of the elderly SRO population.

Some SROs have been reached through social services, recreation programs, nutrition projects, information and referral services that serve as avenues leading to other options. Once there is a trust relationship and communication among service deliverers, the SRO will respond more positively to referrals. This is more likely to occur when the person is sent to a particular individual within an agency, rather than simply to an impersonal bureaucracy.

Conclusion

It is important to understand the reasons intrinsic to creation of the elderly SRO lifestyle and perhaps to prevent a repetition of the syndrome in future years. However, little published research exists on this population group. They remain invisible even in the literature. No single proposal will solve all of the problems of the downtown residents with atypical lifestyles.

Recommendations might include the establishment of an agency support system within the community designed to accommodate the distinctive needs and lifestyles of the SRO population. This might be best accomplished by a team of three or four workers with differing expertise and disciplines who would walk the streets, sit in lobbies, snack bars, short-order cafes, and other areas frequented by elderly SROs.

THE DIOGENES SYNDROME

The Diogenes Syndrome, a poorly understood form of extreme self-neglect, can be characterized as self-abuse. It is named after Diogenes, the Greek philosopher, who lived in Athens, Greece, during the fourth century B.C. and reputedly lived his life in a bathtub surrounded by squalor. He also walked abroad during daylight hours through the streets of Athens carrying a lighted lantern, searching for an honest man.

The Diogenes Syndrome appears not to be a single entity, and there is great diversity among persons exhibiting such symptoms and behaviors. There is also great diversity among cases in cognitive status, psychiatric diagnoses, socioeconomic status, and medical comorbidity.

This condition of neglected self-care, abandonment of the personal environment, social isolation, and a substandard quality of life is regarded as a syndrome and has variously been referred to as senile breakdown, social breakdown of the elderly, or Diogenes Syndrome. There are sufficient common features among this population to indicate that severe self-neglect in old age is a syndrome. Such common features include domestic squalor, personal uncleanliness, and a complete disregard for the deteriorating home environment. Additional characteristics of the syndrome are the collection of useless objects (syllogomania), an indifferent, shameless attitude, and a stubborn refusal of help offered by family or welfare agencies (Ungvari & Hantz, 1991).

Generally they live alone and are frequently known to community agencies for several weeks to a number of years. Some accept home services, such as home help, nursing, and meals. Most, however, repeatedly decline offers of assistance, even to the point of refusing to open the door to callers. These older persons often come to the attention of health care providers when these persons require emergency hospital admission due to falls or collapse.

The acutely-ill old person with a dirty and neglected appearance, in a setting of gross domestic disorder and squalor, is not uncommon, yet has attracted little study. Their homes are often filthy on the outside with peeling paint and broken windows framed by grimy and torn curtains. There are often holes in the walls, the windows replaced by rugs or newspaper, and the original wallpaper unrecognizable. Rotting food, feces, empty bottles, and old newspapers may cover the floor and the few pieces of broken furniture. A pervasive characteristic strong, stale, and slightly suffocating odor hangs over the interior. The individuals are usually dressed in layers of dirty clothing, sometimes covered by an old raincoat or overcoat. When confined to bed, they lie beneath a pile of ragged blankets, clothing, or newspapers. They never appear to undress or to wash, the hair may be long and unkempt, and the exposed surfaces of skin deeply etched with dirt. They rarely apologize for their personal or domestic state. Some may hoard useless rubbish (syllogomania)—newspapers, cans, bottles, and rags, often in bundles and stacks; the size of the collection often seriously encroaches on the living space. Little food is found in the house, and old dishes and moldy scraps are often seen. The telephone and electricity have long been disconnected; the radio, television set, and heater have ceased to function. Life is reduced to the bare necessities in all respects (Ungvari & Hantz, 1991).

They seldom complain of shortage of money, and, for many, poverty does not seem to be a feature. Some own their own homes and have capital assets. In some instance, their careers seemed to have been successful, and they had enjoyed sound family backgrounds, education, and social standing in earlier life as journalists, dentists, musicians, and teachers. When they are admitted to the hospital because of a fall or collapse, they are generally found to suffer from a variety of diseases.

Although somewhat more aloof, detached, shrewd, suspicious, and less well integrated than the general older population, they appear to be intelligent with normal personalities. When psychological assessments are conducted, they reveal good intellectual preservation and higher-than-average intelligence. The tendency to distort reality might explain the lack of concern about living standards.

The syllogomania may have been a distortion of an instinctive drive to collect things. Some have a compulsive habit to hoard objects that might be useful; others lack the initiative to throw away useless items. The significance of this useless hoarding is obscure, but it could provide a feeling of security, and it can be found in the general older population, especially those who experienced the Great Depression in the 1930s.

This syndrome appears to have linkages to losses of a significant other, resulting in total distrust. The condition is found among the poor and the wealthy and cuts across socioeconomic lines. It can be described as a form of self-burial. Some recluses may also harbor animals, such as cats or dogs, in large numbers.

Conclusion

The Diogenes Syndrome is characterized by social withdrawal, self-induced abysmal living conditions, and lack of concern about receiving assistance even in the face of life-threatening situations. They further refuse any assistance to clean their environments or services, such as Meals-on-Wheels even when their nutritional needs are clear. Most of these older persons reject any services.

Many persons who exhibit the characteristics of the Diogenes Syndrome had led successful professional and business lives, with good family backgrounds and upbringing. Personality characteristics showed them to tend to be aloof, suspicious, emotionally labile, aggressive, and reality-distorting individuals. It is suggested that this syndrome may be a reaction late in life to stress in a certain type of personality (Clark, Mankikar, & Gray, 1975). Such self-neglect could also be a generalized reaction to stress brought on by late-life changes, such as financial distress, bereavement overload, alterations in physical status, and enforced isolation (Vostonis & Dean, 1992).

The almost total self-neglect and active refusal of help cannot be fully explained by physical illness or the social situation. Day care center and community care could well be the main lines of management to be favored, rather than hospital admission or institutional placement.

VICTIMS OF DOMESTIC VIOLENCE

Domestic violence is defined as a pattern of coercive control characterized by the use of physical, sexual, and psychologically-abusive behaviors. Domestic violence, or violence within the family, occurs at all levels of society; social factors are not relevant. The rate of incidence can only be estimated as studies include only those persons who are willing to respond to surveys. Underrepresented groups include those who do not speak English, the very poor, the elderly, the homeless, the hospitalized, or the incarcerated.

The actual rates of domestic violence are probably much higher than reported. Physical aggression in intimate relationships is frequent and widespread. There are doctors, ministers, psychologists, and nurses who beat their family members. Violence occurs at least once in two-thirds of all marriages. A woman is beaten every fifteen seconds in the United States, and 2,000 to 4,000 women are murdered by their husbands or boyfriends every year.

Violence is a pattern, a reign of force and terror. It becomes more frequent and severe over time. Only the perpetrator has the ability to stop the violence. A change in the victim's behavior will not cause the abuser to become nonviolent.

As the life expectancy increases, persons who are frail and vulnerable become potential victims for a wide variety of abuses, fraud, and exploitation. The mistreatment and neglect of older persons is largely hidden, shrouded in secrecy and shame. Some older persons suffer from mental health problems or are heavily sedated and are unaware of the circumstances. Older persons are often reluctant to reveal incidents of violence perpetrated against them, particularly when the aggressor is a family member.

Officially reported cases may represent only a small fraction of the actual rate of incidence. Although mandatory reporting laws exist throughout the country, there is a general reticence in admitting that the problem exists, and, as a result, indications of violence are overlooked and unsuspected, and facile explanations are accepted. Such lack of recognition or understanding of the problem can lead to alterations in physical and mental health status, or even death.

Contemporary stress theory as it relates to health is attributed to Hans Selye, who in 1950 published his now-famous work, *The Stress of Life*. Selye defined stress as the rate of wear and tear on the body (Selye, 1976). Examples are physical injury, disease, infection, and psychological and emotional tension. These demands are called stressors, and they have the potential to produce physical and chemical changes in the body to which the person must adjust. Selye named this stress response the general adaptation syndrome (GAS).

Familial Abuse

The violence in American society appears to be escalating, with the American home becoming equally violent. Older Americans run the greatest risk of assault, physical injury, and even murder in their own homes by members of their own families. Because females dominate the older population, the greatest number of incidents involve older women. Victims often are unable to care for themselves, and the perpetrator is usually an adult child.

Maltreatment of older persons shows great variance, and it may be intentional, unintentional, or the result of neglect. Such maltreatment causes harm to the older person either temporarily or over a longer period of time. The often-cited stereotype of a highly dependent White woman over the age of seventy-five who is being physically abused by her son or daughter is only a small aspect of this problem (Bradley, 1996).

The first references to maltreatment of older adults appeared as "granny bashing" in the British literature in 1975 (Frazier & Hayes, 1991). Although all fifty states have laws aimed at preventing the abuse of older persons, the actual extent of the problem is difficult to determine. The types of abuse include not only physical abuse and neglect, financial abuse, psychological abuse, sexual abuse, but violation of rights. Such abuses can include nutritional deprivation; maladministration of drugs; verbal, sexual, and financial abuse; failure to attend to health needs; isolation or confinement; and assault.

Elder abuse often remains invisible. Abused elders are more likely to have marital problems, be intellectually impaired, and to live with others. Although there are many reasons why older people are abused, the most common include deteriorating family relationships, caregivers who have been abused themselves, social isolation, psychopathology of the abuser, and imbalance of power between abused and abuser.

Caring for a sick, dependent elderly person is a challenge for even the most capable person. Some caregivers are themselves elderly and suffer from health problems. When caregivers to older people have little support from within the community, they may suffer intolerable strain that may lead to elder abuse. Disturbed sleep, difficult behavior, and fecal incontinence often result in severe strain on the caregiver and may set the scene for abuse.

Many caregivers express feelings of frustration, despair, and worry over their own well-being. They often feel that the situation is beyond their control. Difficult situations are often compounded by strained family relationships in which, for instance, a son or daughter feels a duty to care for a parent of whom they have never been particularly fond or who has treated them badly in the past. The excessive personal use of alcohol or tranquilizing drugs by caregivers can have a disinhibiting effect, which may lead to emotions being translated into physical actions.

Physical abuse is the most commonly encountered form of elder abuse as it is the most easily recognized. Financial abuse, neglect, and sexual abuse are probably underrecognized and underreported. Some families wait too long to seek nursing home placement for older family members; some keep them alive as long as possible to take advantage of their Social Security checks and use of other assets. Psychological abuse in the form of aggression, humiliation, and intimidation is the most difficult to identify and quantify.

Spousal Abuse

The number of persons who are abused by their spouse, live-in partner, or lover is unknown. It is estimated that 99 percent of the perpetrators are men. Approximately one in five women is physically abused by her partner, and 2 to 3 million are severely assaulted every year. If verbal and emotional assaults were included, the numbers would be much higher (Stets & Strauss, 1990).

Every nine seconds, a woman is battered. More than 50 percent of all women will experience some form of violence from their spouses during marriage. More than one-third are battered repeatedly every year, and it is estimated that one out of twelve women are raped. Between 15 percent to 25 percent of pregnant women are battered. Marital violence cuts across all class and racial lines (Herman, 1992). Until recently, the only public agency officially documenting the existence of marital violence has been the police. Poor people have fewer alternatives and are more likely to call the police than upper- or middle-class people. Homes in wealthier neighborhoods tend to be farther apart, thus neighbors are not likely to be aware of the problem or to hear screams. In poor city neighborhoods, people live closer to one another and tend to be aware of the problems of neighbors.

Drug abuse and alcoholism facilitate the violence, but substance abuse alone does not cause the violence. Battering is the single major cause of injury to women, exceeding rapes, mugging, and even car accidents. More than 1 million abused women seek medical help for injuries caused by battering each year. As many as 50 percent of the female homicide victims are killed by their husbands or lovers (Bean, 1992). The cause of such violence can be linked to the fact that men are normally socialized by this culture to be violent and sexist.

One-half of the women who are abused suffer beatings several times a year. The other one-half may be beaten as often as once a week. The intensity and frequency of attacks tend to escalate over time. Compared to nonabused women, abused women are five times more likely to attempt suicide, fifteen times more likely to abuse alcohol, and nine times more likely to abuse drugs (Bean, 1992).

Pregnancy is a time of increased risk of abuse. There are more incidents of violence during pregnancy. As many as one of fifty pregnant women is physically abused. A past history of abuse is one of the strongest predictors of abuse during pregnancy. Nonpregnant women are usually beaten in the face and chest, while pregnant women tend to be beaten in the abdomen, which can led to miscarriage, abruptio placentae, fetal loss, premature labor, fetal fractures, pelvic fractures, rupture of the uterus, and hemorrhages. Physical abuse during pregnancy may be related to ambivalent feelings about the pregnancy, increased vulnerability of the women, increased economic pressures, and decreased sexual availability.

Unfortunately, abuse of pregnant women is often overlooked by health care professionals even when the victim appears in the emergency department with bruises, cuts, broken bones, and abdominal injuries (Steward & Cecutti, 1993). The long-term effects of such battering during pregnancy, particularly as women grow old, has not been the subject of serious study.

Nonphysical abuse can have equally devastating effects as physical assault. Words can be as damaging as a fist in the face. Emotional abuse often accompanies physical abuse (Jacobson et al., 1994). The damage to self-esteem can last a lifetime and can reverberate in old age. Emotional abuse involves one person shaming, embarrassing, ridiculing, or insulting another either in private or in public. It may include destruction of personal property, or the killing of pets in an effort to frighten or to control the victim. Such statements as "You can't do anything right," and "You're ugly and stupid—no one else would ever want you," are devastating to self-esteem and are long remembered. If they are repeated constantly, the reaction may be to believe them as fact.

Domestic violence often happens without warning and without a buildup of tension. It is a behavioral characteristic that reflects a developed pattern of violence. The woman often knows when she will be struck. A typical cycle occurs when conflict escalates into a violent episode after which the perpetrator begs for the victim's forgiveness. The victim stays in the system because of promises of reform. With the next episode of conflict, the cycle of violence begins again and becomes part of the family dynamics (O'Leary & Vivian, 1990).

The acts that men commit against women are more dangerous and result in more severe injuries. While the victim is being beaten, she is also being verbally abused, often by being called a whore, an incompetent housekeeper, or an inadequate mother. The abuser attacks aspects of life that women use to measure their success: homemaking, child care, attractiveness, sex appeal, and sexual fidelity. Control over the victim is established by repetitive emotional abuse that instills terror and helplessness. Threats of serious harm or threats against other family members keep the victim in a constant state of fear. Such abusive behavior alternates with unpredictable outbursts of physical violence (Koss, Woodruff, & Koss, 1990). Such domestic captivity of women along with traumatic bonding to the batterer often goes unrecognized and without any record made of such life experience in medical records.

Victims may be immobilized by a variety of affective responses to the abuse, such as anxiety, helplessness, and depression. Feelings of self-blame may be expressed in such statements as "If I hadn't talked back to him, he wouldn't have hit me," or "If I were a better wife, he wouldn't beat me." Guilt can contribute to depression, which further immobilizes victims and keeps them from leaving or seeking help. Some women feel they deserve the treatment because it is up to them to make the marriage work. They may experience guilt over the failure of the relationship because of family, religious, or cultural values against divorce or separation. Some experience shame at remaining in the abusive relationship.

Fear contributes to women's inability to leave abusive relationships. Often threatened with death at the idea of leaving, they lie in fear of physical reprisal. Fearing loneliness, some women may believe that being in a bad relationship is better than being alone. Leaving the relationship does not necessarily ensure the end of the abuse. The abuser is often most dangerous when threatened with or faced with separation (Bean, 1992). Some women do not wish to enter or re-enter the workforce, while others fear they may not find another sex partner.

Economic problems that lead to the dependency of the woman on the spouse can compromise her ability to access medical care. Since many battered women marry early, directly out of high school, they have no financial resources of their own and are unsophisticated as to their options. The woman may not have a source of income because the husband will not allow it. If the abuser is arrested, he may lose his job, and the family will be deprived of an income. Further, women have been taught to be submissive in exchange for financial support. In older couples, the abusive treatment may be of a long-standing nature.

Premature Aging

Women who endure violence at the hands of a spouse or a caregiver over prolonged periods of time experience premature aging. Physiological changes that result include internal damages, alterations in heart rate, and debilitating changes in the respiratory system (Koss & Keslet, 1992). Psychological effects lead to a sensation of being frozen in time, undergoing a constant state of fear, and diminishment of behavioral motivations, such as the desire to eat, which leads to food deprivation.

Women who suffer domestic violence over extended periods of time undergo stress, including epinephrin stress response, which exhausts their reserve capacity and compromises their total health. They remain in a state of anatomical anxiety, which causes the body to shoot blood to the brain and heart, burning up all the bodily reserves resulting in undernourishment of other vital organs, such as the lungs or digestive tract (Kemp, Green, Hovanitz, & Rawlings, 1995). High stress brings on a wide range of physical responses and results in changes, such as loss of teeth.

Such women are mentally compromised. They are beaten down and become submissive. They may fear to express an opinion, because their treatment for many years has been one of derision and browbeating. Her needs have been the last to be considered; the spouse's needs were paramount. Such women may begin to neglect themselves on a variety of levels, may turn to alcohol or drugs or use a combination of both, and eventually find they have sleep difficulties and experience depression. Their own health care is neglected, and, if on medication, they can be noncompliant. They may also engage in risk-taking behaviors and general life-threatening behaviors. Some become openly suicidal.

The longer the abusive state lasts, the quieter the victim becomes and is less likely to seek help. They see no avenue of escape and, with a particular kind of tunnel vision, accept their life situation. There is little joy in their lives; friends and relatives avoid them. Some of the avoidance is due to exhaustion on the part of friends and relatives from trying to help or to the deliberate shutting out of avenues of assistance by the victim herself.

The economic conditions frequently force the woman to remain in her current situation. Since a number of women who are now septuagenarians and octogenarians had never been employed outside the home, they are dependent on the spouse for a livelihood. Without financial assistance, the prospect of leaving is not an option. Furthermore, abuse in old age can be more lethal as the woman is not allowed to see a physician for routine medical care.

Society sanctions male violence by neglecting female victims. This social neglect includes a lack of resources, a minimal response to domestic violence, and inadequate laws. Financial resources have been reduced during recent years. An example is the 1992 abolishment of the toll-free national domestic violence hotline due to lack of funding.

The mental health of women is largely dependent on the quality of family life. In a comfortable, deeply fulfilling marriage in which the woman is supported and loved, these conditions promote mental well-being and can influence the strength of the immune system. Such women become ill less frequently. Even those who experience health problems have greater support and confidence to combat such diseases through the support and concern of their spouses and children. In spite of illness, such women can still be happy, optimistic, and encouraged to live as full a life as possible. Such conditions are also conducive to recovery from illness. However, in marriages in which love is absent, such commitment is tenuous at best, and problems, such as financial crises, the aging of the couple, health problems or natural disasters, can lead to a breakdown of the relationship. The family life is beset with problems, disharmony, depression, and violence. Women in such relationships remain because of economic dependence and physical weakness, as well as fear for their lives. These women also sacrifice their health for the sake of their children (Chen, 1999).

In China, women who have been victims of family violence are unwilling to tell others because of the fear of "losing face." They do not dare to protect their own rights and personal dignity. Some have been sexually abused by their husbands for many years and cannot overcome their persistent nightmares related to these incidents. Some women are treated simply as servants, while the husbands have sexual relationships with other women. These wives fear the consequences of being divorced.

Such life experiences can lead to health problems, such as insomnia, nightmares, rapid or irregular heart rates, loss of appetite, and shortness of breath. In addition, depression, tension, experiencing a constant state of fear, loss of self-confidence, and suicidal ideation are potential mental health problems. Such conditions lead to premature aging with weight loss, skin wrinkling, and graying of the hair. Such women may become introverted, taciturn, socially unresponsive, nervous, and exhibit a variety of idiosyncratic or abnormal behaviors. These women are prone to a wide range of health problems, including mental dysfunction, psychoses, high blood pressure, heart disease, cancer, and suicide (Chen, 1999).

Stress Theory

Stress can compromise the total health of the individual, as the body remains for long periods of time at a state of auto-arousal. Since the body rushes supplies of blood to the brain and heart, bodily reserves are exhausted (Horowitz, 1993). Much of such stress is experienced while women are pregnant, causing blood to be shunted away from the fetus.

The general adaptation syndrome (GAS), as described by Selye (1976), attributes stressors, such as physical injury, disease, infection, and psychological and emotional tensions, as having the potential to produce physical and chemical changes in the body to which the person must adjust. Stress thus is responsible for the rate of wear and tear on the body.

The first state in the GAS is the alarm reaction. The stressor is recognized, consciously or unconsciously, and the person is propelled into some type of action, the "fight-or-flight" response. Physiologic changes are mediated through the autonomic nervous system. Hormone levels, blood supply, and oxygen are all increased. The person experiences an intensified level of alertness and anxiety.

In the stage of resistance, the second stage in the GAS, the body attempts to adapt to the stress. Hormone levels readjust, and the body achieves some level of homeostasis in the continued presence of the stress. The person relies on defense mechanisms and coping behaviors during this stage.

In the third stage, the stage of exhaustion, physiologic resources are depleted, and the person is no longer able to resist the stress. The pituitary gland and adrenal cortex are unable to produce hormones, and the immune response becomes depressed. The person's thinking is disorganized, and there is a loss of contact with reality. If the stress continues, the person will eventually die (Wilson & Kneisl, 1992). Stress is strongly identified with the onset of a number of diseases, including Alzheimer's disease that afflicts large numbers of women as they age. Alzheimer's disease has also been linked to the experience of repeated blows to the head.

Psychoneuroimmunology

Psychoneuroimmunology is an area of scientific study that explores the damaging effects of chronic stress on the central nervous system, the body's defense against external infection and aberrant cell division.

The immune system is a surveillance system that protects the body and responds to a person's internal and external environments.

It must distinguish between normal cells and malignant cells, as well as identify and destroy foreign and disease-causing organisms. Examples of autoimmune disorders are Graves' disease, rheumatoid arthritis, ulcerative colitis, ileitis, lupus, psoriasis, myasthenia gravis, and pernicious anemia. The immune system can be damaged, as in Acquired Immunodeficiency Syndrome (AIDS), or it can malfunction, as in allergies and cancer.

There are several ways the brain can influence the immune system. In general, stress leads to negative affective responses and the woman's anger turned inward results in anxiety and depression. These feelings ultimately influence health. Emotions directly affect biological processes that influence a persons's susceptibility to disease (Riggs, Rothbaum, & Foa, 1995). The health of women who experience prolonged periods of stress can be compromised, with many of the disease symptoms becoming manifest in old age. Life expectancy for older women who have been battered can be shortened. In addition, emotions can lead to behaviors, such as smoking or drinking, that increase the risk of diseases, such as pancreatitis, gall bladder problems, and respiratory disorders.

The limbic system, which controls emotions, has many connections to the hypothalamus. When a stressful event occurs, the limbic system stimulates the hypothalamus, which, in turn, stimulates the pituitary gland. The pituitary stimulates the adrenal glands, which mobilize the body's defenses. Stress also stimulates the hypothalamus to activate more neurotransmitters. Because immune cells have receptors for many neurotransmitters, alterations affect their ability to function (Abbas, Lichtman, & Pober, 1991; Vollhart, 1991).

Cognitive and sociocultural stimuli are among the most potent factors in activating the biologic responses to stress. An example is the effect of bereavement on a person's health. After the death of a spouse, the surviving spouse's risk of death is especially high during the first six months. This increased risk may also be related to a depressed immune system that can have far reaching consequences.

When stressful life events occur, people are at increased risk for health problems, mental and physical. Battering produces not only external, but internal injuries. It can affect the pattern of aging and leads to premature aging.

Cardiovascular Disorders

Cardiovascular disorders are one of several categories of disorders considered to be psychophysiologic. They link psychological and cardiac functions and create pathologic conditions in the heart and blood vessels. The most common forms are coronary heart disease and hypertension. Extensive research has been conducted on the relationship between anxiety and stress levels and people who are predisposed to cardiovascular disorders.

The presence of these conditions in older women can also be linked to their stressful experiences as battered women. The increase in behaviors, such as drug abuse, also can lead to cardiac problems. Such abuse can include prescription drugs and drugs prescribed for other family members that are left in the medicine chest. There is a form of pseudolegitimacy in ingesting these drugs because they had been ordered by a physician, even though dosages may be exaggerated.

Cancer

In addition to genetic factors and a high-risk lifestyle, there may be a psychophysiologic component to the cause of cancer. People predisposed to cancer often act as if they do not have any problems in their lives. For some, the fear of conflict that underlies this behavior is related to low self-esteem and fear of abandonment.

The incidence of cancer in older women has not been investigated from the perspectives of particular life experiences, including the experience of prolonged battering.

Respiratory Disorders

Changes in the rate, regularity, and depth of respiration correlate with many emotional states. Changes in respiration are also symptoms of respiratory disorders. Of these disorders, asthma is the most widely studied from a psychophysiological perspective.

There are allergic, immunologic, and psychological factors of asthmatic attacks. Psychologic factors can directly alter the size of the bronchial tubes, leading to an acute asthmatic attack. Asthmatic attacks can be extremely frightening, and this fear may contribute to feelings of helplessness and hopelessness. The incidence of respiratory disorders among battered women as they age has yet to be explored.

Gastrointestinal Disorders

There are many behaviors connected to gastrointestinal functions. Changes in appetite, food intake, digestive function, and elimination occur almost daily in relation to emotional stress. Disorders thought to be psychophysiologic include esophageal reflux and esophageal spasm, hyperacidity of the stomach, and intestinal disorders such as constipation, chronic diarrhea, and ulcerative colitis.

Many of these symptoms are suffered by older women. The relationship between battering and the presence of such symptoms has not been determined. The relationship between poor oral health and tooth loss is an additional concern for battered women. Overeating behavior may also result leading to the onset of diabetes, which frequently does not receive medical attention due to economic or restrictive familial conditions.

Life Expectancy

The life expectancy of battered women may be seriously compromised. It is estimated that for every year of abuse experienced, the woman loses two years from her life expectancy (Lesnoff-Varavaglia, 2001).

The psychological effects of battering are extensive, but physical appearance may also be altered. Broken blood vessels on the face, loss of teeth, excessive weight gain or loss, hair loss, and alterations in gait and posture commonly result. Such physical alterations can also affect the relationship with the spouse.

Such women can also miss developmental milestones. They may even regress developmentally and exhibit dependent or maladaptive behavior (Saundera, 1994). The battering prevents the experiencing of the full human developmental process. The loss of self-esteem, the experience of constant shame and always being at fault, leads to an internalizing of poor self-worth that can result in the belief that this is indeed who she is. If she had done things right in the first place, none of the battering would have occurred. The constant reminder that no one else would want her and that she is stupid and ugly convinces her that all of her life, including her sexual life, depends upon the spouse, and, should he reject her, she would never find another man.

Some of these women have elected to be housewives; part of the success they experience as women is by having married. Unfortunately, many children side with the spouse against the woman as the father is viewed as one who pays the bills. They treat her as unimportant, and her needs are not considered. The woman may also be irritable with the children in her desire to please the spouse. She may become obsessive in her behavior or paranoid causing friction with the children. Some children learn to dislike the mother and do not sympathize with her. They frequently leave home early. She may also hesitate to disappoint her own family by having her marriage fail, and this causes her to remain in an abusive relationship and to deny or hide the abuse.

In effect, the battered woman lives to satisfy someone else's needs, not her own. Since they are really needed, some of these women do not feel rejected nor are they suicidal. They are the host for a parasite who gradually consumes them. Such women have no time to think about themselves or to have thoughts of their own as they are obsessed with the needs of the spouse. They are in a constant state of fear: fear of physical attack and death, and fear of not meeting his expectations. Living in such a state of fear can continue for a number of years.

Most people would consider that a woman is endangered in situations in which a batterer is physically assaultive or directly threatens an imminent assault. There are, however, situations in which the threat is not immediate, but a woman's history of being battered is relevant to her perception of the dangerousness of the situation and its likely outcome based on her unique history with the batterer. When the appraisal of threat by a woman is high and her appraised resources for responding to threat behavior are low, an expected response would include fear or anxiety, physiological arousal, and behaviors intended either to avoid or alter the situation. Actual or threatened death or serious injury, or a threat to the physical integrity of self or others, is defined as a traumatic event within the medical and psychological community (Jacobson et al., 1994).

Post-Traumatic Stress Disorder

Domestic violence can lead to posttraumatic stress reactions, including posttraumatic stress disorder (PTSD) in which certain behaviors or events can cause the battered women to act or feel as if prior severe violence were recurring, even if it is not. This experience may include reliving the experience, illusions, hallucinations, and dissociative flashback episodes, including those that occur on awakening or when intoxicated (American Psychiatric Association [APA], 1994; Kemp, Fawling, & Green, 1991). Violence negatively affects battered women in a variety of other ways, such as economic loss, loss of employment, and increased health care use.

The lack of economic and other tangible resources makes leaving or staying away difficult for some battered women (Dutton, 1992). Without money, transportation, shelter, child care, and a source of income or support, a woman leaving an abusive relationship has no means of providing for herself and her children. Resources, such as shelters and advocacy services, to aid battered women in leaving abusive relationships and establishing independent households, are severely limited in most communities throughout the country. There is further evidence of the battered woman's fear that her abusive partner will escalate his violence toward her at the point she attempts to separate from or end the relationship with him. This is validated, generally, by homicide statistics (Liss & Stahly, 1993). Police response to domestic violence (as opposed to stranger violence) is slower and less likely to result in a written report or a search for evidence (Bachman, 1994).

It has been shown that batterers seek custody at higher rates and are awarded custody no less often than nonbatterers (Edleson & Tolman, 1992). There is often no more powerful obstacle to terminating an abusive relationship than when a woman faces the possibility that her children will be taken from her either through custody decisions that favor the batterer, kidnapping, or homicide. This is an additional way to provide the batterer access to the victim. Within the last decade, the scientific and clinical literature has documented a broad range of emotional, cognitive, physiological, and behavioral sequella to traumatic events such as battering. The complexity and variability of traumatic response to violence has only begun to be understood fully, and its long-lasting effects that can reverberate in old age have yet to be determined. In examining diseases and health problems of women in old age, the factor of lifelong abuse has not been considered.

Some older women, especially those suffering from depression, have given up on life, or at least a life that is free of maltreatment. They await the peace of heaven. Practitioners can also be less inclined to give services or resources to an individual whose life span they view as limited.

Internal injuries, perforated eardrums, damaged spleen or kidneys, punctured lungs, and eye injuries are all possible injuries that can play a role in the rate and type of aging the woman experiences. Physical symptoms can also include old untreated injuries that in old age result in physical discomfort or complications. The woman can experience depression, ranging from mild to severe, and may exhibit suicidal tendencies. The woman may present stress-related, sometimes vague, symptoms, such as insomnia, nightmares, anxiety, extreme fatigue, eczema or hair loss, weight loss or gain, gastrointestinal symptoms, respiratory difficulties, chest pain, pelvic pain, back pain or headaches.

PTSD in elderly persons impairs their ability to deal with subsequent life stress and to negotiate successfully the developmental stages of late life (Weintraub & Ruskin, 1999). Symptoms may be persistent or intermittent, and the disorder may be time limited or chronic. Elderly individuals do not appear more predisposed than young persons to develop PTSD, and symptoms of the disorder are similar across age groups: re-experiencing the trauma, avoidance, and hyperarousal. It is often conveniently relegated to a diagnosis of dementia.

Antidepressants, group therapy, and cognitive-behavioral therapy are presently the mainstays of treatment, although to date no systematic and controlled research has been done on the treatment of PTSD in this age group. There is the possibility that the onset of certain diseases in older women may be attributable to the experience of having been battered.

A stressful marriage greatly affects the health of the persons involved. Since women are usually the victims in such instances, they frequently sacrifice their health to maintain a seemingly traditional family with both parents and children. In some cultures, such as China, the low status of women exacerbates the problem (Chen, 1999). The women may be relegated to a simple housekeeping function while the husband assumes a mistress whom he flaunts before the wife. The loss in self-esteem and deep personal unhappiness often lead to physical illnesses. Some symptoms include insomnia, nightmares, general nervousness, difficulty in breathing, sweating, heart arrhythmia, and emotional instability. Their loss of confidence is reflected in their lack of interest in living and consideration of suicide. Their withdrawal results in silence and great loneliness, and their work performance suffers. Ultimately, such symptoms lead to mental illness, high blood pressure, heart disease, and cancer.

CONCLUSIONS

Service providers need to increase their understanding of the wide array of problems presented by domestic violence to the health of older women. Increased emphasis must be placed on the development of detection, intervention, and prevention strategies. The underlying societal attitudes and institutional policies that permit the maltreatment of the older population requires intensive exploration (Frazier & Hayes, 1991). There is a general reluctance to intervene in family affairs and the difficulty in knowing how to cope with the problem when it is identified.

Although intervention is complicated, it calls for an interdisciplinary approach. It should include health information and support, respite care, day care, home care including nursing, provision of aids and appliances, incontinence advice, financial advice, advocacy, legal or police intervention, rehousing, and institutional care. Removal of older persons from the home should be seen as a last resort and should not be done without their consent. Support services that are provided should deal with specific problems. Since many cases of abuse are due to caregiver stress, interventions should often be aimed at helping caregivers to overcome the problems they face.

Warning signs can include poor family relationships, a history of family violence, low income, and inadequate housing. Caregivers who are emotionally, physically, and socially isolated, who suffer from lack of privacy, or have a history of alcohol or drug abuse or mental illness, can be prone to acts of abuse and violence.

Suspicious circumstances can include unexplained falls, burns, and fractures; bruises in in unusual places, such as the inside of the thigh or pinchmarks on the arms. The provision of inappropriate clothing, being left in wet clothing, or an inappropriate administration of medication by the caregivers are also circumstances that can lead to the suspicion of elder abuse. Signs of sexual abuse can include overt sexual behavior, torn or stained underclothes, genital infection and irritation, "hickies" or "love" bites, and bruising and lacerations in the rectovaginal area. Financial abuse can take the form of unexpected inability to pay bills or a disparity between assets and living conditions (Vinton, 1991).

The effects of battering, particularly at younger ages, can seriously curtail the life expectancy of women and can be conducive to premature aging. It is important to establish the relationship between diseases in old age and traumatic life events, such as battering and maltreatment.

REFERENCES

Abbas, A. K., Lichtman, A. H., & Pober, J. S. (1991). *Cellular and molecular immunology.* New York: Saunders.

American Psychiatric Association. (1994). *Diagnostic and statistical manual of mental disorders* (4th ed.). Washington, DC: Author.

Bachman, R. (1994). *Violence against women: A National Crime Victimization Survey report.* (NCJ-145325.) Washington, DC: Bureau of Justice Statistics, U.S. Department of Justice.

Bean, C. A. (1992). *Women murdered by the men they loved.* New York: Haworth Press.

Bradley, M. (1996). Caring for older people. *British Medical Journal, 313,* 548–550.

Chen, X. (1999, October 11–14). *The quality of marriage and the psychological health of women.* Paper presented at the China–U.S. Conference on Women's Issues, Beijing, China.

Clark, A. N. G., Mankikar, G. D., & Gray, I. (1975). Diogenes syndrome: A clinical study of gross neglect in old age. *The Lancet,* 366–368.

Dutton, M. A. (1992). Understanding women's responses to domestic violence: A redefinition of battered woman syndrome. *Hofstra Law Review, 21* (4), 1191–1242.

Edleson, J. L. & Tolman, R. M. (1992). *Intervention for men who batter: An ecological approach.* Newbury Park, CA: Sage.

Frazier, B. H., & Hayes, K. C. (1991). *Selected resources on elder abuse*. Washington, DC: U.S. Department of Agriculture.

Herman, J. (1992). *Trauma and recovery*. New York: Basic Books.

Horowitz, M. (1993). Stress-response syndromes: A review of posttraumatic stress and adjustment disorders. In J. P. Wilson & B. Raphael (Eds.). *International handbook of traumatic stress syndromes* (pp. 49–60). New York: Plenum.

Jacobson, N., et al. (1994). Affect, verbal content, and psychophysiology in the arguments of couples with a violent husband. *Journal of Consulting and Clinical Psychology, 62* (5), 982–988.

Kemp, A., Fawling, E. I., & Green, B. (1991). Posttraumatic stress disorder in battered women: A shelter sample. *Journal of Traumatic Stress, 4* (1), 137–148.

Kemp, A., Green, B. L., Hovanitz, C. & Rawlings, E. I. (1995). Incidence and correlates of posttraumatic stress disorder in battered women: Shelter and community samples. *Journal of Interpersonal Violence, 10* (1), 43–55.

Koss, M. P., & Heslet, L. (1992). Somatic consequences of violence against women. Archives of Family Medicine,1, 53–59.

Koss, M. P., Woodruff, W. J., & Koss, P. G. (1990). Relation of criminal victimization to health perceptions among women medical patients. *Journal of Counseling and Clinical Psychology, 58* (2), 147–152.

Lesnoff-Caravaglia, G. (2000). *Nutrition and the longevity of battered women*. Paper presented at the International Conference on Nutrition and Aging, Paris, France.

Liss, M. B., & Stahly, G. B. (1993). Domestic violence and child custody. In M. Hatway, & M. Hansen (Eds.), *Recovery from battering: Feminism and family therapy* (pp. 175–187). Newbury Park, CA: Sage.

The National Council on the Aging. (1976). *The invisible elderly*. Washington, DC: Author.

O'Leary, D. D., & Vivian, D. (1990). Physical aggression in marriage. In F. D. Fincham, & T. N. Bradbury (Eds.), *The psychology of marriage* (pp. 323–248). New York: Guilford Press.

Riggs, D., Rothbaum, B. O., & Foa, E. (1995). A prospective examination of symptoms of posttraumatic stress disorder in victims of nonsexual assault. *Journal of Interpersonal Violence, 10* (2), 201–214.

Saundera, D. (1994). Posttraumatic stress symptoms profiles of battered women: A comparison of surveys in two settings. *Violence and Victims, 9* (1), 31–44.

Selye, H. (1976). *The stress of life*. New York: McGraw-Hill.

Stets, J. E., & Straus, M. A. (1990). Gender differences in reporting marital violence and its medical and psychological consequences. In M. A. Straus & R. J. Gesses (Eds.), *Physical violence in American families: Risk factors and adaptations to violence in 8,145 families* (pp. 151–180). New Brunswick, NJ: Transaction Publishers.

Steward, D. E., & Cecutti, A. (1993). Physical abuse in pregnancy. *Canadian Medical Association Journal, 149* (9), 1257– 1263.

Ungvari, G. S., & Hantz, P. M. (1991). Social breakdown in the elderly, I. Case studies and management. *Comprehensive Psychiatry, 32* (5), 440–444.

Vinton, L. (1991). Abused older women: Battered women or abused elders? *Journal of Women & Aging, 3* (3), 5–19.

Vollhart, L. T. (1991). Psychoneuroimmunology. *American Journal of Orthopsychiatry, 61* (1), 84–92.

Vostonis, P., & Dean, C. (1992). Self-neglect in adult life. *British Journal of Psychiatry, 161,* 265–267.

Weintraub, D., & Ruskin, P. E. (1999). Posttraumatic stress disorder in the elderly: A review. *Harvard Review of Psychiatry, 7* (3), 144–152.

Wilson, H. S., & Kneisl, C. R. (1992). *Psychiatric nursing* (4th ed.). Reading, MA: Addison-Wesley.

Chapter 7

GROWING OLD IN PRISON

GARI LESNOFF-CARAVAGLIA

WITH THE INCREASE in the number of older persons within the total population, there is a concomitant increase in the numbers of older persons in specific population categories, including prison inmates. The growth in the number of elderly prisoners reflects both the growth in the elderly population as a whole, as well as the institution of tougher sentencing laws that target violent and repeat offenders. People are currently given longer sentences for which they are not parolable, and, consequently, a larger number will grow old in prison.

A new term has evolved "cellblock seniors" to describe those who have grown old and frail in prison. An eighty-six-year-old man clutching a walker as he shuffles down a prison hallway is not the usual image of a dangerous killer locked up for the good of society. Because elderly people require more medical care, it can cost nearly three times as much to incarcerate them, or about $65,000 a year per inmate. New crops of prisons are surfacing with geriatric wings equipped with oxygen generators and wheelchairs, instead of hand guns and stun guns.

There is an increase in the numbers of older persons among the prison population both as recidivists and as first-time offenders. The prison setting in which they spend their lives has been variously labeled as a correctional institution, the "big house," "stir," or the "slammer."

There are predominantly three types of elderly prisoners. One group is made up of those who committed crimes as younger persons and were sentenced to prison in their youth, and, thus, have lived much of their lives within the prison setting and have grown old in prison. They often live to advanced ages and, since they are completing extended- or life-term sentences, they are known as "lifers." Such inmates frequently spend their youth, middle age, and old age behind bars.

The second group includes those who were committed as older first-time offenders and were sentenced to prison. They committed crimes at the age of fifty-five or older and serve their prison sentences as elderly people.

The third group is made up of career or habitual offenders who move in and out of prison, serving a few years at a time throughout their lives. They have a history of criminal behavior and may have served several sentences in different environments, such as jails, state prisons, or federal prisons. These are the "old cons." Such persons are also referred to as recidivists, repeaters, or as the "revolving-door type."

The majority of older inmates, however, live out their old age in environments geared toward younger prisoners. They face unique problems with respect to mental health, rehabilitation, and parole.

THE AGED INMATE

Aged offenders represent a very special population with specific needs and concerns. They have been given very little attention because it has been common practice to group them with the general prison population that is generally not segregated by age. Older prisoners, however, are forced to acquire coping strategies for a strange and unusual situation at a period in life when their coping mechanisms are considerably diminished (Lesnoff-Caravaglia, 2000). It is for this reason as well, that for the elderly convict, release can be as traumatic as was the original confinement. For those elderly inmates who committed crimes in old age because of shrinking financial resources, release can be especially problematic.

One of the few studies in this area examined the lifestyles of the older prison population (aged fifty-five and older) to determine from psychosocial, biological, and medical perspectives what it was like to grow old in the setting of a prison (Lesnoff-Caravaglia, 1998).

It was clear from the study (Lesnoff-Caravaglia) that the social and psychological aspects of the prisonization experience for the elderly must be understood within the context of their total biological, psychological, and social functioning. Aged inmates needed to be viewed against the backdrop of both the immediate environment they face, as well as within the context of the world they left behind. The nature of aging in a prison community presents unusual challenges. Vocational, educational, and rehabilitation programs are all geared toward the young. Parole criteria are also inappropriate to the lives of the old.

In this study of 101 male prisoners between the ages of fifty-five to eighty-five in two age-integrated correctional institutions, findings revealed concerns by the inmates with respect to the prison environment, health status, psychological well-being, social interaction, and the provision of needed services for older inmates. Results indicated that 72 percent of the older inmates did not receive any special provisions due to age. Many concerns focused on inadequate health care, inappropriate living and bathroom facilities, and difficulties in negotiating the environment. Such problem areas included using bathroom facilities, the stairs, and general problems of mobility. Due to poor medical attention, both acute and chronic health problems went untreated. There was a lack of provision of proper diets for those with special health problems (Lesnoff-Caravaglia, 1998).

Fear of younger inmates was expressed by a large portion of the older inmates (Lesnoff-Caravaglia). There was serious concern over personal safety, including physical harm, psychological pain, stealing of possessions, and abusive treatment that included sexual assault. Due to prison overcrowding, guards are scarce, and the code of silence that prevails in prison ensures that no complaints are registered. Following medical treatment, the physically-vulnerable older victim is returned to the unprotected environment, and the predatory behavior continues.

The importance of providing separate facilities to house only older inmates was frequently expressed. There was strong sentiment that age segregation was a necessity in the prison environment. Younger inmates were described as "different" from older inmates by virtue of the nature of their crimes, as well as their open aggressiveness and hostility. Occupational and recreational activities were largely absent or inadequate. Opportunities for visitations and for greater interaction with family members was restrictive (Lesnoff-Caravaglia, 1998).

Aging prisoners are frequently at the mercy of younger, more aggressive, and difficult prisoners who tend to frighten, to ridicule, or to even harm them. The aged prisoners become depressed, anxious, and consequently dependent on the warden and prison staff for protection.

Some prisoners feel younger in prison. Since many come from impoverished or lower socioeconomic backgrounds, an improvement in health status may clearly result. Older prisoners are not exposed to heavy industry, hard labor, or heavy drinking. They eat regular meals, rest often, and have access to medical care. This is unlikely to be the case among lower-class and working class men outside prison.

Problems can occur with respect to punishment practices. Prisoners who break the rules are placed in solitary confinement, known simply as "solitary" or "the hole." The cell used for such punishment is completely bare with no water or commode and is kept pitch black.

Many older inmates viewed themselves as abandoned by family and society. They felt deprived of friends, employment, and decent accommodations (Lesnoff-Caravaglia, 1998).

Deprivations can lead to atypical behaviors. Prisoners of all ages might adopt a boy–girl posture to encourage sexual interest. Guards bring in girlie clothes, sexually-suggestive pictures, and narcotics. The guards fight among themselves, providing yet another level of tension to an already-hostile environment; departments are at odds with one another; and, all factions may engage in steal-ing from the state. Food deprivation and purposely-poor meals force the inmates to buy food from the canteen that is run by prison officials.

Profiles of Aged Inmates

A profile of an inmate who had been incarcerated in old age is a Black male aged eighty who had spent two and one-half years in a correctional institution. He had been sentenced to six years. He received one visit a year, although he had lost contact with his family and was widowed. "In the streets" (prisoner's reference to the outside world), he had held a variety of jobs but had little formal education. He described his overall health status as good and rated the care provided in the prison as fair, although the food was not suited for an older person. He did not think he had any serious health problems, although he frequently felt ill. He experienced no difficulties in terms of sensory changes or mobility. The majority of his time in prison was spent doing work-related activities as he felt that there was little else to do.

His main concern was personal safety; his fears of younger inmates continues to grow. He is also worried over possibly contracting a serious illness. He does not want to die in prison and often worries about growing older and what this might mean to him in terms of personal safety and his future, once released from prison.

A second profile is of an inmate who spent the greater part of his life in prison. He is a White male, eighty-five years old. He has never had any religious affiliation and is divorced. He has served fifty years in prison and has still twenty more years to serve. His education ended at the sixth grade. He receives no visits and feels abandoned. He is generally depressed and thinks a lot about his death and how he will die.

He described his overall health status as fair, and rated the care he receives as poor. He spends a lot of time worrying about his health. He feels that there are no provisions for persons as they grow old in prison, and that the prison environment was totally inhospitable to an aging inmate. The clothing was inadequate, and the living arrangements are inappropriate, dirty, and crowded. The food served is not geared to older diets and is often inedible. He has great difficulty in using the washroom facilities and the stairs. He experiences hearing and vision loss, as well as foot problems.

He does not like the staff, but does have some friends in the prison. Much of his time is spent reading and watching television, but his main activity is sleeping. He viewed the activities available as inappropriate for older persons, besides he was not interested in leisure-time activities. He maintained that he never thinks about growing old, stating, "I'm old—what's there to think about!" However, he does worry about feeling pain, becoming ill, and the future in general. Some problematic areas for him included drugs and alcohol.

Over the years, his fears have increased regarding the correctional officers, authority in general, and particularly the young inmates. His main concern is the danger presented by the younger inmates. He feels that the staff does little to control them, and that they pose a life-threatening situation for him because of his general weakness and loss of mobility.

He does not look forward to being released from prison. If he could have one wish fulfilled, it would be to die (Lesnoff-Caravaglia, 1988).

Psychosocial Problems

Psychological effects on older inmates can include a high degree of insecurity, fear of pain, a constant fear of illness, more fear of correctional officers and of authority in general, and a heightened fear of young inmates. There is, in addition, a fear of the future and a fear of having no place to live on the outside.

The length of time spent in prison influences the inmate's relationships and reference groups. Society has little place for an elderly prisoner or ex-convict. Cases of not wanting to leave prison when released are common among older men. In one instance, upon release and placed in a nursing home, an older ex-convict returned repeatedly to the prison to throw stones against the watch tower in the hope of being arrested and readmitted.

Marital status, visits with family and kin, and contacts with outside reference groups tend to diminish with the length of imprisonment. The person becomes increasingly more dependent upon the institution for psychosocial support.

Future Concerns

The older population as offenders, not victims of crime, has been neglected in research. Crime committed by older persons will undoubtedly increase as the elderly population grows. Crime-control systems are designed to deal more with youthful offenders than to deal with the aged. For example, putting handcuffs on an older person could result in fractures.

Crimes committed by elderly persons run the gamut from disorderly conduct to homicide. Arrests of elderly persons for crimes of violence, no matter how defined, are increasing. Elderly assaults and homicides are perpetrated on elderly victims and are often the result of the cumulative frustration of marriages grown old, the narrowing of sexual outlets, the irritation and boredom of retirement living, and the feelings of despair and hopelessness—all of which are only too common in elderly populations (Newman, Newman, & Gewirtz, 1984).

Much like crimes committed by younger persons, the root causes of most criminal behavior are to be found in strains in the social fabric of the society as a whole. Elderly crime cannot be understood without viewing the aging of America, the trauma of retirement, the loss of status, and the reduced economic self-sufficiency that so often characterize later years.

When society removes people from its midst, it assumes the responsibility for their care and well-being. This is also the case with older prisoners. The development of special geriatric facilities, such as nursing homes "within walls," may not be a far-fetched notion.

Since systematic studies on aged offenders are extremely limited, ways to ameliorate prison conditions for older inmates have not been given the serious attention they deserve. Unfortunately, too little research has been devoted to this population because the notion of punishment has obscured the need for humane and healthful treatment. Additionally, few, if any studies, have been conducted on the older female inmate. This may be due to the fact that this population is currently so small, but their numbers may swell in the future as well. Research studies need to be conducted that present a picture of "the inside" from an older inmate's perspective.

Prisons are fairly well-prepared to meet the health needs of younger persons, such as sprains and strains, dental hygiene, and hernias. They are not prepared to deal with cardiovascular and respiratory problems, cataracts, osteoporosis, periodontal disease, arthritis, and gastrointestinal problems. Prison medical services are geared toward acute rather than chronic ailments.

Retraining, trade schools, vocational training, and college courses are appropriate for young adults to reintegrate them into society. Such programs have little application for older inmates as they will not be seeking employment. There are no programs to help reintegrate the older inmate into society upon release. They become welfare recipients or recidivists.

The design of prisons is such that inmates must traverse long distances to reach needed services, such as the hospital for sick-call or pill-call. The dining facility is also frequently distant, as is the commissary where they purchase hygienic products or food items. Mobility is seriously compromised if the facility is located in areas where unfavorable weather conditions prevail, such as severe winters. Once they arrive at their destination, older inmates must stand in long lines before they are served. As a result, many limit or forego such services.

The prior world of individuality and autonomy ceases to exist. Privacy narrows in scope to a level of one's thoughts. Availability of different methods by which to manage one's affairs is restricted. Contact with family and friends must be prescribed by the sanctions and controls of the visiting procedure. Exploitation by others, enhanced by the frustration and anger of being a confined person, becomes an everyday conflict (Danto, 1973).

The "rock boss," an inmate leader in a section of a correctional setting; the "punk," the passive recipient of male homosexual attacks; and a "dime dropper," the inmate who is accused of serving as an informer to the formal correctional system are individuals who reflect an adaptation of social roles in a confinement setting (Blake, 1971). The new inmate soon learns that the outside world is restricted and "off limits."

SUICIDE

The conditions in prisons are conducive to suicidal ideation. Both the attitude of personnel as well as prison architecture play a role in the occurrence of a suicide. The "downward mobility" experienced by prisoners is frequently a precipitant of suicide. Prisoners are losers in a very real sense. The inmate group has a high incidence of vulnerability with respect to self-destructive and suicidal behavior.

Since suicide is a behavior pattern that is the outcome of a number of behavioral, environmental, situational, and social forces and conditions, institutions must intervene in the self-destructive lifestyles of its inmate population. The institution must recognize the social structure and personality factors of inmates who are confined in the cell blocks of a prison. During a suicidal attempt, if the rescuer calls for help, the inmate feels he is worthy enough to live. If the rescuer turns a deaf ear, belittles the situation or jokes, he is daring the suicidal inmate to commit suicide; he has told the inmate he is unworthy to live (Danto, 1973). The inmate feels he is carrying out a homicidal plan conceived by the rescuer as he cannot accept responsibility for making the decision to end his life. When an inmate provokes a guard, the guard becomes his "method" of suicide.

There is further evidence of a relationship between alcohol and suicide. Suicidal people are more likely to be found in jails. Some suffer from mental health problems; others act out following drinking. Some persons may consciously or unconsciously arrange to get themselves into jail as a means to control suicidal impulses. There is also a close connection between homicide and suicide.

The combination of pre-existing psychopathology and the prison situation may increase the likelihood of suicide. The prison milieu is run on highly authoritarian lines. Persons are ordered from place to place. Both the physical environment and the social processes that take place there are highly dehumanizing.

To understand predictability of suicide for an individual, one must understand the social process and setting in which one lives. The complexities of a confinement setting are strongly determined by the culture, racial, and ethnic features of those individuals in prison. In most social institutions, there is a normative system, one that has a reward-and-punishment frame of reference. If acceptable behavior is elicited, there are rewards. There is a lack of rewards in the prison system.

The quiet individual receives minimal recognition from the prison system; this individual fails to achieve any identity. The depersonalizing atmosphere of prison helps to reinforce identity loss.

Correctional officers could be better used and their role expanded with regard to intervention in suicidal behavior. Correctional officers are well aware which specific crimes have low social status.

The community offers a considerable number of alternatives for an individual who is suicidal, but the correctional setting offers few or none. Furthermore, there is no exact data on suicide attempts, and the number of unreported cases is probably quite high. Some prisoners exhibit a sociopathic personality with tendencies to act out their aggressive behavior, and, consequently, this group does not attempt suicide. Their increasing presence has somewhat reduced the suicide rate in prisons.

Suicide attempts are sometimes initiated at news of the death of a loved one, particularly the mother. Prolonged separation from significant family members, such as the mother, or abandonment by a wife, can lead to thoughts of suicide. To be incarcerated can be equated to a feeling of death. The person experiences complete loss and initiates a journey into the unknown. This results in great mental strain. Prisoners refer to suicide as "sideways." (He did commit "sideways.")

A razor blade is one of the most coveted possessions of a prisoner; it symbolizes the convict's ability to have a way out in difficult situations and provides a sense of power. In any suicidal act, internal and external factors act together. The primary external factor is the environment in which the person exists; the primary internal one is that person's psychological state.

Incarceration has several traumatic aspects. Repressional forces upon the personality include the experience of an overpowering environment, isolation, and exclusion from the customary social group, and, last but not least, discrimination. A large majority of convicts are psychologically-abnormal personalities who have a particular tendency toward asocial psychopathic and, to a lesser extent, neurotic systems. In an asocial psychopath, outbursts of aggression are expected, even against the self. In neurotics, unconscious guilt feelings have pushed them to their acts. Suicide is the most severe form of self-punishment.

People struggle to live as long as they fear death, but when the fear is of life, death is the only answer. Prisoners are wont to say that if a man wants to commit suicide, he will find a way. While ten years is not life—ten years was more than he wanted to do.

Another motive for suicide results from rape. There is force placed upon some men to become a "little girl" or "sissy." Some inmates after such assaults, commit suicide. Death was preferred to being degraded and dishonored.

The range of available lethal methods is limited in prisons. Prison construction can also present limitations due to the absence of bars or pipes. Hanging is accomplished by using one's own clothing by tearing the clothing in strips; socks and belts are also used, as are bedclothes, such as sheets. When present, cell bars, vents, or ceiling pipes are used. Frequently, there is not enough room to suspend oneself fully without touching the floor. Most of the hangings are accomplished by falling into a sitting position with the legs stretched out on the floor, or the inmate falls into a kneeling position that the inmate maintains. Actually, one strangles oneself to death with real determination. One could stop it at any point by simply standing up.

The time selected is usually from midnight to 8:00 A.M. It is difficult to find a time when people are not present. On an average day in Los Angeles County, 12,000 people are in jail.

Some arrange to be caught with a weapon, so that they can be rescued. Removal of the weapon is usually not sufficient to alter the situation, and counseling and medical treatment may be more effective. Linkages with local community mental health centers could provide some of the necessary treatment.

AGE AND GENDER ISSUES

Crime is traditionally considered as perpetrated by younger men, and, while that appears accurate, prisons in the United States are housing a growing number of older inmates. According to the U.S. Bureau of Justice Statistics, the number of inmates aged fifty-five and older more than doubled from 1981 to 1990 (Morton, 1996).

Older inmates can also be easily overlooked and their needs ignored. However, they are often regarded as having a calming or settling effect on younger inmates. Intergenerational mixing, by contrast, presents a danger to the older inmate.

There are several factors influencing the number of older people in prison. First, there are more older people in the general population, and they are living longer. In the last sixty years, the average life expectancy has increased from fifty-four years to over seventy-five years. At the same time, society's heightened concern about crime and violence has resulted in longer sentences and mandatory incarceration to include life without parole for an increasing number of offenses. Additionally, several jurisdictions including the federal government have abolished parole and limited probation as a sentencing option (Morton, 1996).

Correctional agencies also do not have a single definition of who constitutes an older inmate. Some adopt the age of fifty as the starting point for defining the older inmate because heredity, socioeconomic conditions, lifestyles, and the medical care available to many inmates result in their aging prematurely.

As with general inmate populations, men greatly outnumber women. Approximately 63 percent of those aged fifty and older were incarcerated for violent offenses including murder and sexual assault.

Designing or modifying facilities and programs to foster independence among older inmates, to help them stay in the general population, is cost-effective and provides better community adjustment upon release. For those older inmates who cannot function in the general population, special units can be critical to their survival. Special units or facilities are not widely available for older inmates in state and federal prisons. The National Institute of Corrections in 1985 identified only eleven states that had such units.

One of the most costly aspects of incarcerating older inmates is medical care. Older inmates suffer an average of three chronic illnesses and generate three times the medical expenses incurred by younger prisoners. To keep health care costs from continuing to rise, correctional systems will have to take a long-range approach toward prevention, intervention, early diagnosis, and treatment (Miller, Cohen, & Wiersema, 1995).

Aging causes physiological changes that can affect the practices and procedures of correctional facilities. Taste, smell, touch, sight, and hearing all become dulled. Since they take in less sensory information, older inmates may not be able to respond quickly or appropriately to stimuli. This may be misinterpreted as deliberately not listening or disobeying.

As one ages, the bones become more brittle and lung capacity decreases, resulting in a loss of oxygen throughout the body, including the digestive system that reduces stamina, which, in turn, affects work assignments. Such changes necessitate special diets for older inmates. The kidneys begin to lose mass after age fifty, which can cause frequent urination or incontinence among older inmates. Prostate problems are also a common occurrence.

Medical staff trained to work with older inmates are essential. Older inmates are often uninformed about their bodies or medical treatments. Staff members must ensure that prisoners understand their condition and learn how they can work with medical personnel. Staff must be particularly sensitive to the effects of medication on older inmates; 25 percent of the older patients in hospitals are there as a result of improperly prescribed drugs ordered by their physicians.

Because many older inmates will die in prison, facilities must provide for hospice programs, counseling for terminally-ill inmates, and visits by family, friends, and volunteers. The inmate's right to a living will, medical power of attorney, and other legal matters must also be addressed. When death occurs, counseling will be needed for inmates and staff members who worked closely with the deceased. If there is no family to accept the remains, a funeral or memorial service and a dignified burial service should be provided.

Even disciplinary programs need to be reexamined, because strategies that encourage younger inmates to participate and behave acceptably may not be effective with sixty-year-olds.

A lack of specialized prerelease programs for older inmates and a limited use of outside resources to meet their needs prevail. Reentry programs will need to be modified to ensure that housing, continuity of medical care, and other concerns of the aging are addressed. Inadequate prerelease services may result in older inmates refusing release or otherwise spending more time in prison because they have nowhere else to go.

Staff must be carefully screened and selected on the basis of their interest in and ability to relate to older people. Empathic training models need to be used in their training so as to help them better understand disabling conditions, such as hearing, visual, and mobility impairments.

Women aged fifty and older constitute some 4 percent of the women incarcerated in state and federal prisons in 1990. Because of mandatory sentencing, the war on drugs, longer sentences, and sentence of life without parole, women as a whole make up the fastest growing group of prisoners. If these approaches to crime control continue, the number of older women in prison will increase. Only three systems reported as of 1991 as having special units for older women, compared with fourteen that had them for older men. Prison personnel must also be sensitive to physiological and societal differences between men and women in the development and implementation of programs for older women (Lesnoff-Caravaglia, 1998).

FUTURE TRENDS

Growing old behind bars becomes an increasing possibility as the U.S. prison populations age, crowding worsens, and health care costs increase. Across the United States,

prisoners aged fifty-five and older number approximately 20,000; California, with roughly 2,000, has the largest share (Morton, 1996). Gerontologists and criminologists typically begin tracking older inmates at age fifty-five, although some prisons label people as young as thirty-five and forty as elderly. The two trends that complicate matters include the fact that the aging of the United States, in general, means more older inmates, while mandatory sentences as part of the nation's get-tough stance on crime guarantee more young offenders will grow gray behind bars. States such as Florida, Pennsylvania, and South Carolina have instituted programs that address inmates' changing needs, and, in some cases, are planning for geriatric prisons.

One recommendation is to place some older inmates out of cells and into home-monitoring programs to save bed space for younger inmates more prone to repeat crime. The high costs related to the housing of older prisoners include special diets, excessive supervision, costly medication, and expensive treatments. Dialysis or chemotherapy for one inmate, for example, can cost thousands of dollars annually. Older convicts typically suffer three chronic illnesses behind bars, compared with less than one for younger cellmates (Miller, Cohen, & Wiersema, 1995).

It is important to seek out alternatives that free up prison cells for more violent younger inmates and thus reduce the cost to taxpayers. If older offenders were released into half-way houses or community-care centers, they would be eligible for Social Security, Medicare, veterans' benefits and programs under the federal Older Americans Act. In prison, those benefits stop at the gate.

South Carolina, which houses 340 older offenders, addressed the need in 1983 by opening State Park Correctional Institution in Columbia, designed solely for handicapped and geriatric inmates. Florida is planning to develop measures to deal with issues such as health care for inmates and parolees, community resources that might keep elderly offenders out of prison, barriers to mobility, and the possibility of using pets for companionship (Morton, 1996).

The greatest fear of older inmates is that they will die in prison. It costs thousands of dollars to keep an older inmate alive. For example, one prisoner can take four kinds of medication for arthritis, have had treatments with radiation therapy and chemotherapy, and undergone two major surgeries to remove cancerous tumors from his body. He may also have diabetes, congestive heart failure, hypertension, degenerative-disc disease, and gout.

Meanwhile, low-risk elderly inmates are kept behind bars, often lost in the administrative shuffle. They tend to be invisible, prompted by fear, disability, or dementia to stay out of the way. Many are too afraid or confused to apply for parole, rarely have visitors or have family that might act in their behalf, and go for decades without being written up for disciplinary violations. They often stay well beyond the national average time served for their sentences (Lesnoff-Caravaglia, 2000).

The ironic quality of the U.S. corrections system is that it struggles to release the highest-risk prisoners and keep the low-risk prisoners. A growing number of criminal-justice experts, including Jonathan Turley, a law professor at George Washington University who founded the Project for Older Prisoners based at the George Washington University Law School, maintains that early release of low-risk elderly prisoners should be considered as a way to relieve overcrowding, to cut corrections costs, and to diminish recidivism (Morton, 1996).

NURSING HOMES "WITHIN" WALLS

Due to a lifestyle that often includes substance abuse, poverty, and poor dietary, health, and hygiene habits, older inmates are typically in poorer health than people the same age in the mainstream public. It is not uncommon for an older prisoner to have the body deterioration normally associated with a person ten years older. This is largely due to an abusive lifestyle that results in high-risk persons. Many suffer from hepatitis C, cardiac problems, diabetes, all of the normal chronic ailments except for more drug abuse and sexually transmitted diseases.

Treating any prisoner is a complex undertaking. Security is the primary concern and can complicate treatment. When nurses are hired, for example, they are often told that they are also correctional officers.

Some of the young inmates help the elderly by taking them for a walk through the ward. Many elderly prisoners suffer from pulmonary problems and need daily sessions on respirators. The older amputees who lost limbs because of diabetes rely on the good will of younger inmates to help look after them. Some younger inmates are enlisted to assist older inmates. Some of the younger offenders have been tapped to help care for older inmates. They are known as wheelchair aides, but unofficially are called "the pushers."

It is a long way from certain units to the chow hall, at least two city blocks. Inclement weather, such as snow, can add to the problem. Many must use wheelchairs or use walkers or canes. Most elderly prisoners leave prison in a hearse to the cemetery. Many of the men have outlived or lost contact with family members during their years in prison. Their families have grown old and died.

A steady increase in the number of elderly prisoners has led to a new kind of prison guard—one who must help inmates out of bed, tie their shoes, and sometimes even bathe, feed, and dress them. Corrections officers pride themselves in their counseling ability as much as their riot-control skills.

When an inmate does not respond to an officer's order, it does not always mean he is deliberately disobeying. It might mean that he could not hear the order, or that dementia keeps him from understanding it. Many offenders suffer from dementia and Alzheimer's disease. This creates a real challenge, combined with the prison mentality and the traditional prison structure, where a person is ordered to do something just once before action is taken. It is still important for the staff to keep security in the forefront. The problem may be not one of escaping, but of wandering.

Old prisoners get much sicker and suffer from costly chronic problems. When they are victimized by the young, aggressive inmate or by guards, they tend to sustain greater and longer lasting injuries. Simple things can alter a regular prison setting, such as putting grab bars in key places, colored edges on stairs, taking care that stairwells are not too steep.

Washington state has opened one of the nation's first assisted-living prisons, Ahtanum View Correctional Complex in Yakima. Prisons may, in the future, look more like nursing homes. Personnel, however, face new challenges. For example, how does one break up a wheelchair fight? What is the best way to take down a fractious eighty-year-old offender without fracturing a hip? In one institution, an older person in a wheelchair took care of the prison cats. When one of the younger offenders kicked it and broke its rear leg, a near riot ensued.

The frail elderly often become invisible in prisons. They are low maintenance and not troublemakers. It can be easily overlooked that a frail, quiet older inmate has not eaten in three days. Private medical prisons are also being developed. They will provide a secured medical facility where inmates can serve their time and get the proper care at a fixed rate. This can result in significant savings in the costs of inmate care.

Medical costs for geriatric inmates are very high, running to $6,000 a year for those over age fifty, while medical care for the average younger inmate is approximately $1,000 a year. Those older than sixty-five cost three to four times as much. They have a very high incidence of substance abuse and smoking, suffer from emphysema, and have higher chronic-disease levels, such as hypertension, diabetes, heart disease. Some suffer the effects of a violent life lived on the streets that can leave permanent injuries and disabilities. The cost of medical care for older inmates in state prisons is paid for by state taxpayers. As long as inmates are incarcerated in state prisons, the federal government does not pay for their medical bills (Miller, Cohen, & Wiersema, 1995).

There is a movement growing throughout the corrections industry to release terminally-ill and elderly inmates. This population is costing too much and may lead to a modification in sentencing. There may be a form of release program developed for the terminally-ill and the elderly. It will be an economic decision rather than a social policy and will require some time to implement.

While many older offenders do not require special housing, those who are disabled or infirm should be placed in a protective environment because of the possibility of victimization. Those with chronic illnesses are likely to have increased use of infirmary and hospital services. About 80 percent of those sixty-five or older have some chronic illness requiring long-term care. One of four will require nursing home care. Work and program restrictions are inevitable for this group of offenders, but few departments of corrections have developed alternative programs for the elderly.

CONCLUSION

As prison populations age, the problems facing corrections officials will also change. The specialized needs of this particular segment of the prison population are not only quite different from those of traditionally younger inmates, but they are also extremely diverse within the group. The cost of providing adequate care to meet their needs is increasing and will continue to increase well into this century as the last of the Baby Boomers reach age sixty-five. Areas that will be particularly costly will include the provision of elder-friendly environments that will meet the changing physical, psychological, and social needs of older inmates; programs created specifically for older inmates, not only while in prison but with respect to their future reentry into society; and health care including the costs of treating long-term illnesses and caring for the frail elderly as they grow older.

Older prisoners have little or no probability of committing another offense. However, age alone does not determine whether an inmate will reoffend. Many have only a few years to live. For the lowest-risk prisoners, there can be supervised release; those who are at moderate risk, electronic monitoring; for the highest risk, special geriatric units.

Nursing homes, as an essential feature of the prison environment, appear to be a reality of the future. The construction of new prison facilities consistent with modern design could offset some of the environmental problems. Prisons set aside for the elderly and infirm prisoners are gradually being considered.

REFERENCES

Blake, J. (1971). *The joint.* Garden City, NY: Doubleday.

Danto, G. L. (1973). *Jailhouse blues.* Orchard Lake, MI: Epic.

Lesnoff-Caravaglia, G. (1998). *Growing old in prison.* Paper presented at the International Gerontology Congress, Adelaide, Australia.

Lesnoff-Caravaglia, G. (2000). *Health aspects of aging.* Springfield, IL: Charles C Thomas.

Miller, T. R., Cohen, M. A., & Wiersema, B. (1995). Crime in the United States: Victim costs and consequences. *Final Report to National Institute of Justice.* Washington, DC.

Morton, J. B. (1996). Elderly inmates. In M. D. McShane & F. P. Williams (Eds.), *Encyclopedia of American prisons* (pp. 190–193).

Newman, E. S., Newman, D. J., & Gewirtz, M. L. (1984). *Elderly criminals.* Cambridge, MA: Oelgeschlager, Guss, & Hain.

Chapter 8

THE RURAL ELDERLY

SARA A. QUANDT AND THOMAS A. ARCURY

THE PURPOSE OF THIS CHAPTER is to identify public health issues pertinent to older adults in rural communities. The focus is on identifying the role physical and social factors related to residing in a rural community have on health promotion and disease prevention, as well as the delivery of health care services. Although there is heterogeneity among rural elders, and one must be careful to avoid stereotypes, common features exist that mark the life experiences of many rural elders. In addition, rural communities across the United States today face common constraints in providing health-related services to their older residents.

Basic research and epidemiological investigations have identified an array of practices that promote health—physical activity, balanced diet, health screenings, and avoidance of tobacco. Attention is now needed to the environmental influences on health, and particularly how the environment affects these health-promoting practices (Satariano, 1997). It is with this environmental perspective that the rural elderly should be considered. In this chapter, the rural elderly are defined, and their distinctive characteristics for public health are identified. How public

health services reach the rural elderly is described with emphasis on the several types of service where needs are greatest. In conclusion, two issues—complementary and alternative medicine and religion—that are of growing interest among rural health care providers are considered.

WHO ARE THE RURAL ELDERLY?

Approximately one in four elderly persons lives in a rural environment. Such places are typically characterized by low population density and by populations traditionally dependent on farming and other extractive industries. These characteristics of rural environments set the stage for a number of issues faced by rural elders that distinguish them from their urban and suburban counterparts.

The precise number of rural elders depends largely on the definition of "rural" employed. The U.S. Bureau of the Census (1992a) distinguishes "metropolitan" from "nonmetropolitan" counties. Metropolitan

TABLE 8.1
Highest and Lowest Quartiles of States: Number of Rural Residents Aged Sixty and Over

	Lowest Quartile			*Highest Quartile*	
State	*%*		*State*	*%*	
California	8.7		Vermont	64.8	
New Jersey	8.9		North Dakota	56.8	
Nevada	11.2		West Virginia	56.8	
Rhode Island	11.3		South Dakota	54.8	
Hawaii	11.4		Maine	51.7	
Arizona	11.8		Mississippi	51.6	
Massachusetts	13.3		North Carolina	50.8	
New York	14.3		Arkansas	46.1	
Utah	14.5		Montana	46.0	
Florida	14.6		New Hampshire	45.7	
Illinois	16.5		Kentucky	45.2	
Connecticut	17.5		South Carolina	44.5	

Source: U.S. Department of Health and Human Services, 1996.

counties are those with a city of at least 50,000 people, or containing an urbanized area (city and surrounding urban fringe) of 100,000 or more. A metropolitan area extends to include adjacent counties that are economically and socially tied to it. In 1990, 25.9 percent of persons sixty-five and older lived in nonmetropolitan counties. A second distinction is between "urban" and "rural." In addition to the urbanized areas of 100,000 or more, the Census considers any town of 2,500 or more to be urban. In 1990, 23.6 percent of persons sixty-five and older lived in a rural area. These rural areas can fall within or outside of a metropolitan county (U.S. Bureau of the Census, 1992b).

Table 8.1 lists the lowest and highest quartiles of states, ranked by percentage of persons sixty and older who are rural residents (U.S. Department of Health and Human Services [DHHS], 1996). California has the lowest percentage of rural elders with 8.7 percent, while Vermont has the highest, 64.8 percent. In contrast, Table 8.2 shows highest and lowest quartiles of states by the number of persons aged sixty and older who are rural residents. Alaska has the lowest

number of rural elders (less than 12,000), while Pennsylvania has the most (over 670,000). These rankings help demonstrate the variety of circumstances and environments in which rural elders live. Those with the lowest densities tend to be in the West and Northeast, while those with the highest densities are largely in the Southeast. Only one state—North Carolina—falls in the top quartile for both number of rural elders and percentage of the elderly population that is rural.

As in the United States as a whole, older women outnumber older men in rural areas, and the proportion increases with age, reflecting differential mortality patterns (U.S. Bureau of the Census, 1992b). Within rural areas, there are significant differences between farm and nonfarm residence patterns. More men than women aged sixty-five and older live on farms, reflecting the difficulty for women in living alone on a farm and their greater migration rates to small towns and urban centers if single or widowed. In rural nonfarm locations, women outnumber men. The preponderance of women increases with the greater urbanization of the location.

TABLE 8.2

Highest and Lowest Quartiles of States: Percentage of Residents Aged Sixty and Over Who Are Rural

Lowest Quartile		Highest Quartile	
State	*# Rural Elderly*	*State*	*# Rural Elderly*
Alaska	11,612	Pennsylvania	670,306
Hawaii	19,789	Texas	575,271
Nevada	20,203	North Carolina	554,526
Wyoming	21,978	New York	457,073
Rhode Island	22,376	Ohio	446,008
Utah	29,238	Florida	444,485
Delaware	34,566	Michigan	431,341
New Mexico	55,285	California	366,963
Vermont	57,431	Georgia	339,561
Montana	64,512	Virginia	323,817
North Dakota	67,123	Tennessee	321,319
Idaho	69,974	Illinois	316,491

Source: U.S. Department of Health and Human Services, 1996.

The ethnic diversity of the elderly population is less in rural than in urban areas (U.S. Bureau of the Census, 1992b). Eighty-eight percent of urban elders are white, compared to 93 percent of rural nonfarm and 96.7 percent of farm elders. Minority rural elders tend to be geographically clustered. African American rural elders are most likely to be found in the Southeast, while most Native American rural elders live in the Southwest and Plains.

Rural elders rate their health lower than nonrural elders (Van Nostrand, 1993). Comparing metropolitan and nonmetropolitan respondents for the National Health Interview Survey 1985–87 and 1990, a greater proportion of nonmetropolitan respondents rated their health as fair or poor than in metropolitan respondents (30% vs. 27%) (Van Nostrand, 1993). These findings are significant, because self-rated health has been found across populations to predict mortality, quality of life, and more objective physician assessments of health. The metro–nonmetro difference is quite pronounced for African American respondents. Over one-half of nonmetro rural African Americans rate their health as fair or poor, compared to about one-third of Whites.

WHAT MAKES RURAL ELDERS A SPECIAL POPULATION?

The special nature of the rural elderly population has been discussed at length by a number of analysts (Coward & Krout, 1998; Coward & Lee, 1985; Gesler, Rabiner, & DeFriese, 1998; Krout, 1986; Rowles, 1988; van Willigen, 1989). The issues raised are summarized here to underscore the importance of giving special recognition to rural elders for public health practice. Three elements of the rural context are central to public health practice for older adults: the social environment of rural communities, the culture of rural older adults, and the life histories of rural older adults.

The social environment in which rural older adults live provides special problems as well as special assets for this population. Special problems include isolation, limited availability of services, difficulty with transportation, and restricted economic resources. Special assets include a strong sense of belonging to place and the willingness of family and community members to provide emotional as well as instrumental support.

Rural communities have low population densities (few people per unit of area), and the few population concentrations (towns and cities) are small and widely dispersed. The dispersed nature of the rural population, particularly outside of towns, results in a great risk of social and interactional isolation. The limited population density of rural communities restricts the number and variety of public services, health services, and commercial services. Some of the implications of restricted services in rural communities for the health of rural adults are obvious. For example, there are few primary health care providers and facilities, and very few specialists for elders with chronic conditions, such as rheumatologists and certified diabetes educators. Many rural elders must travel great distances to get primary and specialized health care in their own communities or in urban centers. Other implications of restricted services in rural communities are not as obvious. For example, there are few large grocery stores in rural communities, and many of the smaller food stores cannot carry a diverse inventory of merchandise. Older adults, therefore, have difficulty getting a variety of fresh fruits and vegetables that are not produced locally or are not in season. Older adults with chronic conditions, such as diabetes, may not have ready access to the types of food they require for self-management. Public spaces, such as parks or large enclosed areas such as malls, are also limited in rural areas, thus rural older adults may have less access to safe areas in which to exercise than their urban counterparts. Adding to the problem of scattered services is that of limited transportation. Rural roads are often small and in disrepair;

in some areas, residential roads remain dirt or gravel. This is discussed in great detail later.

Most rural communities have limited economic resources. Land, much of it farm land or undeveloped, is not appraised at high values, and tax rates are low. A high proportion of rural residents are employed in blue-collar and service industries. Rural communities, therefore, have limited resources to fund public health services to rural elders. Any funds used for elder services compete with programs for children and other special populations.

Rural communities have experienced high levels of out-migration since World War II. Those who leave tend to be younger and better skilled. This has implications at several levels. Individual older adults may be left without children or other family members; this can increase the level of social isolation. The community often loses its best potential leaders. The economy of the area suffers as there are fewer persons to support local businesses, making the services available to older adults fewer. Over the last 25 years, there have been additional circumstances that have fundamentally changed rural life. The farm crisis of the 1980s left some midwestern areas in dire straits (Tickamyer & Duncan, 1990). Lichter and McLaughlin (1995) described some areas as rural ghettos, because poverty and lack of economic opportunity rival that characteristic of urban centers.

Recent changes have acted to increase diversity in rural off-farm employment, especially for women (Bokemeier & Tickamyer, 1985). Some rural areas have experienced an influx of immigrant workers for new low-wage industries, such as meat and poultry processing (Lamphere, 1992), changing the local culture and creating new demands for public health resources.

Some rural communities have experienced population growth, particularly growth in retired older persons (Longino & Smith, 1998). These retirement destination areas (e.g., Florida, Arizona, and North Carolina) have amenities that older adults want. The effect of these older migrants is varied. They tend to bring income, pay taxes, lead to the creation of more service-sector jobs, and not compete for existing jobs. In contrast, immigrants can add to the strain on public services. To the degree that these migrants differ from the local populations, there is potential for culture clash and community disruption.

Despite these negative aspects of rural living for older adults, notable positive features exist. Rural elderly who age in place profess a strong attachment to their rural communities (Rowles, 1988). In particular, they value their social networks of kin and neighbors. These networks provide significant instrumental as well as emotional support. Groger (1983) documented the flow of resources (money, land, assistance) between rural generations. Quandt and colleagues found that a constant exchange of food, some of it in significant quantities and other merely token, reinforced friend, neighbor, and kin-relations, making both givers and recipients feel integrated into their rural communities (Quandt, Arcury, Bell, Vitolins, & McDonald, 2001).

These feelings of attachment to place and people have traditionally been reinforced by local rural institutions, such as schools, churches, newspapers, and stores. As schools and churches consolidate and national companies replace local ones, the community centeredness valued by older residents has been reduced.

The culture shared by the residents of rural communities can be diverse in many ways. For example, health beliefs often vary by ethnicity and class. However, rural culture includes several general characteristics that transcend ethnicity and class. Educational attainment in rural areas is low. This is particularly true of older generations, many of whom went to school in one-room school-

houses and who left school for work before completing high school. Public health programs for these rural elders must be geared to those with low educational attainment. Residents of rural communities are conservative and traditional. Rural older adults are generally very religious and participate in conservative Christian denominations. There is a strong sense among rural residents of independence and self-reliance, the belief that people should take care of themselves. Such beliefs tend to place value on family and friend networks for help, rather than government programs.

The common life history of many rural elders shapes the beliefs, behaviors, and current health status seen in this population. A large proportion have done manual labor throughout their lives. This includes farming, mining, forestry, and, for some, manufacturing. Such work is dangerous, and thus the lifetime experience with occupational injuries and illnesses is high. In addition, such labor-force participation rarely brings high wages or pensions, so that income and assets in old age are limited. Many rural elders had little access to professional medical care in their youth. This shapes both attitudes, a predisposition to self-care, for example, as well as adult health status.

The cultures and social environments of rural communities contain significant variation. As the demographic characteristics of rural older adults vary from community to community and region to region, so does the social environment, culture, and life history of these rural elders. There is generational as well as ethnic, class, gender, and spatial variation. As younger generations age, the rural communities in which they grow old will become less isolated and have more services. These newer generations of older adults have greater educational attainment and a greater proportion have worked in less physically demanding occupations than older generations.

Therefore, it is important that public health programs directed at the rural elderly consider who the elders being addressed are in time as well as place.

PROVIDING PUBLIC HEALTH SERVICES TO RURAL ELDERS

The public health system in rural communities must contend with economic, spatial, and cultural constraints to meet the needs of older residents. Because the needs of older adults have little overlap with those of younger residents, the provision of services almost always reflects the tension of allocating scarce resources among diverse population segments.

The focus of public health for older adults is long-term care, those services that help older adults continue to live independently in the community. The sources of long-term care range from informal care to formal services provided by governmental and private organizations. The focus of long-term care includes preventive services, as well as services needed to deal with disability and chronic disease.

Informal Care

Health needs of older adults are met first through informal-care networks. Within these networks, spouses are the most usual caregivers. Because rural elders are more likely to be married than those in urban areas, they are more likely to be able to draw on spousal assistance. Rural couples have been found to hold very traditional ideas about gender roles (Stoller & Lee, 1994), and these tend to favor men when it comes to health issues. Stoller and Lee argue that rural elders see women as more naturally caring (Stoller & Lee, 1994).

This is borne out by their concerns for men's health that may result in men following better diets and engaging more often in other health-promoting behaviors.

Adult children form the second tier of informal assistance. Because rural elders have more children, on the average, than urban elders, and are less likely to be childless, there may be a rural advantage (Stoller & Lee, 1994). However, within rural areas, there are clear differences in the availability of children. Rural nonfarm elders have the least access to children, due to the limited economic and educational opportunities for younger people in many rural towns. Elders who dwell on farms have the greatest access to children, particularly sons, as they are involved with the farm enterprise. Reflecting the traditional rural gender roles, sons tend to provide services related to the farm–transportation, home repair, or yard work. Kivett (1988) reports that rural fathers receive significantly less help in health-related areas from sons, in comparison to that received by mothers from daughters. She further notes that there is no evidence that daughters-in-law provide a level of support that is equivalent to the level of support provided by daughters (Kivett, 1988).

Friends and neighbors appear more likely to fill gaps in support networks in rural areas than in urban settings. Elders who have aged in place have friends with whom they share decades of experiences. Their assistance tends to be for fairly low level, although important, functions, e.g., checking on the well-being of elders and sharing excess garden produce (Quandt et al., 2001; Rowles, 1981). Van Willigen (1989) notes that elders withdraw from such neighborly exchanges when they become too frail or have resources too limited to reciprocate in some way for assistance. Thus, the role of friends and neighbors as helpers for older rural adults is quite limited.

Voluntary organizations form another tier of informal care support for elders. Although there are not rural–urban differences in participation in voluntary organizations, rural elders are advantaged over the urban in participation in church-related activities. A greater proportion of elders in rural communities belong to churches and participate more frequently. While there are regional differences, the church appears to be a support organization for those elders who are lifelong rural residents. Rural values support traditional religious orientations, and, in the absence of other foci, churches are centers of activities in many small towns. African American communities, in particular, have centered activities around the church, and these churches are a source of emotional and material support. However, little is known about the churches' ability to provide long-term support. Greater numbers of women have entered the workforce, the network of women in churches who can assist others may not be as large as in the past.

The other types of voluntary organization important for rural elders are agricultural organizations. The Grange has been a traditional multigenerational family-based organization in the Midwest and West. The Cooperative Extension Service administers a number of programs throughout the United States. Traditionally, homemaker clubs have been a focus for women, offering instruction on food- and health-related topics. However, similar to most organizations in rural communities, the Cooperative Extension Service is oriented toward all age groups, and programs for older persons compete for resources with those intended for other age groups.

Senior centers constitute another voluntary organization for older adults. While participation in senior centers is limited in urban (12.5%) and suburban (14.0%) areas, 14.8% of rural nonfarm elders participate in activities sponsored by senior centers (Krout, Cutler, &

Coward, 1990). Krout (1998) notes that there are more senior centers per population in rural areas. These centers are a focal point for activities, frequently providing transportation, health screenings, and other services needed by elders.

Hired home-based services supplement the informal care networks of elders. Available data suggest that rural elders are disadvantaged relative to urban elders in the availability of such services (Krout, 1998). For those with economic means, hired help paid for by the elder or a caregiver is the most available source of home-based services. However, such arrangements are sometimes problematic for rural elders. Although paying for services may allow the older person to maintain a sense of independence, payment may conflict with rural values of cooperation and sharing. Quandt and colleagues found that rural elders in several contexts noted that helpers would not accept payment, or that the elders were reluctant to offer (Quandt et al., 2001; Quandt, Arcury, McDonald, Bell, & Vitolins, 2001; Quandt, McDonald, Arcury, Bell, & Vitolins, 2000). Stoller and Lee (1994) point out that rural elders are not accustomed to paying for services, particularly at wages usual for the service industry, and this hampers their ability to hire and to retain help for in-home services.

Formal Care

The Older Americans Act authorizes funds to states for a variety of formal, community-based services. These include health and social services, such as senior centers, transportation, nutrition, home health care, adult day care, respite services, and chore services. Most of these services are developed and administered by the 670 local Area Agencies on Aging (AAAs) throughout the United States. In rural areas, these AAAs are particularly important because of the lack of other private organizations that provide services, as well as groups to whom AAAs can subcontract services. Krout (1986; 1998; 1991) has noted that rural AAAs provide fewer services than those in urban areas, and offering a service often does not guarantee that it is available throughout the area served by the rural AAA. Distances and caps on numbers of clients that can be served restrict access for many services.

There is considerable variation among rural communities in the types and amounts of services offered, but some generalizations have been offered. Most of the delivery models used have been developed in urban areas and co-opted for rural. Often the service providers have not been trained to understand the differences between rural and urban communities and to plan specifically for rural elders. Because little evaluation has been conducted of rural formal services, service providers have little insight into what works and what does not. At least some of the problems faced in developing rural programs is due to the way regulatory and funding policies have disadvantaged rural areas (Krout, 1998). There are four types of formal services for which needs and service delivery requirements differ significantly in rural communities from urban.

Transportation Services

Transportation is a major unmet need of older Americans as they seek to maintain mobility and independence, while coping with age-related physical and social changes (Burkhardt, Berger, Creedon, & McGavock, 1998). Its importance in rural areas cannot be overestimated. Older adults in many rural areas have fewer transportation options compared to their urban and suburban counterparts. At the same time, rural residences,

services, and facilities are spatially dispersed. When formal transportation services are absent or insufficient, rural older adults must drive private cars, be dependent on family and friends, or pay high fees to informal drivers to secure necessary health services (e.g., groceries, prescription medicine, health care), or their needs for these services are not met (Quandt, McDonald, Arcury, Bell, & Vitolins, 1999). Transportation is considered a major barrier to the use of health services by service providers and older adults in rural communities (Arcury, Quandt, Bell, McDonald, & Vitolins, 1998).

According to 1995 Nationwide Personal Transportation Study (NPTS) data (Center for Transportation Analysis, 2001), 86 percent of all trips and 91 percent of all miles traveled in the United States are by private vehicle. Older adults are even more likely than the general population to depend on private vehicles to meet their transportation needs. According to the same NPTS data, 89 percent of trips by adults aged sixty-five and older are by private vehicle. A survey of rural Iowa residents aged seventy-five and older showed that 92 percent of trips made the previous day were by private car; 6 percent were on foot, while less than 1 percent involved use of public transportation (Foster, Damiano, Momany, & McLeran, 1995).

According to NPTS data, adults sixty-five years and older make fewer (3.4 vs. 4.4) and shorter (6.5 vs. 9.1 miles) trips than their younger counterparts. Older adults as a group also limit the times and situations in which they drive. They drive less at night, during rush-hour traffic, on congested streets and freeways, and when weather and road conditions are bad (Benekohal, Michaels, Shim, & Resende, 1994; Chu, 1994; Rothe, 1990). While these self-imposed reductions and limitations in driving have a positive effect on safety, little is known about their impact on mobility.

Many women in rural communities never learned to drive. Women are more likely than men to stop driving, as are persons with lower incomes, those who are no longer employed, those with others living in the same household, and urban versus rural residents (Chipman, 1998; Kington, Reuben, Rogowski, & Lillard, 1994; Marottoli et al., 1993). Age itself is strongly correlated with driving and, to a lesser extent, so are a number of medical conditions common to aging (Ball et al., 1998; Campbell, Bush, & Hale, 1993; Kington et al., 1994; Owsley, Stalvey, Wells, & Sloane, 1999).

When questioned directly about why they stopped driving, older adults most commonly cite health and vision problems, or simply a lack of comfort driving or loss of confidence in their ability to drive safely (Hakamies-Blomqvist & Wahlstrom, 1998; Kington et al., 1994; Persson, 1993; Rabbitt, Carmichael, Jones, & Holland, 2000). Financial and economic reasons are also cited (Rabbit et al., 2000). Loss of comfort in driving is sometimes triggered by involvement in a crash or by a near-crash situation (Stutts, Wilkins, & Schatz, 1999). Although most studies of driving cessation have been conducted on urban populations, Johnson (1995) obtained similar results from a sample of elderly men and women living in a very rural section of the western United States. Burns (1999) suggested that a possible explanation for older adults' discomfort with driving may be a decline in navigational abilities (sense of direction, ability to read signs while stopped and moving, identifying left-right directions, etc.). In a study of rural elders, Quandt et al. (1999) found strategies, such as avoiding night driving, taking routes with only right turns, and even driving with one wheel off the shoulder of the road, used by elders to compensate for reduced comfort with driving.

A number of researchers have drawn a link between driving and quality of life. Cut-ler (1975) followed a sample of 104 elderly persons in a small Ohio community over a period of two and one-half years, and found that after controlling for subjective health, family income, age, sex, and residential location, those with transportation (i.e., able to drive and with access to a car) were significantly more likely to have stable or increasing life-satisfaction scores than those without transportation. In a more recent study of rural older adults' decisions to stop driving, interviews with individuals who had recently given up their license revealed feelings of regret and social isolation (Johnson, 1995). Loss of a driver's license has routinely been equated with loss of independence and diminution of one's sense of self-worth (Burkhardt et al., 1998; Eisenhandler, 1990; Stutts et al., 1999). Older women are particularly vulnerable to mobility loss, since they are more likely than men to give up driving, to live alone, and to be poor (Eberhard, 1999; Siegel, 1996).

Stamatiadis, Leinbach, & Watkins (1996) view transportation as a crucial link to community resources for the rural elderly in meeting a variety of needs. In their study of rural elderly travel, they noted that, in addition to transportation for such critical needs as medical care, transportation for social and recreational purposes is important to the physical and mental well-being and should constitute an important policy objective.

There is very little available information about the strategies older adults adopt for meeting their transportation needs once they curtail driving or stop altogether. The fact that they typically end up traveling less, and being unhappy with their inability to travel where they need or want to go, suggests that the strategies practiced are not entirely satisfactory. Again examining NPTS data (Center for Transportation Analysis, 2001), one finds that with increasing age, older adults are less likely to drive themselves and more likely to ride as a passenger in a car. Over 70 percent of adults aged sixty-five to sixty-nine are drivers when travelling in private vehicles, compared to only 49 percent of adults aged eighty-five and older. This suggests that a primary strategy for older adults unable to drive is to have someone else drive them. This other person is most frequently a spouse (for women) or other family member (most often a daughter or son), but it can also be a friend or other nonrelative (Burkhardt et al., 1998). However, in rural areas where there is an absence of formal transportation alternatives, family members and friends or neighbors cannot always meet the transportation needs of elderly persons, forcing some older adults to continue to drive despite their deteriorating abilities and the risk to their own and others' safety (Stamatiadis et al.,1996).

Few older adults use a paid driver or rely on taxis, busses, special transportation for the elderly, or other forms of public transportation. Overall, less than 2 percent of the trips made by older adults are by public transportation (NPTS, 1995). Reasons offered by older adults for not using public transportation include inconvenience, cost, security and safety, and the simple fact that public transportation does not go where they want to go, when they want to go there (Burkhardt et al., 1998; Stutts et al., 1999). Beyond these reasons, only a minority of older adults have regular public transportation available to them. This is especially true for those who live in rural areas.

Seldom do rural communities have inexpensive public transportation. Many rural communities have initiated free van services for their older and disabled populations to address this need. However, travel on these van services must often be scheduled at least a day before traveling, and the traveler must spend the extra time of going to the destinations of other passengers and waiting for them. Rural elders therefore are limited in their ability to travel to public services (congregate meal sites, health fairs, clinics), to shop for food, to obtain medical care, or to obtain prescriptions. One of the positive aspects of some rural communities is that some retailers are willing to deliver food and prescriptions to older adults at no charge (Quandt, Arcury, & Bell, 1998).

Nutrition Services

Because adequate nutrition is important for disease prevention and health promotion, nutrition services are critical for a range of health issues. In addition, nutrition services can contribute to the well-being and quality of life of older adults because food and the act of eating embody core social and cultural values (Quandt, 1999).

Older adults in general are considered to be at nutritional risk because of the biological and social changes that accompany aging (Quandt et al., 1998). Absorption of some nutrients is impaired, and the actual requirements for nutrients may increase. The lower physical-activity levels of many older adults require them to ingest fewer calories. As a result, they are likely to consume lower than recommended levels of vitamins and minerals, unless ways are found to increase the nutrient density of the diet (Vitolins et al., 2000a). This is made more problematic by the fact that older adults' mechanisms of hunger and satiety are less efficient, reducing their ability to regulate their intake of energy (Roberts et al., 1994). Drug interactions and poor oral health also pose problems for getting adequate nutrients (Marcus, Kaste, & Brown, 1994; Roe, 1989; Rolls, 1992). Changes in social and personal circumstances, such as retirement, reduced income, and widowhood, can all change what, how, and with whom older adults eat. Eating alone has been cited as a risk factor for eating fewer and less adequate meals (Davis, Murphy,

Neuhaus, & Lein, 1990; McIntosh & Shifflett, 1984; Quandt, Vitolins, DeWalt, & Roos, 1997).

While these changes affect all adults, regardless of residence, those in rural areas may well be at greater risk due to issues of lower-income, education, and health status (Ralston & Cohen, 1994). Getting adequate food can be harder due to the more limited inventory of rural grocery stores and higher prices. Transportation for shopping is a problem for many. In contrast, the tradition of home food production found in many rural communities may enhance the nutritional resources available to rural elders (Quandt, Popyach, & DeWalt, 1994).

Data to evaluate the nutritional status of rural elders are sparse. Studies have been conducted in local populations, at different times, with different sampling frames, and using different data collection techniques. Because of the heterogeneity of rural populations, it is impossible to make generalizations concerning nutrient intakes. The region from which the greatest number of studies have emerged is the southeastern United States. In this region, characterized by a large number of rural elders and minority rural elders, income, education, and ethnicity make a difference in diet and nutritional status. Data from a variety of studies show that a substantial proportion of older adults eat fewer than three meals per day (Kolasa, Mitchell, & Jobe, 1995; Lee, Templeton, & Wang, 1995; Quandt, Vitolins, DeWalt, & Roos, 1997). Such eating patterns are associated with lower dietary quality and lower nutrient intakes. Lee and colleagues (1991) found that African Americans had poorer nutrient intakes than Whites in a sample from eleven southern states. However, ethnic differences disappeared when socioeconomic status was taken into account. In comparing dietary intakes of rural White, African American and Native American elders from rural North

Carolina, Vitolins, and colleagues (2000a) found that African American males have significantly lower intakes of a number of nutrients than other men, although there were no ethnic differences among women.

The use of vitamin and mineral supplements is widespread across the U.S. population, including older adults. Because of the lower activity level and generally lower intakes of foods among the elderly, achieving satisfactory dietary intakes through foods alone is difficult for many older persons. Lee and colleagues (1991) found that 34 percent of rural elders used supplements, and that their total nutrient intake was higher than that of nonusers. Vitolins and colleagues (2000b) found 47 percent of elders used supplements and had higher total intakes. However, when diet and supplements were assessed separately, Vitolins and colleagues (2000b) found that supplements tended to be used by those whose diets were already adequate, rather than those needing supplemental vitamin and mineral intakes. Thus, nutrition counseling may need to be directed toward more effective use of supplements in rural populations.

Title III nutrition programs, congregate meals, and home-delivered meals, are available in most rural communities. Congregate meals are designed to provide social interaction, as well as a nutritious meal, while home-delivered meals are intended to assist disabled or homebound individuals and their spouses. Because of the dispersed population, rural areas face significant obstacles in providing meal services to all eligible elders. For congregate meals, participants without personal transportation must be provided van service to a central site. To maximize the number of clients served, some programs operate vans on different routes each day. Distance and transportation also limited home-delivered meals. Program regulations constrain travel times for prepared foods, and volunteers must be recruited to deliver meals

(McDonald, Quandt, Arcury, Bell, & Vitolins, 2000; Quandt & Rao, 1999).

Food security is a concern in rural populations, as lower incomes and transportation difficulties may prevent elders from having an ensured supply of adequate food. Declines in functional status and loss of spousal assistance often force elders to reduce gardening and other home food production. An Urban Institute study of hunger among the elderly found that most elders in rural Kentucky dealt with food shortages by "belt-tightening" actions—such as eating smaller meals and making do—rather than actively trying to access food pantries and other emergency sources (Quandt & Rao, 1999). Rural values of self-sufficiency and experience with seasonality of work and income may make rural elders less likely than their urban counterparts to seek assistance (Quandt et al., 2001). Quandt and colleagues found some rural elders reluctant to use nutrition programs because they perceived them as a form of "welfare," but they were willing to accept food shared by friends and neighbors. Food sharing fit better with rural values, but it was not a reliable source of food (Quandt, Arcury, Bell, Vitolins, & McDonald, in press; Quandt, Arcury, McDonald, Bell, & Vitolins, in press).

The central role of food and nutrition in health promotion and disease prevention make this an area of concern for public health programs. Rural areas have fewer private services that can support the nutritional needs of older adults, and, as a result, there tend to be fewer options to Title III services for rural elders than for those in other areas.

Health Promotion and Preventive Services

Delaying the onset of disability and dependence is recognized as a goal for public health across all segments of the population. While this applies to rural populations, there has been relatively little research directed specifically at barriers to health promotion in rural elderly populations. Similarly, there is little evidence about differences from urban elders in availability of health-promotion programs, rates of participation, and successful approaches to health promotion (FallCreek, Muchow, & Mockenhaupt, 1994). The assumption that rural elders are more active and healthier than other elders may lead to the conclusion that health-promotion services are less needed in rural areas, but the assumption is not supported by data.

Several factors may limit health promotion among rural populations. They include poverty and availability of health professionals and their services. There has been a gradual expansion of preventive services covered by Medicare, an important factor in the rural population where private-insurance coverage is lower and poverty is higher than among urban elders. Medicare has shifted from its original focus on acute and in-hospital care to include such services as influenza and pneumonia vaccines, and cancer screenings (Pap, mammography, colorectal examinations). Bone-mineral-density testing and diabetes self-management have recently been added for the management of chronic disease. However, two areas of health promotion most linked to functional decline and disability—smoking cessation and nutrition counseling—are still not covered. Particularly in rural tobacco-producing areas, smoking has been an accepted practice, and attempts at cessation must deal with the way that tobacco has been integral to the economic and social processes of these communities.

Successful models of health promotion in rural populations must take into account the restrictions of physical environment, as well as rural values. Physical inactivity, which has been identified as a focus for health promotion across the population, is an example of the obstacles faced in rural health promotion (Anonymous, 1998). In a comparison of rural and urban older women, Wilcox and colleagues (Wilcox, Castro, King, Housemann, & Brownson, 2000) found that rural women, particularly those in the South and those with less education, were more sedentary than urban. Rural women cited more barriers to leisure-time physical activity, including lack of access to facilities, street lights, and sidewalks. In addition, rural women reported not seeing others exercise, less social support for exercise, and greater interference of caregiving demands with physical activity. Minority women (African American and Native American) were particularly likely to be sedentary and to cite barriers to leisure-time physical activity. Because many rural residents spent their working years in occupations that were physically active, engaging in such activities during leisure hours is not an established habit. Misra, Quandt, & Aguillon (1999) found that physical activity among older adults did not seem to be as strongly associated with other health-promoting behaviors (e.g., nutrition) as might be expected. Such findings suggest that the promotion of active lifestyles in older rural populations may need to address different issues than promotion in a nonrural population.

Some rural health-promotion programs have centered on the rural church and its role as a focus for rural life. The Black Churches United for Better Health Project tested a church-based intervention to improve fruit and vegetable consumption in rural North Carolina (Campbell et al., 2000). They were successful in enlisting the help of minority rural congregations from a variety of denominations to conduct nutrition classes, change the dietary intake at church-sponsored events, and promote increased fruit and vegetable intakes through pastoral sermons and printed materials. The program was success-

ful at increasing fruit and vegetable intakes among adults, including older adults. Other church-based programs have trained lay health advisors who can spread health-promotion advice through social networks (Eng, 1993). Churches have also been used to promote smoking cessation and health screenings.

The rural shortages of health professionals across all of the allied health fields present a barrier to preventive services and health promotion. Much of the recruitment of health professionals into rural areas has centered on acute-care personnel. Public health departments have responsibility for prevention in all age groups, thus the competition for scarce personnel places elders at a disadvantage. In rural areas, most health-promotion programs have been administered by Area Agencies on Aging or by the United States Department of Agriculture (USDA) Cooperative Extension Service.

FallCreek et al. (1994) cite several models of successful health promotion projects for rural elders. They stress that a variety of approaches can be used to overcome the barriers of the rural environment. For example, use of interactive videos or train-the-trainer programs allows volunteers or laypersons to run health-promotion sessions and reduces the need for health professionals. Inclusion of traditional practices (e.g., foods or physical activities) will make programs fit better within the cultural milieu of the rural community. Because so much of the care of elders takes place through informal caregiving, programs on health-promotion issues for elders that are actually aimed at their caregivers may be an effective way to provide information. A variety of ways can be devised to reduce dependence on face-to-face contact for programs. Some have used mailed printed material to contain costs. Although there are always issues with regard to vision and literacy, careful development and distribution of printed materials may be effective in many circumstances. However, because some mental and physical health problems of rural adults may be related to social isolation, attention to communication strategies that minimize isolation should be sought, while trying to contain costs. This could include the use of telephone, of contacts by other personnel who normally see elders (e.g., letter carriers), or incorporation of health messages into existing events, such as church programs and congregate meal programs. In many instances, older adults can be reached by multigeneration programs that address younger adults (e.g., cancer-screening programs and nutrition). This reduces the competition for resources among programs and draws on the rural values of family.

Mental Health Services

There have been no comprehensive epidemiological surveys of mental health and mental disorders that permit definitive characterization of rural elders or differentiation of their mental health status from that of other older adults. The Epidemiological Catchment Area program of National Institute of Mental Health (NIMH) and National Institute on Aging (NIA) surveyed approximately 20,000 elderly persons across five areas (Robins & Regier, 1991). In Durham, NC and St Louis, MO, the samples included both rural and urban elderly. Within these sites, no striking differences were found between rural and urban residents, nor were any differences consistent across locations.

Even if rural populations experience mental illness rates comparable to urban and suburban populations, the prevalence in rural communities may be fairly high. Dowart (1990), for example, estimates that 15 percent to 25 percent of the rural elders sixty-five and over have some type of psychiatric illness.

Reynolds and Kupfer (1999) report that one in six older patients seen in general medical practice is depressed. In a survey of executive directors of AAAs, Bane, Rathbone-McCuan, & Balliher (1994) found a fairly uniform ranking of mental health problems for elders across rural and mixed planning and service areas. Loneliness and depression were ranked as the common problems, followed by memory impairment, anxiety, and grief. Drug use and psychiatric disorders, such as paranoia and personality disorders, ranked much lower.

Aspects of the rural environment may contribute to mental illness. Out-migration of children, loss of spouses, and failing health all can exacerbate the isolation rural elders already experience. In a study of 3,000 rural elders in Iowa, Russell, Cutrona, de la Mora, & Wallace (1997) found that loneliness predicted admission to nursing homes and decreased time to admission. In addition, the life courses that many elders have followed with low educational attainment and manual-labor occupations may lead to false-positives on screening instruments such as the Mini-Mental Status Examination (Keefover et al., 1996).

Two problems impede improving the mental health of rural elders: limited availability of services and low usage. Cutbacks in services and closure of rural hospitals where elderly have traditionally obtained care have led to fewer services and greater distance to services in rural communities (Neese, Abraham, & Buckwalter, 1999). Fortney, Rost, Zhang, & Warren (1999) examined data on geographic accessibility and treatment for depression and found that those with greater travel time were less likely to obtain care in accordance with Agency for Health Care Research and Quality guidelines. Rural areas have fewer trained mental health professionals. For acute and chronic mental conditions, most rural elders lack access to geriatric psychiatric specialists. Community mental health services are also less available in rural communities than those that serve a mix of rural, suburban, and urban elders. Bane et al.'s (1994) survey of AAAs showed that a basic list of mental health services was provided by 62 percent of AAAs. Some, such as telephone reassurance and mental health screening, had an availability greater than 88 percent. Others, such as adult day care, mental health outreach, and grief support were available in less than 70 percent. Almost all services listed were less available in rural areas, and may not always be available for the entire, dispersed rural population in an area (Bane et al., 1994).

A variety of studies have shown low rates of utilization of mental health services by rural elders (Durenberger, 1989; Office of Technology Assessment, 1990). While this can in part be attributed to access, it may also be linked to a rural value system that stresses "making do," sees use of assistance as a sign of weakness, and stigmatizes mental illness (Buckwalter, Smith, & Caston, 1994; Heltsley, 1976). Bane (1997) suggests that a case manager approach, using various outreach and educational models, may be helpful in overcoming these cultural barriers.

Additional Issues for Providing Public Health Services

Two issues linked to rural values and belief systems should be considered when analyzing public health and the rural elderly. The first, religion, has been mentioned throughout this chapter; the information that follows summarizes research specifically on health and religion. The second, complementary and alternative medicine, is of increasing interest throughout the health professions.

Religion and Health among Rural Elderly

Religion has a prominent place in rural U.S. culture, and there are cultural differences between rural and urban society in the emphasis on religion (Chalfant & Heller, 1991). While strongly religious elders are found everywhere, religion has a central role in the belief systems of people who live in more rural places. Conservative Christian religion is extremely salient to those who live in rural communities. This pervasive nature of religion for rural-community residents has been documented for African Americans (e.g., McAuley, Pecchioni, & Grant, 2000; Nye, 1993), as well as for Whites (e.g., Peacock & Tyson, 1989; Scott, 1995; Titon, 1988). The great importance of religious belief and performance of religious practices among the older residents of rural communities has an acknowledged relationship to their health.

The importance of relationships between religion and health among older adults is demonstrated in the work of several scholars (e.g., Koenig et al., 1997; Koenig et al., 1998; Koenig et al., 1999; Koenig, Larson, & Weaver, 1998; Krause, 1997; Krause, Chatters, & Meltzer, 2000; Krause, Ingersoll-Dayton, Ellison, & Wulff, 1999; Levin, Larson, & Puchalski, 1997; Levin & Taylor, 1997), the emphasis of the joint-research programs on religion and aging funded by the Fetzer Foundation and NAI, and the efforts to develop better measures of religiosity (Fetzer Institute, 1999). However, while the strength of religious belief in rural communities is acknowledged, there is little research on religion and spirituality and health in rural communities (exceptions include Arcury, Quandt, McDonald, & Bell, 2000; McAuley et al., 2000; Mitchell & Weatherly, 2000).

Both organized religion and individual religiosity are important to public health among older rural adults. Religious organizations (churches) are foci for providing formal services and instrumental support, as well as social and emotional support to rural elders (e.g., Rowles, 1985, 1986). Rural churches are important institutions for facilitating public health programs. For example, the nutrition intervention for cancer prevention in rural North Carolina was based in churches (Campbell et al., 2000). The National Institutes of Health (NIH) has supported the development of manuals for using churches as sites for public health programs (e.g., George, Daniel, Worthington, & Malcom, 1994; National Institutes of Health, 1992). Rural churches are often the sites of direct programs to older adults, such as congregate meal programs and home-delivered meal programs. Church members usually help their older congregates when the congregates are ill and often provide direct help with such needs as home repairs.

Individual religiosity or spirituality is related to health status, health beliefs, and health behavior among older elders. Mitchell and Weatherly (2000) show that religiosity is positively associated with mental health among rural older adults in eastern North Carolina. McAuley et al. (2000) discuss how rural older African Americans and Whites describe the place of religion in their health beliefs. They found that African Americans were more likely than Whites to have specific role expectations for God in the experience of their health and illness (McAuley et al., 2000). Arcury, Quandt, McDonald, and Bell (2000a) show how African American, Native American, and White rural elders integrate religious beliefs and behaviors into their health self-management practices.

The understanding of roles of organized and individual religion in the health of rural elders must be further developed. The potential of churches as avenues for providing public health services must be better realized in a manner that does not infringe on individual beliefs. The ways that individuals incorporate religious practice and spirituality into their health behaviors need to be better understood.

Complementary and Alternative Medicine Use among Rural Elderly

Americans use a great deal of complementary and alternative medicine (CAM) (Eisenberg et al., 1993; Eisenberg et al., 1998). CAM use by older adults has positive aspects. Individuals are taking greater interest and responsibility for their health, and there is an expansion of the biomedical model to a more holistic model of health. There is, in addition, an increased respect for cultural diversity (Astin, Pelletier, Marie, & Haskell, 2000). However, the increased use of CAM also has negative aspects. These include individuals' discontinuing use of proven and effective therapies for unproven, ineffective, and even harmful therapies; the ill effects of interactions of CAM and prescribed medicines; and financial losses incurred from aggressively marketed fraudulent products (e.g., Bigby, 1998; Jarvis, 1999).

CAM use should be high among rural older adults, and understanding this CAM use is important for public health practice in rural communities. Rural communities have historically had less access to formal medical care than urban and suburban communities (see Gesler & Ricketts, 1992; Ricketts, 1999). Through necessity, the residents of rural communities made use of home and folk remedies, as well as use of folk practitioners. Rural populations have had lower incomes and higher rates of poverty than urban and suburban populations and were less able to afford conventional medical care. In addition, the types of employment of many residents in rural areas, such as agriculture and small business, have resulted in a lower proportion of rural residents having health insurance, reducing further rural residents' ability to afford conventional medical care. The cultural systems of rural communities are generally conservative and traditional. Given the traditional values and limited cosmopolitan tendencies of rural communities, the types of CAM used by rural residents would be less likely to include "new-age" therapies (e.g., aroma therapy) and those that are imbedded in non-Western religious traditions (e.g., acupuncture, meditation), and more likely to include Western folk and home therapies.

However, knowledge of the prevalence of CAM use and types of CAM used by rural older adults remains an area of conjecture. There has been virtually no research on CAM use in rural elderly populations (or in any elderly U.S. populations for that matter [Astin et al., 2000]). Kirkland, Mathews, Sullivan, and Baldwin (1992) present several chapters that discuss the use of folk remedies as part of rural and minority culture in the southeast United States. There has been some empirical research on the use of CAM in rural communities and in the general southeast United States. For example, Mathews reports on the practice of "rootwork" among African Americans in eastern North Carolina (Mathews, 1987). However, because this investigation focused on the belief system surrounding rootwork, the distribution of this belief system in the general African American or rural population of this region is unclear. Cavender and Beck (1995) conducted a survey of 102 respondents aged sixty and older in a rural western Virginia community with a predominantly White population. They found general knowledge of home and folk medicines, and their older respondents reported that their parents made moderate use of home and folk remedies. However, these contemporary older adults made little use of home and folk remedies and relied largely on conventional medical care. Arcury, Quandt, Bell, et al. (2000) draw on data from a multi-year ethnographic study in two rural North Carolina counties. Their sample of 108 individuals aged seventy and older included African American, Native American, and White men and women. They found that home and folk remedies and vitamin and mineral supplements were used by most of these older adults. Men and women did not differ in CAM use. African and Native American elders used home and folk remedies more than White elders; White and Native American elders used vitamin and mineral supplements more than African American elders.

CAM use has the potential for improving as well as diminishing the health of rural elders. The indications are that rural older adults tend to use home and folk tonics and remedies rather than alternative systems of care, such as homeopathy. A great deal more effort must be directed at understanding CAM use among rural older adults. Additional studies of CAM use are needed to assess regional variation. Health care providers should be aware that a large number of their patients use CAM and may need counseling to minimize CAM-drug interactions.

CONCLUSIONS

Knowledge of many issues related to public health and the rural elderly is limited. Large-scale studies focused solely on rural elders are rare, and the numbers of rural residents in large national studies is often too small for meaningful separate analysis. This lack of firm knowledge is made even less certain by the constant change of rural communities, as population migration and changes in communication alter the population composition and rural way of life.

Despite this lack of knowledge, one can conclude that many public health-related services are more difficult to provide in rural settings. There needs to be creative new models of service delivery developed for diverse rural communities, rather than simply adapting those from urban areas. Social and cultural studies of the rural elderly make it clear that approaches to public health need to be culturally appropriate and sensitive to the belief systems of older adults.

Perhaps the greatest challenge for the future lies in the changes one can expect in rural elders. The current eighty-year-old resident of a rural community, born in 1920, differs significantly from a sixty-year-old son or daughter, born in 1940. From a life course perspective, it is clear that the coming generation of elders will be different from their parents. They will enter old age with different experiences and different health exposures. Their expectations for health and functioning may be different, and they will have had a lifetime of experience with modern medicine. The challenge for public health is to provide appropriate services for rural elders today, and to be adaptable to the elders of the next generation.

REFERENCES

Anonymous. (1998). Self-reported physical inactivity by degree of urbanization–United States, 1996. *MMWR–Morbidity & Mortality Weekly Report, 47,* 1097–1100.

Arcury, T. A., Quandt, S. A., Bell, R. A., McDonald, J., & Vitolins, M. Z. (1998). Barriers to nutritional well-being for rural elders: community experts' perceptions. *The Gerontologist, 38,* 490–498.

Arcury, T. A., Quandt, S. A., Bell, R. A., & Vitolins, M. Z. (2000). Complementary and alternative medicine use among rural older adults. Manuscript under review.

Arcury, T. A., Quandt, S. A., McDonald, J., & Bell, R. A. (2000). Faith and health self-management of rural older adults. *Journal of Cross-Cultural Gerontology, 15,* 55–74.

Astin, J. A., Pelletier, K. R., Marie, A., & Haskell, W. L. (2000). Complementary and alternative medicine use among elderly persons: One-year analysis of a Blue Shield Medicare supplement. *Journals of Gerontology: Medical Sciences, 55A,* M4–M9.

Ball, K., Owsley, C., Stalvey, B., Roenker, D., Sloane, M., & Graves, M. (1998). Driving avoidance and functional impairment in older drivers. *Accident Analysis and Prevention, 30,* 313–322.

Bane, S. D. (1997). Rural mental health and aging: implication for case management. *Journal of Case Management, 6,* 158–161.

Bane, S. D., Rathbone-McCuan, E., & Galliher, J. M. (1994). Mental health services for the elderly in rural America. In J.A.Krout (Ed.), *Providing community-based services to the rural elderly* (pp. 243–266). Thousand Oaks, CA: Sage.

Benekohal, R. F., Michaels, R. M., Shim, E., & Resende, P. T. V. (1994). Effects of aging on older drivers' travel characteristics. *TRR, 1438,* 91–98.

Bigby, M. (1998). Snake oil for the 21st century. *Archives of Dermatology, 134,* 1512–1514.

Bokemeier, J., & Tickamyer, A. (1985). Labor force experiences of nonmetropolitan women. *Rural Sociology, 30,* 51–73.

Buckwalter, K., Smith, M., & Caston, C. (1994). Mental and social health of the rural elderly. In R. T. Coward, C. N. Bull, G. Kulkulka, & J. M. Gallaher (Eds.), *Health services for rural elders* (pp. 203–232). New York: Springer.

Burkhardt, J. E., Berger, A. M., Creedon, M., & McGavock, A. T. (1998). *Mobility and independence: Changes and challenges for older drivers.* Bethesda, MD: Ecosometrics.

Burns, P. C. (1999). Navigation and the mobility of older drivers. *Journal of Gerontology: Social Sciences, 54B,* S49–S55.

Campbell, M. K., Bush, T. L., & Hale, W. E. (1993). Medical conditions associated with driving cessation in community-dwelling, ambulatory elders. *Journal of Gerontology, 48,* S230–S234.

Campbell, M. K., Motsinger, B. M., Ingram, A., Jewell, D., Makarushka, C., Beatty, B., Dodds, J., McClelland, J., Demissie, S., & Demark-Wahnefried, W. (2000). The North Carolina Black Churches United for Better Health Project: Intervention and process evaluation. *Health Education & Behavior, 27,* 241–253.

Cavender, A. P., & Beck, S. H. (1995). Generational change, folk medicine, and medical self-care in a rural Appalachian community. *Human Organization, 54,* 129–142.

Center for Transportation Analysis. (2001). www-cta.ornl.gov/npts/1995/doc/index.shtml.

Chalfant, H. P., & Heller, P. L. (1991). Rural/urban versus regional differences in religiosity. *Review of Religious Research, 33,* 76–86.

Chipman, M. L. (1998). To drive or not to drive: The influence of social factors on the decisions of elderly drivers. *Accident Analysis and Prevention, 30,* 299–304.

Chu, X. (1994). *The effects of age on the driving habits of the elderly: Evidence from the 1990 National Personal Transportation Study* (Rep. No. DOT-T-95-12). Washington, DC: U.S. Department of Transportation.

Coward, R. T., Krout, J. A. (Eds.). (1998). *Aging in rural settings: Life circumstances & distinctive features.* New York: Springer.

Coward, R. T., & Lee, G. R. (1985). An introduction to aging in rural environments. In R. T. Coward & G. R. Lee (Eds.), *The elderly in rural society* (pp. 1–55). New York: Springer.

Cutler, S. J. (1975). Transportation and changes in life satisfaction. *The Gerontologist, 15,* 155–159.

Davis, M. A., Murphy, S. P., Neuhaus, J. M., & Lein, D. (1990). Living arrangements and dietary quality of older U.S. adults. *Journal of the American Dietetic Association, 90,* 1667–1672.

Dowart, R. A. (1990). Managed mental health care: Myths and realities in the 1990s. *Hospital and Community Psychiatry, 41,* 1087–1091.

Durenberger, D. (1989). Providing mental health care services to Americans. *American Psychologist, 44,* 1293–1297.

Eberhard, J. W. (1999). Safe mobility for senior citizens. *IATSS Research, 20,* 29–37.

Eisenberg, D. M., Davis, R. B., Ettner, S. L., Appel, S., Wilkey, S., Van Rompay, M., & Kessler, R. C. (1998). Trends in alternative medicine use in the United States, 1990–1997: Results of a follow-up national survey. *JAMA, 280,* 1569–1575.

Eisenberg, D. M., Kessler, R. C., Foster, C., Norlock, F. E., Calkins, D. R., & DelBanco, T. L. (1993). Unconventional medicine in the United States: Prevalence, costs, and patterns of use. *The New England Journal of Medicine, 28,* 246–252.

Eisenhandler, S. A. (1990). The asphalt identikit: Old age and the driver's license. *International Journal of Aging and Human Development, 30,* 1–14.

Eng, E. (1993). The Save Our Sisters project—A social network strategy for reaching rural black-women. *Cancer, 72,* 1071–1077.

FallCreek, S., Muchow, J., & Mockenhaupt, R. E. (1994). Health promotion with rural elders. In R. T. Coward, C. N. Bull, G. Kukulka, & J. M. Galliher. (Eds.), *Health services for rural elders* (pp. 182–202). New York: Springer.

Fetzer Institute. (1999). *Multidimensional measurement of religiousness/spirituality for use in health research: A report of the Fetzer Institute/National Institute on Aging working group (with additional psychometric data).* Kalamazoo, MI: Author.

Fortney, J., Rost, K., Zhang, M., & Warren, J. (1999). The impact of geographic accessibility on the intensity and quality of depression treatment. *Medical Care, 37,* 884–893.

Foster, N. S. J., Damiano, P. C., Momany, E. T., & McLeran, H. T. (1995). Travel patterns of rural elders. *Transportation Quarterly, 49,* 51–65.

George, Y. S., Daniel, A. B., Worthington, V. L., & Malcom, S. M. (1994). *The AAAS Black Church Health Connection Project: Hands on Life Sciences Activities.* Washington, DC: American Association for the Advancement of Science.

Gesler, W. M., Rabiner, D. J., & DeFriese, G. H. (1998). Introduction to research on rural health and aging issues. In W. M. Gesler, D. J. Rabiner, & G. H. DeFriese (Eds.), *Rural health and aging research: Theory, methods and practical applications* (pp. 1–13). Amityville, NJ: Baywood Publishing.

Gesler, W. M., & Ricketts, T. C., III, (Eds.). (1992). *Health in rural North America.* New Brunswick, NJ: Rutgers University Press.

Groger, B. L. (1983). Growing old with or without it. *Research on Aging, 5,* 511–526.

Hakamies-Blomqvist, L., & Wahlstrom, B. (1998). Why do older drivers give up driving? *Accident Analysis and Prevention, 30,* 305–312.

Heltsley, M. E. (1976). The aged in small town, U.S.A. *Journal of Home Economics, 68,* 46–50.

Jarvis, W. T. (1999). Quackery: The National Council Against Health Fraud perspective. *Rheumatic Disease Clinics of North America, 25,* 805–814.

Johnson, J. E. (1995). Rural elders and the decision to stop driving. *Journal of Community Health Nursing, 12,* 131–138.

Keefover, R. W., Rankin, E. D., Keyl, P. M., Wells, J. C., Martin, J., & Shaw, J. (1996). Dementing illnesses in rural populations: The need for research and challenges confronting investigators. *Journal of Rural Health, 12,* 178–187.

Kington, R., Reuben, D., Rogowski, J., & Lillard, L. (1994). Sociodemographic and health factors in driving patterns after 50 years of age. *American Journal of Public Health, 84,* 1327–1329.

Kirkland, J., Mathews, H. F., Sullivan, C. W., III, Baldwin, K. (Eds.). (1992). *Herbal and magical medicine: traditional healing today.* Durham, NC: Duke University Press.

Kivett, V. R. (1988). Older rural fathers and sons - Patterns of association and helping. *Family Relations, 37,* 62–67.

Koenig, H. G., Cohen, H. J., George, L. K., Hays, J. C., Larson, D. B., & Blazer, D. G. (1997). Attendance at religious services, interleukin-6, and other biological parameters of immune function in older adults. *International Journal of Psychiatry in Medicine, 27,* 233–250.

Koenig, H. G., George, L. K., Hays, J. C., Larson, D. B., Cohen, H. J., & Blazer, D. G. (1998). The relationship between religious activities and blood pressure in older adults. *International Journal of Psychiatry in Medicine, 28,* 189–213.

Koenig, H. G., Hays, J. C., Larson, D. B., George, L. K., Cohen, H. J., McCullough, M. E., Meador, K. G., & Blazer, D. G. (1999). Does religious attendance prolong survival? A six-year follow-up study of 3,968 older adults. *Journals of Gerontology. Series A, Biological Sciences & Medical Sciences, 54,* M370–M376.

Koenig, H. G., Larson, D. B., & Weaver, A. J. (1998). Research on religion and serious mental illness. *New Directions for Mental Health Services, 80,* 81–95.

Kolasa, K. M., Mitchell, J. P., & Jobe, A. C. (1995). Food behaviors of southern rural community-living elderly. *Archives of Family Medicine, 4,* 844–848.

Krause, N. (1997). Religion, aging, and health: Current status and future prospects. *Journal of Gerontology: Social Sciences, 52B,* S291–S293.

Krause, N., Chatters, L. M., & Meltzer, T. (2000). Using focus groups to explore the nature of prayer in late life. *Journal of Aging Studies, 14,* 191–212.

Krause, N., Ingersoll-Dayton, B., Ellison, C. G., & Wulff, K. M. (1999). Aging, religious doubt, and psychological well-being. *Gerontologist, 39,* 525–533.

Krout, J. A. (1986). *The aged in rural America.* New York: Greenwood Press.

——. (1991). Rural area agencies on aging - An overview of activities and policy issues. *Journal of Aging Studies, 5,* 409–424.

——. (1998). Services and service delivery in rural environments. In R. T. Coward & J. A. Krout (Eds.), *Aging in rural settings: Life circumstances & distinctive features* (pp. 247–266). New York: Springer.

Krout, J. A., Cutler, S. J., & Coward, R. T. (1990). Correlates of senior center participation–A national analysis. *Gerontologist, 30,* 72–79.

Lamphere, L. (1992). *Structuring diversity: Ethnographic perspectives on the new immigration.* Chicago: University of Chicago Press.

Lee, C. J., Templeton, S., & Wang, C. (1995). Meal skipping patterns and nutrient intakes of rural southern elderly. *Journal of Nutrition for the Elderly, 15,* 1–14.

Lee, C. J., Tsui, J., Glover, E., Glover, L. B., Kumelachew, M., Warren, A. P., Perry, G., Godwin, S., Hunt, S. K., McCray, M., & Stigger, F. E. (1991). Evaluation of nutrient intakes of rural elders in eleven southern states based on sociodemographic and life style indicators. *Nutrition Research, 11,* 1383–1396.

Levin, J. S., Larson, D. B., & Puchalski, C. (1997). Religion and spirituality in medicine and education. *JAMA, 278,* 792–793.

Levin, J. S., & Taylor, R. J. (1997). Age differences in patterns and correlates of the frequency of prayer. *Gerontologist, 37,* 75–88.

Lichter, D., & McLaughlin, D. (1995). Changing economic opportunities, family structure, and poverty in rural America. *Rural Sociology, 60,* 688–706.

Longino, C. F., Jr., & Smith, M. H. (1998). The impact of elderly migration on rural communities. In R. T. Coward & J. A. Krout (Eds.), *Aging in rural settings* (pp. 209–226). New York: Springer.

Marcus, S. E., Kaste, L. M., & Brown, L. J. (1994). Prevalence and demographic correlates of tooth loss among the elderly in the United States. *Special Care in Dentistry, 14,* 123–127.

Marottoli, R. A., Ostfeld, A. M., Merrill, S. S., Perlman, G. D., Foley, D. J., & Cooney, L. M. (1993). Driving cessation and changes in mileage driven among elderly individuals. *Journal of Gerontology: Social Sciences, 48,* S255–S260.

Mathews, H. F. (1987). Rootwork: Description of an ethnomedical system in the American South. *Southern Medical Journal, 80,* 885–891.

McAuley, W. J., Pecchioni, L., & Grant, J. A. (2000). Personal accounts of the role of God in health and illness among older rural African American and White residents. *Journal of Cross-Cultural Gerontology, 15,* 13–35.

McDonald J., Quandt, S. A., Arcury, T. A., Bell, R. A., & Vitolins, M. Z. (2000). On their own: Nutritional self-management strategies of rural widowers. *The Gerontologist, 40,* 480–491.

McIntosh, W. A., & Shifflett, P. A. (1984). The influence of social support systems on dietary intake of the elderly. *Journal of Nutrition of the Elderly, 4,* 5–18.

Misra, R., Quandt, S. A., & Aguillon, S. (1999). Differences in nutritional risk and nutrition-related behaviors in exercising and nonexercising rural elders. *American Journal of Health Promotion, 13,* 149–152.

Mitchell, J., & Weatherly, D. (2000). Beyond church attendance: Religiosity and mental health among rural older adults. *Journal of Cross-Cultural Gerontology, 15,* 37–54.

National Institutes of Health. (1992). *Churches as an avenue to high blood pressure control.* Bethesda, MD: National Institutes of Health (NIH).

Neese, J. B., Abraham, I. L., & Buckwalter, K. C. (1999). Utilization of mental health services among rural elderly. *Archives of Psychiatric Nursing, XIII,* 30–40.

Nye, W. P. (1993). Amazing grace: Religion and identity among elderly black individuals. *International Journal of Aging and Human Development, 36,* 103–114.

Office of Technology Assessment. 1990). Health care in rural America. (Rep. No. OTA-H-434). Washington, DC: U.S. Government Printing Office.

Owsley, C., Stalvey, B., Wells, J., & Sloane, M. E. (1999). Older drivers and cataract: Driving habits and crash risk. *Journal of Gerontology: Medical Sciences, 54A,* M203–M211.

Peacock, J. L., & Tyson, R. W., Jr. (1989). *Pilgrims of paradox: Calvinism and experience among Primitive Baptists of the Blue Ridge.* Washington, DC: Smithsonian Institution Press.

Persson, D. (1993). The elderly driver: Deciding when to stop. *The Gerontologist, 33,* 88–91.

Quandt, S. A. (1999). Social and cultural influences on food consumption and nutritional status. In M. E. Shils, J. A. Olson, M. Shike, & A. C. Ross (Eds.), *Modern nutrition in health and disease* (9th ed., pp. 1783–1792). Baltimore: Williams & Wilkins.

Quandt, S. A., Arcury, T. A., & Bell, R. A. (1998). Self-management of nutritional risk among older adults: Conceptual model and case studies from rural communities. *Journal of Aging Studies, 12,* 351–368.

Quandt, S. A., Arcury, T. A., Bell, R. A., Vitolins, M. Z., & McDonald, J. (2001). The social and nutritional meaning of food sharing among older rural adults. *Journal of Aging Studies, 15,* 145–162.

Quandt, S. A., Arcury, T. A., McDonald J., Bell, R. A., & Vitolins, M. Z. (in press). Meaning and management of food security among rural elders. *Journal of Applied Gerontology.*

Quandt, S. A., McDonald J., Arcury, T. A., Bell, R. A., & Vitolins, M. Z. (1999). Driving and transportation strategies of rural elders. *The Gerontologist, 39,* 302.

Quandt, S. A., McDonald J., Arcury, T. A., Bell, R. A., & Vitolins, M. Z. (2000). Nutritional strategies of elderly widows in rural communities. *The Gerontologist, 40,* 86–96.

Quandt, S. A., Popyach, J. B., & DeWalt, K. M. (1994). Home gardening and food preservation practices of the elderly in rural Kentucky. *Ecology of Food and Nutrition, 31,* 183–199.

Quandt, S. A., & Rao, P. (1999). Dimensions of hunger among the elderly in a rural community. *Human Organization, 58,* 28–35.

Quandt, S. A., Vitolins, M. Z., DeWalt, K. M., & Roos, G. (1997). Meal patterns of older adults in rural communities: Life course analysis and implications for undernutrition. *Journal of Applied Gerontology, 16,* 152–171.

Rabbitt, P., Carmichael, A., Jones, S., & Holland, C. (2000). *When and why older drivers give up driving.* London: AA Foundation for Road Safety Research.

Ralston, P. A., & Cohen, N. L. (1994). Nutrition and the rural elderly. In J. A. Krout (Ed.), *Providing community-based services to the rural elderly* (pp. 202–220). Thousand Oaks, CA: Sage.

Reynolds, C. F., & Kupfer, D. J. (1999). Depression and aging: A look to the future. *Psychiatric Services, 50,* 1167–1172.

Ricketts, T. C., III. (Ed.). (1999). *Rural health in the United States.* New York: Oxford University Press.

Roberts, S. B., Fuss, P., Heyman, M. B., Evans, W. J., Tsay, R., Rasmussen, H., Fiatarone, M., Coritella, J., Dallal, G. E., & Young, V. R. (1994). Control of food intake in older men. *Journal of the American Medical Association, 272,* 1601–1606.

Robins, L., & Regier, D. (1991). *Psychiatric disorders in America: The Epidemiologic Catchment Area Study.* New York: Free Press.

Roe, D. A. (1989). Drug-nutrient interactions in the elderly. In H. N. Munro & D. E. Danford (Eds.), *Nutrition, aging and the elderly* (pp. 363–384). New York: Plenum Press.

Rolls, B. J. (1992). Aging and appetite. *Nutrition Reviews, 50,* 422–426.

Rothe, J. P. (1990). *The safety of elderly drivers: Yesterday's young in today's traffic.* New Brunswick, N.J.: Transaction Publishers.

Rowles, G. D. (1981). The surveillance zone as meaningful space for the aged. *Gerontologist, 21,* 304–311.

——. (1985). The church as a focus of support for the rural elderly. *Gerontologist, 25,* 97.

——. (1986). The rural elderly and the church. *Journal of Religion and Aging, 2,* 79–98.

——. (1988). What's rural about rural aging–an Appalachian perspective. *Journal of Rural Studies, 4,* 115–124.

Russell, D. W., Cutrona, C. E., de la Mora, A., & Wallace R. B. (1997). Loneliness and nursing home admission among rural older adults. *Psychology & Aging, 12,* 574–589.

Satariano, W. A. (1997). Editorial: The disabilities of aging–looking to the physical environment. *American Journal of Public Health, 87,* 331–332.

Scott, S. L. (1995). *Two sides to everything: The cultural construction of class consciousness in Harlan County, Kentucky.* Albany, NY: State University Press of New York.

Siegel, J. (1996). *Aging into the 21st century* (Rep. No. HHS-100-95-0017). Washington, DC: Administration on Aging, U.S. Department of Health and Human Services.

Stamatiadis, N., Leinbach, T. R., & Watkins, J. F. (1996). Travel among non-urban elderly. *Transportation Quarterly, 50,* 113–121.

Stoller, E. P., & Lee, G. R. (1994). Informal care of rural elders. In R. T. Coward, C. N. Bull, G. Kukulka, & J. M. Galliher (Eds.), *Health services for rural elders* (pp. 33–64). New York: Springer.

Stutts, J. C., Wilkins, J. W., & Schatz, S. (1999). *The decision to stop driving: Results of focus groups with seniors and family members.* Rep. No. Paper presented at the 78th Annual Meeting of the Transportation Research Board, January 1999, Washington, DC.

Tickamyer, A., & Duncan, C. (1990). Poverty and opportunity structure in rural America. *Annual Review of Sociology, 16,* 67–86.

Titon, J. T. (1988). *Powerhouse for God: Speech, chant, and song in an Appalachian Baptist Church.* Austin, TX: University of Texas Press.

U.S. Bureau of the Census. (1992a). *Census of population and housing, 1990: Public use microdata samples U.S.* (machine-readable data files). Washington, DC: Author.

——. (1992b). *Census of population and housing, 1990: Public use microdata sample U.S. technical documentation.* Washington, DC: Author.

U.S. Department of Health and Human Services. (1996). *Rural residence of older Americans: State-by-state* statistical tables based on the 1990 Census of Population and Housing. (Rep. No. HHS-100-95-0017). Washington, DC: Author.

Van Nostrand, J. F. (1993). *Common beliefs about the rural elderly: What do national data tell us?* (Rep. No. DHHS Publication No. [PHS] 93-1412). Hyattsville, MD: National Center for Health Statistics.

van Willigen, J. (1989). *Gettin' some age on me: Social organization of older people in a rural American community.* Lexington, KY: University Press of Kentucky.

Vitolins, M. Z., Quandt, S. A., Case, L. D., Bell, R. A., Arcury, T. A., & McDonald, J. (2000a). Ethnic and gender variation in the dietary intake of rural elders. *Journal of Nutrition for the Elderly, 19,* 15–29.

——. (2000b). Vitamin and mineral supplement use by rural older adults. *Journals of Gerontology: Medical Sciences, 55A,* M613–M617.

Wilcox, S., Castro, C., King, A. C., Housemann, R., & Brownson, R. C. (2000). Determinants of leisure time physical activity in rural compared with urban older and ethnically diverse women in the United States. *Journal of Epidemiology and Community Health, 54,* 667–672.

V. ENVIRONMENTAL ASPECTS OF AGING AND PUBLIC HEALTH

Chapter 9

ENVIRONMENTAL HEALTH AND AGING

Michele Morrone

INTRODUCTION

ENVIRONMENTAL HEALTH SCIENCE is the segment of public health that addresses the interrelationship between the environment and human health. Environmental issues that impinge upon the domain of public health include food safety, drinking water quality, indoor air quality, outdoor air quality, wastewater management, solid and hazardous waste management, and vector control. One of the major goals of environmental health practice is to prevent the spread of disease through the management of environmental issues. Environmental health is the first line of defense against illness, and, as such, it has major implications for the maintenance of optimal health for older populations.

Environmental health became a profession in the late twentieth century, and its development has consistently contributed to the decline of disease. The field of environmental health is factor in current population-age distribution since it has eliminated deaths that could have resulted from many pathogens. Many of the positive directions of public health during the last millennium are the result of improved environmental health practices. These successes include motor vehicle safety, safer workplaces, control of infectious diseases, safer and healthier foods, and fluoridation in drinking water (CDC, 1999). With all of the successes of the past 100 years, the future for the profession looks even more challenging. According to Fielding (1999), environmental health as a practice faces many challenges in the future including a "fragmented public health infrastructure," an "aging population," and "irreversible changes in environmental health determinants" (p. xiii).

The fact that people are living longer today can be attributed to the successes of public health initiatives in the twentieth century (Kerschner & Pegues, 1998). The extended life expectancy is changing the face of public health as health professionals work to

149

ensure that "the quality of life is not compromised by the quantity of life" (Fredman & Haynes, 1985, p. 2). As one result of the increased life expectancy, cancer has surfaced as a major cause of death among people sixty-five and older, prompting medical professionals to call cancer a disease of aging (Ershler & Longo, 1997; Greenberg, 1987). In a somewhat perverse way, environmental health professionals have contributed to increases in cancer because life expectancy is increasing due to the success of programs to control acute infectious diseases that previously killed millions of people. Recently, however, several environmental diseases are emerging or reemerging, and these diseases have the potential to threaten the health of all people, but especially the aging population.

The environment plays a critical role in human health, and those over the age of sixty-five are helping researchers to understand the health impacts of the environment. Pedersen and Svedberg (2000) summarized studies conducted on twins who were reared in different environments and noted some significant associations between early environmental exposures and disease in the elderly. They highlight studies of a bacterium known as *Helicobacter pylori* that is suspected to be related to ulcers in adults. In these studies, the elderly twin who had ulcers also had antibodies to *H. pylori,* indicative of an exposure to the bacterium at some stage in life. The twin with the ulcer was also more likely to have been raised in poverty than the twin without an ulcer. This led the authors to conclude that the environmental exposures during the course of a lifetime are critical factors in the health of the elderly.

Almost without exception, people over the age of sixty-five are more susceptible to disease, and, therefore, more susceptible to adverse health impacts related to poor environmental health. One of the major issues facing public health professionals today is the spread of infectious diseases that have never been seen before or were thought to be under control. This chapter first discusses these emerging and re-emerging diseases, highlighting some important infectious diseases that may affect the aging population. The focus then shifts to a discussion of environmental diseases transmitted by food, water, vectors, and air that are likely to be of concern to public health professionals who work with the aging.

EMERGING AND RE-EMERGING ENVIRONMENTAL DISEASES

Past research confirms that the aging population is more susceptible to infectious diseases than other segments of the population (Ginaldi et al., 1999; Pawelec, Solana, Remarque, & Mariani, 1998). As people age, their immune systems become compromised, and they are unable to effectively resist many infectious agents (Wick & Grubeck-Loebenstein, 1997). Since a major goal of environmental health is to prevent disease, decreased immunity is especially important to public health professionals who manage the environment (Yoshikawa, 1997). The aging population presents serious challenges to environmental health professionals due to the population's predicted increase in numbers, compromised immune systems, and the viability of infectious diseases.

According to Farmer (1996), the late 1980s and early 1990s "has been one of the most eventful in the long history of infectious disease" (p. 259). Perhaps of greatest concern to public environmental health professionals are new and reemerging diseases. Emerging infectious diseases are those that are either new or "have existed but are rapidly increasing in incidence or geographic range" (Morse, 1995, p. 7). Emergent diseases surface when public health professionals least expect them. For example, the 1993 hantavirus outbreak in the southwestern United States took public health officials by surprise. The pathogens that cause emerging diseases, such as hantavirus, are not under surveillance by public health officials; therefore, they are only addressed after people have already become either seriously ill or are dead. Pathogens emerge as a public health threat for many reasons, not the least of which is the susceptibility of the host—an aging population, is more susceptible to many pathogens and thus contributes to emerging diseases (Morris & Potter, 1997).

Re-emerging diseases are those that were thought to be controlled through efforts, such as vaccination and surveillance, but are now resurfacing as health threats. As discussed in more detail later, tuberculosis (TB) is an example of a re-emerging disease that has the potential to adversely affect the aging population. TB is an airborne disease that is especially problematic in institutional settings, such as nursing homes and hospitals. Many public health officials are alarmed at the drug-resistant strains that have emerged in recent years due to nosocomial transmission (Rullán et al., 1996).

Nosocomial infections are those that are spread in institutional settings, such as hospitals and nursing homes. *Haemophilus influenzae* (Hib) is an example of an infectious disease prevalent in institutional settings. Heath et al. (1997) conducted a case study of Hib in an Australian nursing home and concluded that "Hib can cause clusters of serious disease among the elderly—at least in institutions" (p. 180). Other nosocomial infections of concern in long-term care facilities include antibiotic resistant strains of *Staphyloccocus aureus*.

Institutional care does not prompt as great a concern as do people over sixty-five who live on their own or in community settings. However, the fact that such a large percentage of the aging population is choosing to live on their own means that infectious diseases may be more difficult to control. Institutional settings offer the opportunity for infectious disease control that are not available in apartments and retirement communities. The aging population who live on their own are responsible for their own infection control; this means that environmental health professionals may assume more prominent educational roles in the future.

The public health system in the United States and across the globe is not ready for the pending threats of emergent and re-emergent diseases. There are limited funds and programs in place to manage diseases that are new or were once thought to be under control. Lederberg (1997) cautions that nations have become "complacent" about infectious disease due mainly to a reliance on antibiotics. There has been a shift in focus from acute diseases caused by infectious agents to chronic illnesses. According to Lederberg:

> Whether the life expectancy curve continues to rise smoothly or whether it has some jagged declines depends on what we do about the transmission of infectious disease, including foodborne disease. (1997, p. 417)

Environmental health practice has played a major role in reducing the prevalence of infectious diseases across the globe. Improvements in sanitation have directly reduced the spread of many infectious diseases. Nonetheless, infectious diseases continue to be the cause of deaths of millions of persons throughout the world each year. This is particularly true of respiratory infections, diarrhea, and tuberculosis (Hinman, 1998). New and re-emergent diseases that are of concern to health professionals can be spread through food, water, vectors, and air.

FOODBORNE DISEASES

Controlling pathogens that are transmitted through the food supply is a major focus of environmental health science and practice. Every year, millions of people become ill from ingesting disease-causing organisms in their food. In most cases, these illnesses can be prevented through proper food-sanitation techniques, including temperature control and time management.

The aging population contributes to the public health problem of foodborne pathogens because they are more susceptible to these pathogens (Altekruse, Cohen, & Swerdlow, 1997; Altekruse & Swerdlow, 1999). According to the Food and Drug Administration's Center for Food Safety and Applied Nutrition (CFSAN, 1999), older persons are at greater risk to serious illness from exposure to foodborne pathogens. A compromised immune system and a decline in the effectiveness of the digestive system are two of the reasons why the elderly are considered an "at-risk" population in relation to foodborne illnesses.

Among the foodborne pathogens that are emerging as public health concerns are campylobacter, *e. coli* 0157:H7, listeria, and salmonella. All of these pathogens lead to various levels of gastrointestinal distress and, in some cases, can result in death. These pathogens are either relatively new to environmental health specialists or are new strains of well-known pathogens. The reasons for the emergence of many foodborne pathogens include a globalization of the food supply as nations now routinely consume food from other countries, the overuse of antibiotics to protect investments in livestock, and inadequate surveillance systems due to limited public health resources (Tauxe, 1997).

Outbreaks of foodborne illnesses are different than they were just a short time ago; they are no longer localized events that can be traced to an improperly cooked and served meal at a "church supper." It is becoming increasingly common for a portion of the food supply to be transported from other countries–the United States consumes grapes from Chile, shrimp from Vietnam, and specialty foods are imported from virtually anywhere across the globe. Transporting food from one country to another, or one continent to another, offers opportunities for transporting infectious agents as well. Pathogens that were thought to be mainly associated with undercooked meat are now surfacing in fresh produce that is shipped all over the world. The changing nature of the food supply could create additional problems for the aging population because they are no longer able to rely on food-preparation methods that they may have used for many years to keep their food safe.

In addition to global markets of food products, there is some evidence suggesting food producers rely too much on antibiotics as preventive measures to protect livestock. In many instances, antibiotics are consumed regularly as part of the feed. While this does protect economic interests on the farm, the reliance on antibiotics can lead microorganisms to adapt into antibiotic resistant strains. The public health implications of infectious diseases that are not treatable with current antibiotics are enormous.

The major problem with foodborne-illness surveillance is that most cases of illness are not associated with outbreaks, consequently public health professionals are not able to conduct epidemiological investigations regarding them. Most environmental and public health professionals involved in food safety agree that foodborne illness is grossly underreported, and that there are many more cases of illness than those that they have quantified. Some of the most common and dangerous foodborne pathogens are discussed.

Campylobacter

Campylobacter is the leading cause of foodborne diarrheal illness in the United States with as many as 2.4 million cases every year (Altekruse, Stern, Fields, & Swendlow, 1999), recently exceeding salmonella as the major cause of gastrointestinal distress (Satin, 1999). Campylobacter is associated with the consumption of meats and poultry, and the epidemiology of the illness is being studied worldwide (Galmés & Martinez, 1997; O'Sullivan, Fallon, Carroll, Smith, & Maher, 2000).

Campylobacter is rarely associated with foodborne illness outbreaks; cases of this illness occur somewhat "sporadically" (Sharp & Reilly, 1994). There are probably many more cases of campylobacter illness since, in most instances, the diarrhea is mild, and people generally recover in a short time. If one ingests the *Campylobacter jejuni* bacteria, it is likely that diarrhea will follow in three to five days. In some cases, vomiting may accompany diarrhea, and the symptoms of the illness can last for up to one week. Some unfortunate individuals may experience recurrent symptoms for nearly a month after exposure. Although the illness is mainly associated with eating contaminated food, it is possible to ingest the bacteria by not following good hygienic procedures when coming into contact with domestic animals, including livestock.

As with any gastrointestinal illness, the aging population is at risk for complications resulting from diarrhea and vomiting. The greatest risk is dehydration, and individuals stricken with a foodborne illness must take precautions to avoid it.

Escherichia Coli 0157:H7

E. coli is an emerging foodborne pathogen that is becoming a major public health threat not only due to the seriousness of the illness, but also to the costs associated with surveillance and treatment (Elbasha, Fitzsimmons, & Meltzer, 2000). The new strain of e. coli, 0157:H7, was first identified in 1982, and recent outbreaks of this strain have been associated with apple cider, lettuce, and alfalfa sprouts.

E. coli is a dangerous infection that can lead to kidney failure and death, especially in people with compromised or undeveloped immune systems, such as the elderly and children. In the case of e. coli, it is not the bacteria itself that causes illness, it is the toxin that develops in the body after the bacteria has been expelled. In discussing the public health impacts of *E. coli* 0157:H7, Chapman (1995) reports that, since the 1982 outbreaks in Oregon and Michigan, additional reports of the illness have been sporadic. However, when there are outbreaks, they are generally very severe, and high mortality rates are reported among the elderly. Recently, five people have been confirmed dead in Canada from e. coli that was in a drinking water source.

A main public health concern with regard to e. coli is that only a very small amount of the bacteria results in illness. This means that a person does not have to eat an undercooked hamburger, rather, just the act of preparing the hamburger can lead to illness associated with ingesting the bacteria. The spread of this bacteria by food-preparation methods is one good example of how the aging population may need some re-education in food-sanitation procedures. Since *E. coli* 0157:H7 is a new strain of a common bacteria, increased caution must be exercised in home kitchens to prevent cross-contamination.

Listeria

In 1998, a national outbreak of listeriosis occurred, resulting from the consumption of deli meats and hot dogs. Listeriosis is caused by the bacteria *Listeria monocytogenes* which is ubiquitous in nature. The main sources of this bacteria in the food supply are meats and poultry products. One of the major factors that contribute to the danger of this bacteria is that listeria flourishes in cold temperatures, thus refrigerating meats contaminated with this bacteria may enhance their growth.

People with healthy, uncompromised immune systems will usually not become ill from ingesting listeria; however, this bacteria can be deadly to immunocompromised individuals. Pregnant women and the elderly are most susceptible to this foodborne pathogen. There is a 63 percent fatality rate for adults over sixty who have contracted listeriosis (Satin, 1999). The listeria bacteria can lead to meningitis and encephalitis.

Salmonella

Salmonella is a pathogen familiar to most individuals who prepare food. It is mainly found in poultry products and undercooked eggs. One reason that the aging population may be at greater risk from salmonella has to do with cooking procedures. Many elderly people employ cooking methods based on past experiences that could lead to undercooked meals. Salmonella is also spread by contaminated utensils, thus sanitation is a chief means of preventing the spread of this bacteria.

By some accounts, salmonella species cause up to 40 percent of all foodborne outbreaks (Blumenthal, 1995). The symptoms of salmonella food illness surface twenty-four to forty-eight hours after exposure and can include diarrhea and vomiting. In most instances, the body can rid itself of the bacteria in three to four days, however, as with all gastrointestinal illnesses, the elderly may be at greater risk to suffer more serious health effects.

WATERBORNE DISEASES

Cryptosporidiosis, cholera, and diphtheria were the focus of many environmental health programs in the twentieth century. Great strides were made globally in minimizing these illnesses; however, there is some evidence that these diseases are seeing a resurgence. In discussing waterborne illnesses, Page (1987) explains that, although incidence of waterborne diseases in developed countries has declined; this decline is based on technology that may lead to complacency. He also argues that bacteria is prevalent in almost all water supplies, leading to constant low-level exposures, but age is one factor that determines whether illness occurs.

The public water supply in the United States is one of the safest in the world, due to filtration and disinfection techniques. The problem, however, is reliance on technology. Public water systems draw their water from polluted rivers and lakes and rely on technology to clean the water for drinking purposes (Okun, 1999). It is cheaper for water companies, public and private, to treat polluted water rather than to search for a source of relatively unpolluted water. The implications of such actions are clear. If there is a problem with treatment, even if it is temporary, the likelihood people will become ill increases dependent upon the water source.

Although environmental health practitioners are especially concerned about microbiologicals in drinking water, there are also concerns about chemicals. Chemical contaminants can include pesticides, fertilizers, and residual chemicals from the disinfection process. Drinking-water quality management is a balancing act, as environmental health professionals focus on keeping people healthy in the short term, while minimizing the risk of chronic illnesses.

Cryptosporidiosis

Guerrant (1997) explains that the parasite cryptosporidium is not new, but it is drawing increasing attention from public health professionals because of its recent activity in institutional settings such as long-term-care facilities. Cryptosporidium causes extended periods of diarrhea and can result in serious health effects to immunocompromised individuals. Furthermore, it is of great concern to environmental health professionals because the bacteria appears to be resistant to common water-disinfection methods.

The most prominent outbreak of cryptosporidiosis occurred in 1993 in Milwaukee, Wisconsin. As the result of equipment failure at the water treatment plant, more than 400,000 people became ill from ingesting the parasite. More than 100 people died from complications attributed to the gastrointestinal distress associated with the illness. The outbreak cost more than $53 million and has led some to call cryptosporidium "one of the most important new contaminants needing control in drinking water" (Smith & Rose, 1998, p. 14).

Cholera

Although it may be quite rare to hear of outbreaks of cholera in developed countries, the organism that causes this diarrheal illness is always present in the environment. *Vibrio cholerae* is a bacterium that thrives in warm water and can cause illness both by ingestion of the bacterium directly or by contact with an infected person. Although industrialized countries may have less of a concern with cholera, it is somewhat common to see outbreaks of this disease in developing countries. Africa, in particular, houses countries with some of the highest rates of cholera worldwide (Birmingham et al., 1997)

Recent outbreaks of cholera include one in Nigeria in 1996 in which more than 1,300 people were treated. In discussing the Nigerian outbreaks, Lawoyin, Ogunboded, Olumide, and Onadeko (1999) argue that cholera is a major public health threat on a global level because it is becoming endemic in

many developing countries, and some people may be carriers of the disease organism without symptoms. Worldwide travel may, therefore, play an important role in the spread of the disease across the globe. Watery diarrhea and vomiting are the two major symptoms of cholera; however, dehydration can occur quickly. It can be treated relatively easily, but young children and the elderly face increased likelihood of death from dehydration.

Cholera has great potential to become a future health threat for several reasons. One is based on the predicted changes in global climate. As Borroto (1998) suggests, if predictions about global warming are accurate, *V. cholerae* will thrive, and more people across the globe will be at increased risk from contracting the disease. It is an illness that may focus public health professionals' attention on vaccination and education to prevent its becoming a major cause of illness and death.

Diphtheria

The bacteria that causes diphtheria is *Corynebacterium diphtherae* and exposure to this bug has largely been controlled through water-sanitation techniques and immunization. Although countries have different immunization protocols, most children in the United States should be immunized with the diphtheria–pertussis–tetanus vaccine (DPT) by the time they enter elementary school. In addition, there are protocols for children to receive boosters of this vaccine.

There has been some emerging concern about recent outbreaks of diphtheria in Eastern Europe, in particular among adults. One possible reason, as explained by Galazka and Robertson (1996), for the resurgence of diphtheria among adults is that due to successful environmental health practices *C. diphtherae* is no longer ubiquitous in the environment. For people to retain immunity from a toxin after a vaccine is no longer effective, they must be exposed to low doses of the toxin. This is not happening in the case of diphtheria; children are immunized to resist the toxin, but the toxin is generally not available to maintain the immunity. Therefore, when an adult is exposed to the toxin, perhaps during travel or from inadequately treated drinking water, the adult may become very ill. Galazka and Robertson recommend boosters for adults to curb the spread of this disease.

Chlorine and Other Chemicals

Since the early 1900s, chlorine has played the major role in ensuring the safety of drinking water around the globe. It is the most common method of drinking-water disinfection because it effectively kills many microbiological contaminants. There are emerging concerns about the use of chlorine as a disinfectant due to recent research identifying chemical by-products of the disinfection process; in particular, there is emerging evidence of an association between chlorine and cancer. The relationship between consumption of chlorinated drinking water and cancer is an area that is undergoing considerable research, but it is also an area that involves serious methodological challenges including conducting retrospective studies of cancer. Schenck, Wymer, Lykins, and Clark (1998) argue that the data linking chlorinated drinking water to cancer has so far been inconclusive, but this may still be an important public health issue in the future. The implications of finding a direct connection between chlorine in drinking water and cancer include not only managing cancer, but identifying a less risky alternative to disinfection.

Chlorine can react with organic substances in water to produce chemicals known as trihalomethanes (THMs) such as chloroform (Yu & Cheng, 1999). When the source water contains naturally-occurring bromide, the THM dichlorobromomethane can result

from the disinfection process. These THMs may pose a more significant cancer risk than chloroform and bromoform alone (Nokes, Fenton, & Randall, 1999). Gibbons & Laha (1999) suggest that the formation of disinfection by-products has led to the extremely profitable bottled-water industry in the United States. However, they argue that purchasing bottled water is not a necessary expense because results from studies they conducted in Florida show THMs in municipal tap water to be well within regulated maximum contaminant levels.

To create even further public health challenges in ensuring the safety of drinking water, there is evidence suggesting that chlorine may not be the most effective disinfection method to control some bacteria such as *Legionella pneumophila*. Kool, Carpenter, & Fields (1999) conducted a case-control study on nosocomial outbreaks of Legionnaires' disease. They found a significant association between use of chlorine alone and occurrences of the illness. Hospitals using water disinfected with chlorine followed by secondary disinfection with monochloramine (a mixture of ammonia and chlorine) were less likely to have been involved in an outbreak of the disease. As discussed later, Legionnaires' disease tends to affect individuals over the age of fifty more than other age groups; therefore, findings about the efficacy of chlorine to control the bacteria are relevant to the aging population.

VECTORBORNE DISEASES

Vectors are insects, including ticks and mosquitoes, that transmit disease to humans. Environmental health professionals are becoming increasingly concerned about the resurgence of vectorborne diseases, such as malaria. There are several reasons for the resurgence in the past twenty years, including the fact that the public health system is failing to adequately monitor the spread of these diseases (Gubler, 1998). Another issue associated with the spread of vectorborne illness is population density; the closer people live together, the easier it is for these diseases to spread. Living situations housing many people who are susceptible to illness in close quarters are ripe for an outbreak of a disease caused by pathogens from vectors.

Population distribution is related to population density, but distribution also refers to geographical locations of population. As an example, in the United States, suburban areas are growing more rapidly than urban or rural areas. As people move to suburban areas, they may be constructing homes in areas that are prime tick habitat and, therefore, contributing to the spread of tickborne diseases such as Lyme disease and Rocky Mountain Spotted Fever (Greenberg, Feinberg, & Pomeroy, 1998). Tickborne diseases such as Lyme disease are emerging as serious infectious diseases in the United States.

Lyme Disease

Lyme disease was first discovered in 1975 in Lyme, Connecticut, when an unusually large number of children began experiencing symptoms of juvenile arthritis. Environmental health professionals identified the vector as the deer tick, which is smaller than the common dog tick and, therefore, more difficult to control. Lyme disease is treatable if it is caught early, but it can lead to chronic illnesses, such as arthritis.

Lyme disease offers an example of how emerging diseases are as much a function of social factors as they are of biological factors (Schrag & Wiener, 1995). In the case of Lyme disease, population ecology, or distribution of the population in the United States, has been a major factor in the emergence of this disease. As land-use changes, and people move

to more rural areas, their opportunities for contact with deer and the vector that carries Lyme disease increases. Mayer (2000) sums up the role of social factors in the spread of infectious diseases as follows: "The emergence and resurgence of infectious diseases is as much a matter of social, ecological, and geographical change as it is of smaller scale molecular or microbiological phenomena" (p. 938).

The bacterium responsible for Lyme disease is *Borrelia burgdorferi* and is one of the most common vectorborne diseases in the United States. The disease is becoming increasingly common in other countries as well. In a study conducted in Germany, Huppertz, Böhme, Standaert, Karch, and Plotkin (1999) examined 313 cases of Lyme disease during a twelve-month period. They found the highest rates of Lyme disease in children and the elderly. They explain that there may be many factors contributing to the increase in numbers of Lyme-disease cases, including better reporting. Nevertheless, they suggest that the greatest factor may be the increase in incidence of infected vectors, concluding that surveillance efforts for the vector must be increased across the globe.

Malaria

Malaria is emerging as an important vectorborne disease worldwide. Although the Anopheles mosquito is the vector for this disease, the causes of malaria's resurgence are many. According to Molyneux (1998), the reason for epidemics of malaria is interaction between "social, economic, political, ecological, climatic, and development change" in areas where malaria is endemic (p. 932). These changes combined with the fact that the vector is highly adaptable to environmental change, including its ability to resist many pesticides (Garfield, 1999), suggest that future epidemics of malaria can be expected. In studying malaria in Argentina, de Casas, Verhasselt, Carcavallo, and Boffi (1998) confirm that social factors, such as population mobility, socioeconomic status, and household sanitation, are just as important as physical factors of climate, vegetation, and presence of water as breeding sites for the vector.

Malaria has generally been linked with death in children under the age of five; however, there is new evidence suggesting that the age profile of health effects from malaria may be changing (Alles, Mendis, & Carter, 1998). As with many infectious diseases, people must be constantly exposed to low levels of the pathogen in order to obtain or maintain immunity. In the case of malaria, as with diphtheria discussed earlier, opportunities for low-level exposures are being minimized by environmental health practices; thus, in the event of an exposure, people who are not immune may become quite ill or even die.

Malaria is of particular concern because it is a parasitic disease that may not produce clinical symptoms in infected individuals quickly. Therefore, mosquitoes can feed from an infected person before the symptoms emerge, become infected, and then transmit the parasite to another host. Therefore, travel is an important factor in the spread of this disease as it is with many of the communicable diseases.

AIRBORNE DISEASES

Many diseases of the elderly caused by airborne pathogens are the results of nosocomial transmission. Nosocomial diseases have the greatest effect on the aging population and upon those who are immunocompromised. Environmental health professionals work to minimize the spread of nosocomial disease by evaluating ventilation systems in institutional settings as well as advising about infection-control techniques.

Because indoor air quality is an important emerging health threat, Ziegenfus (1987) focused mainly on this issue in his chapter in the book *Public Health and the Environment.* He argues that indoor-air-quality issues will become one of the most important environmental health issues of the future, emphasizing the fact that most people spend eighty to ninety percent of their time indoors. Influenza, tuberculosis (TB), and Legionnaires' disease are three of the diseases caused by airborne pathogens in the indoor environment. Each of these diseases presents unique challenges to public health professionals because of its ability to spread quickly and, particularly in the case of TB, its emerging resistance to antibiotics. One of the "major forces" in the rising nosocomial infection rate is "antimicrobial use in hospitals and long-term care facilities" (Weinstein, 1998, p. 418). Compounding the risk to the elderly is that patients often are transferred from hospitals to nursing homes and bring the antibiotic strains of many illnesses back with them to long-term care facilities.

Influenza

Influenza is caused by a virus, and there are outbreaks and global epidemics of influenza every year. It is a major cause of death in the elderly population (Fredman & Haynes, 1985). In presenting their recommendations for vaccinating people against influenza, the Center for Disease Control and Prevention's (CDC) Advisory Committee on Immunization Practices (ACIP, 2000) note that people who are sixty-five and older have the highest rates of serious illness and death from influenza. ACIP is also concerned about those who are in the fifty to sixty-four age group, and their year 2000 recommendations include immunizing all people aged fifty and over. People who live in nursing homes, retirement communities, or assisted-living facilities should also be vaccinated.

Tuberculosis

TB is caused by an airborne bacteria that can remain suspended in air for extended periods of time. Recent concerns of public health professionals are with antibiotic-resistant strains of the TB bacterium. These strains create serious challenges to health care professionals.

Institutions, such as nursing homes and prisons, are showing increases in TB activity. One reason why TB is a problem in many institutions has to do with the age of some of these facilities. Older facilities do not meet current standards for indoor-air control that are in place to prevent the spread of airborne diseases. The CDC issued guidelines in 1998 for nursing homes related to screening for TB. The new guidelines include a two-step skin test for all health care workers and nursing home patients (Greenberg et al., 1998).

Legionnaires' Disease

Legionella pneumophila is a bacteria that thrives in cooler temperatures; it can be both air- and waterborne, although most cases of legionella in hospitals have been linked to drinking water (Kool, Carpenter, & Fields, 1999). The legionella bacteria escape the water source, become airborne, and are inhaled. This bacteria was responsible for an outbreak of legionellosis in Philadelphia in 1976. It is of particular concern to the elderly because it can cause pneumonia in people over fifty.

Legionnaire's disease manifests itself as pneumonia and can be deadly to individuals with chronic respiratory problems and other ailments affecting the immune system. Although nosocomial transmission of the pathogen accounts for only about one-fourth of the cases of Legionnaires' disease, the mortality rate for patients who became infected in hospitals is almost twice as high as those who were infected in the community (Ruef,

1998). This statistic emphasizes the importance of environmental health controls in hospitals and institutions.

Outdoor-Air Pollution

Outdoor air pollution comes mainly from two sources: motor vehicles and stationary sources. In the United States, motor vehicle exhaust is a leading cause of nitrogen oxides which react with sunlight to form ground-level ozone, also known as smog. All across the country, there are communities that post "ozone action days" when ozone levels are so high in the immediate area that residents with compromised respiratory systems, such as asthmatics and the elderly, should not venture outdoors. Population growth means an increase in motor vehicle use, and population distribution in the United States is occurring in such a way that further exacerbates the situation. That is, as more people move from pedestrian-friendly cities, to car-friendly suburbs and fringe areas, motor vehicle use will continue to grow.

Motor vehicles also substantially contribute to particulate matter (PM) pollution—fine particles of soot and dust that carry pollutants that can be inhaled. Although the respiratory effects of PM are well-documented, there is debate about the level of exposure that can lead to adverse health effects. Furthermore, some research suggests that the elderly may suffer PM-related health effects more than other age groups, and that these effects may include cardiopulmonary (heart–lung) problems. Chapman, Watkinson, Dreher, and Costa (1997) summarize epidemiological evidence supporting cardiopulmonary effects from exposure to PM. The elderly who have pre-existing cardiopulmonary conditions are especially susceptible, Chapman and colleagues explain that PM exposure can lead to increased mortality and hospitalization rates in the elderly. They conclude that it will be a "public health burden" to conduct more "carefully-designed research" relative to the cardiopulmonary effects of PM matter on older adults (Chapman et al., 1987).

Air pollution and the weather may not directly cause illness in the elderly, but they may increase the symptoms of chronic illnesses. Gazerro, Inelman, Secco, and Gatto (1996) conducted a study in a town in Italy with a high percentage of people over the age of sixty-five to assess the relationship between the environment and health of the elderly. They concluded that, although it is difficult to make causal links between environmental factors and disease, there are notable changes in elderly health related to environmental conditions (Gazerro et al., 1996). As examples, they note that the clinical symptoms of chronic illnesses, such as emphysema and arthritis, worsen in relation to air pollution and weather patterns.

Heat stroke and heat-related deaths are more prominent among the elderly than any other age group. In one study in Japan, more than one-half of the heat-related deaths during a twenty-five-year period were people either under four or older than seventy (Nakai, Itoh, & Morimoto, 1999). If predictions about global warming are accurate, the average annual temperature will rise in the future. Many scientists believe that global warming is resulting from human-made pollutants emitted from the burning of fossil fuels. Therefore, air pollution creating a rise in temperature may eventually lead to more heat-related effects on the elderly.

CONCLUSION

Because the population is aging, great demands will be made on the environmental health departments of public health agencies.

The many challenges will include minimizing the spread of disease through environmental media, such as food, water, vectors, and air. Environmental health professionals understand the importance of protecting special populations, such as children and the elderly; however, resource constraints often limit their ability to do so. To minimize the adverse effects on the aging population, good environmental planning today is required.

The most promising indication that environmental planning is becoming more of a priority is found in *Healthy People 2010* (Department of Health and Human Services [DHHS], 2000). The Healthy People planning initiatives began in the late 1970s and are updated on a regular basis. There are two goals of *Healthy People 2010.* The first is to increase both the quantity and quality of life. Environmental health is among twenty-eight focus areas in the Healthy People plan. Environmental health objectives include reducing exposure to outdoor-air pollution and improving water quality.

Goals and objectives in plans such as *Healthy People 2010* can focus public health attention, but, in the absence of effective environmental controls, education becomes critical. Educating the sixty-five-and-older age group about proper sanitation procedures to minimize their risk of illness from infectious diseases will remain an important component of all environmental health programs. When effective, education is expensive. Reaching a special population, such as the elderly, will increase costs of environmental-education programs. Even though education can be expensive, it is still the most cost-effective disease-prevention mechanism.

Environmental health professionals' main role is prevention, but a disturbing trend in public health will have long-term consequences on the ability of agencies to address prevention. This trend involves reduction in funding for surveillance of environmental diseases. For example, in some states, the once-prominent mosquito-surveillance programs suffered serious cutbacks in the late 1990s, to the point where there is virtually no surveillance by public health agencies occurring in these states.

Calabrese (1986) sums up the public health challenge regarding the elderly eloquently when he states:

> Age-related differences are important for regulatory agencies to consider because these differential susceptibility patterns over a lifetime affect us all. Thus, in contrast to genetic predispositions which may affect relatively small subsets in the population, aging factors at some time affect all people. Thus these findings require serious appraisal because the public health concerns are enormous. (p. 277)

REFERENCES

Advisory Committee on Immunization Practices. (2000). Prevention and Control of Influenza. *Morbidity and Mortality Weekly Recommendations and Reports, April 14, 2000, 49* (RR03), 1–38.

Alles, H. K, Mendis, K. N., & Carter, R. (1998). Malaria mortality rates in South Asia and in Africa: Implications for malaria control. *Parasitology Today, 14* (9), 369–375.

Altekruse, S. F., Cohen, M. L., & Swerdlow, D. L. (1997). Emerging foodborne diseases. *Emerging Infectious Diseases, 3* (3), 285–293. Retrieved April 21, 2000, from the World Wide Web: www.cdc.gov/ncidod/eid/vol3no3/cohen.htm.

Altekruse, S. F., Stern, N. J., Fields, P. I., & Swerdlow, D. L. (1999). *Campylobacter jejuni:* An emerging foodborne pathogen. *Emerging Infectious Diseases, 5* (1), 28–35. Retrieved April 21, 2000, from the World Wide Web: www.cdc.gov/ncidod/vol5no1/altekruse.htm.

Altekruse, S. E., & Swerdlow, S. L. (1996). The changing epidemiology of foodborne dis-eases. *American Journal of Medical Science, 311* (1), 23–29.

Birmingham, M. E., Lee, L. A., Ndayimirije, N., Hersh, B. S., Wells, J. G., & Deming, M. S. (1997). Epidemic cholera in Burundi: Patterns of transmission in the Great Rift Valley Lake region. *The Lancet, 349* (9057), 981–85.

Blumenthal, D. S. (1995). Infectious agents in the environment. In D. S. Blumenthal & A. J. Ruttenber (Eds.), *Introduction to environmental health* (2nd ed., pp. 71–102). New York: Springer.

Borroto, R. J. (1998). Global warming, rising sea level, and growing risk of cholera incidence: A review of the literature and evidence. *GeoJournal, 44* (2), 111–120.

Calabrese, E. (1986). *Age and susceptibility to toxic substances.* New York: John Wiley & Sons.

CDC. (1999). Achievements in public health, 1900–1999: Changes in the public health system. *Morbidity and Mortality Weekly Reports, December 24, 1999, 48*(50), 1141–1147.

CFSAN. (1999). *Seniors and food safety.* Retrieved April 21, 2000, from the World Wide Web: http://vm.cfsan.fda.gov/~dms/seniorsb.html.

Chapman, P. A. (1995). Verocytotoxin-producing *Escherichia coli:* An overview with emphasis on the epidemiology and prospects for control of *E. coli* 0157. *Food Control, 6* (4), 187–193.

Chapman, P. A., Watkinson, W. P., Dreher, K. L., & Costa, D. L. (1997). Ambient particulate matter and respiratory and cardiovascular illness in adults: Particle-borne transition metals and the heart-lung axis. *Environmental Toxicology and Pharmocology, 4* (3–4), 331–338.

de Casas, C., Verhasselt, Y., Carcavallo, R. U., & Boffi, R. (1998). Environmental risk factors for diseases transmitted by vectors: A case study in North Argentina. *GeoJournal, 44* (2), 121–127.

Department of Health and Human Services. (2000). *Healthy People 2010-Conference edition. Chapter 8: Environmental health.* Retrieved April 21, 2000, from the World Wide Web: web.health.gov/healthypeople/Document/HTML/Volume1/08Environmental.htm.

Elbasha, E. H., Fitzsimmons, T. D., & Meltzer, M. I. (2000). Costs and benefits of a subtype-specific surveillance system for identifying *Escherichia coli 0157:H7* outbreaks. *Emerging*

Infectious Diseases, 6 (3), 293–297. Retrieved May 15, 2000, from the World Wide Web: www.cdc.gov/ncidod/eid/vol6no3/elbasha. htm#1.

Ershler, W. B., & Longo, D. L. (1997). Aging and cancer: Issues of basic and clinical science. *Journal of the National Cancer Institute, 89,* 1489–1497.

Farmer, P. (1996). Perspectives: Social inequalities and emerging infectious diseases. *Emerging Infectious Diseases, 2* (4), 259–269. Retrieved April 21, 2000, from the World Wide Web: www.cdc.gov/ncidod/eid/vol2no4/farmer. htm.

Fielding, J. E. (1999). Public health in the 20th century: Advances and challenges. *Annual Reviews in Public Health, 20,* xii–xxx.

Fredman, L., & Haynes, S. (1985) An epidemiologic profile of the elderly. In H. T. Philips & S. A. Gaylord (Eds.), *Aging and public health* (pp. 1–41). New York: Springer.

Galazka, A. M., & Robertson, S. E. (1996). Immunization against diphtheria with special emphasis on immunization of adults. *Vaccine, 14* (9), 845–857.

Galmés, A., & Martines, J. F. (1997). Acute *Campylobacter jejuni* gastroenteritis in Majorca. *Journal of Clinical Epidemiology, 50,* 29S.

Garfield, R. (1999). Malaria control in Nicaragua: Social and political influences on disease transmission and control activities. *The Lancet, 354* (9176), 414–418.

Gazerro, M.. L., Inelman, E. M., Secco, G., & Gatto, R. A. (1996). Elderly people: state of health and living environment. The case of Budrio (northern Italy). *Health & Place, 2* (2), 115–123.

Gibbons, J., & Laha, S. (1999). Water purification systems: A comparative analysis based on the occurrence of disinfection by-products. *Environmental Pollution, 106* (3), 425–428.

Ginaldi, L., De Martinis, M., D'Ostilio, A., Marini, L., Loreto, M. F. Corsi, M. P., & Quaglino, D. (1999). The immune system in the elderly I. Specific humoral immunity. *Immunologic Research, 20* (2), 101–108.

Greenberg, M. R. (1987). Health and risk in urban-industrial society. In M. R. Greenberg (Ed.), *Public health and the environment* (pp. 3–24). New York: Guilford Press.

Greenberg, R. N., Feinberg, J. E., & Pomeroy, C. (1998).The hot zone–1997: Conference on emerging infectious disease. *Emerging Infectious Diseases, 4* (1), 135–142. Retrieved April 22, 2000, from the World Wide Web: www.cdc.gov/ncidod/eid/vol4no1/newsnote. htm.

Gubler, D. J. (1998). Resurgent vector-borne diseases as a global health problem. *Emerging Infectious Diseases, 4* (3), 442–450. Retrieved March 15, 2000, from the World Wide Web: www.cdc.gov/ncidod/eid/vol4no3/gubler. htm.

Guerrant, R. L. (1997) Cryptosporidiosis: An emerging, highly infectious threat. *Emerging Infectious Diseases, 3* (1), 51–57. Retrieved April 21, 2000, from the World Wide Web: www.cdc.gov/ncidod/eid/vol3no1/guerrant. htm.

Heath, T. C., Hewitt, M. C., Jalaludin, B., Roberts, C., Capon, A. G., Jelfs, P., & Gilbert, G. L. (1997).·Invasive *Haemophilus influenzae* type B disease in elderly nursing home residents: Two related cases. *Emerging Infectious Diseases 3* (2), 179–182. Retrieved April 2000, from the World Wide Web: www.cdc.gov/ncidod/eid/vol3no2/heath.htm.

Hinman, A. R. (1998). Global progress in infectious disease control. *Vaccine 16* (11/12), 1116–1121.

Huppertz, H. I., Böhme, M., Standaert, S. M., Karch, H., & Plotkin, S. A. (1999). Incidence of Lyme borreliosis in the Würzburg region of Germany. *European Journal of Clinical Microbiology and Infectious Diseases, 18* (10), 0697–0703.

Kerschner, H., & Pegues, J. A. M. (1998). Productive aging: A quality of life agenda. *Journal of the American Dietetic Association, 98* (12), 1445–1448.

Kool, J. L., Carpenter, J. C., & Fields, B. S. (1999). Effect of monochloramine disinfection of municipal drinking water on risk of nosocomial Legionnaires' disease. *The Lancet, 353* (9149), 272–277.

Lawoyin, T. O., Ogunboded, N. A., Olumide, E. A. A., & Onadeko, M. O. (1999). Outbreak of cholera in Ibadan, Nigeria. *European Journal of Epidemiology, 15,* 367–370.

Lederberg, J. (1997). Infectious disease as an evolutionary paradigm. *Emerging Infectious Diseases, 3* (4), 417–423. Retrieved April 21, 2000, from the World Wide Web: www.cdc.gov/ncidod/eid/vol3no4/lederber.htm.

Mayer, J. D. (2000). Geography, ecology and emerging infectious diseases. *Social Science & Medicine 50* (7–8), 937–952.

Molyneux, D. H. (1998). Vector-borne parasitic diseases–An overview of recent changes. *International Journal for Parasitology, 28* (6), 927–934.

Morris, J. G., & Potter, M. (1997). Emergence of new pathogens as a function of changes in host susceptibility. *Emerging Infectious Diseases, 3* (4), 435–441. Retrieved May 31, 2001, from the World Wide Web: www.cdc.gov/ncidod/cid/vol3no4/morris.htm

Morse, S. S. (1995). Factors in the emergence of infectious diseases. *Emerging Infectious Diseases, 1* (1), 7–15. Retrieved April 21, 2000, from the World Wide Web: www.cdc.gov/ncidod/eid/vol1no1/morse.htm.

Nakai, S., Itoh, T., & Morimoto, T. (1999). Deaths from heat-stroke in Japan: 1968–1994. *International Journal of Biometeorology, 43* (3), 0124–0127.

Nokes, C. J., Fenton, E., & Randall, C. J. (1999). Modelling the formation of brominated trihalomethanes in chlorinated drinking waters. *Water Research, 33* (17), 3557–3568.

Okun, D. A. (1999). Historical overview of drinking water contaminants in public water supplies. In Commission on Geosciences, Environment and Resources (Eds.), *Identifying future drinking water contaminants* (pp. 22–32). Washington, D.C.: National Academy Press.

O'Sullivan, N. A., Fallon, R., Carroll, C., Smith, T., & Maher, M. (2000). Detection and differentiation of *Campylobacter jejuni* and *Campylobacter coli* in broiler chicken samples using a PCR/DNA probe membrane based colorimetric detection assay. *Molecular and Cellular Probes, 14* (1), 7–16

Page, G. W., III. (1987). Water and health. In M. R. Greenberg (Ed.), *Public health and the environment* (pp. 105–138). New York: Guilford Press.

Pawelec, G., Solana, R., Remarque, E., & Mariani, E. (1998) The impact of aging on innate immunity. *Journal of Leukocyte Biology, 64* (6), 703–712.

Pederson, N. L., & Svedberg, P. (2000). Behavioral genetics, health and aging. *Journal of Adult Development, 7* (2), 65–71.

Ruef, C. (1998). Nosocomial Legionnaires' disease–Strategies for prevention. *Journal of Microbiological Methods, 33* (1), 81–91.

Rullán, J. V., Herrera, D., Cano, R., Moreno, V., Godoy, P., Peiró, Castell, J., Ibañez, C., Ortega, A., Agudo, L. S., & Pozo, F. (1996). Nosocomial transmission of multidrug-resistant *Mycobacterium tuberculosis* in Spain. *Emerging Infectious Diseases, 2* (2), 125–129. Retrieved May 15, 2000, from the World Wide Web: www.cdc.gov/ncidod/eid/vol2no2/downrull. htm.

Satin, M. (1999). *Food alert: The ultimate sourcebook for food safety.* New York: Checkmark Books.

Schenck, K. M., Wymer, L. J., Lykins, B. W., Jr., & Clark, R. M. (1998). Application of a Finnish mutagenicity model to drinking waters in the U.S. *Chemosphere, 37* (3), 45–64.

Schrag, S. J., & Wiener, P. (1995). Emerging infectious disease: What are the relative roles of ecology and evolution? *Trend in Ecology and Evolution, 10* (8), 319–324.

Sharp, J. C. M., & Reilly, W. J. (1994). Recent trends in foodborne infections in Europe and North America. *British Food Journal 96,* (7), 25–34.

Smith, H. V., & Rose, J. B. (1998). Waterborne Cryptosporidiosis: Current status. *Parasitology Today, 14* (1), 14–22.

Tauxe, R. V. (1997). Emerging foodborne diseases: An evolving public health challenge. *Emerging Infectious Diseases, 3* (4), 425–434. Retrieved April 21, 2000, from the World Wide Web: www.cdc.gov/ncidod/eid/vol3no4/tauxe. htm.

Weinstein, R. A. (1998). Nosocomial infection update. *Emerging Infectious Diseases, 4* (3), 416–420. Retrieved April 21, 2000, from the World Wide Web: www.cdc.gov/ncidod/eid/vol4no3/weinstein.htm.

Wick, G., & Grubeck-Loebenstein, B. (1997). The aging immune system: Primary and secondary alterations of immune reactivity in the elderly. *Experimental Gerontology, 32* (4–5), 401–413.

Yoshikawa, T. T. (1997). Perspective: Aging and infectious diseases: Past, present, and future. *Journal of Infectious Diseases, 176* (4), 1053–1057.

Yu, J. C., & Cheng, L. (1999). Speciation and distribution of trihalomethanes in the drinking water of Hong Kong. *Environment International, 25* (5), 605–611.

Ziegenfus, R. C. (1987). Air quality and health. In M. R. Greenberg (Ed.), *Public health and the environment* (pp. 139–171). New York: Guilford Press.

Chapter 10

SAFETY AND THE ELDERLY

TIMOTHY J. RYAN

INTRODUCTION

INJURY REDUCTION as a goal of public health providers is not only an ethically desirable target, but, with the burgeoning aging-baby-boomer population entering this age category, a financially necessary objective as well. According to the National Center for Health Statistics (Kramarow et al., 1999), the U.S. population over the age of sixty-five is expected to be 70 million by the year 2030. Accounting for a projected 20 percent of the total population at that time, this group's impact on the health care needs of the country will be significant. For that reason alone, steps taken to decrease the possibilities of injuries to the elderly, or to hasten recovery from such injuries, constitute important, prospective public health actions.

Injuries suffered by the aged are in many respects no different than those visited on all age groups in the population. Causes of such injuries are as varied as the exposures of the individual: electrical shocks, broken glass or sharp object injuries, farm implement accidents, and exercise-related stress injuries. Much like the very young population, composed of infants and children, the elderly as a

group have a number of notable and peculiar risk- and outcome-modifying factors that must be considered with respect to their exposure to traumatic injury. These injury-enhancing factors affect nearly 80 percent of all persons seventy years of age or older (Kramarow et al., 1999) and include physiological changes, such as blindness, hearing loss, arthritis, osteoporosis, mental- or physical-disease states, and levels of medication. Acting singly or in conjunction with one another, such alterations can serve to increase the burden of injury to the aged.

According to the Institute of Medicine's Committee on Injury Prevention and Control , the ability to intervene or ameliorate injury causes is a relatively recent public health concept. Prior to the late 1960s, human injuries were regarded as either random and unavoidable occurrences ("accidents" or "acts of God"), or as consequences of malevolence or carelessness (Institute of Medicine [IOM], 1999). In 1968, Haddon advanced the idea that the etiology of injury could be described by the interaction of environmental factors with human factors. Using uncontrolled or unintentional energy release (kinetic, thermal, electrical, chemical, and radiation) as the

Phases	Factors				
		Individual Behavior	Agent	Physical Environment	Socio-economic Environment
	Pre-event				
	Event				
	Postevent				

Figure 10.1. Haddon's energy control matrix. Note: Adapted from IOM, 1999.

causative agent of injury, Haddon identified a structure whereby potential injury-causing events could be evaluated at one of three points to effectively intervene for the purposes of injury reduction. The three control points were termed the preevent phase (prior to the energy release), the event phase (i.e., the uncontrolled energy release), and the postevent phase. These three control points were subject to modification by both human factors and environmental conditions. Under the intervention model created by Haddon, a 3-phase × 4-factor matrix can be constructed (Figure 10.1). Cost-effective injury control in this scheme can be effected by rank ordering the most likely effective combination of energy release phase and factor.

Traumatic injuries commonly experienced by older persons include a number of well-characterized outcomes, including falls, motor vehicle accidents (MVAs), and a diverse miscellaneous grouping including burns, hypothermia, drowning, and poisoning. These areas of injury have long been recognized, and, consequently, a reasonably competent infrastructure for data collection about their prevalence exists. Research into injuries among the elderly must focus on changing causes for these injuries, or on other

factors (e.g., demographics) responsible for greater or diminished accident occurrence. Although the popular press frequently gives voice to concerns about the prevalence of persons living in nursing homes (Shapiro, 1998), in actuality only a small percentage of the elderly population resides in institutions. Greater than 90 percent of elderly persons reside in private homes, either with family members or alone. Thus, many of the risk factors present in the domestic setting prevail throughout older ages for all but the most incapacitated persons, and, as a result, it is the home rather than the institution where accident-prevention efforts may be most efficacious.

FALLS

Elderly injuries caused by falls are the leading cause of morbidity and mortality within this segment of the total population. Falls resulting from all causes are the leading cause of injury-attributable deaths in those over sixty-five years of age, accounting for approximately 9,000 fatalities on an annual basis in the United States alone (Hoyert, Kochanek, & Murphy, 1999). Although never described as such, in traditional public health parlance, elderly falls constitute a pandemic in that one of every three elderly adults experiences a fall each year (Tinetti, Speechley, & Ginter, 1988). Finally, among older adults, falls are the most common cause of injuries as well as the most prevalent reason for hospital admissions attributable to trauma (Fife & Barancik, 1985).

The predominance of falls as an injury issue among the aged population poses a conundrum of causality. At issue is whether such persons are at increased risk of injury primarily as a result of elevated exposure to traumatic occurrences owing to a greater number of falls, or if this group is more prone to serious injury from any fall event as the result of biologically related predisposing host factors connected to age. It is possible that the injury rates, known to increase by age among community-dwelling elderly people (Sorock, 1988) are confounded by a higher exposure to falling incidents. The inability of fall victims to accurately recall (and thus report) their falls may, therefore, reduce the true fall-incidence rate, thereby artificially elevating the injury morbidity rate among the elderly. For example, Peel reports that over 30 percent of all falls were not accurately recalled by the elderly, and that there was a statistically significant difference in fall recall attributable to whether or not the individual was injured (Peel, 2000).

Confusion as to the exact etiology of falls among the elderly arises when host factors mediating the individual's role in a given fall episode are considered. In his review of the many factors related to falls in the elderly, Sattin presents eight host-dependent risk factors potentially affecting the injury outcome of a fall incident (Sattin, 1992). Those factors are shown in Table 10.1, along with two other fall-related injury factors (injury agent and environment). While the inclusion of "age" among the factors listed may, at first, seem circularly repetitious, as a category it includes a variety of physiologic changes that occur with advancing age that may adversely affect a fall-incident outcome. These include arthritis, diminished muscle strength, decreased joint flexibility, decreased collagen elasticity, and general discomfort and pain. "Sex" is listed as a factor in that women and men may have different outcomes for a similar fall incident (Sattin, 1992).

The other host factors included in Table 10.1 are more directly explained, for the most part, in terms of the role they play in elderly falls and injuries. The predisposition of frail, elderly women with osteoporosis to fall-related injury is well-known, and the cause—decreased bone resistance to mechanical energy with an attendant rise in the risk of fractures—well-documented (Sattin, 1992; Tideiksaar, 1986). Chronic diseases associated with elderly falls are primarily related to cardiac diagnoses and include the following: syncope, conduction disorders or dysrhythmias, hypertensive disorder, and ischemic heart disease. Anemia and diabetes have also been linked with fall injuries in a population-based study (Sattin et al. [1990], as cited in Sattin, 1992). Specifically how gait and balance abilities translate into fall hazards is uncertain, but it is recognized that elderly person with fall histories typically exhibit an uncoordinated gait in addition to poor control of both body position and posture.

Clear vision ability is extremely important insofar as fall avoidance is concerned. Visual acuity, depth perception-contrast-sensitivity, peripheral vision, visual perception, dark adaptation and glare tolerance are all vision-related host factors that can interact with other injury elements, most notably environmental factors, to increase the risk of falls in the elderly population. Sattin (1992) lists "mental status" as a host-related risk factor because at least six studies have linked it with fall injuries. Although this factor figures

TABLE 10.1
Sattin's Risk Factors for Falls Among the Elderly

Host	Injury Agent	Environment
Age, Sex	Mechanical energy	Lighting
Osteoporosis	Impact position	Stairs
Chronic diseases	Impact location	Rugs, flooring
Gait, balance		Bathtubs
Vision		Shelving
Mental status		Footwear
Medication use		Streets, walkways
Alcohol use		

Source: Sattin, 1992

Note: The U.S. government has the right to retain a non-exclusive, royalty-free license in and to any copyright covering this paper.

prominently in more insidious morbidity or mortality of the aged (e.g., hypothermia-related deaths), confusion, impaired judgment, distraction, agitation, or a lack of awareness can all be associated with heightened risk of a fall and related injury (Fierro & Jenkins, 1997). For their mostly predictable effects on equilibrium, gait, balance, vision, or mental state, the impacts of certain medications and recreational alcohol use have obvious and intuitive potential outcomes on the exposure of the elderly to fall incidents.

Not only do host factors complicate any attempts to formulate a coherent public health approach to injury prevention related to falls, but so too do agent (energy) and environmental factors. Despite long-standing knowledge of Haddon's energy-factors construct, there is a dearth of information about attempts to use energy control for fall prevention. This is likely because of the desire and need for unrestrained mobility by the elderly population. The basic physics of mechanical-energy transference remain unchanged (i.e., force = mass × acceleration). Where force acts as an injury agent upon the elderly, the predominant variable is the individual proper, and individual physiological resistance to such forces. From this perspective, force and its effect on fall-injury severity is secondary to the individual. Thus, as an

agent, energy and mechanical force effectively become host-factor dependent. Environmental factors, however, are much more directly related to the incidence of falls and, therefore, of some importance in a discussion of injury outcomes from falls among an aged population.

Environmental factors important to the etiology of falls may be defined as those fall factors attributable to extrinsic conditions present when a fall takes place. Alternately, an exclusionary definition of environmental factors would include all fall causes not distinctly linked to either the host or a mechanical force. Whereas control of host- or energy-related factors may be difficult or not possible, mitigation of environmental hazards is comparatively straightforward and easily accomplished by the individual or by those acting on behalf of an elderly person. Because environmental conditions have been implicated in up to one-half of all fall injury events (Sattin, 1992), recognition of such factors is crucial to the development of effective control efforts. Common examples of environmental factors that are found in homes as well as in public places are shown in Table 10.2.

The public or home environments traversed by the elderly population are no different than those experienced by all adult segments of the population. Churches, restau-

TABLE 10.2
Domestic and Public Environmental Fall Factors

	Factor	*Rationale*
Domestic	Bathroom fixtures	Slippery bottoms, insufficient load-bearing capacity, too low—cause fall when exiting
	Furniture: Tables, chairs, stools	Obstruct travel path; too low—cause fall when exiting
	Electrical cords	Trip, stumble hazards
	Carpets, rugs	Trip, stumble hazards
Public	Debris, rubbish	Slips, trips
	Ice, snow, wet walking surfaces	Slips
	Pedestrian traffic signals	Too short to allow comfortable crossing pace
	Pools, showers	Slips
Both	Illumination	Glare, collision hazard; dim auditorium aisles
	Stairs	Too many; risers or treads nonconforming (too high or too deep, respectively); too steep
	Handrails	One side only
	Thresholds	Trip hazards, stumble hazards

rants, governmental offices, public sidewalks, parking lots, and, of course, homes, constitute the universe of walking surfaces addressed by the elderly. The diversity of environments encountered by the elderly, however, may be decreased, with their exposure to fall opportunities limited to more routinely visited places (e.g., senior centers, churches, outpatient-care facilities). This may be fortuitous in one regard, in that fall hazards unique to a specific location will be avoided if the location is never visited. Unfortunately, that same unique hazard is probably more likely to result in a fall in an elderly person who, because of individual host factors, cannot identify or otherwise avoid it. For this reason the elimination of all potential environmental-fall factors, regardless of perceived importance, should be the public health goal.

Although the intention of fall prevention through environmental-factor modification is easily understood, scientifically proving the efficacy of various control approaches is made difficult by the inability to conduct meaningful prospective studies. Most studies of environmental-fall-injury outcomes have

been descriptive only, lacking rigorous control populations for comparison (Sattin, 1992). Accordingly, studies of the impacts of environmental factors are mostly retrospective or longitudinal, and often based more on institutional populations than on the healthy, independent elderly groups. Sattin notes another difficulty with respect to the lack of uniformity among fall survey instruments, most notably checklists. Although numerous variations of these exist, they are for the most part unstandardized, have no clear definitions other than those serving the interests of the investigator developing them, and may, in fact, lack validity and reliability.

MOTOR VEHICLE ACCIDENTS

According to the American Association of Retired Persons (AARP), presently one-third of all active motor vehicle drivers are aged fifty-five or older (AARP, 1992). Presently, approximately 13 percent of U.S. drivers make up the categorical definition of "older drivers" (i.e., sixty-five years old or older) according to the National Center for Injury Prevention and Control (NCIPC; Stevens et al., 1999). As a category, this group is expected to experience a two-thirds increase over current levels by the year 2030 (Transportation Research Board, 1994). Thus, elderly-driver numbers can be expected to swell to upwards of one in four of all drivers within the next thirty years. Because of their overrepresentation in MVAs, such a dramatic demographic shift portends significant changes in terms of elderly involvement in MVAs, MVA injuries, and MVA fatalities. Because of overall population safety, infrastructure needs, and direct costs attributable to those increases, the opportunities and needs with respect to elderly drivers is emerging as a major public health focus area.

The facts concerning MVA-related incidents among older drivers are somewhat alarming. Quoting from a CDC report concerning the elderly and MVA (Stevens et al., 1999):

1. from 1990–1997, there were 55,000 MVA fatalities in this age group,
2. this number reflects a 14% increase in the number of motor vehicle traffic related deaths for those over 65 years of age,
3. there were 1.9 million nonfatal injuries for this group in the same reporting period,
4. these injuries reflect almost a 20% increase in the number of motor vehicle injuries in the periods reported,
5. as the U.S. population grows, so too grows the number of elderly drivers, and
6. although they represent only 13% of the population, the elderly currently account for 17% of all MVA fatalities.

Despite the power of these numbers, what exact role the elderly play in national injury statistics, and the threat posed by this age group to society, is far from obvious. For example, although it is true that MVA deaths per 100,000 are higher for those seventy years or older, it is also true that this rate is second to that of drivers aged less than twenty-five years (NCIPC, 1999). Even though the proportions of older drivers is expected to increase, and the accidents from this group have, to date, demonstrated a disproportionate increase relative to other segments of the population, they do not represent the most serious group of hazardous drivers. From a public health perspective in which Years of Potential Life Lost (YPPLL) is a major factor, clearly it is the younger-driver age group where the most pressing issues rest.

There is compelling evidence that as a group, the elderly self-select away from dangerous driving conditions and situations. Elderly drivers are reported to drive fewer miles at lower speeds in less busy traffic during daylight hours (Zhang, Lindsay, Clarke, Robbins, & Mao, 2000). The elevated risks posed by seventy-years-or-older drivers is modified to an indeterminate extent by the fact that such drivers make up such a small proportion of the licensed driving population. Yet in the case of drivers aged seventy-five-plus, their fatality rates per mile driven exceed even the highest risk groups (those aged sixteen to nineteen) (Massie, Campbell, & Williams, 1995). For Canadians, whose elderly driving population can be assumed to mirror that of the United States, the percentage of aged drivers with licenses was found to decline with advancing age, demonstrating a negative association between disability and license holding (Millar, 1999). Ultimately, one is lead to the inference that a preponderance of statistical findings indicate that if the elderly experienced the same driving exposure in terms of frequency and conditions as do the majority of all drivers, then the accident, injury, and fatality rates for the elderly would be greater.

This conclusion is supported to some extent by determinations of fault from past accidents. Cooper (1990) found that drivers aged seventy-five and older were at fault for approximately four of five accidents in which they were involved. Fault increases with age, so that drivers aged sixty-five and over were responsible for 75 percent of fatal crashes in which they were involved, while drivers aged twenty-six to forty were at fault in 39 percent of such accidents (Hakamies-Blomqvist, 1993). Thus it would appear that responsibility for crashes and age-adjusted incidence rate of MVA-related fatalities are highly correlated and follow the "U"-shaped distribution reported by the Insurance Institute for Highway Safety (Figure 10.2). It should be noted that these statistics include a small proportion (17%) of incidents involving pedestrians, and thus are not exclusively MVA-fatalities.

It appears that the situation with respect to MVA in the United States is changing relatively quickly. In just the last decade, it was reported that crash rates for the elderly population had declined in the 1974–1988 timeframe, as compared with younger drivers (Stutts & Martell, 1992). Evans (1988) reported that while risks to elderly drivers indeed increased at older ages, the increases were small compared to the substantial reductions in distances driven with increasing age. However, among these same elderly drivers the total number of MVA-related fatalities increased by 30 percent between 1990 and 1997. In addition, nonfatal injuries increased by 21 percent in this same period. Such increases cannot be termed small no matter what other mitigating factors are involved (Stevens et al., 1999).

If these increases in fatalities are limited to the elderly population, one possible question to be asked is whether or not older drivers impose an excess risk of death or injury on other road users. In answer to that query,

Dulisse (1997) linked 1991 crash data from police reports to hospital discharge data in Wisconsin. He reported that drivers aged sixty-five to seventy-four did not increase excess risk of injury or fatality to others drivers, whereas drivers aged seventy-five and older were "over- associated" with increased injuries to drivers in other age groups (although the actual numbers were very small) (Dulisse, 1997). It is notable that from 1986 to 1996, the number of licensed drivers aged seventy years or older has increased by nearly 50 percent, and, that, with the aging of the population, that number will increase (National Highway Traffic Safety Administration, 1997). Whatever the total number of excess injuries or fatalities were reported by Dulisse (1997; 0.26 per 100 million driver miles), it is logical to assume it will shortly double. If this assumption becomes fact, then Dulisse's conclusions may need to be revisited insofar as they hold public health implications for society.

While some of the facts concerning MVA outcomes associated with the elderly are contentious or ambiguous, the injury-risk factors unique to this group are not. As for all injury studies, the use of host, agent, and environmental factors can help provide a better understanding of the importance of age-related-incident outcomes. Clearly, host factors, such as the mental and physical skills desirable for safe driving, deteriorate with age. Well-known host age-related variables include cognitive impairment, decreased muscle strength, increased nerve-impulse conduction time (i.e., impaired reaction time), poorer vision, and reduced night vision (Morgan & King, 1995). After adjusting for all other factors, these host characteristics in elderly drivers produced odds ratios (OR) for fatal-injury crashes of 1.37, 1.42, and 2.26 for those aged seventy to seventy-four, seventy-five to seventy-nine, and eighty and older, respectively, as compared with cohorts (Zhang et al., 2000). The same study reported

Motor Vehicle-Related Deaths per 100,000 Population, by Age and Sex, 1996

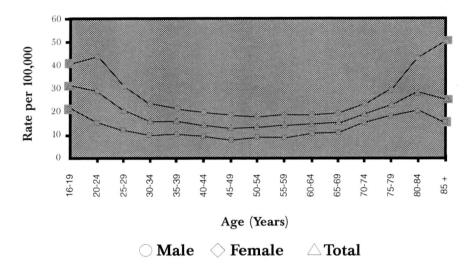

Figure 10.2. "U"-shaped traffic-fatality distribution. Source: Insurance Institute for Highway Safety, 1996.

that drivers aged seventy-five to seventy-nine with medical or physical conditions were five times more likely to have fatal MVAs than same-aged drivers with no such conditions. Somewhat counter-intuitively this study found that drivers eighty and older were only three and one-half times more likely to suffer fatalities as compared with same-aged drivers lacking medical or physical conditions. Use of alcohol by an elderly driver in a fatal MVA was seen in 6.5 percent of such crashes, as compared to the use of medications (4.2%) (Zhang et al., 2000).

Agent factors are contributing factors in MVAs involving the elderly in several ways. Vehicles overtaking another vehicle, typically at increased speed (i.e., kinetic energy), produced an OR = 5.6 with respect to in-

creased risk of fatality to the elderly driver. Furthermore, in accidents where speed were in excess of about 45 mph, the OR = 10.99 (95% confidence interval) when comparing fatal to minimal damage MVAs (Zhang et al., 2000).

Environmental conditions of notable concern to an aged population include road-surface condition, weather, and light. As noted earlier, as measured by the number of miles driven under various, adverse environmental conditions, such as wet roads or poor lighting, the elderly tend to limit their exposure to hazardous driving environments. Probably because of this fact, over two-thirds of all fatal MVAs involving the elderly occur under clear-weather conditions on dry roads (Zhang et al., 2000).

HYPOTHERMIA, BURNS, AND OTHER INJURIES

Morbidity and mortality among the elderly are led by natural causes, such as cardiovascular diseases, followed by falls and MVAs. After accounting for these three leading causes of death among the aged, the diversity of causes increases as the number of injuries and fatalities attributable to any given cause decreases. Among these secondary unnatural causes are hypothermia, burns, institutional (nosocomial) insults, poisonings, and violence and aggression.

Hypothermia

Hypothermia is defined medically as a central body temperature of less than or equal to 95 degrees Fahrenheit, and it constitutes a medical emergency since persons so affected are at greater risk of death (Hector, 1992). According to the Centers for Disease Control and Prevention (Fierro & Jenkins, 1997), season, geography, and age are all factors important in the etiology of accidental hypothermia. Specifically, hypothermia deaths are predictably more prevalent in the winter months, even in milder climates. Geographic locations subject to extreme cold or mountainous or desert terrain are also associated with increased hypothermia fatalities. In one study, almost one-half (49%) of deaths for which hypothermia was the underlying cause, the decedents were sixty-five years or older (Fierro & Jenkins, 1997). Figure 10.3 illustrates the average annual death rate, broken down by age and sex, attributable to hypothermia.

Male deaths from hypothermia exceed those of females at all age groups, as seen in Figure 10.2. In addition to sex, host factors, such as mental state (e.g., Alzheimer disease, alcohol intoxication, medications, mental illness), can affect an individual's susceptibility to this risk. Environmental factors and race are also important. For example, colder-than-normal winters for a typical location may serve to temporarily elevate hypothermia-related deaths. Associated with this, race-specific differences, such as social or economic variables, may act to increase an individual's exposure to cold temperatures, or access to protective clothing or shelter (Fierro & Jenkins, 1997).

Burns

Not only do low-temperature extremes present special hazards to an aged population, but so too do elevated temperatures, such as found in fires or hot bath water. Deaths from fire are the fifth leading cause of injury death among people sixty-five years old and older (Gulaid, Sacks, & Sattin, 1989). The elderly, as well as the very young or mentally disabled, are at elevated risk of morbidity and mortality from burns and scalds. Deaths from residential fires occur disproportionately in the southern United States and are higher among persons aged sixty-five or older (NCIPC, 1996). Of 173 patients with burn injuries, 21.4 percent were aged sixty-five or older when that same age group accounted for only 12.4 percent of the total U.S. population (Byrom, Word, Tewksbury, & Edlich, 1984). In the United States in 1988, over 5,000 persons were killed in over 500,000 house fires, and an additional 23,000 persons were left injured. In a Canadian study, the highest house fire death rates, 3.2 per 100,000 per year, occurred in those aged eighty years or older (Chernichko, Saunders, & Tough, 1993).

Causes for increased risk of burns and scalds in the elderly population are many and multifactorial. They include an inability to lower injuriously-high water heater temperature controls (Adams, Purdue, & Hunt, 1991), blood-alcohol levels, living in mobile homes,

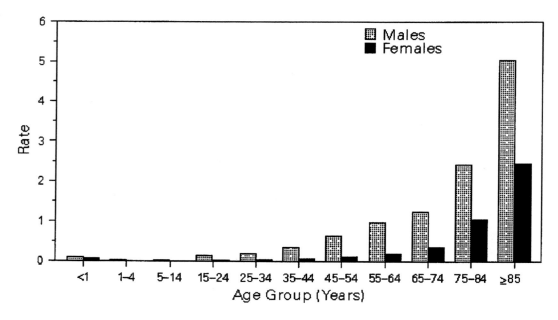

Figure 10.3. Hypothermia Death Rates per 100,000 by Age Group and Sex (1979–1994). Source: Fierro and Jenkins, 1997.

use of smoking products (Chernichko et al., 1993), reduced skin sensitivity to elevated temperatures, and inability to quickly or effectively remove oneself from tubs of scalding water (Graitcer & Sniezek, 1988). As for all segments of the population, the availability of a properly installed and working smoke detector—or lack thereof—is a significant factor affecting fire outcomes in residential settings.

Other Injuries

Fire

The current demographic trends in the United States and abroad indicate that the effect of fire as a public health concern is destined to increase over the next several decades unless public health interventions focused on this age group are designed and put in place. As the population of older persons

increases to over one in five by the year 2030, the residential-fire death toll may similarly be expected to climb (Gulaid et al., 1989). In addition to the elevated mortality expected, higher health care costs should be expected in that fifty-day hospital stays are the average for the burned population (Carroll et al., 1995). Although the survival rates of all burn victims have improved significantly in the last several decades, and most patients are eventually able to return home after discharge, almost one-third (27%) of the oldest burn victims (i.e., those aged seventy-five years and older) ultimately require permanent placement in extended-care facilities (Larson, Saffle, & Sullivan, 1992).

Poisoning

Poisoning is the fourth most frequent cause of injury-associated death among the elderly, and adverse drug reactions are the most frequent cause of fatality within this category. In general, the term poisoning includes unintentional ingestion, overdoses, or adverse reactions to drugs or alcohol, as well as suicides and overdoses or adverse reactions to illegal substances. Deaths from unintentional poisonings increase sharply among those seventy-four years and older (NCIPC, 1996). Of the unintentional subcategory of poisonings, most are caused by mental confusion or forgetfulness, resulting in the ingestion of extra doses of medications, by mistakes in the identification of medications, through use of an improper route of administration, or as the result storing prescriptions improperly (Haselberger & Kroner, 1995). Women are more likely than men to mistakenly take an excess of medication, as reported in poison control center data (Kroner, Scott, Waring, & Zanga, 1993).

While children six years and under constitute the majority of poisonings, it is the older-aged patient who is more likely to die or require hospitalization from accidental poisonings (Haselberger & Kroner, 1995; Klein-Schwartz, Oderda, & Booze, 1983).

Drowning

For all ages, drowning ranks as the fourth leading cause of unintentional injury in coastal locations, specifically Los Angeles County (O'Carroll, Alkon, & Weiss, 1988). The total number of elderly drownings each year is relatively small at approximately 500 persons. Nevertheless, that number makes drowning the fifth leading cause of unintentional-injury death among those sixty-five years and older (NCIPC, 1996). A major risk factor for such fatalities is bathtubs, according to National Center for Health Statistics data, and there is frequently an association of falling with drowning among persons aged sixty years old (Budnick & Ross, 1985). Other risk factors re-

ported by Budnick and Ross, in addition to age, include sex (males have a threefold greater incidence of drowning than do females), race, and location, for which Pacific and Mountain states had higher rates for bathtub deaths only. As with most unintentional injuries and fatalities, alcohol plays a significant role in drownings across all age groups.

Outside drowning appears to be associated most closely with prevalent risk sources in an area. Patetta and Biddinger (1988) found that two of five drownings occurred in freshwater, whereas Nichter and Everett (1989) reported that bodies of salt water were implicated in almost one-half of all Florida fatalities. In Los Angeles, the largest proportion of drownings took place in private swimming pools (O'Carroll et al., 1988). Somewhat interesting drowning appears to be a preferred means of suicide in some localities, such as Florida, where suicide accounted for 29 percent of drowning deaths among those sixty years and older and 44 percent among those eighty years and older (Nichter & Everett, 1989).

STRATEGIES FOR PREVENTION

Public health measures to improve the safety of the physical environment for an aging population deserve heightened attention owing to the increasing proportion of the aged in the total U.S. population. It is in the best interests of all stake holding parties—government, health care providers, insurance agencies, infrastructure providers, working persons, and, of course, the elderly—to begin to research, design, and implement more effective strategies for the prevention of morbidity and mortality in elderly persons. In the majority of approaches, what might best serve an aged population will almost certainly benefit persons in all age groups, especially the young. With ever-lengthening life spans among its citizens, society must turn its attention toward efforts that can help improve the quality of life for this segment of the population.

Requisite actions to be taken toward injury prevention can be both administrative and engineered, depending on the injury to be addressed and the extent to which technology or infrastructure issues can play a role in hazards abatement. For example, basic-awareness training on the hazards of scalding water can be used in some situations for elderly caregivers or residents to decrease the incidence of such injuries. Concomitantly, information about the availability and effectiveness of thermoregulator valves might be widely disseminated to infrastructure providers and elderly homeowners. For many of the causes described in this chapter, injury reduction can best be advanced through efforts in multiple areas including education, heightened awareness, regulation, engineering, and field-trial research.

In the earlier description of traumatic injury, the concept of host–agent–environment was introduced. For prevention actions aimed at falls, this same construct can be used to ameliorate and minimize both fall occurrence and, to a much lesser extent, adverse outcomes. The NCIPC recommends three host-specific and a variety of environmental actions to be taken to prevent falls among the elderly (NCIPC, 1999). Host factors include strength, balance, and coordination, all of which can be controlled to reduce falls. In addition, NCIPC recommends a review of medications taken by the elderly individual, since, either singly or in combination, some may cause light-headedness resulting in a fall. Finally, because of the increasing frequency of vision problems with age, vision checks of eyeglass prescriptions and screening for vision-reducing pathology, such as cataracts, is

recommended. In a similar fashion, environmentally related actions have been advised by the NCIPC and others (Sorock, 1988; Tideiksaar, 1986). Frequently mentioned in this category is addition of "grabber" bars in bathrooms, and the elimination of various trip hazards presented by loose rugs, objects on floors, such as books, magazines, and electrical wires. Less quantifiably effective measures include the correction of poor lighting, fixing missing or loose handrails, and lowered kitchen cabinet heights.

It must be pointed out that the effectiveness of environmental controls for the reduction of falls among the elderly is a somewhat controversial topic, and that a number of notable studies have questioned the utility of such controls as compared with other public health intervention options. Carter, Campbell, Sanson-Fisher, Redman, & Gillespie (1997) concluded that as of yet no causal link between the presence of environmental hazard and falls in older people has been established, and that more definitive work needs to be conducted. Acknowledging the counterintuitiveness of simple and obvious environmental-abatement actions, Sattin, Rodriguez, DeVito, & Wingo (1998) state that modern fall-prevention actions directed at environmental hazards may have less potential effect than previously thought (although the effectiveness of bathroom grab bars is recommend for further evaluation). Finally, in their study of 3,182 independently living persons aged sixty-five, Hornbrook, Stevens, and Wingfield (1994) found that an intervention effort aimed at environmental and behavior effects only reduced falls by 7 percent overall and did not decrease the likelihood of falls requiring medical treatment. In the face of such studies, any public health intervention aimed primarily at environmental factors to reduce falls should be carefully examined.

From a classical viewpoint directed at the elimination of the fall agent (in all cases, gravity), infrastructure changes to remove potential energy inherent in different living-area floor levels can be recommended. While such an effort will have no effect on many fall incidents, it would be beneficial in the notable exceptions of floor and step mishaps. Sorock (1988) notes that among elderly people, the most frequent and costly injuries from falls are associated with floors and stairs or steps, and promotes construction of residences for the elderly without stairs, thresholds, outside steps, or curbs. One further recommendation is to design energy-absorbing surfaces for use in high-probability impact areas, such as bathroom or bedside floors.

With respect to MVA injury and fatality prevention, the CDC–NCIPC recommends multifaceted interventions specifically tailored to the risks and needs of the older driver. These include efforts to improve the safety of vehicles, infrastructure design elements to improve traffic and pedestrian safety, and behavior modification not only of older drivers, but of passengers and pedestrians as well (Stevens et al., 1999). Vehicle-safety changes are frequently technology driven, with the latest developments including reduced-glare, high-output headlights, knee bars, and interior side-impact padding and airbags. Infrastructure-design-element changes could include larger road signs that are illuminated at night, slower designated speeds on streets, or the installation of median islands on wider roadways. Besides rigorous enforcement of existing traffic laws for all pertinent age groups, some state governments have turned to regulatory strategies centered on licensing to address the increased risks posed by some elderly drivers. In some cases, driving privileges are restricted, such that the individual may only drive at certain times of day, in certain geographic locations, or on specified road types. In addition, most states mandate physician reporting of certain age-related driving impairments, and several jurisdic-

tions are now introducing reduced license terms for older drivers (NCIPC, 1997). In larger population centers, increased presence and use of public transportation remains an affordable and relatively safe method of mobility for many elderly persons.

The explosive growth of microelectronic devices that occurred since the 1950s, largely as the result first of the transistor and then the integrated circuit, is primarily responsible for the dramatic decrease in fire fatalities among all age groups in recent decades. Due to these advances such technology became affordable and practical by way of the home smoke detector and fire alarm. Most residential fires occur in the heating months of December through March, when home-heating devices account for a preponderance of such incidents. Along with careless smoking, both types of causes can be mitigated through public health programs aimed at supplying residences with functioning smoke detectors. While such low- or no-cost detector "give away" programs have not always been directly linked with decreased fatalities (Gorman, Charney, Holtzman, & Roberts, 1985), their absence has been clearly associated with an increased risk of death in fire occurrences (Runyan et al., 1992). Public education and heightened awareness of careless smoking and safe heater use are two administrative-type interventions that round out public health efforts to minimize fire-related injuries among the elderly.

Scalding burns are easily prevented through existing technology, such as thermoregulator valves. Numerous life-threatening burns to elderly persons can be easily averted through the use of such devices, as well as by simply lowering hot-water-supply-heater thermostats. A similar approach mentioned by others included engineering controls in both kitchen and bath areas designed to lower temperatures to minimize scalding burns (Lewandowski, Pegg, Fortier, & Skimmings,

1993). However, one study found that even among elderly burn patients who realized the potential for tap-water scalding, these same individuals had not lowered the settings of their water heater in order to avoid future injury (Adam, Purdue, & Hunt, 1991). The authors conclude that behavior modification rather than public health awareness efforts would be more successful in reducing such burns.

Several studies have recommended poisoning-prevention steps that are classified as either pre-event or postevent, where efforts are aimed at prevention and case management, respectively (Haselberger & Kronger, 1995; Oderda and Klein-Schwartz, 1984). Of interest from the public health perspective is the pre-event, or prevention, stage. In addition to medication organizers designed to help the elderly track and use their prescriptions appropriately, manufacturer and pharmacy actions to better label and package medicines have been recommended.

Drowning prevention is a difficult goal, in that falls as well as suicide by drowning can obfuscate or bias attempts to measure the utility of specific interventions. Nevertheless, environmental controls have been demonstrated to be effective for the very young and thus, by extension, might reasonably be anticipated to work for the elderly population. Fencing of pools to avoid access by mentally confused persons, and the use of grab bars and slip-resistant surface coatings are both recommended as engineering approaches to drowning prevention (Nichter & Everett, 1989). Because of the psychological element linked to this type of injury, counseling has also been suggested as a means of reducing such injuries (Budnick & Ross, 1985). O'Carroll, Alkon, and Weiss (1988) caution that public health professionals must not rely solely on national drowning-site statistics for the development of effective local efforts, in that local or regional patterns of morbidity and mortality may differ significantly from national findings.

CONCLUSION

The elderly represent a special at-risk segment of the population with respect to injury morbidity and mortality. Not only are they more likely to disproportionately suffer from certain accidental causes, but their healing is oftentimes complicated by one or more host factors related to poor health immediately prior to the injury. The elderly population of the United States is large and growing. Injuries in this population have more variable outcomes than similar injuries for other groups, and injuries in the elderly are more frequently fatal than like-trauma in other groups. For these reasons, the importance of injury reduction among the elderly as a public health focus is emerging. It is contingent upon all stake holders connected to this demographic group to recognize the developing issues with respect to elderly safety and to direct resources toward novel and effective ideas for their cost-effective resolution.

REFERENCES

Adams, L. E., Purdue, G. F., & Hunt, J. L. (1991). Tap-water scald burns. Awareness is not the problem. *Journal of Burn Care and Rehabilitation, 12* (1), 91–95.

American Association for Retired Persons (AARP). (1992). *Graduated driver licensing: Creating mobility choices.* Washington, DC: Author.

Budnick, L. D., & Ross, D. A. (1985). Bathtub-related drownings in the United States, 1979–81. *American Journal of Public Health, 75* (6), 630–633.

Byrom, R. R., Word, E. L., Tewksbury, C. G., & Edlich, R. F. (1984). Epidemiology of flame burn injuries. *Burns, Including Thermal Injury, 11* (1), 1–10.

Carroll, S. M., Gough, M., Eadie, P. A., McHugh, M., Edwards, G., & Lawlor, D. (1995). A 3-year epidemiological review of burn unit admissions in Dublin, Ireland: 1988–91. *Burns, 21* (5), 379–382.

Carter, S. E., Campbell, E. M., Sanson-Fisher, R. W., Redman, S., & Gillespie, W. J. (1997). Environmental hazards in the homes of older people. *Age and Ageing, 26,* 195–202.

Chernichko, L., Saunders, L. D., & Tough, S. (1993). Unintentional house fire deaths in Alberta, 1985–1990: A population study. *Canadian Journal of Public Health, 84* (5), 317–320.

Cooper, P. J. (1990). Differences in accident characteristics among elderly drivers and between elderly and middle-aged drivers. *Accident Analysis & Prevention, 22* (5), 449–508.

Dulisse, B. (1997). Older drivers and risk to other road users. *Accident Analysis & Prevention, 29* (5), 572–582.

Evans, L. (1988). Older driver involvement in fatal and severe traffic crashes. *Journal of Gerontology, 43* (6), S186–193.

Fierro, M., & S. R. Jenkins, Centers for Disease Control and Prevention. (1997). Hypothermia-related deaths–Virginia, November 1996–April 1997. *MMWR December 12, 1997, 46* (49), 1157–1159.

Fife, D., & Barancik, J. I. (1985). Northeastern Ohio trauma study III: Incidence of fractures. *Annals of Emergency Medicine, 14,* 244–248.

Gorman, R. L., Charney, E., Holtzman, N. A., & Roberts, K. B. (1985). A successful city-wide smoke detector giveaway program. *Pediatrics, 75* (1), 14–18.

Graitcer, P. L., & Sniezek, J. E. (1988). Hospitalizations due to tap water scalds. *MMWR CDC Surveillance Summaries, 37* (1), 35–38.

Gulaid, J. A., Sacks, J. J., & Sattin, R. W. (1989). Deaths from residential fires among older people, United States, 1984. *Journal of the American Geriatrics Society, 37* (4), 331–334.

Haddon, W., Jr. (1968). The changing approach to the Epidemiology, prevention, and amelioration of trauma: The transition to approaches etiologically rather than descriptively based. *American Journal of Public Health, 58* (8), 1431–1438.

Hakamies-Blomqvist, L. (1993). Fatal accidents of older drivers. *Accident Analysis & Prevention, 25* (1), 19–27.

Haselberger, M. B., & Kroner, B. A. (1995). Drug poisoning in older patients. Preventative and management strategies. *Drugs and Aging, 7* (4), 292–297.

Hector, M. G. (1992). Treatment of accidental hypothermia. *American Family Physician, 45,* 785–792.

Hornbrook, M. C., Stevens, V. J., & Wingfield, D. J. (1994). Preventing falls among community-dwelling older persons: Results from a randomized trial. *The Gerontologist, 4* (1), 16–23.

Hoyert, D. L., Kochanek, K. D., & Murphy, S. L. (1999). Deaths: Final data for 1997. *National Vital Statistics Reports, 47* (19), 1–104. Hyattsville, MD: National Center for Health Statistics.

Institute of Medicine (IOM). (1999). The injury field. In R. J. Bonnie, C. E. Fulco, & C. T. Liverman, (Eds.), *Reducing the burden of injury advancing prevention and treatment* (pp. 18–38). Washington, DC: National Academy Press.

Insurance Institute for Highway Safety (IIHS). *Facts, 1996 Fatalities: Elderly.* Arlington, VA: IIHS, 1997.

Klein-Schwartz, W., Oderda, G. M., & Booze, L. (1983). Poisoning and the elderly. *Journal of the American Geriatrics Society, 31* (4), 195–199.

Kramarow, E., Lentzner H., Rooks, R., Weeks, J., & Saydah, S. (1999). *Health, United States, 1999 with Health and Aging Chartbook* (DHHS Pub No. [PHS] 99-1232-1; 9-0477) (pp 1–27). Hyattsville, MD: National Center for Health Statistics.

Kroner, B. A., Scott, R. B., Waring, E. R., & Zanga, J. R. (1993). Poisoning in the elderly: Characterization of exposures reported to a poison control center. *Journal of the American Geriatrics Society, 41* (8), 842–846.

Lewandowski, R., Pegg, S., Fortier, K., & Skimmings, A. (1993). Burn injuries in the elderly. *Burns, 19* (6), 513–515.

Larson, C. M., Saffle, J. R., & Sullivan, J. (1992). Lifestyle adjustments in elderly patients after burn injury. *Journal of Burn Care and Rehabilitation, 12* (1), 48–52.

Massie, D. L., Campbell, K. L., & Williams, A. F. (1995). Traffic accident involvement rates by driver age and gender. *Accident Analysis & Prevention, 27* (1), 73–87.

Millar, W. J. (1999). Older drivers–A complex public health issue. *Health Reports, 11* (2), 59–71.

Morgan, R., & King, D. (1995). The older driver–A review. *Postgraduate Medical Journal, 71,* 525–528.

National Center for Injury Prevention and Control (NCIPC). (1996). *Major causes of unintentional injuries among older persons: An annotated bibliography.* Atlanta, GA: Centers for Disease Control and Prevention.

——. (1997). *Motor vehicle-related deaths among older American fact sheet.* Retrieved May 15, 2000, from the World Wide Web www.cdc.gov/ncipc/factsheets/older.htm.

——. (1999). *Check for safety: A home checklist for older adults.* Atlanta, GA: Centers for Disease Control and Prevention.

National Highway Traffic Safety Administration. (1997). *Traffic safety facts 1996: Older population.* Washington, DC: Author.

Nichter, M. A., & Everett, P. B. (1989). Profile of drowning victims in a coastal community. *Journal of the Florida Medical Association, 76* (2), 253–256.

O'Carroll, P. W., Alkon, E., & Weiss, B. (1988). Drowning mortality in Los Angeles County, 1976–1984. *JAMA, 260* (3), 380–383.

O'derda, G. M., & Klein-Schwartz, W. (1984). Poison prevention in the elderly. *Drug Intelligence and Clinical Pharmacy, 18* (3), 183–185.

Patetta, M. J., & Biddinger, P. W. (1998). Characteristics of Drowning Deaths in North Carolina. *Publich Health Reports, 103* (4), 406–411.

Peel, N. (2000). Validating recall of falls by older people. *Accident Analysis and Prevention, 32* (3), 371–372.

Runyan, C. W., Bangdiwala, S. I., Linzer, M. A., Sacks, J. J., & Butts, J. (1992). Risk factors for fatal residential fires. *New England Journal of Medicine, 327* (12), 859–863.

Sattin, R. W. (1992). Falls among older persons: A public health perspective. *Annual Review of Public Health, 13,* 489–508.

Sattin, R. W., Rodriguez, J. G., DeVito, C. A., & Wingo, P. A. (1998). Home environmental hazards and the risk of fall injury events among community-dwelling older persons. *Journal of the American Geriatrics Society, 46,* 669–676.

Shapiro, J. P. (1998, November 16). John Glenn's mixed message on aging. In *U.S. News and World Report.* Retrieved May 8, 2000, from the World Wide Web http://www.usnews.com/usnews/issue/981116/16old.htm.

Sorock, G. S. (1988). Falls among the elderly: Epidemiology and prevention. *American Journal of Preventive Medicine, 4* (5), 282–288.

Stevens, J. A., Hasbrouck, L., Durant, T. M., Dellinger, A. M., Batabyal, P. K., Crosby, A. E., Valluru, B. R., Kresnow, M., & Guerrero, J. (1999). Surveillance for injuries and violence among older adults. *CDC Surveillance Summaries, December 17, 1999. MMWR 1999, 48* (SS-8), 27–50.

Stutts, J. C., & Martell, C. (1992). Older driver population and crash involvement trends, 1974–1988. *Accident Analysis & Prevention, 24* (4), 317–27.

Tideiksaar, R. (1986). Preventing falls: Home hazard checklists to help older patients protect themselves. *Geriatrics, 41* (5), 26–28.

Tinetti, M. E., Speechley, M., & Ginter, S. F. (1988). Risk factors for falls among elderly persons living in the community. *New England Journal of Medicine, 319* (26), 1701–1707.

Transportation Research Board. (1994). *Transportation Research Circular No. 429: The licensing of older drivers.* Transportation Research Board, Washington, DC: Author.

Zhang, J., Lindsay, J., Clarke, K., Robbins, G., & Mao, Y. (2000). Factors affecting the severity of motor vehicle traffic crashes involving elderly drivers in Ontario. *Accident Analysis & Prevention, 32,* 117–125.

VI. TECHNOLOGY AND AGING

Chapter 11

SQUARING THE CIRCLE: DEMOGRAPHY AND TECHNOLOGY

GARI LESNOFF-CARAVAGLIA

MODERN SCIENCE had its initiation during the late sixteenth and early seventeenth centuries. Its evolvement was due not so much by the acquisition of new knowledge about the world, but as a new way of thinking about that world in the broadest sense (Hatton & Plouffe, 1997). Such scientific theorizing can lead to the discovery of creative practical applications that largely stem from such new connections or relationships of thoughts and ideas. In a similar vein, alterations in the composition of the world population have served to foster new perspectives. The increase in life expectancy and the increasing presence of older members within societies has led to new horizons in scientific development and its practical applications.

Technological innovation has irretrievably altered the course of human lives. It continues, however, to evoke strong positive and negative reactions. The introduction of a new technology brings in its wake the possibility of unforeseen inherent occurrences that are the result of the presence of the technology along with its potential malfunction. For example, the development of the ship carried with it the potential of shipwreck, the train of train wrecks, the automobile of automobile accidents, and the airplane of plane crashes. Some such disasters, such as nuclear accidents, can have far-reaching effects. Media technology has the potential to alter human frames of reference by supplanting the real world with fleeting inconstant images. Medical technology has the capacity to make physical encroachments, such as the taking over of biological functions (the pacemaker, for example). The human body through the procedures of transplants can be regarded as being controlled by technology (Armitage, 2000).

Increases in life expectancy to ages of 125 and beyond can also potentially embody the notion of the unforeseen as accidents in that advances in technology are responsible for increases in life expectancy. The effects of such life extension upon society and the individual have yet to be determined. The advent of "mercy killing" legislation in some nations may lead to new views of what constitutes "life" and the appropriate timing of death. In addition, the future may hold totally new diseases and disabilities that result from the increases in life expectancy. There may well be future references to the "accident" of old age.

TECHNOLOGY: THE PRACTICAL APPLICATION OF SCIENCE

The practical application of science can be at either the levels of high technology or low technology. On occasion, simple solutions on the level of low technology, such as redesigning tools or altering home environments, have more practical outcomes. Some high-technology streams, such as genetics, robotics, informatics, and communication technology, provide the potential for very powerful and controversial applications. For example, the science of genetics is leading to the possibility of predicting such conditions as heart disease and Alzheimer's disease.

In industrial applications, robotics has meant freeing labor from unwanted repetitive tasks, as well as freeing up labor for more important tasks. It has also been instrumental in effecting speed of production permitting automobile manufacturers, for example, to complete a car in thirty-two seconds. Such applications of robotics can be used to meet human needs, as well. The most important feature of the application of robotics so far is that it has provided a certain amount of dignity for the individual who is helped. It offers the promise of being able to do things for oneself that normally require a caregiver to perform. For example, fetch-and-carry systems could routinely deliver various supplies to the rooms of some nursing home residents. A robotic system, Helpmate, is being used in hospitals to deliver late trays and to perform errands.

Communication is probably the most important feature of human experience—removing isolation and preventing depression. Although most of today's elderly have had little experience with computers, the evidence, although scant, indicates that they are receptive to using the new technology, either "as is" or when tailored to their needs. The elderly of the future are likely to be more open to using computers because of exposure to them throughout their lifetimes, as well as their recognition of the empowerment aspects inherent in being abreast of new technology.

Computer-Assisted Health Instruction

The use of computer-assisted health instruction is a logical extension of self-care and self-help. The growing use of information technologies for educating the public about maintaining health, and preventing or treating disease, is rapidly increasing the number of software programs on health education and management.

The relevance of this technological phenomenon for use by and for the elderly has not yet been widely recognized in either the private or public sector; however, the use of information technologies, particularly the microcomputer, could help the elderly maintain independent living and is likely to be particularly effective when used in conjunction with physicians and other health care providers.

Expanding the knowledge base also provides older clients with information that allows them to judge the quality and appropriateness of treatment modalities. By becoming sophisticated consumers, they are also in the position to initiate malpractice suits. While some such actions are justifiable, others are brought against the health care professional to fatten retirement coffers.

Future computer use by patients is expected to reach beyond providing them with information about their health status to become a virtual "hospital on the wrist." The concept of the hospital on the wrist includes a computer, a microminiature analyzer, and drug reservoirs with electronic probes capable of monitoring changes in the body, measuring vital signs, analyzing blood and enzymes, cardiac monitoring, and comparing findings with expected values for the individual wearing it. The device would be able to communicate with computers of the wearer's physician as well as with computers in hospitals or other medical institutions and could administer drugs directly through the skin. It could also signal the patient when direct medical care was needed.

As envisioned, the hospital on the wrist does not offer the patient total medical autonomy but includes interactions between the patient, the patient's computer, and the computers of health professionals. Computers and telecommunications now in use by patients for health purposes are oriented to assisting physicians and other health professionals with patient management in various health settings.

Computer-assisted health care that complements professional care may enable chronically-ill people to remain in their homes when they wish to do so. A number of factors point to an increase in the proportion of the chronically-ill population who may choose home care over institutional care in the future. Moreover, advances in medical technology now allow services to be provided at home that once required an institutional setting. Reductions in size and complexity have made many machines portable. Telecommunication equipment connecting patients and health professionals can facilitate their interaction and enhance the quality of care.

"Smart" sensors—those incorporating microprocessors—currently sense and measure blood pressure, pulse rates, body temperature, blood glucose, and electrical activity of the heart. Measurements of other physical functions have been developed for use in rehabilitating handicapped patients; those that have the potential for computer-based processing may be applicable for monitoring the health status of segments of the older population. Computer technology can enable hospital-based approaches for managing chronic diseases to be expanded to the home.

Computers that monitor such household functions as turning on and off lights, radios, and televisions, and providing wake-up service by voice synthesizers that speak preprogrammed messages could be programmed to remind elderly persons of medication times, instruct them on diet and medical care practices, and remind them of physician and other health professional visits. Devices could be programmed to track medicinal intake and periodically dispense medicines. A bedside, automated programmable dispensing machine has been developed for use in hospitals that may be adaptable for use in the home.

Medical Devices and Instrumentation for the Elderly

The human body is endowed from birth with many natural defenses, including autoimmunity and redundancy of tissues, organs, and parts, enabling it to resist the changes that come with age, disease, and trauma. As human beings age, such natural defenses gradually fail and may require replacements. The growing number of medical devices and instrumentation that has characterized modern health care, along with transplants, may well substitute for loss of such natural defenses. This may also pave the way for the technological control of human bodily functions (Quivery, 1990).

Society has rejected two of the most obvious remedies of the past, hiding the disability or hiding the disabled. Alternatives are now available in aids that are attractive, and that would be used without reservation, and, in some cases, even with pride. Such aids run the gamut from the vast array of visual aids to prosthetic devices and footgear.

Initially, technical aids were not always popular with the professionals in institutions and with society in general. Much work had to be done to create a degree of acceptance for the aids; it was easier in some cases than in others. The fact that many professional people are uncomfortable with technical devices and resist their introduction has been all too evident. This has been particularly the case in introducing new devices to facilitate patient mobility and those that alter existing routines in patient care.

Technological advances in the medical-device area have had a profound impact on patient survival and improved quality of life. The benefits have been particularly notable for chronic diseases or dysfunctions that become more prevalent with increasing age (Coombs, 1994). Technologies that have increased life expectancy include advances in public hygiene and sanitation, reductions in infectious diseases, and continued improvement and accessibility of general health care. Today's medical devices can improve the functioning of, and, in some instances, replace body parts that have deteriorated due to age or disease. Some examples include dental prostheses that are used in cases of tooth loss, artificial knees, hip prostheses, and mechanical aids that help with problems of mobility.

The most significant contributions have been made in the area of implantable systems. These include intraocular lenses, heart valves, urethral sphincters, penile implants, cochlear implants, electrical pain control, cardiac pacemakers, defibrillators, artificial joints, and drug pumps. In each instance, the intent is to return the patient to a situation as close to normal as the state of the art permits. By virtue of their being implanted, these devices become

relatively transparent to the patient. They tend to free the patient of the responsibility as well as the emotional involvement that may accompany the disease (Harris, 1983).

With the advances in home health care, the older population can receive intravenous medications in a home setting instead of the hospital. This helps prevent environmental confusion in that companionship and security in familiar surroundings are available. Services, such as homemakers, allow older persons to maintain mobility in the household. Video- and audiocassettes are helpful in rehabilitation. Large type is available in health instruction magazines and with medical instructions. National organizations such as the Arthritis Foundation and the American Cancer Society have grown significantly and help pave the way for the latest medical discoveries.

Ethical dilemmas abound with respect to when, where, and how to use such medical interventions. They involve the deliberations of physicians, social workers, and third-party payers who become, in fact, gatekeepers in terms of health care allocation. When would a person be considered too old to be given a particular device? What is the rationale for keeping older persons alive when they suffer from irreversible brain disease or dementia? The responses to such questions become increasingly more complex as medical technology and science continue to advance and to provide alternative-treatment possibilities. Technology now can control the timing and quality of individual demise.

Fears of Technology

The impersonal quality and the anonymity frequently associated with technological development also carry with them the fear that the society itself will be swallowed up by the "machine." Any form of civilization based on technology that might minimize the role of the individual also gives rise to the fear that particular persons or groups of individuals might be regarded as extraneous to the mainstream of society and thus expendable. This fear may be particularly experienced by older persons for whom the quality of life is closely linked to social participation and particular significance as individuals. The diminishment of coping skills and dependency on others for assistance is for some a humiliating and frustrating experience. The diminishment of roles for older persons, both in the world of work and within the family itself, has also fostered a perception of the world as a place accessible only to those who are not only more physically able, but who are also more in consonance with the contemporary culture, that is, the age of technology.

An additional fear is that the presence of machines could dictate the nature of human lifestyles. For example, the aged might be expected to avail themselves of particular machines and to adapt their lives accordingly. Loss of mobility might mean not ever going outdoors again as a television screen can transmit environmental information to the homebound individual. Not to accept such a substitution might mean being regarded as someone who is "acting out" or aberrant in behavior, uncooperative, mentally ill, or even possibly suicidal. The range of choice, due to the presence of the machine, may become seriously circumscribed. What was intended as freedom may result in a fettering of human personal decision. Will acceptance of the machine become the basis for determining what is normal in old age? To grow old alongside one's machines may be the expected model Lesnoff-Caravaglia, 1987). The contemporary image of the older person spending hours before the television set may have already prepared the first stage in this evolution. When to say "no" to the machine increases as an ethical dilemma, particularly when the machine may mean the extension of life, or the prolongation of death, or possibly a little of each.

The fear of the "takeover" by technology is nonetheless very real. Because of their independent source of power and their semiautomatic operation even in their cruder forms, machines have seemed to have a reality and an independent existence apart from the user. The most durable conquests of the machine, however, lay not in the instruments themselves, but in the modes of life made possible via the machine and in the machine (Mumford, 1963). The refrigerator and the automobile are but two common examples of machines that have altered existence. Few would willingly return to the days of the icebox or travel by foot.

The clue to modern technology was the displacement of the organic and the living by the artificial and mechanical. In the past, the irrational and demonic aspects of life had invaded spheres where they did not belong. It was a step forward to discover that bacteria, not evil brownies, were responsible for curdling milk and that an air-cooled motor was more effective than a witch's broomstick for rapid long-distance transportation (Mumford, 1963).

Fears of technology, however, can be practically dispelled if it is recognized that the machine developed as a parallel or complement to the kind of society that evolved. As part of such total development, the machine shares with society a common past, present, and future. The machine thus has no role apart from that which society chooses to give it. The difference between the First and Second Industrial Revolutions may lie, however, in the intense rapidity with which various contemporary technologies are introduced and applied. Nonetheless, the technical triumphs of the machine cannot be separated from the general human achievements of a particular era.

No matter how completely technology relies on the objective procedure of the sciences, it does not form an independent system, like the universe. One cannot ignore the psychological as well as the practical origins of the machine. Technology exists as an element in human culture, and it promises well or ill to the same degree that the social groups that exploit it promise well or ill (Lesnoff-Caravaglia, 1999).

The Brave "Old" World

The world has taken another step in a unique evolutionary process. The notion of the physical world as being linked to an evolutionary process has long been held, but the fact that the material construct of the world—the world created by human ingenuity—has also developed and grown in a manner strongly suggestive of an evolutionary progression is recent.

For example, if arms are not long enough to reach a desired object, artificial means are developed for either reaching the item or for grasping the item and having it brought close. To speak to an individual who is miles distant, there is no longer the necessity to devise special drums or whistles to attract attention, to make smoke signals, or even to write. To witness an activity that is occurring some distance away, the individual does not have to move physically, but can have the incident portrayed over a screen. To move to a location that is at some distance, there is no need to worry about personal physical endurance or to plan on how much food to dry and store in preparation for a trip.

In this particular evolutionary process, the capability to perform certain actions is augmented without physical changes to the person. People do not grow longer, sharper teeth or claws; instead they invent tools or methods for processing materials. The tele-phone has become the new voice and ears; the television new eyes; the automobile and airplane feet, while the computer is the messenger. For sustenance, unfortunately, the invention has been "fast food."

This is the first time in human history that so many persons have lived long enough to reach the age of sixty-five and beyond. This is the first time in human history that technology has intruded so definitively into personal, individual life space extending to the world of work, recreation, family life, health care, and religion.

Today it is possible to consider intervention and prevention strategies in caring for older persons that were inconceivable as recently as ten years ago. This capability, in turn, has fomented debates in the areas of ethics, economics, and health care that have troubled the very fabric of society. Such issues, as they impinge upon public health, personal autonomy, and decision making, play a significant role in determining the level of independence and freedom accorded older individuals. They also raise the spectre of the amount and kind of dependence the presence of technology fosters and give rise to the question: Will such accelerated advances in technology eventually lead to super playpens for the elderly in the form of automated homes? Although automated homes may be regulated by older persons, they may create an electronic lifestyle that permits social interaction of a very particular kind. Such restricted social interaction could obviate the need for the physical presence of other human beings. It could result in a kind of inertia by which one could participate in everything that happens throughout the world without the need to be physically present (Virilio, 2000).

In contrast, the increase in the numbers of older persons and persons with disabilities could present problems that only the presence of large amounts of new technology can resolve. Future life may be conducted in an atmosphere of limited human interaction, with technology providing life support, communication, and entertainment from an encapsulated environment. The life of the astronaut may be duplicated for those of extreme age who present with serious disabilities. The situation of many older persons already resembles that of the astronauts in space, and the resemblance may increase in the near future. Older persons, much like astronauts, frequently exist in a restricted environment that is beset by problems related to activities of daily living, physical activity, and recreation.

With advancing age, the issue of dependency becomes very real. There is a slow erosion of the locus of control in the lives of persons as they live into the eighth and ninth decades of life. Such an altered locus of control may well increase in the future unless technological interventions are instituted.

Furthermore, the crisis in health care personnel has led to an even closer scrutiny of the potential uses of technology in health care environments. If there are insufficient numbers of persons available to perform services, machines (robots) must do the work. For example, with the reduction in adequate numbers of personnel, clerical work often performed by nurses can be more efficiently accomplished by computers, allowing nurses more time for one-on-one nursing care (Englehardt, 1989).

Another example is in the lifting and moving of patients. This can be more easily and safely accomplished through appropriate devices, thus reducing the number of staff required, as well as lessening the severity of back problems sustained by health care personnel. The debate with respect to "high touch versus high tech" has virtually vanished from the scene because it is now patently clear that it is possible to increase high touch only when aided by the presence of high tech.

Lifestyles of caregivers, such as family members, can be appreciably ameliorated through the introduction of technologies in the home environment. The ability to remain in control of one's life even in very advanced old age allows for individual dignity and self-esteem. Both elements are significant factors in the maintenance of physical and psychological well-being.

States of dependency are made up of a variety of factors. They include experiencing multiple chronic symptoms; a limitation on personal options, dependency on the physical environment that was once taken for granted; and dependency on persons drawn from the family unit or public agencies. To grow old and to be well has not been a common human experience. Increases in life expectancy means that persons can live long lives without experiencing many limitations. Once they begin to experience some restrictions, dependency becomes a source of deep and abiding frustration.

SHRINKING OF THE PERSONAL WORLD

Just as the expansion of the world is a gradual and often overwhelming experience for the young child , the subtle contraction of the world and one's capability to experience it, is also fraught with fear and questioning on the part of older persons. Older individuals tend to use less and less of what can be termed *the total environment*. This gradual restriction often begins when the person leaves the world of work at retirement. A second point at which there is a reduced level of participation in the outside world occurs when the individual experiences the onset of a chronic illness. Further restrictions occur as the individual ages and sensory deficits, such as vision or hearing losses, become more intensified. Such physical alterations can at times be sufficiently severe to constitute a need to alter individual lifestyle. A frequent change is to limit outside activities, with a concomitant increased usage of the home environment.

Home environments are used at a much higher rate by older persons due to physical constraints, economic difficulties, and even psychological conditions such as fear. The location of the residence of the person plays an important role in the perception of safety within the environment and the view of the outside environment as being essentially hostile. Such a restriction to the home environment leads to what can be termed a *basic-needs orientation*. Requirements for the carrying out of activities of daily living (ADLs) take on increasing importance as the limitations due to senescent changes and disabilities due to disease continue to escalate.

Independence in this shrinking environment continues to be eroded, and there is the necessary enlistment of outside resources. The entrance of other family members, health care personnel, social service agencies, and a host of other assistive groups into the individual's private life means the lessening of decision-making power by the older person. As one gradually loses control of one's personal life due to illness, immobility, or sensory loss, the control of that life is assumed by outside agencies. Such a decrease in control is usually followed by further constrictions of the individual world.

Even when the person continues to reside at home, there is a progressive diminished use of all of the home space and features. Such diminished use can begin with the individual's not using the basement, attic, garden, or garage. Outdoor activity is reduced and eventually ceases. Particular rooms of the home are no longer used, such as the living room, dining room, study, or spare bedrooms. Should the person have dif-

ficulty using stairs, the bedroom may be moved to a first-floor room and use made of a first-floor bath when it exists. Some home modifications may be necessary to effect such a move. The individual may remain on the second floor if such accommodations to a first level are not possible.

Restrictions of the life space eventually center on "areas of survival." These areas are the kitchen, the bathroom, and the bedroom. The circle of experience appreciably narrows, and control slowly, but inexorably, moves away from the individual. As the person continues to age and become more dependent, even possibly bedfast, the locus of control becomes more decidedly assumed by outside agencies. The final area of control, the most personal, is taken over by someone else at the bedside.

The types of activities that usually suffer some restriction generally fall into the categories of instrumental activities of daily living (IADLs) or ADLs. Although many of these activities are considered routine, their performance reflects on individual functional capabilities. Problems in the performance of such activities are frequently the basis for a determination as to whether or not the person can live independently and whether institutionalization needs to be considered.

One intervention that can help offset some problems is the development of augmentative technologies that permit persons to perform many of the activities necessary for independent living. Decreasing abilities to use particular appliances, to use the entire living space, or to provide for the accommodation of sensory losses, reduced mobility, and the reduction in physical strength can all be counteracted by modifications of existing homes or the construction of homes that are prosthetic in nature. The conventional home may be a lethal environment for the elderly. Just as environments for special populations, such as children, take into account their special needs, environments for older persons require a careful assessment to determine their suitability.

The concept of designing products and environments so that they are usable to the maximum number of age groups is known as universal design. Such design applications can effectively extend the number of years a person can remain and function at home. This is of particular significance for older persons for whom the housing of preference is one's own home. A simple series of inexpensive alterations, such as adding more lighting or including press-on or motion-sensor light switches, dual-sided banisters on stairways, adjustable countertops, lever controlled door knobs, carpets with a tight weave to prevent tripping, or installing safety bars or handheld showers in the bathroom, can make such a choice a reality. Since the elderly spend more time at home than any other demographic group, a constant upgrading or retrofitting of their homes to keep up with changing capabilities is an important health issue.

Furthermore, the functional capability of the individual allows for decision making in terms of how life will be scheduled and structured. Deciding how to spend one's day, or what the daily menu will be, is often regarded as routine and a matter of course. When such decisions must be made in concert with other individuals, or when decisions regarding such issues are determined solely by others, the locus of control has effectively moved away from the individual. When such control includes areas such as dressing, feeding, and toileting, the loss of control become almost complete.

The situation becomes one that can possibly be best described as "Maslow in reverse." In Maslow's pyramid (1968), persons satisfy lower basic needs and move up to the top or pinnacle of the pyramid to reach a personal sense of achievement in intellectual or spiritual arenas. Older persons have spent their lives in striving to reach the top of the pyramid, and many achieve this task successfully. Now that they are at the top of the pyramid and are aged, they must move downwards or backwards, and this is a negative progression that is not happily accepted. To move down the slope of the pyramid means preoccupation with psychological and biological functioning. Furthermore, since such basic needs had once been mastered, there may be anger and frustration at having to attend so exclusively to meeting these needs again, particularly when one's tolerance and ability to cope are waning. This move also constitutes a radical change in self-image, and those intellectual, spiritual, or professional achievements that form part of self-identity pale against the reality of negotiating a steep flight of stairs or opening a food container. For older persons, intellectual, professional, spiritual, aesthetic, and avocational growth seems to have been dismissed, disregarded, or diminished in meaning.

Physical movement also is restricted as the environment shrinks. Contrary to the dictates of human health requirements, older persons become more sedentary and engage in less exercise. Part of this reduced physical activity results from reduced participation in the environment because of physical or environmental barriers. Environmental barriers can include the structure of the home, its layout, and the presence of stairs. Storage space and appliances may be difficult to access or use, thus cutting back on the person's activity. Shrinkage of the environment due to the nature of the environment itself means that there is a lack of fit between the person and the environment. Such a lack of consonance means that the person is less stimulated by the environment and finds it to be more of a frustration. Increasingly, drawing away from the environment and curtailing their ability to manipulate the environment to their own best advantage results in persons losing control of their lives, and, eventually, of themselves. Both physical and mental deterioration may result, and it is at this juncture that a loss of interest in life may manifest itself. Coupled with such negative views of the self are the feelings of impotence and uselessness, which can lead to suicidal ideation.

The social climate in which many older persons experience aging is often bereft of caring friends and family members. Support groups may not be available due to several factors, including three principal ones: death, distance, and divorce. Some persons practice an avoidance of community groups or agencies in fear of the discovery of their inadequacies and potential placement in a nursing home. Family members may also decide to avoid older family members out of fear of being expected to participate in their care which may be arduous and tedious.

The longer a person lives, the greater is the likelihood of the experience of the death of a loved one. Such death experiences may be multiple, and the person begins to feel like "the last leaf" and to question the purpose of continued existence. Due to the shrinking of the world, fewer persons are available to fill the gaps left by the dead.

Not only do the elderly suffer from the death of persons, but they are also plagued by distance. They themselves may have moved a number of times during their lifetimes and not have developed lasting friendships. Relatives, due to the mobility of society, may be scattered across the globe. Despite the advertisements of telephone companies, long-distance calling is not an effective substitute. Relationships are maintained only through persistent and ongoing contact, and distance attenuates many once-close relationships.

Divorce effectively divides older persons from potential support groups. Women who are divorced in old age have difficulty in finding new partners. Men are more likely to re-build personal lives with new partners due to the greater presence of older women and society's sanction of older men's marrying women of much younger ages. A man can have two or three families throughout life, whereas many older women are limited to one. The longer life expectancy afforded women continues to exacerbate this problem.

With the increase in the divorce rate, younger women may develop complicated family patterns over time with ties that include a variety of nonblood relatives. Divorced parents frequently are estranged from children or have a series of children, both of their own and of their succeeding partners, such that responsibility for the older parent is often muddied. There is much confusion about with whom the moral responsibility for an aging parent lies. Should it be the daughter who has never lived in the mother's home? A step-granddaughter? The deceased husband's natural daughter who resided with them while attending high school?

When children are available, they are faced with responsibilities for several sets of older relatives. These may include one's own parents, parents-in-law, aging aunts and uncles, and older siblings. In addition, they have responsibilities to their own immediate families and may have to work to contribute to the family income.

Technology and Aging

It is also important to bear in mind that the elderly are not the handicapped. Their concerns and problems may stem from similar dysfunctions, but the problems of the elderly are precipitated and experienced in old age and are often brought on by the process of normal aging. It is also important to note that there is insufficient anthropometric data on the elderly. Not enough is known about reaching capabilities or the strength potential of older persons. Functional body measurements are needed that define not only what the elderly are, but what they can do in terms of body movements, ambulation, arm and leg reaches, and task performance–the kinds of data needed by engineers who deal with the design of housing, health and chronic-care facilities, transport vehicles, appliances and equipment, and prostheses. Most of the studies done in these areas have been based on males in their mid-20s, leaving a serious research gap. Much of the application of technology also assumes its usage by younger clients and must be modified to suit the needs and capabilities of older persons (Howell, 1994). This is particularly true of the development of wheelchairs.

To provide for a continuity of experience for older persons, surveys or assessments of homes should be an ongoing activity. Such inventories or assessments can evaluate what is presently available to the individual, as well as what can be added to the environment to ensure greater independence. There needs to be a degree of choice permitted the older person in the inclusion or dismissal of particular technologies. As changes are required to adequately accommodate the needs of older persons, home arrangements and the additions of technologies need to be a steady feature of the provision of care. Since accidents figure so prominently in the health care of older persons, safety is an important aspect of all home assessments and contributes to the reduction of overall health care expenditures.

Providers of services to the elderly can also use many of the housekeeping technologies, with the added bonus of having those chores that are boring, repetitive, demeaning, or overly fatiguing performed through mechanical means. The presence of technological devices can significantly add to the interpersonal exchanges between caregiver and client due to less time being given to routine activities. The cost of such home health care would be markedly reduced due to lower labor costs.

Education and Attitudes

To introduce a wide array of technologies, the attitudes not only of older persons, but of caregivers, researchers, industrialists, and the general public must be taken into account. Do these groups agree as to what types of technologies are appropriate? Is the negative attitude toward all things old, including people, a deterrent? An educational program to counter such negative views and attitudes needs to be instituted at a variety of levels. In particular, marketing individuals and industry must be led to see this new and growing market as one to explore. The aging bias that is seen in research must be offset by a recognition that new advances in technologies that can be used with the elderly are often of such universal design that they can be widely employed by all age groups.

The introduction and acceptance of new technologies is a human problem of long standing. For example, a newspaper editorial in 1834 said of a medical instrument:

> "That it will ever come into general use, notwithstanding its value, is extremely doubtful because its beneficial application requires much time and gives a good bit of trouble, both to the patient and the practitioner because its hue and character are foreign and opposed to all our habits and associations. There is something ludicrous in the picture of a gray physician proudly listening though a long tube applied to the patient's thorax."

That *London Times* editorial was criticizing the introduction of the stethoscope (Lesnoff-Caravaglia, 2000).

LOSSES IN OLD AGE

The range of losses experienced by older persons cannot be equated with losses experienced at any other time in an individual's personal history. Many of these losses are of a permanent nature and strike at the very heart of personal identity: work role, social role, loss of sensory acuity (Who is prepared to grow old and blind?), the death of nearly everyone one has known, and an alteration in the relationship between the self and the environment. When physical, economic, and familial changes are the norm, individuals begin to question their personal identity. Neighborhood changes are often viewed as a form of death. Once initiated, many of these changes are irreversible.

Furthermore, social roles undergo change without the person's being able to intercede in such alteration. They are caught in the flow of time. In role repetition, for example, the aged mother frequently experiences the return of her adult children to the home, and she repeats her nurturing role. Adult children return to the home for a variety of reasons. Examples include the return of the ill and aging son by the daughter-in-law, or the return to the home of an adult daughter whose husband has divorced her and left her for a younger woman.

In role equivalence, both mother and son may be residents in the same nursing home and are both regarded by society at large as "old." Generational differences are snuffed out. Aging families engage in discussion of the merits of nursing homes in much the same way they once discussed the advantages of particular schools or colleges. Family visits may be carried out by moving from floor to floor of the same nursing home or through visits in different departments of the same hospital.

In role reversal, the mother is frequently the recipient of care by children who may in fact become her "guardians." Such role alteration is fraught with resentment and discomfort on both sides. People are not prepared to be long-living neither economically (The recent barrage of sale of the jewels of famous aging women provides a good contemporary example.) nor psychologically. Never in the history of humankind has this opportunity for such long life presented itself to so many as a common projection of self.

Another factor that has important implications for the acceptance and use of technologies is the fact that the older population is made up principally of females. Females generally have received little exposure to things mechanical or technical. One exception is the older female population of the former Soviet Union. Following World War II, with the male population practically decimated, Russian women had to take on all forms of labor. The herculean effort undertaken by the women is today commemorated by a national Russian holiday. This is also why nursing home residents (principally women) in Russia are accorded the status of war veterans.

HEALTH CARE

The fit or lack of fit between the person and the environment has a determining effect upon when aging occurs and how the process is made manifest. The environment as the locus for aging provides a significant point of interaction that largely influences why particular changes are experienced with advancing age. Environments that do not adequately match the needs and interests of the elderly often serve to accelerate the aging process, resulting in premature aging. Prosthetic environments that are malleable to the needs and interests of the elderly can be regarded as augmentative in that they serve to extend the capacities of aging persons and are geared toward promoting continued maximal functioning.

Traditional home, institutional, and work environments can maximize or restrict optimal functioning in the elderly. The incorporation of both high and low technologies in such key settings can offset the decrements of age. Such interventions can be person oriented or environment oriented. Person-oriented changes include such adaptations as dentures, cosmetic surgery, and organ transplants. Environment-oriented changes have taken on a wide variety of constructs derived from computer technology. Electronic cottages that permit people to continue to conduct a variety of occupational roles while remaining in the home setting are but one example.

Through an electronically controlled environment, control can be exerted through the interaction with a finger, the eye, or the voice. Behavior is accommodated to the type of control to be effected and the capabilities of the user. The only exceptions might be the acts of eating, washing, dressing, or toileting. The blind or paralyzed person can be viewed as the model for the visually or mobilely disabled occupant of the intelligent home (Virilio, 2000). A remote control provides the power to control the domestic environment. The user's energy and motor body triggers the use of the domestic functions. Environmental control can lead to a sedentary society with the home activity analogous to the activity of astronauts moving around in high orbit (Virilio, 2000). This can produce a type of fixedness resulting in a seated or couched individual as a prototype of the future.

In much the same way that the experience of a life long lived is altering the needs and wishes of the elderly, their own increasing sophistication and knowledge of their own health status and the health care system convince them that most traditional health care settings are inappropriate. As the educational level, political acumen, and economic status of the elderly continue to rise, the demand for health care within the home setting or the community will also increase.

Not only does technology provide the freedom for the making of personal decisions, but it also frees caregivers from routine activities and allows for more time to be spent in meaningful personal interactions. The use of robots, for example, in health care settings can increase the quality of care and the level of job satisfaction—two principal concerns of health care providers and their employees. Robots can be developed to assist in the activities of daily living, as well as for the provision of respite to caregivers. Reminding technologies can be developed set to the speed of understood speech and can use the caregiver's voice or that of a family member (Engelhardt, 1989). Examples of ways in which robotics can be used in health care settings include the following:

> transfer of patients (lifting),
> housekeeping,
> ambulation,
> physical therapy,
> depuddler (cleaning of human and pet wastes),
> surveillance,
> physician assistance,
> nursing assistance,
> patient assistance,
> fetch and carry, and
> cognitive rehabilitation.

The successful use of such technologies rests largely on attitudes of caregivers, patients, and family members.

The robotic systems that will serve the needs of the most severely disabled individuals will be those that have a high degree of machine intelligence. The need for sensitive and delicate touch will be mandatory in a robotic aid intended to help lift or to transfer a paralyzed patient whose body or garments must be handled with a confident but gentle touch.

Automated Guided Vehicle Systems technology is already performing materials-handling tasks in industry. This same technology can be used in an institutional health care environment to transport meals, drinks, and personal items to patients. Such a mobile robotic device could also move from patient to patient, collect vital-signs data, and, with two-way communication, provide a link with the centralized nursing station. Robots can perform tasks that health care providers find boring, repetitive, degrading, or dangerous. Robotic technologies hold the possibility for playing a role in both patient therapy and therapist training. A system that can deliver range-of-motion exercises for muscle maintenance, if properly designed, can also serve as a teaching tool for student therapists because it could be programmed to mimic certain disabilities.

There are currently a number of technologies that have broad applicability and not only serve in a rehabilitative capacity, but provide freedom for a broad range of activities. Examples of technologies with such liberating features include eyeglasses, hearing aids, pacemakers, talking books, and Kurzweil reading machines. Furthermore, devices, such as eyeglasses, have no side effects and open up a broad arena of activities for the user in the vocational as well as avocational spheres of life. Devices for the elderly must find such a broad market base to ensure their development, usage, and acceptability as ordinary features of life.

Equally important are those features of daily life that can promote and encourage the taking on of responsibilities by patients. One such possibility lies in the development of reminding technologies. In developing reminding technologies, it is important to place sufficient emphasis upon the reaction of the older person to the technology. Such concern

must focus upon how the information is delivered, that is, whether the speed is appropriate, and whether the rate at which the information is given is meaningful. Whether such information is accepted to the point of provoking action or a response may be related to the gender or language of the speaker.

It is even conceivable that robots can be designed that can make the environment so sensitive that it can provide respite care. Sensitive monitoring instruments can serve to offset accidents and to develop an environment that focuses upon intervention and prevention rather than simply custodial or policing care.

Technology and Long-Term Care

With the increase in life expectancy, individuals will increasingly survive into ages where the prevalence of chronic and debilitating conditions rises significantly. Eighty percent or more of persons over the age of sixty-five have at least one identifiable chronic disease or condition, the most common being arthritis, impaired hearing or vision, diabetes, chronic heart conditions, respiratory problems, and some degree of mental failure. Technological advances potentially provide a means for dealing with at least some of the disabilities often associated with aging and that frequently lead to the need for costly long-term care.

The health of the caregivers and the health of the care receiver must be jointly considered. What benefits the caregiver can result in less staff turnover. For example, the technology that can be employed for patient lifting and moving may not be immediately perceived as having such a beneficial effect, but the reciprocal nature of the provision and the receipt of care is too often lost. The incorporation of technology into long-term-care settings thus plays a dual role that enhances the environment from both the perspective of the patient and the care provider.

Technologies for caregivers can include devices and procedures to facilitate and improve caregiving. Long-term care has traditionally been labor intensive, with little emphasis on technology. Few labor-saving devices are used, and caregivers, including both informal and paid personnel, often receive little or no training in efficient methods of care. As a result, staff turnover is very high in long-term-care facilities, and families and other informal caregivers become overburdened and exhausted.

The relationship between technology and aging underscores the importance of functional ability for maintaining the independence of the elderly, along with maximizing their options and improving their quality of life. The growth of the aging population is likely to increase the demand for long-term care and the need for assistance, principally for those age eighty-five and older who face a combination of incapacitating and largely unavoidable infirmities.

Technology has been the major factor in the growth of the older population and the increase in longevity. Technology can now respond by providing both knowledge and ways to apply that knowledge in the long-term care setting. It is clear that a major challenge into the twenty-first century will be the maintenance of the health and functional ability of the older population, particularly as the proportion of those of advanced age continues to rise.

TECHNOLOGY AND THE WORLD OF THE OLDER WOMAN

The gap between current technological innovation and its application in the human environment has markedly affected where, how, why, and even when women age. The lack of "fit" between the person and the environment is particularly striking in the world of the older women and has resulted in premature aging and the escalation of disease states. The absence of alterations in environments, such as public places, dwellings, and institutions frequented by older women, has circumscribed their lives and caused them to age more rapidly and to experience higher rates of illness than their chronological age alone might warrant. The ignoring of such factors is not only an indication of gender bias, but is a reflection of social apathy and the fact that linking technology to aging has become an academic exercise with few roots in reality.

The much discussed SMARTHOUSE has left no one the wiser. Older women continue to live in antiquated environments, and the much condemned "grab-bar mentality" has remained as the only signal advance. The freedom and independence to be afforded by recent technological advances has not been reflected in the home setting, in institutions providing services to older women, nor in the lifestyles of older women. Despite such advancements in technology, older women continue to live in an obsolete world.

The environment as the locus for aging largely influences why particular physiological and psychological changes are experienced with advancing age. Public and private environments that do not adequately match the needs and capabilities of older women often serve to accelerate the aging process. Inhospitable environments are responsible for the increase in stress that accompanies aging, as well as increasing the potential for accidents and reducing healthful behaviors such as meal preparation, personal hygiene, and physical activity.

Prosthetic or adaptive environments that are technologically malleable can serve to extend the capacities of aging women and to promote continued maximal functioning. Robotic and artificial intelligence in human–machine integration provides unprecedented opportunities for maximizing the functional potential of women as they age. Yet, the home environment continues unchanged, and "home" becomes less sweet and more lethal as its occupants age.

Advances, such as alteration of the living environment to include automated and self-monitoring devices, automated assistance in activities of daily living, and home surveillance and safety features, have long been discussed, but have resulted in few applications. The new gravity-free devices for mobility and new microelectronic advances for the delivery of social services and home health care have yet to surface in practice.

Even the more spectacular biological interventions have been without an echo. Artificial or assistive insemination has radically altered reproductive possibilities for older women, even after menopause. Such advances have led some nations to consider the instituting of laws to prevent older women from being impregnated after reaching a certain age. One argument that is presented to support such legislation is that the older woman would be too old to nurture these children of late life. It is interesting to note that such an argument has never been advanced when the aged parent is a male. The capability to successfully implant a uterus is a new effort to overcome menopause and to continue female fertility indefinitely. In contrast to the discovery of Viagra®, this discovery did not make headlines. In the meantime, Viagra® has become a term as commonplace as Kleenex®.

Ways of incorporating both high and low technologies to offset the risks inherent in an antiquated and unresponsive environment seem to have escaped researchers, academicians, and industrialists. The savings in health care costs alone, it would appear, would have caught the attention of governing bodies, that is, if they were not all principally male. The environment in which women age, is older than they, and substantially more wrinkled.

CONCLUSION

Technology is being increasingly coupled with the unprecedented historical event of a burgeoning older population. The presence of large numbers of persons aged sixty-five or older throughout the world is leading to changes as novel and dramatic as those experienced during the First Industrial Revolution. Such population changes, experienced for the first time with no historical models to draw upon, are necessitating wide-scale alterations within society that only a uniting of this demographic phenomenon with technology can hope to meet. Such changes were only just beginning to be felt at the end of the nineteenth century, were made manifest during the twentieth century, and will blazon forth in the twenty-first century, creating what can be easily regarded as the Second Industrial Revolution.

The aging of the nation has meant that as larger portions of the population have diminished capacities for coping with the activities of daily life, there has been a concomitant decrease in the labor force of younger persons capable or willing to assist with such tasks. The absence of support groups in the home, such as children, spouse, or relatives due to distance, divorce, death, or the advanced old age of adult children, has also meant that reliance upon people as an appropriate resource is no longer a real alternative. The provision of such services must come from a new source–technology. If sufficient numbers of people are not available to perform requisite tasks, then machines must take their place.

Every phase of human existence, from the provision of necessities to sustain life to modes of recreation and to participation in the world of work, requires alteration. New techniques that will keep more people healthy and active and longer-lived can also be harnessed to the workplace to make the work environment more hospitable to the older worker. Technology from such a perspective can serve as a liberating force for the older population.

Acceleration in technological advances, coupled with increases in the aging population, has led to an unavoidable convergence of these two major societal trends. What the blend can look like is largely dependent upon attitudes toward the elderly and the appropriate usage of technologies in areas such as home heath care, education, work–retirement schemes, and adaptive lifestyles. As the population continues to age, it is likely that increasing numbers of those aged eighty-five or older will face incapacitating and largely unavoidable infirmities. The relationship between technology and aging underscores the importance of functional ability in maintaining the independence of the elderly, maximizing their options, and improving their quality of life. Technology has been the major factor in increasing life expectancy; technology can further respond by providing additional knowledge and avenues to enhance the quality of life in advanced old age.

The societal effects of technological change and the aging of the population are only partly foreseeable. Nonetheless, there is likely to be an increase in the prevalence of chronic diseases that can impair the older person's ability to function independently. This, in turn, will lead to a growing need for social and health care services as part of a continuum of care including long-term care, ambulatory care, and home health care. There will be an increase in the demand for medical care of acute illnesses, as well.

Changes in living arrangements will also affect the provision of care. The significant changes in family structure and housing alternatives can result in more older individuals living alone. Persons over the age of sixty-five can also have aged living parents and relatives for whom they may have some responsibilities and obligations.

The aging of the population raises critical concerns for employment, the retirement system, transportation, health care, recreation, and housing. The increases in the number of persons aged sixty-five and older have occurred because of technological advances that have resulted in better control of infectious and chronic diseases and improved standards of living. New technologies under development today suggest continued change in longevity and functional capacity. It is clear that the aging of the population will fundamentally change the future economic and social fabric of the world.

Most current projections regarding the impact of an aging population, however, assume an elderly population with characteristics similar to those of persons living in the present day, such as withdrawal from the work force, declining health, increased need for hospitalization and nursing care, and other characteristics that suggest a highly dependent sixty-five and older age group. Improved health care, increased understanding of the physiology of aging, and continued advances in technology may well alter the characteristics of the elderly of the future. In addition, applications of computers, robotics, telecommunications, and other technical innovations in the home and workplace may provide new opportunities for increasing independence, productivity, and quality of life for the elderly.

When the contemporary world is looked on from a historical perspective, it is clear that there has been an evolutionary progression. Planes have become the wings dreamed of by Daedalus, and people do walk on water, albeit on the decks of ships. Astronauts have explored the moon and found that it was not made of green cheese, and scientists have discovered that it is not brownies who curdle milk, but bacteria.

New mysteries are being constantly uncovered in the world of the computer, robotics, and a host of other systems with equally complex features. Once a technology is invented, it usually advances to be perfected again and again. The process of aging is equally irrevocable; populations will continue to age in large numbers. The late premier of the former Soviet Union, Nikita Khruschev, was quoted as having observed that the world has moved in one generation from the outhouse to outer space (Lesnoff-Caravaglia, 1999).

REFERENCES

Armitage, J. (Ed.). (2000). *Paul Virilio. From modernism to hypomodernism and beyond.* Thousand Oaks, CA: Sage.

Coombs, F. (1994). Engineering technology in rehabilitation of older adults. *Experimental Aging Research, 20,* 201–209.

Engelhardt, K. G. (1989). Health and human service robotics: Multi-dimensional perspectives. *International Journal of Technology and Aging, 2*
(1), 6–41.

Harris, R. (Ed.). (1983). *Medical devices and instrumentation for the elderly.* Arlington, VA: Association for the Advancement of Medical Instrumentation.

Hatton, J., & Plouffe, P. B. (1997). *Science and its ways of knowing.* Upper Saddle River, NJ: Prentice Hall.

Howell, S. (1994). The potential environment: Home, technology and future aging. *Experimental Aging Research, 20,* 285–290.

Lesnoff-Caravaglia, G. (Ed.). (1988). *Aging in a technological society.* New York: Human Sciences Press.

——. (1999). Ethical issues in a high-tech society. In T. Fusco Johnson (Ed.), *Handbook on ethical issues in aging* (pp. 271–288). Westport, CT: Greenwood Press.

——. (2000). *Health aspects of aging.* Springfield, IL: Charles C Thomas.

Lesnoff-Caravaglia, G., & Klys, M. (1987). Lifestyle and longevity. In G. Lesnoff-Caravaglia (Ed.), *Realistic expectations for long life* (pp. 35–48). New York: Human Sciences Press.

Maslow, A. (1968). *Toward a psychology of being* (2nd ed.). New York: Van Nostrand Reinhold.

Mumford, L. (1963). *Technics and civilization.* New York: Harcourt, Brace & World.

Quivery, M. (1990). Advanced medical technology: Finding the answers. *International Nursing Review, 37* (5), 329–331.

Virilio, P. (2000). *Polar inertia.* (P. Camiller, Trans.). Thousand Oaks, CA: Sage.

Chapter 12

SECURITY AND THE ELDERLY

Timothy J. Ryan

INTRODUCTION

To begin to understand the issue of security of the elderly U.S. population, one must first understand characteristics of that population, such as its age distribution, fears, and vulnerabilities. For example, no other age segment of the population is described as being generally "paralyzed with fear" with regard to becoming victims of criminal activity (Barthel & Lansky, 1994; Young & Stein, 1990). Not only are these existing characteristics important, but equally significant are the dynamics of population change, especially the effects resulting from the aging of the Baby Boomer generation (i.e., those born in the two decades following World War II). Finally, shifting demographics need to be considered in that the nature and types of crimes vary by location, socioeconomic status, and race. Due to these factors, discussions of personal safety and security matters with respect to the older population must begin with a clear understanding of the composition of that population.

Using U.S. Department of Justice (DOJ) definitions, "The elderly" is taken as a syn-

onym for persons age sixty-five or older. This age group is composed of over one in eight U.S. residents and made up 12.7 percent of the U.S. population in 1997 (Klaus, 1999). The older population of the United States is significant and growing, with women constituting the majority of the older population. Contrary to popular notions about the residences of the elderly, only a small proportion of older persons reside in institutions. The majority of elderly persons are community dwelling with a sizable proportion, particularly women, living alone (Kramarow, Lentzner, Rooks, Weeks, & Saydah, 1999). Thus, the nation, as a whole, is presented with a growing, more-vulnerable-than-average population that is also at risk with regard to crimes in the community.

According to the most recent data available, 13 percent of the U.S. population was sixty-five years of age and over in 1997 (Klaus, 1999). Americans live longer than ever before, and persons who survive to age sixty-five today can reasonably expect to live an additional eighteen years. In 1970, one in ten Americans were older than sixty-five; in 1990, one in eight persons fell into this age grouping. Once the Baby Boomer cohort averages sixty-five or older (sometime after 2030), the U.S. Bureau of the Census projects one in five will be sixty-five years old or older (Bachman, Dillaway, & Lachs, 1998). This population will be more diverse than at present. For example, in 1997, older persons made up a larger proportion of the non-Hispanic White population compared with other racial and ethnic groups. However, the older non-Hispanic White population is growing more slowly compared with other groups, and, thus, the 2030 population will almost certainly be more ethnically diverse. Therefore, any socially related crimes associated with different racial populations and their neighborhoods can be assumed to be changeable over the next three decades. Because the poverty rate is higher among older Black and Hispanic persons compared with older White persons (Kramarow et al., 1999), security issues correlated with impoverished neighborhoods (e.g., drug-related crimes) should be expected to track with these demographic changes in the U.S. population.

Some perspective of the importance of crime as a cause of morbidity and death among the elderly is essential. Despite their heightened fears of crimes against persons, such as violent assaults (Pain, 1995), it is the chronic diseases, such as heart disease, cancer, stroke, and chronic obstructive pulmonary diseases, that are the leading causes of death among the older population. This does not, however, rule out the legitimacy to concerns of crime specifically directed at the older, at-risk population.

Owing to declining physical and mental abilities, such as decreased locomotion, eyesight, and hearing, the elderly make easy targets for certain crimes. Specifically, visual and hearing impairments among older persons increase sharply with age. In 1995, 13 percent of persons seventy to seventy-four years of age were visually impaired, compared with 31 percent of persons eighty-five

years of age and older. For hearing impairments, the prevalence rose from 26 percent of persons seventy to seventy-four years of age to 49 percent of persons eighty-five years of age and older (Kramarow et al., 1999). Perhaps because of these limitations, compared with violent-crime victims in other age groups, elderly victims of nonlethal violence were less likely to use self-protective measures, such as arguing with the offender, running away, calling for help, or attacking the offender (Klaus, 1999).

As a consequence, society can anticipate a growing elderly population that is less able on the average to defend itself from crime. Despite mental or physical weaknesses, the major hazards to the population are the well-recognized chronic diseases associated with old age, and not crime in general. However, perhaps in recognition of its own susceptibilities, this population tends to fear crime and acts accordingly (e.g., venturing outside of the home less frequently). What then, are the true risks to the elderly in the United States from crime?

U.S. CRIME STATISTICS FOR THE ELDERLY

The Bureau of Justice Statistics of the U.S. Department of Justice keeps many of the most-telling data relating to crime in the U.S. directed at, or committed by, the elderly. Much of what follows must necessarily draw heavily upon those sources. As stated earlier, since population trends will dictate changing crime patterns, the reader is referred to the DOJ web site (United States Department of Justice [DOJ], 1999) for the latest compilations and reports.

Between 1992 and 1997, the average population of persons age sixty-five or older was 31.3 million. These elderly were victims of 2.7 million property and violent crimes,

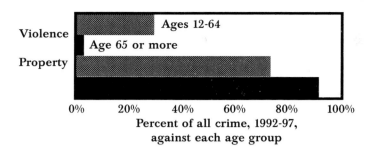

–Violence made up
27% of crimes against
persons ages 12-64,
compared to 6% of
crimes against persons
over 64.

Figure 12.1. Property crimes outweigh violent crimes among the elderly. Source: U.S. DOJ, 1999.

with property crimes far outweighing violent crimes (Figure 12.1). Specific categories of crimes committed against the elderly were as follows:

1. 2.5 million property crimes (household burglary, motor vehicle theft, and household theft),
2. 46,000 purse snatchings or pocket pickings,
3. 165,000 nonlethal violent crimes (rape, robbery, and aggravated and simple assault), and
4. 1,000 murders.

As noted previously, the elderly are less likely to be the victims of violent crime (Klug, 2000). In fact, during the 1992–1997 study period, the elderly made up 15 percent of the population age twelve or older but accounted for only 7 percent of all measured crimes (Klaus, 1999). Compared with much younger segments of the U.S. population, the elderly therefore experience less violence and fewer property crimes. This finding is important to note relative to the more popular notion of the elderly as an at-risk population for all criminal activity. On the average, in the same analysis period for every 1,000 persons at their age level, persons age sixty-five and older experienced only five violent crimes, while those younger than age twenty-five experienced over 100 (Klaus, 1999). Empirically, just 5 percent of all homicides occur among persons sixty-five years and older: Homicide is a far greater problem among younger adults (Stevens et al., 1999).

Although they have less exposure to all measured crimes, as a group the elderly do have a specific-crime-risk profile (types of crimes, locations, times, race) to which they fall victim. As just indicated, the elderly are disproportionately affected by property crimes with more than nine in ten crimes against the elderly fitting the definition of property crimes; fewer than four in ten crimes against persons aged twelve to twenty-four fit the definition of property crimes. White females are at the lowest risk of property crimes (Figure 12.2). Probably for the reasons mentioned previously, robbery accounts for one-fourth of the violent crimes against persons age sixty-five and older, whereas this same criminal act accounted for less than one-eighth of the violent crimes experienced by the majority of non-elderly adults (i.e., those aged twelve to sixty-four). This heightened vulnerability is confirmed by anecdotal information; for example, it is common law-enforcement knowledge that the undercover decoy most likely to attract a street robber is an officer disguised as an older woman (Young & Stein, 1990).

FIGURE 12-2. WHITE FEMALES AT LOWEST RISK OF PROPERTY CRIMES

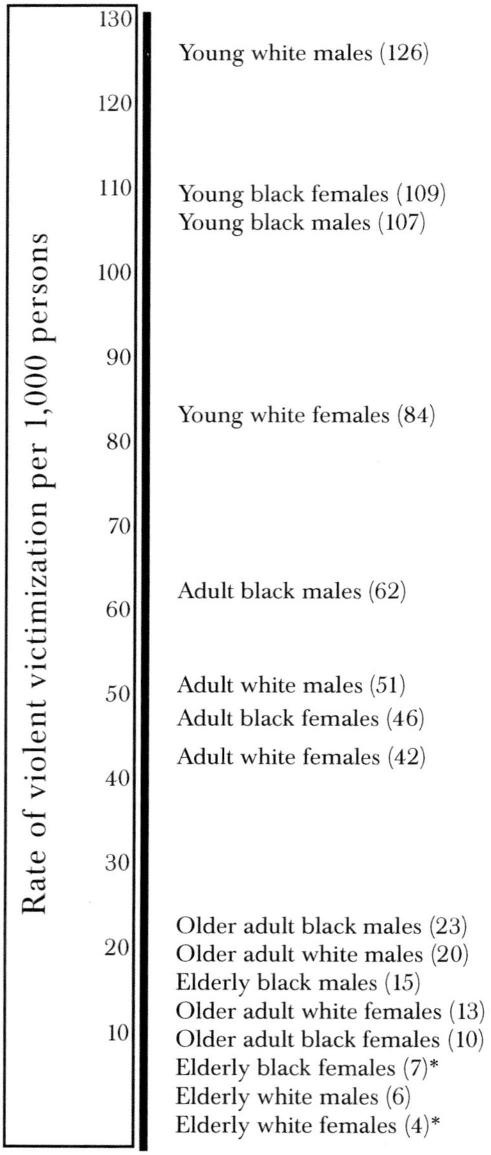

Rate of violent victimization per 1,000 persons

130	
120	Young white males (126)
110	Young black females (109)
100	Young black males (107)
90	
80	Young white females (84)
70	
60	Adult black males (62)
50	Adult white males (51)
40	Adult black females (46)
	Adult white females (42)
30	
20	Older adult black males (23)
	Older adult white males (20)
	Elderly black males (15)
10	Older adult white females (13)
	Older adult black females (10)
	Elderly black females (7)*
	Elderly white males (6)
	Elderly white females (4)*

Note: This report applies the following age categories: · Young (ages 12-24) · Adult (ages 24-49) · Older adult (ages 50-64) · Elderly (age 65 or older)

* This apparent difference between elderly females is not statistically significant.

Source: U.S. DOJ, 1999.

Additionally, due to generalized fears and physical or mental failings, older persons often do not venture far from their homes. Consequently, most crimes against the elderly are more likely to occur in or near their homes in daylight hours. According to Bachman et al. (1998), elderly men were more likely to be robbed at or near a private residence compared to all other groups (49%), as compared with nonelderly adult males, who were the least likely to be robbed at such locations (22%). Older Blacks are victimized at a rate twice that reported for Whites in a number of crime categories, including community and household crimes (7.6 per 1,000 Black vs. 3.6 per 1,000 White). This same over representation of Blacks to Whites is found for violent household crimes, where the rate for African Americans sixty-five and older is 154 per 1,000 as compared to 71 per 1,000 for Whites (Johnson-Dalzine, Dalzine, & Martin-Stanley, 1996). Finally, vulnerability clearly plays a determining factor in sexual assaults of the elderly in that intimidation by physical force was reported to be all that was necessary to subdue victims in most cases (Muram, Miller, & Cutler, 1992). Furthermore, elderly women (representing arguably the most vulnerable victims) were the most likely robbery victims to face unarmed offenders (Bachman et al., 1998).

Clearly, it is property crime and not violence that constitutes the majority of crime occurring against the elderly (Table 12.1). Furthermore, the elderly had lower victimization rates than any other age groups for all types of violent and property crime measured by the National Crime Victimization Survey (NCVS) conducted for 1992–97. As shown by this data, compared to the majority of nonelderly adults, the elderly were

1. Five times less likely to be victims of robbery,
2. Twelve times less likely to be victims of aggravated or simple assault,

3. One-half as likely to be victims of burglary, and
4. Three times less likely to be victims of motor vehicle theft or theft.

It is important to note that the NCVS does not interview members of any type of institutionalized population, thus crimes occurring in those settings are missed. In particular, violence, abuse, neglect, theft, or other victimization of older persons in nursing homes are not measured through the survey. In addition, the NCVS does not measure kidnapping, crimes against businesses, fraud (including telemarketing scams), and other economic or "white-collar" crimes. Data for all crimes compared between the elderly and nonelderly U.S. population are presented in Figure 12.3.

Race and sex are both significant factors in terms of perpetrators of crimes against the elderly. Males committed 60 percent of the murders of both elderly and younger victims, and Whites committed a larger proportion of the murders of persons age sixty-five and older than other adult persons. Similarly, males committed over three-fourths of the nonlethal violence against elderly persons, and White offenders committed almost one-half of all such crimes. Almost one-half of the nonlethal violence against persons age sixty-five or older involved a White offender and a White victim, with roughly one-fifth of nonlethal acts involving a Black offender and a White victim. Only one-eighth of nonlethal violence directed at the elderly involved both a Black offender and a Black victim (Klaus, 1999).

Although suicide might be described as a "crime against self," it is most often a violent act. Firearm use was the predominant suicide method for both men and women. In fact, firearm-related suicides accounted for 70 percent of all suicides during the years 1990 through 1996, while poisoning was the second most prevalent method.

TABLE 12.1.
Crimes Against the Elderly

Crime Type	Crime Count	Percent
Victimizations of Households 65 and Older		
Total crimes	2,694,290	100
Personal crimes	212,420	7.9
Crimes of violence	166,330	6.2
Murder	1,000	4.0
Nonfatal violence	165,330	6.1
Rape/Sexual assault	3,280	0.12
Robbery	40,950	1.5
Total assault	121,100	4.5
Aggravated assault	34,050	1.3
Simple assault	87,050	3.2
Personal theft	46,090	1.7
Property Crimes	2,482,870	92.1
Household burglary	623,790	23.2
Motor vehicle theft	124,930	4.6
Theft	1,733,160	64.3

Note: Adapted from National Crime Victimization Survey, as cited by Klaus, 1999.

While those aged sixty-five and older represent approximately 13 percent of the U.S. population they account for nearly one-fifth of all age-grouped suicides. Suicide among the elderly remains a significant problem despite evidence showing it to be in decline for both men and women (Figure 12.4). Approximately 43,000 (20%) of the 216,631 suicides that occurred in the United States from 1990 through 1996 involved adults aged greater than or equal to sixty-five years. This number represents an absolute decrease of 8.4 percent, from 6,394 in 1990 to 5,855 in 1996, as well as a 16 percent decrease in suicide rates for this age group (from 20.6 to 17.3 per 100,000 persons) (Stevens et al., 1999). Both race and sex account for significant differences in terms of who commits suicide among the elderly. As seen in Figure 12.5, the majority of suicides are committed by Whites, followed by Hispanics and Blacks. Also notable on Figure 12.5 is that among the elderly, suicide seems to decline with increasing age. Rates of suicide are highest among the youngest of those sixty-five and older, and decline with each age decade. Men accounted for 82 percent of suicides among those sixty-five years and older and, for the 1990–1996 reporting period, their rate decreased 15 percent (from 41.6 to 35.2 per 100,000 persons). For women, the rate decreased 25 percent, from 6.4 to 4.8 per 100,000 persons (Stevens et al., 1999).

EMERGING ISSUES

A topic of growing concern and media attention has been termed "elder abuse." The general definition of elder abuse typically includes mistreatment of the elderly that is inflicted by a family member, friend, caregiver, landlord, or stranger, as opposed to self-neglect (which is often a result of mental deterioration or other disabilities). It may consist of passive neglect, psychological abuse, financial abuse, active neglect, or physical abuse.

Types of crime	Average annual, 1992–97	Average annual rates per 1,000 persons or households		
		All	65 or older	Less than age 65
All crimes	40,581,530			
Crimes of violence	10,511,850	48.9	5.3	56.4
Murder	20,580	0.1	0.0	0.1
Nonfatal violence	10,491,270	48.8	5.3	56.3
Rape/Sexual assault	441,070	2.1	0.1	2.4
Robbery	1,209,260	5.6	1.3	6.4
Total assault	8,840,940	41.2	3.9	47.5
Aggravated assault	2,284,190	10.6	1.1	12.3
Simple assault	6,556,760	30.5	2.8	35.3
Personal theft	402,120	1.9	1.5	1.9
Property crimes	29,667,550	292.2	117.3	338.3
Household burglary	5,326,780	52.5	29.5	58.5
Motor vehicle theft	1,664,550	16.4	5.9	19.2
Theft 22,676,220	223.4	81.9	260.6	
Number of households		101,518,080	21,161,850	80,356,230
Population, age 12 or older		214,789,200	31,296,350	183,492,860
Number of crimes		40,581,530	2,694,290	37,887,250

Note: "Household head" means only that this person provided information about household characteristics and data on burglaries, motor vehicle thefts, or property thefts occurring within the household

Figure 12.3. Rates of violent and property crimes, U.S. 1992–1997. Note: Klaus, 1999.

The Calgary Regional Health Authority (CRHA, 2000) uses the following five criteria to critically delineate elderly abuse:

1. *Financial abuse.* Believed to be the most common form of abuse. It includes theft, mismanagement of money, or the sale of property without consent.
2. *Physical abuse* such as grabbing, hitting, hair-pulling, or physical restraint.
3. *Mental or psychological abuse* such as ridicule, threats, humiliation, or destruction of personal belongings.
4. *Physical or emotional neglect* that may include withholding food, medical care or support. It should be noted that neglect may be deliberate or it may be due to a lack of knowledge of the needs of the older person.
5. *Caregiver or institutional abuse* that may include physical containment or unreasonable restrictions being forced on the person.

According to CRHA, while abusers may vary, they are typically family relatives of the older person—sons, daughters, or spouses.

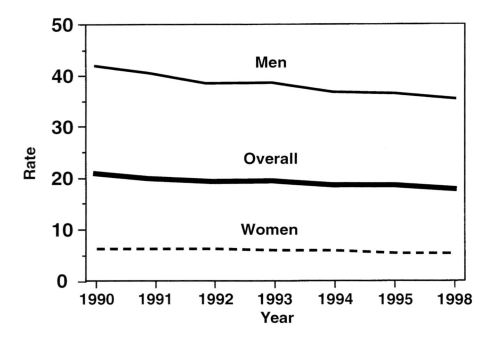

Figure 12.4. Suicide rates* among those 65 and older, 1990–1996. Note: Stevens et al., 1999. * Per 100,000 population.
Source: National Center for Health Statistics, CDC.

Some relatives have problems with alcohol or drug abuse while others have problems with stress, which can be a trigger for abuse. Older people are often reluctant to talk about ill treatment because they are embarrassed, deny that it is happening to them, or believe that it will soon stop. They may be ashamed of how their family members behave, or they fear being admitted to an institution. Some aged persons are unable to speak out because of memory or language problems.

While the NCVS cannot report on such instances of elderly abuse, it does report violent crimes to those sixty-five and older by any person. Such data is obtained from the Uniform Crime Reports. Klaus reports (1999) that for persons aged sixty-five or older, as for other age groups, most violence measured by the NCVS is simple assault (see Table 12.1).

Simple assault is defined as an attack without a weapon, resulting either in no injury or in a minor injury, such as cuts or bruises. Simple assault includes attempted attacks and verbal threats to attack or to kill the victim.

More serious injuries from assailants known to the elderly person do occur and because of their value systems, elderly adults can be more prone to stay in abusive relationships (particularly if the situation promotes family stability, social interaction, or economic benefit) (Anetzberger, 1997). Based on recent averages, it can be expected that each year relatives or close acquaintances injure about 36,000 persons aged sixty-five or older and kill about 500 (Figure 12.6). Victims of murder over age sixty-four were two times more likely than victims between ages twelve and sixty-four to have been killed by

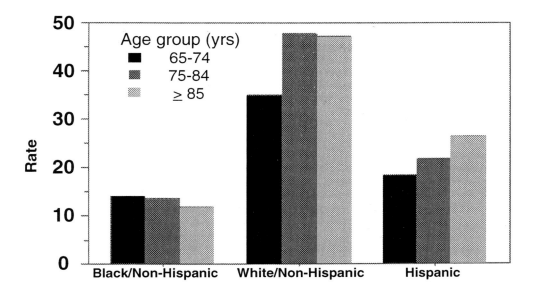

Figure 12.5. Suicide rates* by race/ethnicity among those 65 and older, 1990–1996. Note: National Center for Health Statistics, CDC, 1999. * Per 100,000 population. Suicide rates by ethnicity were excluded from the analysis for three states during the years when they did not record ethnicity data: Louisiana (1990), New Hampshire (1990–1992), and Oklahoma (1990–1996).

relatives or intimates. Perhaps not surprisingly, and mirroring other elderly crime locations, violence by relatives or persons well-known to the victim was more likely to occur in the victim's home.

In addition to elder abuse, fraud is emerging as a crime targeted toward the elderly. According to the U.S. Office of Consumer Affairs, fraud is an extremely large and profitable activity in this country. With revenues over $100 billion per year, if it were a legitimate business, fraud would rank next to Exxon, the third largest Fortune 500 company in the United States (Harris, 1995). Of that value, approximately 40 percent of such fraudulent efforts involve telemarketing scams according to U.S. Department of Justice figures (Direct Marketing, 1998), costing

elderly victims an estimated $40 billion each year. Given the increasing elderly population and some unique vulnerabilities to fraud by that group, crimes of this type directed at the elderly can be anticipated to increase significantly in the ensuing decades.

Referred to as "whoopies" by one convicted con man, Well-Off Older People (as well as all aged persons in general) have at least four characteristics that make them uniquely vulnerable to fraud. This is especially true for communications-based scams, in that a 1993 Federal Bureau of Investigation (FBI) sting operation of suspect telemarketing firms concluded that one in three targeted victims were elderly persons. Greater assets and holdings, an abundance of leisure time with too many empty hours, emotional isola-

Each year on average between 1992 and 1997, a relative, intimate, or close acquaintance injured about 36,000 persons age 65 or older and killed about 500

	Average annual elderly victims per year, 1992–97
Nonlethal violence committed by —	
Total	36,290
Relatives and intimates	15,040
Others well known to victim	21,250
Murder committed by —	
Total	500
Relatives and intimates	260
Others well known to victim	240

Figure 12.6. Elderly abuse. Note: Klaus, 1999.

tion predisposing to more receptive interactions, and anxiety and worries over money are all factors making the elderly more vulnerable to scams than other age segments of the population (Harris, 1995).

The elderly are more prone to be targeted for white-collar crime because of their relatively high assets. Citing 1991 Bureau of the Census numbers, Harris (1995) reports that the median household net worth for those sixty-five and older was $88,192. With fewer responsibilities in retirement, some elderly persons are more prone to respond to junk mail or unsolicited telephone "opportunities" simply to use their time available. In conjunction with that vulnerability, those persons who are more isolated may welcome an opportunity to engage in conversation with unknown scam artists solely for the initial reason that they are lonely and have not had human interaction for some extended period. Somewhat ironically, some elderly persons may be victimized financially by their very motivation to secure or pass on their accumulated assets. Costs of long-term care are well-known to the aged community, and, in an effort to avoid the high costs of institution-

alization, some elderly persons are taken advantage of by unscrupulous caretakers or children. A common example might be receiving shoddy workmanship or inferior building materials at an elderly person's residence, as a result of the resident's desire to continue to occupy it and not a more expensive assisted-care dwelling.

Finally, there is some proof that the traditional explanations for the increased vulnerability of the elderly are valid. A trusting nature coupled with difficulties in hearing or seeing can make the elderly more easily beholden to relative strangers for daily assistance, such as check writing, house cleaning, or odd-jobs completion. The changing world around the elderly may also make them susceptible to fraudulent practices nonexistent in their collected living experiences. For example, a 1993 American Association of Retired Persons survey found that of those sixty-five and older, only 40 percent of respondents knew that 1-900 telephone calls are typically charged on an expensive per-minute basis (Harris, 1995).

Perhaps for these same reasons, some elderly are left behind insofar as new technology is capable of providing safeguards to their homes and property. One of the most prevalent applications of such new security measures is in the form of centrally monitored intrusion, fire, and panic alarm systems. Provided by a great variety of local, regional, and national suppliers (e.g., Brinks, ADT, GE, Pinkerton, and others), home alarms have become much more common and affordable owing to advances in electronics semiconductor technology over the last decade. Despite their availability, there are obstacles to acceptance by older persons. Chief among these is the rigid adherence to system activation-deactivation protocols, in conjunction with sometimes difficult to remember, let alone enter, passwords. For example, one system sold by ADT requires the resident to enter at least a four-digit code into a centrally located system interface within thirty seconds of entry to the home. This time limit can be too short if the travel distance to the keypad is excessive, if the occupant has moderate mental difficulties in remembering the password, or if distractions exist when entering (e.g., preventing a pet from getting out, or setting down groceries). Difficulties like these increase with the age of the occupant, in that memory and locomotion abilities show an inverse relationship to age. With some notable exceptions, other high-tech solutions to security issues are equally limited to the elderly for similar reasons.

Vehicle antitheft systems are a good example of technological advances that can be used effectively by older persons. Often termed "keyless entry" by marketers, such systems can simultaneously activate–deactivate an automobile alarm system with the press of a single button. This technological advance is beneficial not only because of its interconnectability with the vehicle alarm system, but also because it eliminates fumbling for a door key, which, in turn, leaves the owner at risk for a shorter period of time.

Other security advances, however, are less adaptable to an aged population. Personal alarms, which require the would-be victim to immediately locate and actuate them, are a poor choice for an older person suffering from typical age-related physical limitations such as failing eyesight, diminished tactile senses, or arthritis. For the same reasons, video-monitoring systems may be of little utility to an older person. Typically employed at entrances to a building, closed-circuit-television monitoring systems have been available for many years. However, only recently has their use become more widespread, owing, again, to methods of mass production and electronic's advances. As of this writing, it is possible to buy off the store shelf a complete system for less than $100, well within the means of many elderly. Although such systems can help keep entrances secure, their applicability to the elderly is severely limited by very small screen size, moderately complex setup and installation, or even the remote control used to operate them. According to information supplied through many Geriatric Research, Education, and Clinical Centers (GRECC, 1999), as persons' abilities decline with age, the physical qualities of objects are increasingly used as cues for their use. Even then, what can be seen or touched may be misused. With respect to a video-monitoring system, for example, elderly persons with more diminished faculties might attempt to control the TV, VCR, or even the ceiling fan with the remote provided for the security system. In more advanced cases, all remote controls might be confused with such seemingly unrelated items as push-button telephones, radios, or lights.

One of the more unusual emerging issues of the aging population entails caring not only for greater numbers of community-dwelling persons or those institutionalized in long-term care facilities, but also for aging criminal offenders. According to the National

Institute of Corrections (NIC), the national percentage of inmates fifty years of age and older has increased significantly in recent years (NIC, 2000). Coupled with this increase is a self-reported lack of knowledge among correctional practitioners regarding issues such as elderly care economics, programmatic approaches available, and changing management systems in meeting the needs of this population. Longer prison sentences, the rise of infectious diseases, and limited availability of in-prison programs coupled with a lack of resources, enhance the possibility that this specific elderly population may be forgotten, deteriorate to a poorer condition, and thereby become a financial burden to society. Presently a research need, this issue of the aging population will need to be constructively addressed for public health as well as humanistic reasons.

IMPACTS OF CRIME ON THE ELDERLY

Not only do the elderly possess a number of unique victimization characteristics, they also suffer from victimization in a number of indirect or secondary ways not felt by other nonelderly adult segments of the population. Fear for themselves as well as their heirs, emotional isolation, ruinous financial loss, or life-long debilitating (or even fatal) physical outcomes can all act singly or in combination to deleteriously affect the prevalent mental outlook of elderly persons. As if suffering from the direct criminal activity were not difficult enough, crime outcomes on the elderly can have what Young and Stein (1990) have termed *the double sorrow,* which occurs when the elderly suffer vicarious victimization in the aftermath of a crime committed against a friend, child, or grandchild.

As pointed out by Bachman et al. (1998), one of the clearest findings about crimes against the elderly is the negative association between age and the probability of becoming a victim of violent crime. Despite being less frequent victims, the fear of any crime has a life-altering effect on many elderly. Behavioral adjustments to living with this fear may be both rationale and less advised, and include the following:

1. limiting social activities,
2. avoiding going out at night, and avoiding certain places,
3. curtailing hospitality to strangers,
4. moving out of life-long neighborhoods,
5. adding locks, dogs, security systems, or weapons to the household, and
6. participating in crime-prevention efforts.

The stress caused to the elderly population from such fears is not easily quantified, but its prevalence and potency are well-reported (Barthel & Lansky, 1994; Johnson-Dalzine et al., 1996). Emotional tolls taken by crime can mount for the elderly; many have already come to terms with their growing vulnerability, and a criminal violation can leave them humiliated and less able to productively function—possibly for the rest of their lives (Young & Stein, 1990).

In addition to emotional suffering placed upon the elderly following direct or vicarious victimization, they may also suffer financially as well as physically. Almost by definition, a retired person typically has no upwardly financial earning power and must subsist on a fixed income. Whereas a robbery or burglary of younger persons may be recovered from by future earnings, the elderly victim may be hard hit from such crimes and poorly situated to financially recover from losses. This is especially true with respect to fraud aimed at an elderly person's liquid assets such as cash, savings, bonds, or stocks. Because of their physical frailty or mobility, direct crime outcomes may lead to secondary, even life-threatening injures for the elderly victim. In the case of thefts of money or assets, such crimes pose a double issue in that the aged victim may already face proportionately higher fixed costs for health care, assisted living, or special transportation (Young & Stein, 1990).

Medical and health-related outcomes among the elderly as a direct result of crime directed at them are important. While elderly women are the least likely robbery victims to be assaulted by armed offenders, as a subgroup they are the most likely to sustain physical injuries as an outcome of such an incident. Although less than one in three assault victims are typically injured in an assault, greater than 50 percent of those so injured required medical care for those injuries. This pattern is similar to the need for care in the aftermath of elderly robbery victims injured in such incidents (Bachman et al., 1998).

PREVENTION AND CONTROL

Similar to safety issues related to the elderly, crime directed at them must be viewed as an area in which action can be implemented to reduce the incidence of morbidity and mortality. While crime intervention is perhaps not the most traditional arena of public health activity, many of the efforts using more classical, communicable disease or chronic health-improvement models can be used successfully in this area. Indeed, such efforts must be considered now in that the aging Baby Boomer generation will soon be entering that segment of the U.S. population sixty-five and older and swelling its ranks. Rising crime trends, such as those reported in this chapter, can be studied with the intent of

reducing or abating further increases owing to burgeoning numbers among the elderly.

What specific public health steps should be taken is determined by the violence or crime to be combated. With respect to violent crimes, and especially crimes in which the elderly are physically injured, the elderly person must receive appropriate treatment in the immediate aftermath of the victimization. Such treatment needs (beyond medical) can best be met by readily available and skilled victim-services providers. Young and Stein (1990) call for the addition to victim-service components to existing programs in place at locations, such as senior centers, and for the expansion of victim-assistance programs staffed by those with skills in working with older people.

In cases of the much more prevalent property crimes, the first step toward crime reduction should come from seeking out local law enforcement crime-prevention programs. Virtually all police departments have an individual or unit assigned to the prospective reduction of crimes, such as burglary. At no cost to the elderly requestor, a uniformed police officer visits the home and conducts a security audit. Such audits can be helpful in identifying weaknesses in the natural defenses present at a home. Because property crimes against the elderly are most likely to occur in or close to the home, information that can be used to better safeguard a domicile, its contents, and occupants is potentially quite valuable for crime deterrence as well. With many elderly persons, however, information alone is not sufficient. Those aged eighty and older, in particular, find it increasingly difficult to act on information regardless of its apparent or true beneficial nature. For this reason, community-provided services to assist those sixty-five and older with home-security upgrades are very useful. Services needed may be minimal and simple, such as minor drilling or screwing to install added hinges or locks. When cost for either hardware or installation labor is at issue, longstanding and trusted community providers might be looked to for assistance with both.

When elder abuse is at issue, a first step might be an awareness campaign that seeks to help community members as well as caretakers, adult children, and other potential abusers clarify what constitutes abuse. With a community-accepted definition in place for elder abuse, it is much more likely that strangers or other casual observers might also be relied on for reporting of potential cases of abuse. In addition to awareness, work on developing an enhanced infrastructure for the support of the physical, mental, and social needs of the elderly is recommended. By having additional or part-time care options available to family members, stress related to the full-time care needs of a semidependent elder might be safely diffused. Much elder abuse can be prevented through educational programs and support for families in such predicaments.

Insofar as fraud aimed at the elderly is concerned, police and citizen groups can directly fight back. In states with sizeable elder populations, such as Florida, New Jersey, and California, law enforcement agencies have created special units to deal with the targeted victimization of the elderly. Involvement of the members of the affected community has been somewhat successful in at least one such effort conducted in Florida (Harris, 1995). There, "Senior Sleuths" was created. Constituting a group of some 400 elderly persons recruited by the Florida Attorney General's office, members checked the truthfulness and honesty of a variety of consumer providers of elderly goods. Hearing aids, drugs, and automotive parts were among the areas they examined. This involvement effort proved successful in finding a variety of unscrupulous groups targeting the elderly (for example, auto repair shops and tire dealers that

assessed extra charges to elderly customers for unnecessary services). When family members are accessible to elderly parents, their heightened awareness and vigilance to telephone scams, bogus sweepstakes, and check overages by caretakers can reduce such losses. Actions, such as home visits with an eye toward numerous junk mail offers, accumulations of mostly worthless "prizes" from contests, and checkbook reviews, can help identify problems and perpetrators.

Because older adults have high suicide rates, there is a need for suicide-prevention activities directed at older adults. Any such actions must be cognizant of the fact that elderly suicides vary by age, race, and sex, and, therefore, prevention strategies need to be tailored to the specific demographic characteristics of these groups. Strategies for reducing suicide rates among older adults include training primary-care providers to better recognize suicidal risk factors, such as depressive disorders, and to make appropriate referrals. An identification of protective factors in preventing suicide among older adults should also be researched so that it may be integrated into prevention strategies. Community-based interventions to identify and treat persons at risk also have been shown to be effective. Other prevention strategies include senior peer-counseling programs, suicide-prevention efforts that target persons at high risk, improvements in mental health services through suicide-prevention centers, and programs that increase awareness of risk factors and protective factors among persons who have frequent contact with older adults (Stevens et al., 1999).

REFERENCES

Anetzberger, G. J. (1997). Elderly adult survivors of family violence: Implications for clinical practice. *Violence Against Women, 3* (5), 499–514.

Bachman, R., Dillaway, H., & Lachs, M. S. (1998). Violence against the elderly. *Research on Aging, 20* (2), 183–198.

Barthel, J., & Lansky, E. (1994). How crime has victimized us over 50s . . . and what we can do about it. *New Choices for Retirement Living, 34* (7), 18–26.

Calgary Regional Health Authority. (2000, July). *Your health: Abuse of the elderly.* Retrieved May 31, 2001 from the World Wide Web www.crha-health.ab.ca/healthconn/items/elder-ab.htm.

Direct Marketing. (1998). Recently released report highlights seriousness of telemarketing fraud. *Direct Marketing, 60* (9), 7.

Geriatric Research, Education, and Clinical Center. (1999). *Caregiving Guidance Functional Level 3.5.* (8 pp). Dementia Care Clinic. Minneapolis, MN: Veterans Administration Medical Center.

Harris, M. J. (1995). Elder fraud. *Money, 24,* 144–150.

Johnson-Dalzine, P., Dalzine, L. & Martin-Stanley, C. (1996). Fear of criminal violence and the African American elderly: Assessment of a crime prevention strategy. *The Journal of Negro Education, 65* (4), 462–469.

Klaus, P. A. (1999). *Crimes against persons Age 65 or Older, 1992–97.* (41 pp). Washington, DC: Bureau of Justice Statistics, U.S. Department of Justice.

Klug, E. (2000). Elderly less likely to be victims of violent crime. *Corrections Today, 62* (2), 14.

Kramarow, E., Lentzner, H., Rooks, R., Weeks, J., & Saydah, S. (1999). *Health, United States, 1999. With Health and Aging Chartbook.* Centers for Disease Prevention and Control US DHHS. Hyattsville, MD: National Center for Health Statistics.

Muram, D., Miller, K., & Cutler, A. (1992). Sexual assault of the elderly victim. *Journal of Interpersonal Violence, 7* (1), 70–76.

National Institute of Corrections. (February 18, 2000). Solicitation for a cooperative agreement—"Managing long term aging offenders and offenders with chronic and terminal illnesses." Department of Justice. *Federal Register, 65* (34), 8446–8447.

Pain, R. H. (1995). Elderly women and fear of violent crime: The least likely victims? *British Journal of Criminology, 25* (4), 584–598.

Stevens, J. A., La Mar, H., Durant, T. M., Dellinger, A. M., Batabyal, R. V., Crosby, A.E., Valluru, B. R., Kresnow, M., & Guerrero, J. L. (December 17, 1999). Surveillance for injuries and violence among older adults. *Morbidity and Mortality Weekly Report, 48* (SS08), 27–50.

U.S. Department of Justice. Selected findings from Bureau of Justice Statistics. Edited by Ronet Bachmsn. Retrieved May 31, 2001, from the World Wide Web: www.ojp.usdoj.gov/bjs/pub/ascii.txt.

Young, M. A. & Stein, J. H. (1990). Elderly crime victims: The double sorrow. *Aging, 360,* 36–37.

VII. HEALTH SERVICES AND THE OLDER ADULT

Chapter 13

HEALTH SERVICES: PUBLIC POLICIES INFLUENCING THE HEALTH OF OLDER ADULTS

KATHERINE E.W. WILL

HEALTH SERVICES AND OLDER ADULTS

IN THE UNITED STATES older adults are generally considered by the general public to be senior citizens at age sixty-five. This has primarily been attributed to the retirement opportunity that Social Security benefits and Medicare coverage has brought within the last three decades. However, even though the older adult is categorized as retired, that adult is quite capable of maintaining a routine lifestyle for approximately another twenty years after retirement before significant physical functions are impaired.

Activities of daily living (ADLs) include such tasks as bathing, dressing, eating, toileting, and ambulating, and are evaluated to assist with determining functional and independence status. Usually, the older adult does not experience a serious decline in physical functions until the mid-eighties. According to the 1990 United States Census survey, only 12 percent reported difficulties with ADLs (U.S. Department of Commerce, 1995). Bathing tends to be the first ADL to be limit-

ed; whereas, eating usually is the last to be affected.

Another commonly utilized measurement of physical capability includes the instrumental activities of daily living (IADLs). Such tasks include telephoning, shopping, balancing the checkbook, housekeeping and cooking meals. These hallmarks are considered in evaluating physical function and independence in the community. Shopping is the primary IADL deficit in those over the age of eighty-five according to the United States (U.S. Department of Commerce, 1995).

Schneider & Guralnik (1990) found that both ADL and IADL abilities decrease with the aging process. However, the older women observed more disabilities than the men. In the seventy-five to eighty-four-year-old cohort, the women can expect a 28 percent decline while the men can expect an 18 percent decline in both abilities. The women who are eighty-five and older can anticipate a 62 percent decline, whereas the men in the same age cohort can anticipate a 46 percent decrease.

219

In addition to the physical-function assessment, independence may be affected by social, mental or emotional factors. For example, if the individual is suffering from depression, that individual may not possess the motivation to prepare meals nor bathe on a regular basis. Grief may lead to physiological problems, such as dietary disturbances, fatigue, and insomnia. Alzheimer's disease and other forms of dementia can cause the elder to have memory lapses, difficulty with communication, confusion, anxiety, or aggressive behavior.

It is a specific disease or condition's signs and symptoms that lead older adults to seek care, but Evashwick (1996) maintains that functional disabilities are the primary reason for extended care. The continuum of care incorporates services with a focus on high acuity, such as hospitals, through services that target community programs, such as health promotion and housing.

Evashwick (1987) identified seven separate major services encompassing over sixty distinct services in the continuum of care model. The major categories include: Extended Care, Acute Care, Ambulatory Care, Home Care, Outreach, Wellness–Health Promotion, and Housing. Table 13.1 lists the various health care services that may be available to older persons in their communities. However, dependent upon the size of the local community, there may be limited access to such diverse services.

The various services provided on the continuum are funded and supported by a variety of sources. Still, some are likely to be covered by private-insurance entities, while others are more likely to be paid by the consumer. Some services are subsidized through governmental sources, while others are not. State subsidies, such as Medicaid, may vary between states for the same type of service, such as assisted living.

Therefore, public policy related to health service provisions for the elderly is diverse.

Public health decision makers will be increasingly asked to provide a multitude of services to maximize independence in a variety of settings, but not drain the country's health care dollars. However, the United States has never experienced the involvement of caring for such a large elder population with the advantages (and disadvantages) of advanced medical technology.

INFORMAL NETWORKS

Informal networks have dominated the care provided to elders for decades in the United States. Prior to the enactment of the Kerr-Mills Act in 1960, an amendment to the Social Security Act of 1935 and contributor to the Medicaid funding system that currently funds a substantial about of care to older adults, the dependent aged population was cared for in family homes. In fact, family and friends provide between 80 and 90 percent of care over an extended period of time (Doty, Liu, & Wiener, 1985). Other common sources of care included neighbors and charitable organizations, such as churches.

Family members have traditionally provided informal care in some of the following ways: personal care, transportation, housekeeping, and errand running. For instance, a spouse may assist with the toileting and bathing needs for weeks or months after a cerebrovascular accident (CVA), which is commonly called a stroke. It is also common for children of elders to shop for groceries or to transport elders to medical appointments. During illnesses, a parent may temporarily live with a child so that extra attention can be given. Many family members cite the desire to care as based on love, financial need, an obligation to help someone who has previously cared for them, or to reduce the risk of institutionalization.

TABLE 13.1
Services of the Continuum of Care

Extended	**Home Care (continued)**
Nursing centers	Home visitors
Step-down units	Home-delivered meals
Swing beds	Homemaker and personal care
Nursing home follow-up	Caregivers
	Respite
Acute	
Medical/surgical in-patient unit	**Outreach**
Psychiatric in-patient unit	Screening
Rehabilitation in-patient unit	Information and referral
Interdisciplinary assessment team	Telephone contact
Consultation service	Emergency response
Transportation	
Ambulatory	Senior membership programs
Physicians' offices	Meals on Wheels
Outpatient clinics	
Interdisciplinary assessment clinics	**Wellness–Health Promotion**
Day hospitals	Educational programs
Adult day care centers	Exercise programs
Mental health clinics	Recreational and social groups
Satellite clinics	Senior volunteers
Psychosocial counseling	Congregate meals
Alcohol and substance abuse care	Support groups
Home Care	**Housing**
Home health–Medicare	Continuing-care retirement communities
Home health–private	Independent senior housing
Hospice	Congregate care centers
High-technology home therapy	Adult family centers
Durable medical equipment	Assisted living centers
	Intermediate care centers for the mentally retarded

Source: Evashwick. (1987). Definition of the Continuum of Care, Managing the Continuum of Care. C. Evashwick & L. Weiss (Eds.), Rockville, MD: Aspen Publishers, Inc., 1987.

The profile of a caregiver is one of a female spouse in her early sixties who ranks her own health as good or excellent. About one-third of the informal caregivers are working, and only about five percent are also caring for children under the age of eighteen. Most enjoy their labors of love and dedication.

Couch, Daly, and Wolf (1999) found that the presence of minor children in married-couple households is connected to increased time spent devoted to domestic production, reduction in labor-market hours, and decreased monetary transfers to parents. However, it does not lead to a decrease in time spent helping parents. For unmarried women, young children lead to increased time spent in the home and a reduction in time in the labor market and in parent care.

Caregivers and Stress

Caregivers typically begin caring for elders when minimal assistance is required, and due to increased needs of the elder over time, the tasks continue for longer than originally anticipated. For instance, the spouse of an individual who has experienced a heart attack may begin caregiving after hospital discharge by assisting with exercise in between home-health visits. With the additional strain of poor vision that cannot be remedied, the caregiver takes on more responsibilities, such as transportation and yard work. This increased physical and psychological stress on the caregiver may not only affect the care given to the elder but may be connected with negative health outcomes for the caregiver. Caregivers are especially vulnerable to psychological stress immediately following the onset of the elder's disease or condition.

However, there is conflicting information related to caregiver stress. According to the longitudinal analysis of the National Long-Term Care Surveys, primary informal caregivers have a very low incidence of burnout (Boaz & Muller, 1991; Kasper Steinbach, & Andrews, 1990; Liu & Manton, 1989; McFall & Miller, 1992). This lends support to the claims that caregivers have an ability to overcome the challenges of caring for loved ones for extended periods of time. Many caregivers indicate that they experience more satisfaction than stress from providing care. It appears that many caregivers who experience high levels of stress from caring for someone, also derive high levels of satisfaction (Doty & Miller, 1993; Miller 1989).

The role of caregiver stress plays an important role in determining public policy because limitations on caregiver involvement may increase costs of providing similar services through private and public entities. Therefore, it is advantageous to consider expanding caregiver provisions, such as respite care or adult day services, to complement community services. This has the potential to delay or eliminate the need for more expensive services, such as home health, assisted living, or nursing center care.

Elder Abuse

Elder abuse in the United States is not uncommon. According to the National Elder Abuse Incidence Study (U.S. Department of Health and Human Services, 2001), approximately 450,000 elders in domestic settings were abused and/or neglected in 1996. Elders who self-neglect account for about 100,000.

Abuse of an elder can be profiled in different ways. For example, the victim may be observed with signs and symptoms of poor hygiene, malnutrition, lack of medications, and dehydration. Most elder victims are over the age of seventy-five, and most abuses are family members who are providing care to the relatives. Some are living in the same household, while others live apart. Common types of abuse include the following:

1. *Neglect:* The failure or refusal to provide necessary care to another under responsibility. An example of abuse is when a daughter leaves a mother under her care, who is incapable of toileting or preparing meals, alone with no outside attention while the daughter goes to work

2. *Abandonment:* The desertion of a person by an individual who has the responsibility of caring for that person. An adult child who leaves on vacation for two weeks with no basic provisions for a disabled parent under that adult child's care, such as food, bathing, and medications, could be guilty of abandonment.

3. *Physical abuse:* The use of force on an elder that can cause injury, pain or

disability. For instance, a caregiver who pushes an individual under his care to sit down to guarantee compliant behavior is physically abusive.

4. *Emotional abuse:* The use of verbal or nonverbal tactics to cause distress, anguish, or pain to another human being is considered emotional abuse. The caregiver who continuously threatens to cease caring for the parent in the home, which causes the parent to cry for hours, may be emotionally abusing the elder.

5. *Sexual abuse:* Nonconsensual sexual contact of any type is sexual abuse. This may even include inappropriate touching during bathing depending on the circumstances.

6. *Financial exploitation:* Financial exploitation includes the unauthorized or illegal use of a elder's funds, property, or other assets. Although there are obvious cases, exploitation might include the unauthorized withdrawal of funds by a daughter from a joint checking account to pay a utility bill for the separate home in which the daughter resides alone.

Self-neglect, where the elder's own behaviors threaten personal well-being, is also considered a form of abuse. In fact, self-neglect accounts for the highest number of elder abuse cases. The next most common form of abuse is neglect, which accounts for approximately 60 percent of the reported cases. Physical abuse follows by representing about 15 percent of the reported cases, and financial exploitation accounts for about 12 percent.

State laws differ with respect to definitions of elder abuse. Most physical, sexual, and financial exploitation cases are considered crimes. In additional to the more conventional authorities, the Adult Protective Services (APS) is the public organization responsible for investigating allegations of elder abuse.

Community professionals attempt to learn more about the causes of elder abuse. Care provided to an older adult can be stressful. The responsibilities of the caregiver may be relatively light when initiated, but increase over time as the condition or disease declines. These added responsibilities may have a negative impact on the rates of elder abuse.

Additionally, the extended family's configuration may change. It is not uncommon to see that the number of caregivers for a parent has decreased from three to one, as a result of the decline of the parent's health status. This increases the burdens of the remaining caregiver, especially related to time constraints and less discretionary time. Abuse may follow these difficult situations. Risk factors include the caregiver's perception of stress, history of violence or abuse in the family, high acuity of the elder, substance abuse of the caregiver, or mental illness of the caregiver.

Public policy may play a significant role in decreasing the number of elder abuse cases. Title XIX of the Social Security Act covers services for the indigent, such as social services, adult day care, and respite care. Although the Medicaid regulations vary from state to state, many include provisions for clients living in their homes. However, these funds are limited, and advocates in some states are targeting campaigns to increase these funds.

Social services block grants through Title XX of Social Security Act also include provisions for community programs. For example: Homemaker, chore assistance, adult day care, adult foster care, and mental health services are available to those over the age of sixty. These programs can provide support systems so that the caregiver can accomplish tasks, such as grocery shopping, or have some personal time for relaxation.

The Older Americans Act is available to those over the age of sixty. It provides funding for those in need of nutrition services, such as home-delivered meals, transportation, information and referral services, in-home services, and social-recreational programs. It also funds the state ombudsman program that serves as a liaison between the client and service organization.

Other Informal Care Providers

Family members are frequently the source of caregiving, but other sources do exist in communities throughout the country. For example, churches have a strong history of orchestrating the means to assist the elder in remaining in the home environment. Congregational members of the churches commonly provide transportation, meals, chores, or visits that decrease the reliance on formal health care networks.

Other groups have organized to provide similar services. For example, youth groups, such as the Boy Scouts and Girl Scouts, assist with grocery shopping or snow removal. Adult groups, such as the Kiwanis or retired teacher's organizations, furnish assistance for elders. One would be remiss in not acknowledging the thousands of neighbors who deliver diverse services to the elders during routine weeks throughout the year. These caregivers donate thousands of hours to assist elders to remain in the communities with minimal, if any, cost to the public funding sources.

FORMAL SERVICES AND NETWORKS

The formal services of care for the elderly are directed toward physical, social, emo-

tional, and spiritual components. Some organizations, such as hospitals, focus on the acute needs of the elder, while others target the chronic or long-term-care needs. For instance, routine physician visits and lunches provided by the community Meals-on-Wheels program may enable the client to remain in a good health status for two or three years with minimal contact with other formal services.

Unlike the younger population, elder services typically involve chronic conditions, such as cardiovascular disease, cancer, cerebrovascular accidents (strokes), or cancer. These health states or episodes commonly exceed ninety days, and, thus, contacts with one or more organizations are common. The formal services and networks have diverse organizational structures and funding sources. Additionally, communities vary with regard to the types of services provided. Generally, communities with larger populations possess more diverse formal services compared to those with smaller populations.

Unfortunately, the elder who requires care in the formal system experiences a disintegrated system. Acute care is usually offered in a hospital setting and is primarily funded by Medicare (Title XVIII of the Social Security Act). However, if skilled nursing or rehabilitation is required after hospitalization, another setting, such as a nursing and rehabilitation center, may be necessary. There are, however, in some instances provisions for the elder to simply relocate to another section of the hospital to continue such services. Medicare and private-pay sources, such as insurance or out-of-pocket monies, fund skilled nursing and rehabilitation. Extended stays are generally covered by out-of-pocket sources, and then Medicaid sources after personal assets have been exhausted.

It is no surprise that elders, and family members, frequently are confused by the different possible health care settings and funding sources. Some elders possess secondary medical insurances to cover the expenses beyond Medicare, which can compound the confusion and distress. Patients and families frequently debate health care, bills for months after discharge, due to the complexities of working with different health care providers.

Although there are an extensive number of formal services available to elders, seven will be noted in this chapter. They include the following:

1. hospitals and ambulatory care centers,
2. home health agencies,
3. nursing and rehabilitation centers,
4. assisted living–residential care centers,
5. physicians and primary care clinics,
6. community services, and
7. palliative care and hospice services.

Mental health services are also an important component of the health care delivery system for older adults and have been included in Chapter 4 and 5.

Hospitals and Ambulatory Care Centers

The primary focus of hospitals related to elder care is to address acute needs. This generally means that the clinicians save lives and treat to cure. For example, an elder undergoes by-pass cardiac surgery to repair vessels damaged by cardiovascular disease, or an elder is treated with radiation therapy to eradicate the body of cancer cells.

In some cases, the hospital clinicians focus on the stabilization of elders. The elder who is suffering a stroke may be treated with a medication to decrease the risks of severe outcomes. Once the patient is stabilized, physical and occupational therapy are commonly ordered in the hospital to gain maximum functional status.

Ambulatory-care centers, or outpatient-surgery centers, provide another option for acute-care services. These centers generally provide short-term services, such as surgeries, following which the patient is expected to return home the same day. Unless there are complications, elders do well in these types of settings. Home health professionals, such as nurses and therapists, may assist the patient after discharge to resume normal activities.

The primary source of funding for elder hospitalization and ambulatory care is Title XVIII of the Social Security Act or Medicare. Those over the age of sixty-five are entitled to this federal health-insurance program. Medicare contains two parts: Part A, which is funded in part by Federal Insurance Contribution Act (FICA) payroll taxes, covers many of the costs for inpatient hospital, Part B is financed by monthly premiums by those who wish to participate and helps pay for physician services and other medical supplies not covered by Part A. Medicare beneficiaries have the opportunity to enroll in managed-care organizations (MCOs) in many locations throughout the country.

The continued financial stability of the Medicare program has been questioned in recent years. Over the last three years, predictions regarding the solvency of Medicare have varied. Estimates generated by the General Accounting Office (GAO), the Congressional Budget Office (CBO), and the Department of Health and Human Services (DHHS) have been confusing. The cutback provisions to the Medicare program, as the result of the 1997 Balanced Budget Act (BBA), were expected to generate about $115 billion in savings from hospitals, nursing centers, and home health agencies. In reality, those cuts will likely reach $212 billion and have already caused significant turmoil in the health care industry. Nursing centers have been especially burdened with the financial strains, and at least a half-dozen national corporations declared bankruptcy in the first half of the year 2000. However, the first six months of 2001 have shown some encouraging signs of an industry emerging from a challenging economic period.

According to current governmental estimates, Medicare will remain financially viable until at least the year 2025. At this point, the concern is that the consequences of the financial cutbacks will adversely affect the quality of care and safety delivered. Several professional trade associations, such as the American Health Care Association (AHCA), and consumer groups, such as the American Association of Retired Persons (AARP), have coordinated efforts to restore lost funding through the BBA.

There will be almost 70 million elderly and disabled persons eligible for Medicare by the year 2025 (Scott, 2000). The U.S. gross domestic product (GDP) directed toward Medicare is expected to almost double from 2.7 percent in 1998 to 5.32 percent in 2025, providing the GDP continues to grow at the present rate. Changes in the economy could cause the financial burden of Medicare to be affected.

Other sources of hospital and ambulatory care funding include managed-care programs, private insurances, and out-of-pocket patient funds. These other funding sources are also active in implementing changes that reduce the costs of acute health care.

Home Health Agencies

Formal home health services have existed in the United States for approximately 100 years. Public health nurses and voluntary Visiting Nurse Agencies (VNAs) tackled the problems associated with community sanitation, poor personal hygiene, and high infant and maternal mortality rates in the early 1900s. From about 1920 to 1960, many hos-

pitals initiated postdischarge care at home for the patient who had been admitted for acute conditions. Additionally, some hospitals began home health programs for the chronically ill who were episodically discharged for long periods.

The Joint Committee on Chronic Disease produced a significant report in 1956 that established guidelines for home health care organizations to promote quality standards for participants (Benjamin, 1993). This Commission Report emphasized the importance of physician involvement, which historically had been minimal, and the recommendation to expand the role of homemakers or personal aides. Coordinated, interdisciplinary teams were also advocated. However, much concern was voiced publicly about the risk of drastic increases in costs if these services were subsidized by the government. The public was reluctant to approve higher taxes to fund services that might be misused or used frivolously. Special concern was expressed for the projected high costs of homemaker or personal aide costs.

Therefore, when Medicare was passed in 1965, the home health benefit available in Part A promoted the use of home health as a substitution for the more expensive acute-care services. A three-day hospitalization stay was mandatory before home benefits were available, as well as physician certification and periodic recertification. Physical, occupational, and speech therapies, skilled nursing, medical social services, personal aide, and medical supplies and equipment were covered for those who required intermittent services and were homebound. Part B of Medicare could be accessed and had similar coverage except a co-payment of 20 percent prohibited many low-income elderly from using the services.

In addition, in 1965, Medicaid started covering home health services as an optional component for state programs. This provided an alternative for the indigent elderly who had exhausted other resources and wanted to remain in their homes. By 1967, home health care was categorized as a mandatory benefit for Medicaid.

Medicare coverage was expanded during the early 1970s to include persons with end-stage renal disease and adults with permanent disabilities. The Social Services Block Grant Amendments in 1974 (Title XX) increased funding for home health services and encouraged states to consolidate social services and to expand homemaker benefits. Also during this approximate time period, Title III of the Older Americans Act (OAA) established a network of Area Agencies on Aging (AAA). These agencies provided housekeeping or chore services for older adults, as well as beneficial information related to accessing services through other organizations. Title VII of OAA prompted funding for home-delivered meals, frequently known as Meals-on-Wheels, and congregate meals in local communities.

Insurance carriers and managed-care organizations have also incorporated home health benefits over the years. Medicare standards continue to be the guidelines for other payer sources. However, privately funded payers generally provide home health services to those under the age of sixty-five, or for those Medicare recipients who use a private payer as a secondary funding source.

The Medicare Hospice Benefit, which will be discussed further in this chapter, was initiated in 1982 as the result of pleas from the public to fund other providers, in addition to hospitals, for terminally-ill older adults. This permitted elders to choose a less-sterile environment and to be cared for by professionals who emphasized quality of life, comfort, and compassion over aggressive care to prolong life.

Nursing and Rehabilitation Centers

Nursing and rehabilitation centers across the United States serve two primary extended-care populations. First, they provide services to the stabilized or low-acuity resident who possesses chronic conditions, such as cardiovascular disease, cerebrovascular accidents, diabetes, or dementia. Second, centers provide highly skilled care and rehabilitation services to those who have recently experienced a significant health disease or condition and are in need of skilled nursing or rehabilitation therapy. Most patients admitted for rehabilitation will return to the home environment within several weeks.

Medicare pays in part for the first 150 days per episode in a nursing center and rehabilitation center based upon federal qualifications. This federally funded insurance program pays 100 percent for the first twenty days, and 80 percent for days 21 through 150 of a qualified stay. Thereafter, it is the financial responsibility of the patient to fund additional expenses. Due to the high expenses of care and a risk of losing personal assets, some people maintain secondary insurances that begin after the Medicare resources are exhausted. Due to the gap in care between hospital and nursing-rehabilitation care, some people have enrolled in managed-health-care plans or Medigap programs that commonly boast more care for the money.

Residents of nursing and rehabilitation centers who do not require a higher level of care, are typically funded by out-of-pocket funds or Medicaid, which combines federal and state funding resources. According to regulations, residents must use personal assets before the state-administered Medicaid will initiate funding. This policy has received negative feedback in some circles because some people believe that Medicaid sources should be available to all citizens, regardless of assets. Therefore, some states have developed and initiated aggressive retrieval programs that prevent people from divesting their assets to family members or other benefactors, prior to access for care in the center. This process is referred to as Medicaid estate planning and enables an elder to look indigent via documentation, but retain wealth through legal maneuvers. However, when Medicaid is activated by the elder, the expense falls upon the taxpayers.

The policy implications for not receiving these personal funds to pay for services are significant. Since the Omnibus Budget Reconciliation Act of 1993, states have been required to recover the costs associated with Medicaid long-term-care services from estates of enrollees who have expired. Unfortunately, data reveals that estate-recovery programs are only able to retrieve a small proportion of long-term-care expenditures. Less than one percent of all nursing home expenditures were recovered in 1995 (Wood & Sabatino, 1996). Several states have devoted more attention to these collection efforts in recent months to reduce the use of governmental subsidies.

Private insurance is another viable funding source for nursing and rehabilitation centers. Unfortunately, private insurers pay only about one percent of nursing center costs. Elders generally cite the high costs of premiums as being the primary obstacle in securing private insurance. The insurance industry believes that this relatively-new insurance product is just in its infancy, and that continued consumer education will increase the use of private insurance. Public decision makers hope that more consumers will purchase insurance to offset some of the subsidies for elder care.

Residential Care-Assisted Living Centers

Residential-care centers, also called assisted-living residences, are a relatively new option to the long-term care segment of the health care industry. The forerunner of residential-care centers was the small boarding home that generally cared for a half-dozen elders who required light assistance with such daily tasks as bathing, meal preparation, or medication reminders. Organizations increased in size during the last twenty years and moved from the traditional setting, as a community family house, to a multi-unit physical plant. In many instances, the custodial care originally provided developed into a higher level of care.

States have observed vast changes in the types of residents served and the number of units developed, especially during the last decade. As a result, some states have developed regulations to guide the placement of acceptable acuity residents, as well as the minimum quality standards for residential-care centers. For example, a resident may only be allowed to receive a maximum of ninety days of skilled nursing care before that resident is required to seek placement in another setting, such as a nursing and rehabilitation center. Some states prohibit skilled nursing care to be delivered by the residential-care-center staff, due to conflict of interest, and mandate that the skilled care be provided by an external source that is not owned or affiliated with the residential-care center.

Funding for residential services varies from state to state. According to the Assisted Living Federation of America (ALFA), slightly more than 40 percent of the states provide some type of funding subsidies for residential-care centers. Such Medicaid waiver programs may pay for all or part of assisted-living expenses. In addition, the insurance industry promotes products that include assisted-living services. Unfortunately, most products are out of reach economically for low- and middle-income elders.

Authorities do not agree on the effect that subsidized funding for residential-care centers has on total expenditures for long-term care. Some indicate that use of residential care reduces the need for more expensive nursing and rehabilitation, and, thus, reduces the total dollar amount spent on care. However, others argue that as elders "age in place" the combined charges associated with residential care and home health care, to address the higher levels of acuity, exceed what nursing and rehabilitation centers charge.

With the number of elderly projected to increase for the next thirty years, the policy implications are important. As a nation, the United States will very likely struggle with how to care for older adults in a cost-effective environment. Medical technology has given patients, and their families, many opportunities, but at what price?

Physician Services

Regular visits by elders to physicians generally permit the physician to keep abreast of chronic medical conditions and diseases, as well as to treat new ones. Older adults made approximately twelve visits to their physicians in 1996 according to the *U.S. Vital and Health Statistics* (2000). Medicare Part B assists payment for physician services and medical supplies for those elders over the age of sixty-five. At this time, Part B does not include coverage for prescription medications, which can account for a large portion of the monthly income. This means that for those individuals on fixed incomes a difficult choice must be faced—whether to purchase medications or to pay utility bills. Some elders choose to self-adjust their medications by

either not taking the full dosage, or by eliminating drugs that they perceive to be less important. Frequently, this self-adjustment compounds the problem, and the elder runs the risk of experiencing negative consequences, which can include costly hospitalization. Thereby, the out-of-pocket expenses for the elder have increased after actions to decrease the out-of-pocket expenditures. This also generally drives up the Medicare or other funding costs.

Due to the high costs of medications and subsequent public attention from different community groups, such as AARP, there has been much attention directed toward improvements in the Medicare system. The new reform plan, championed by the Bush administration, adds a prescription drug benefit to the federal health care program. The political decision makers also have choices to initiate fundamental changes in the Health Care Financing Administration (HCFA) that streamline operations and emphasize state involvement. The Republicans have developed a plan that would cost nearly $40 billion over five years and would offer drug benefits via private-insurance companies for a maximum of $6,000 yearly. The Republican proposal offers a choice of plans, whereas Clinton's proposal maintained one vehicle for procurement.

Community Services

Community services throughout the country also play an important role in assisting elders to remain independent. Although the services vary from state to state, many are funded through the OAA and the community-based organizations. This array of services is commonly referred to as the Aging Network, and the general purpose of the funding is to provide support services to elders that enhance their ability to remain independent through an acceptable level of well-being.

The U.S. Administration on Aging (AOA), which administers the OAA, is located within DHHS. The primary functions of the AOA include the following:

1. to develop and promulgate regulations guiding the implementation of the OAA at the state and local level,
2. to distribute funding to the states and territories,
3. to monitor the implementation of the OAA at the state level,
4. to coordinate with other federal departments,
5. to advocate for aging services at the federal level, and
6. to implement directly Title IV: Training, Research, and Discretionary Projects.

Title III covers home- and community-based services that target resources for the provision of supportive services. State units on aging (SUA) are the entities charged with the coordination of activities at the state level. The Long-Term Care Ombudsman Program (LTCOP) has the responsibility to investigate complaints regarding care in long-term-care centers within the state. The SUAs also have the responsibility of overseeing the Area Agency on Aging (AAA) that implements the provisions of the OAA at the local level. The primary responsibility of each AAA is to develop a comprehensive plan for services for older adults. Each AAA, with the assistance of the community advisory council, conducts a community-needs assessment, and then develops a strategic plan to address the needs of older the adults.

Based upon the needs assessment, the AAA is charged with program development. For example, respite services may be desirable. Respite services provide the family member or friend with time off from caring for the client on a full-time basis. Such temporary services can be provided in the home via a volunteer or via a paid staff member in the home or institutional setting, such as a nursing center. It is common for AAAs to work with other community agencies to enhance programs for the older adult.

AAA also receives some funding for direct services that are mandated, such as employment and congregate and home-delivered meals. Other common services pertain to transportation, legal services, in-home services, and information and assistance. AAAs may find it advantageous to fund services such as adult day care, home repair, respite care, case management, or other options that would enhance the quality of life for the elder population in the community. The law requires that any service provided with funding from OAA is free of charge to those over the age of sixty (regardless of income) or to a spouse of someone meeting the age requirement.

Title III of the OAA also provides minimum amounts, although a wide variety, of disease-prevention and health-promotion activities. Funds can be used by the AAA for programs focusing on health screening, nutrition education, health-promotion materials, and physical fitness activities. Some AAAs determine that continuing programs are in the best interest of the elder population and use the funds for annual health-screening clinics.

Title VI provides funding directly from the AOA to tribal councils and Native Hawaiian organizations. The purpose is to dedicate federal funding for the two minority groups, and the funding can be used for the programs identified in Title III.

Due to easy access to Aging Network services and the growing increase in the older population, there is concern that current levels of resources may be limited. Policy implications most likely will focus on elder program-eligibility criteria and whether to fund elders based on needs or to continue providing services based on community services.

Wisconsin: A State Redesigning Family Care

The Department of Health and Family Services (DHFS) has been in the process of redesigning its long-term care plan to address the needs of the older adult who requires financial assistance for long-term care services. A comprehensive assessment to evaluate the need for long-term care services is a major component, as well as provision to permit dollars to follow the consumer. Once eligibility is determined, the older adult works with a social worker and nurse to arrange for care or support services. Wisconsin included the funding pathway to address the perceived "institutional" bias of the Medicaid program.

The Family Care program, currently being piloted, was developed with the input from older adults, advocates, state-policy professionals, and service providers. In the long run, Family Care will be a flexible benefit for all long-term care services. It will include the Community Options Program (COP), which covers services for those remaining in the home, as well as covering nursing centers, assisted living, community-based residential centers, transportation, and therapies. Aging and Disability Resource Centers will provide unbiased, professional advice about options and "one-stop shopping."

Participation in the program is on a volunteer basis, but those who choose Family Care will be entitled to a "Medicaid-funded, tailor-made" package of services. One of the advantages, compared to the previous system, is that there will be no waiting list for participation. A sliding-scale fee-for-service is in effect, as well as a spousal-impoverishment-protection policy.

Wisconsin funded approximately $12 million for both the 1999–2000 and the 2000–2001 fiscal years. The remaining necessary funds, which are in excess of $200 million, will be state funds reallocated from existing programs and federal sources. As more people transfer into the Family Care option, funds will be transferred to the appropriate service source. There are no county-match funds necessary for participation.

Palliative Care and Hospice Services

The philosophy of palliative care and hospice services was initiated in Great Britain in 1967 by Dame Cicely Saunders who founded St. Christopher's Hospice. Through this endeavor, attention was directed toward symptom-management (physical), as well as the psychological, social, and spiritual concerns of the patients. Successful initiatives investigated and promoted improved pain-control interventions and public education strategies. Additionally, St. Christopher's promoted programs to better care for dying patients and their families.

The hospice movement began in the United States in the 1970s. The creation of the National Hospice Organization (NHO) in 1978 provided a national forum to discuss common missions for the terminally ill who most frequently were cancer patients. Quality standards for hospices and education opportunities were also major agenda items.

In 1982, national support for palliative and hospice services prompted Congress to legislate the Tax Equity Fiscal Responsibility Act (TEFRA) and to expand the Medicare coverage to include hospice. Many private-insurance companies also began to recognize the cost-effectiveness and national support and included hospice benefits. Many states also incorporated hospice benefits under state Medicaid programs.

Technological advances related to the medical care of patients in the United States have dramatically increased over the last twenty-five years. Clinicians are frequently able to treat conditions that previously were untreatable and extend lives for weeks, months, or years. However, these new advances also can bring new challenges, such as side effects, lifestyle changes, and use of increased resources. People with terminal or life-threatening conditions, such as cancer, chronic obstructive pulmonary disease (COPD), renal disease, Acquired Immunodeficiency Syndrome (AIDs), and Alzheimer's disease can live longer, more productive lives compared to previous generations.

Palliative care and hospice services are components of the health care delivery system that address the needs of those patients with terminal illnesses. The older adult may be diagnosed with a terminal illness with a projected continued life span of a few weeks, or a few months. Comprehensive definitions of palliative care embrace physical, psychological, social, spiritual, and interpersonal characteristics to meet the complex needs of the patient and family. The World Health Organization (WHO) defines palliative care as "the active total care of patients whose disease is not responsive to curative treatment" (Critchley et al., 1999, p. 40). The primary goal of palliative care is to enhance the quality and meaning of life and death (Zalot, 1989). The focus changes from cure to comfort.

Hospice services are frequently requested by the older adult or family member when aggressive curative treatment is unsuccessful. Aggressive treatment of symptoms replaces aggressive treatment of disease. The focus turns to the quality of remaining life with special concern toward pain and symptom management, and psychosocial and spiritual-support services. Hospice providers recognize dying as part of the living process. Hospice professionals honor life, but do not facilitate nor delay death.

The hospice team is a multidimensional specialized group trained in the physical, psychosocial, spiritual, and economic needs of the terminally ill. Professional clinicians, as well as volunteers, share in the mission of providing a suitable quality of life. Core interdisciplinary team members include the following:

1. patient's attending physician,
2. hospice physician,
3. registered nurses and licensed practical nurses,
4. medical social workers with counseling background,
5. spiritual counselors,
6. pharmacist,
7. dietitian,
8. art–music therapists,
9. family caregiver, and
10. trained volunteers.

The coordinated efforts of the team are guided by the plan of care that is goal directed with major influences by the patient and family.

As noted earlier, the Hospice Medicare Benefit is the primary payer for older adults. Anyone covered under Part A is eligible to receive hospice care related to terminal conditions when the following conditions are met: (a) physician certification that life expectancy is expected to be six months or less, (b) the elder chooses hospice benefits over standard Medicare benefits, and (c) hospice services are rendered by a Medicare approved provider.

Under this benefit, four levels of care are eligible for Medicare reimbursement: routine home care, continuous care, inpatient respite care, and general acute inpatient care. Two ninety-day periods followed by an unlimited number of sixty-day benefits periods are covered. Hospice-care coverage includes:

1. physician services,
2. nursing services (intermittent),
3. medical social services,
4. counseling,

5. physical and occupational therapies,
6. speech-language pathology,
7. medications,
8. home health aides and homemaker services,
9. medical supplies and equipment,
10. respite care,
11. short-term inpatient care, and
12. bereavement services (continued support to family for maximum of thirteen months after death).

Patients may transfer to another Medicare-certified hospice once during each benefit period. Hospice benefactors may also discontinue services at any time and return to cure-oriented care.

In addition to the therapeutic value of hospice to the elder and the elder's family, studies suggest that such care provisions may be more cost-effective than other end-of-life provider choices. The Medicare Hospice Benefit Program Evaluation found that Medicare saved about $1.25 for every $1.00 spent on hospice care for the first three years of hospice benefit. Much of the savings were derived from the last few weeks of life. The National Hospice Study (NHS) indicated that cost savings in the last few weeks or months of life were primarily due to the substitution of home-care days for hospital in-patient days (NHPCO, 2000).

A 1995 Lewin-VHI study commissioned by the National Hospice and Palliative Care Organization (NHPCO), indicated that for every $1.00 Medicare spends on hospice services, it saves $1.52 in Medicare Part A and Part B expenses. The study also suggested that patients using hospice services during the last year of life incur about $2,700 less in costs compared to those not on the Medicare Hospice Benefit (NHPCO, 2000).

According to NHPCO, there are approximately 3,100 planned or operational hospices in the United States, Puerto Rico,

and Guam today (NHPCO, 2000). NHPCO estimates that hospice programs served at least 700,000 Americans in 1999, or about 29 percent of all who died. The average length of enrollment was forty-eight days and the median length of service was twenty-nine days. In 1997, Medicare expended about $2 billion of its $200 billion budget on hospice services to 382,989 patients receiving 19 million days of hospice care. In 1995, 65 percent of hospice patients were covered by Medicare, 12 percent were carried via private insurance, 8 percent by Medicaid, and the remaining had other sources of payment.

Hospice providers have strong reputations across the country and should no longer be viewed as isolated entities. Unfortunately, some insurance carriers or other funding sources make the decision to refer to a hospice without an acceptable transition by the older adult. The transition between an aggressive, active plan of treatment that targets a cure and one that plans for a comfortable closing to life is not often a quick or easy matter. Therefore, some patients and their families have been pushed by the clinicians into hospice care.

Others, fortunately, have experienced the option of personally choosing hospice services. Many initiate contacts because the battle has been long, and the body is worn. They have a strong drive to enjoy whatever time is remaining with family and friends. Hospice professionals and trained volunteers can assist them to maximize their independence, comfort, and dignity in different environments.

HEALTH CARE PLANNING FOR THE ELDERLY

Planning for the health care needs of the elderly in the United States has historically been episodic. Typically, a problem or issue has presented itself, and a funding source has addressed it. For example, the Medicare program (Title XVIII of the Social Security Act) was initiated in 1965 to focus on acute-care needs of the those over the age of sixty-five, and the Medicaid program (Title XIX of the Social Security Act) also started that year to address the long-term care needs of the indigent elderly. Both Medicaid and Medicare also have provisions to cover other specialized populations. In addition, the OAA was passed in 1965 to fund nutrition programs, supportive services like transportation, and the state ombudsman service. Social service block grants were funded through Title XX (Social Security Act) in 1974 to provide community-based services. Thus, the country does not possess a history of a coordinated, coherent long-term care planning process or policy. This is especially relevant in view of the anticipated increase of older adults in the upcoming decades. The number of people over the age of sixty-five will increase from 39 to 69 million between 2010 and 2030 (Preston, 1996). For the first time in U.S. history, the number of citizens under the age of eighteen will be fewer than those over the age of sixty-five. At the core of many discussions is the debate related to the financial solvency of Medicare's Hospital Insurance Trust Fund. Research studies investigating the projected Medicare funds for the future have been inconclusive and will be highlighted later in this chapter. However, regardless of the funding specifics, there are several variables that will need to be addressed in relation to planning for the health needs of the elderly. These include the following:

1. concentration on chronic-disease management,
2. medical technology,
3. alternative-treatment approaches,
4. end-of-life decisions,
5. consumer advocacy and satisfaction,

6. integration on continuum of care providers to maximize efficiency, and
7. control of expenditures and alternative-funding sources.

Concentration on Chronic-Disease Management

The number of acute infectious diseases has decreased significantly in the last few decades as the result of improved sanitary conditions, pharmaceutical agents, and technology. Diseases, such as polio and cholera, that killed thousands after the turn of the century are now controllable with immunizations, medications, good sanitary conditions, or personal hygiene. However, the public focus on acute diseases, which are usually short in duration and caused by a pathogen, has been replaced with chronic diseases and conditions that affect the health care planning process.

A disease, condition, or disorder is generally considered chronic if it persists for longer than three months. Chronic diseases typically are not caused by pathogens, but by lifestyle choices, aging, environmental conditions, or occupational situations. For instance, lack of exercise and poor nutritional habits are directly related to cardiovascular disease that generally is treated for years. The three leading causes of death in the sixty-five-and-older population are heart disease, cancer, and cerebrovascular accidents (CVAs) or strokes.

Unfortunately, some acute and some chronic conditions can result in long-term health care needs. A diabetic may require nutritional and exercise education and counseling soon after diagnosis, but twenty years later need a prosthetic device as the result of a limb amputation due to poor circulation. A series of CVAs can leave the elder with partial paralysis combined with deteriorating cognitive functioning. These scenarios are commonly played out over the course of many years. Therefore, the elder may interact with different providers on the continuum of care. A hospital is used to stabilize a CVA that may be followed by therapy in a nursing-rehabilitation center, and home health aides may assist the elder with household chores after discharge. Follow-up physician visits continue for extended periods of time due to the seriousness of the condition, as well as for other medical conditions that may warrant medical attention. The same elder may have another CVA during the next five years and follow a similar path of interactions with the health care continuum.

The devastating effects of some diseases and conditions can cause handicaps or disabilities. Another common term used for handicap or disability in the health care field is impairment. Regardless of the term, the relevance is associated with the possible consequences of the decreased independence in elders. Loss of independence can jeopardize self-sufficiency, work or vacation schedules, mobility, freedom from medical care, and self-esteem. Generally, elders in the United States have a strong desire to be in control of their daily activities and not to rely on family or community members for assistance.

There is a growing body of evidence to indicate that health promotion in the elderly can provide positive outcomes. Education and public awareness targeted toward the benefits of seeking emergency care within the first two hours of chest pain may decrease the damage to the heart and reduce the costs associated with medical care. Similarly, smoking cessation of the elderly may decrease some of the associated respiratory complications, such as persistent coughing or a suppressed immune system. Exercise is connected to decreased rates of depression. Educating the public about the different types of health care providers can reduce the unnecessary visits to clinicians.

Therefore, health care planning efforts should include health promotion for older adults. The potential to prevent or to decrease the severity of diseases is extensive and greatly untapped. The three primary benefits of incorporating health promotion into the health care planning agenda include the potential to lengthen independence, to enhance self-esteem, and to reduce health care costs.

Medical Technology

Advances in medical technology have assisted with the eradication of diseases and reductions in discomfort for many procedures and surgeries. Noninvasive procedures have replaced invasive ones, such as the elimination of kidney stones that were once surgically removed but now are crushed with laser technology. Technology has also enhanced diagnostic capabilities that can permit treatment to begin earlier in some circumstances. In the last few decades, thousands of hip replacements have been performed, as well as cataracts removed to improve the quality of life for elders.

Most overwhelming, medical technology is desirable and successful in the United States. Public and private funding for research and development has surpassed most other developed countries. However, the challenges rest not with the innovation but with the public perception that technology is the panacea for the health care system. Society places greater value on technology than other variables, such as nutrition, exercise, vitamin supplements, conversation, and other alternatives.

This interest or reliance on technology may be due to the economic systems that drive the health care system. Reimbursement for hospitals and some other providers focus on the provision of high-tech services. The people in the United States have become accustomed to the latest and best technology and pharmacological interventions available. Knowledgeable patients may even demand the newest treatment despite the long-term effects in the hope that it will be beneficial. This scenario is especially evident in new experimental drugs for life-threatening conditions that have not been fully evaluated by the authorizing organizations, such as the Food and Drug Administration (FDA).

The growing challenge related to medical technology and health care planning is the financing, efficacy, and effectiveness of such innovations. It appears that expensive technical approaches may be used by clinicians in some cases when more basic medical and psychosocial interventions might be more beneficial (Mechanic, 1999). As the number of elders continues to increase, the cost of this continued reliance on technology, combined with additional research focusing on medical care alternatives, will play a more significant role in public policy.

Alternative-Treatment Approaches

Unconventional practices associated with treatments for elimination of illnesses and injuries or decreasing discomfort have not been widely accepted in the United States during the last fifty years. Frequently, these alternative approaches to medicine have not been approved by the U.S. scientific community, although many are used in other countries. However, with the establishment of the Office of Alternative Medicine (OAM) in 1991 in the National Institutes of Health, more research studies are currently being conducted.

Positive outcomes are being expressed by patients and practitioners that lend support for continued efforts to seek and use unconventional treatments. Common disciplines include:

1. *Ayurvedic medicine* originated from traditional Indian practices and focuses on meditation, herbs, minerals, exercise, and nutrition to purify the imbalances of the body. Purification practices and rejuvenation therapies play a role in the healing process.

2. *Acupuncture* is a technique that started in ancient China and involves the insertion of needles into the skin, muscles, or tendons at meridian points. Various meridian points represent body parts, and a healthy condition is expected when the yin and yang (energy modes) are harmonious.

3. *Chiropractic treatment* is based on the concept that healing can occur through spinal manipulation. Many chiropractors today acknowledge that pathogens, hormones, and other variables influence the course of a condition and work with medical physicians. Some focus solely on musculoskeletal disorders. Insurance policies cover chiropractic manipulation in many cases for musculoskeletal conditions.

4. *Clinical ecology* is founded on the concept that hypersensitivity to some food or chemicals can cause medical conditions, such as depression, headaches, pains, cognitive difficulties, and other common concerns. Clinical ecologists claim that the contaminants adversely affect the immune system.

5. *Homeopathy* heals symptoms of a condition by using similar substances as the causative agents in healthy people. Remedies include plant components, minerals, and other substances diluted.

6. *Naturopathy* is based on the idea that medical conditions are due to the of-

fense of nature's laws. Such diseases or conditions are the consequences of toxins in the body. Naturopathic treatments include certain natural foods, herbs, vitamins, massage, and body manipulation.

7. *Religion* is founded on the belief of a higher being that can heal the body. Some, however, believe that the church serves as a safety net from being isolated during illness.

Evaluating alternative treatment practices is difficult at this time. Ongoing studies are investigating the effectiveness and other factors. Research initiatives at the present time are focusing on the following related to common elder conditions:

1. imagery for asthma,
2. acupuncture for depression,
3. manual palpation for constipation,
4. massage therapy for postsurgical recovery,
5. ayurvedic medicine for Parkinson's disease,
6. biofeedback and relaxation for diabetes, and
7. hypnosis for chronic pain.

Professional licensure and education requirements for practitioners vary according to the individual state. This is another avenue to pursue to evaluate quality.

Alternatives to traditional forms of medicine and health care in the United States are being used at an increased frequency. Outcome measurements are beginning to demonstrate some advantages, such as reduced costs with acceptable medical achievements, to these unconventional options. Therefore, it seems relevant to consider these opportunities in health care planning strategies.

End-of-Life Decisions

Morbidity and mortality rates increase as people age. Per capita expenditures for Medicare participants sixty-five years and older were $3,519 in 1993 but vary among age cohorts (National Center for Health Statistics, 1995). For example, per capita expenditures were $2,238 among elders between the ages of sixty-five and sixty-six in 1993, whereas expenditures were $5,083 for those over the age of eighty-five. Although the eighty-five-and-older age cohort is small in relationship to other cohorts, this group is expected to increase from 3.6 million in 1995 to 8.5 in 2030.

Periodically, public opinion or policy makers suggest that large amounts of financial resources are expended on elderly patients at the end of life. However, Mechanic (1999) insists, based upon data between 1976 to 1990, that the proportion of funds used in the last year of life has remained the same. Thus, the argument that a significant amount of resources is wasted on the attempt to extend life is questioned.

Scitovsky (1994) presented evidence indicating that average expenditures in 1988 for Medicare participants who died during the year were $13,316 compared to average expenditures of $1,924 for those elders who lived. The average cost for those who died was inversely related to age with $15,346 expended for those in the sixty-five to sixty-nine cohort and $8,888 for those over the age of ninety. Scitovsky found that this trend was associated with a variety of conditions, such as pneumonia, diabetes, and cardiovascular disease. Few elderly received the aggressive treatments known in the United States, such as artificial respiration.

It will be necessary to continue research investigating end-of-life decisions that may influence health care policy. Some physicians are uncomfortable with the cessation of treatment, exclusive of palliative care, even when the probability of positive outcomes is minute. Additionally, patients and families, commonly, and expectantly, have difficulty with determining the time to cease aggressive treatment. However, the hospice movement in the United States has accomplished great strides in the development of programs to assist the patients, families and caregivers dealing with end-of-life issues. Future health planning endeavors should consider expanded educational and public-awareness campaigns to disseminate information to the public. Consideration should also be given to reimbursement issues, such as respite and counseling for caregivers.

Consumer Advocacy and Satisfaction

Better educated and knowledgeable consumers are becoming more involved in health care decisions compared to a decade ago. Communication technology, coupled with increased health awareness, has prompted a variety of advocacy groups. AARP is one of the largest consumer groups and provides information pertaining to the aging process, health promotion, health care providers, and retirement planning. Other groups are more geared toward specific conditions such as the national Alzheimer's Association and the Arthritis Foundation. Individual states commonly have affiliations, and some metropolitan communities may have chapters.

Consumer-advocacy groups have the ability to unite constituents for the synergistic benefit of greater voice and political power. Historical voting trends indicate that older citizens vote more frequently than their younger counterparts. Older adults are also more likely to contact their politicians than

younger adults. This consumer behavior could greatly influence national and state policy, especially as the United States is faced with more citizens than ever in the history of the federal program being eligible for Medicare benefits.

Providers on the continuum of care are increasingly becoming interested in consumer satisfaction. This is a direct result of better informed clients, patients, and families that are influenced by enhanced communication skills. Increased involvement is health care means that more consumers are asking questions about providers, success rates of treatment, licensure requirements for professionals, and costs. More consumers than ever before are comparing services on the continuum, initiating dialogue with clinicians, and researching options related to health care.

Consumer-satisfaction research related to elder health care services is limited. Within the last five to ten years providers have initiated consumer-satisfaction questionnaires as a tool to monitor quality of care. Professional credentialing organizations, such as the Joint Commission on Accreditation for Healthcare Organizations (JCAHO), advocate active feedback with patients. The President's Advisory Commission on Consumer Protection and Quality in the Health Care Industry developed the "Consumer Bill of Rights and Responsibilities." The goal of this document is to serve as a foundation for additional legislation, although many believe it was founded to curtail MCOs.

The "Bill of Rights" targets MCOs by addressing consumer issues connected with appropriate health care information: the right to be treated in a nondiscriminatory manner; the right to choose the health care provider; the right to appeal denials or other payment differences; the right to participate in the decision-making process; and the right to have emergency care reimbursed. Some states are also in the process of adopting legislation to promote consumer involvement in personal health care.

The elderly population is a diverse group that is expected to grow in cultural diversity in the future. Their needs will be as diverse as their personalities, and the different providers on the continuum of care will be likely to offer a variety of services in many geographic locations. However, according to research conducted by Krothe (1997), elders are primarily interested in controlling their day-to-day activities. Elders have a distinct desire to be independent and choose when to eat, sleep, and bathe. They do not look forward to assistance by family or community members. The home and its contents represent elders' accomplishments throughout their lives, and, therefore, they prefer to remain in the community setting for as long as possible. Information, such as this which was obtained from elders, will become increasingly important for the development of informed policy development.

Health care planning in the future will be consumer driven (Pratt, 1999). Consumers are better informed and educated and will increasingly demand to be active in making health care choices. Due to the large numbers of elders who use a large proportion of health care services, legislators and private enterprise will depend more and more on these elders' viewpoints and recommendations.

Integration on Continuum of Care to Maximize Efficiency

Health services for the elderly consume a large portion of state and federal budgets. Nursing homes and home health care accounted for about 12 percent of personal health expenditures in 1995, and were almost 14 percent of all state and local health care spending (Levit et al., 1996). Medicare covers skilled nursing and rehabilitation needs of the elderly for a maximum of 150 days. Less than 5 percent of the elderly currently enroll in private-insurance programs that could cover health care and assisted-living expenses that exceeded Medicare coverage. Therefore, elders must use private assets to pay for care until such financial resources are depleted. They are then eligible for the federal-to-state-funded Medicaid program that is the primary source of public funding for long-term care for the elderly. Due to the increase in the aged population, enhanced technology, and inflation factors, expenditures associated with long-term care are expected to more than double in inflation-adjusted dollars between 1993 and 2018 (Weiner, Illston, & Hanley, 1994).

There is growing support across the country to drastically reform the existing health care system by integrating acute- and long-term care services through managed care, or other payer types. Supporters claim that Medicare and Medicaid shift costs between each other due to the separation of financial responsibilities. Some arguments focus on the lack of coordination for elders as they go between social agencies and medical providers. Frequently, medical providers know little about the social services the patient is receiving in the community that permit the patient to remain independent. Furthermore, there is no coordinated information system to share such knowledge between organizations. The delivery system is reliant on the patient to communicate the various interactions, which can be difficult for elders whose cognitive abilities may have declined. Good communication can also be hampered when an elder experiences short, rushed visits with clinicians.

Lack of coordination between providers on the continuum of care may also be observed for competitive reasons. Elders may remain in more-expensive hospital settings for rehabilitation related to a hip fracture compared to a less-costly nursing and rehabilitation center because admission has been to the hospital first. The patient may remain in the expensive hospital setting for extended periods of time until eligibility documentation can be completed for less-expensive long-term care environments. Fragmented services are regarded as responsible for the increase in costs, especially administrative, related to elder care.

Proponents of an integrated system also suggest that consumer satisfaction would be improved because the duplicate efforts would be less likely. Such efforts include duplicating unnecessary assessments, diagnostic tests or procedures, office visits, and documentation. "One-stop shopping" has been promoted, and elders, generally, are interested in the concept. Some also suggest that the quality of care would improve because the integrated health care system would likely have better communication.

Opponents of an integrated delivery system cite that competition is good for the "check and balance" of health care. They also project that administrative costs will remain virtually equal in the integrated system compared to the existing system due to the expansion of patient contacts per time period. Another disadvantage of the integrated system is that managed-care providers, insurance companies, or other funding sources do not possess the knowledge related to long-term care, and quality of care would suffer due to lack of proficient skills. The third point of opposition is related to the fear that cost shifting would occur, and funds would be directed away from long-term care areas to acute care where expenses are generally higher. The fourth concern is that long-term care environments will become more clinical or medically oriented due to the association with acute-care environments. This is especially feared since the long-term care providers are developing less clinical settings, such as assisted-living centers, which have

been well-received across the United States in the last decade.

Policy makers are becoming increasingly interested in the discussions associated with system reform. The two primary reasons for increased interest is due to more elders desiring to remain in their homes and the potential to be more cost-effective. However, research remains inconclusive regarding the projected cost savings related to extended-care expenditures (Alecxih, Lutzky, & Corea, 1996; U.S. General Accounting Office, 1994; Wiener & Stevenson, 1998).

States have also become involved by sponsoring demonstration projects that evaluate different approaches to expanding home- and community-based services (HCBS) or integrating health care services. Capitated payment programs for Medicaid-funded health care services include the following: the Arizona Long-Term Care System (ALTCS), the Minnesota Senior Health Option (MSHO), the Monroe County, New York Continuing Care Networks (CCNs), Texas STAR+PLUS, and Program of All-Inclusive Care for the Elderly (PACE).

ALTCS: Elderly with a high risk of institutionalization, a physical disability, mental retardation or other developmental disabilities are eligible for this capitated long-term care program. ALTCS is mandatory for those under the state managed-care programs and is administered by the Arizona Health Care Cost Containment System. Providers are paid a capitated rates that covers both acute- and long-term care services.

MSHO: Elders who live in seven counties in the Minneapolis–St. Paul area have the opportunity to participate in this demonstration project. There is a choice between three managed-care plans that cover acute- and long-term care services. Participants must be dually eligible for

Medicaid and Medicare, and the state administers the program through a single contract. Minnesota holds waivers for Medicaid and Medicare.

CCNs: Monroe County, New York, is also a demonstration voluntary program for dually eligible elders. CCN covers primary-, acute-, and long-term care services under a capitation payment system. The reimbursement is risk adjusted based on the elder's functional status.

Texas STAR+PLUS: This program is mandatory for Medicaid enrollees, and optional for Medicare. Those who are dually eligible and choose from one of the three managed-care organizations for Medicare services also receive an unlimited drug benefit. STAR+PLUS integrates the delivery of acute- and long-term care services and operates under a Medicaid-managed care waiver and Medicaid HCBS waiver.

PACE: Older adults over the age of fifty-five, or older in some states, who meet Medicaid-eligibility criteria have the option to join this program that integrates primary-, acute-, and long-term care services. Adult day and home health care are important vehicles to this program. Although this program was originally a demonstration program, the BBA of 1997 established PACE as a permanent program. Multidisciplinary teams use a combination of funding sources (e.g., Medicaid, Medicare and private insurance) to secure services.

A thrust toward community-based long-term care is founded on the assumption that the capitation efforts that reduced the expensive hospital expenditures will also force costs to decrease in long-term care. Capitation appears to provide a financial incentive to postpone or to avoid institutionalization. However, there is no evidence to substantiate this for the extended-care population. The analyses from the demonstration programs identified will provide information related to appropriate placement, expenditures, and the significance to federal- and state-funding programs.

Control of Expenditures and Alternative-Funding Sources

Policy makers are also investigating other means to reduce the costs of health care for the elderly. Some of these avenues have already been implemented to provide some short-run relief to the costly delivery system. Others are being explored to determine the value to the public in terms of public costs savings, as well as the effect on the quality of care.

Reducing Reimbursement Rates

The BBA of 1997 repealed the Boren Amendment that was included in the Omnibus Reconciliation Act of 1980. This amendment guided how states reimbursed nursing homes and required that reasonable and adequate resources be allocated to fulfill quality-of-care and safety requirements as established by state and federal regulations. Consequently, the states have the ability to establish reimbursement rates.

Some states reimburse nursing centers for Medicaid beneficiaries at rates lower than Medicare or private sources, and, thus, it is not as financially advantageous to admit Medicaid participants. Some centers have decided to decertify Medicaid beds because the costs of providing those services exceed the daily reimbursement rates. The costs associated with federal and state regulations in nursing centers is high, and centers risk poor inspections, and, consequently, the possibility of expensive, civil monetary penalties, (or mandated closure) if reimbursement is insufficient to address the standards.

Therefore, reducing reimbursement rates can also reduce the number of beds in the system, although it may shave costs from the state budget. The risk is that elders with compromised health states will not have other community services available and access to long-term care services will be limited. This can be especially traumatic for elders living in rural areas who cannot support a variety of long-term care services due to a relatively small population.

Limit Quantity of Beds Via Certificate-of-Need (CON)

Another mechanism to control the costs of long-term care is to limit the supply of nursing-facility beds. CONs grant permission to an organization to add beds, construct new buildings, or renovate existing structures, all of which have the potential to increase the costs, especially Medicaid. Therefore, almost one-half of the states currently have moratoriums on adding to the number of beds within a geographic location. However, critics of this cost-controlling mechanism cite problems in this approach to controlling costs. First, the reduction in beds does not address the issue that elders continue to require health assistance as they age. Elders do not have access to nursing and rehabilitation care in all communities. Second, the aged population is expected to increase significantly, and the moratorium on beds will probably only delay increasing costs as a result of the expanding population. Third, residential care–assisted-living centers are reimbursed by Medicaid in some states. It will be necessary to monitor growth to more completely understand the costs associated with long-term care.

Alternative-Funding Sources

Medicaid was not established to be the primary source of payment for long-term care services. The intent, in part, of the federal-to-state-funded program was to provide financial resources to lower-income elderly and to those who are medically indigent. Similarly, Medicare was established to assist with health care costs. As personal expenditures increased, supplemental coverage for Medicare became widely used and different types of Medigap insurance policies became available. Medigap options are available on an individual basis through publicly sponsored programs or from insurance companies. The majority of elders have secured some type of supplemental insurance for Medicare. According to Short and Vistnes (1992), three-fourths of Medicare beneficiaries have purchased some form of Medigap coverage. Almost 60 percent have only one policy. Morrisey (1993) found that the profile of a Medigap buyer consisted of a younger white elder with more education.

According to Jensen and Morrisey (1992), employer-sponsored plans are generally more extensive than those available from insurance sources. The majority of employer-sponsored enrollees retire from companies with more than 1,000 employees (Morrisey, Jensen, & Henderlite, 1990). Unfortunately, there are a large number of people who do not have access to such benefits by virtue of the employer's size or unawareness of such information.

In additional, there has been debate with regard to the security and continuation of employer-sponsored health benefits. The Employee Retirement Income Security Act of 1974 (ERISA) governs benefit plans but has less restrictions on retiree health benefits than on the pension benefits (Melbinger & Culver, 1992). Tax laws regulate that the employer can only reduce retiree health benefits if those benefits are offset by other benefits, higher wages, or both (Jensen, Morrisey, & Marcus, 1987). However, with the drastic rises in recent years of health care and associated costs, employers have attempted to find avenues to reduce such benefits in the long run. This may jeopardize the access to health care for some retirees and place a larger reliance on personal funds that might already be allocated to items such as medications and utilities. A greater financial dependence on public funding may also be noticed in the future as the result of altered employer-sponsored retiree programs.

The effects of supplemental coverage on the utilization of health care services are less known. According to Manning, Newhouse, Duan, Keeler, & Leibowitz (1987), supplemental coverage usually increases the use of Medicare's expenditures. Another study by Scheffer (1988) indicated that Medicare expenses rise by 0.2 percent for each 1 percent in private supplemental insurance. Additional research investigations would assist in the endeavor to accurately plan for public health policy.

Financial incentives for employers may be advantageous in the future from a policy development standpoint in an effort to reduce reliance on public subsidies. In additional, incentives for consumers who do not overuse health care resources may be useful. Health care educators also encourage increased awareness and instruction to reduce the excessive health care use or duplication of services.

CONCLUSION

The continuum of care for the elderly population in the United States is in a period of transition. The traditional health care system, in recent years, that primarily encompassed the physician, hospital, and nursing home is being broadened. This expansion is driven primarily by consumer demands and a public focus on the increasing costs associated with caring for the older population for extended periods. Policy decision-makers are challenged by the expected growth in the elderly population that is expected to increase from 39 million in 2010 to 69 million by 2030 (Preston, 1996). Constituents are expected to face some challenging decisions as the United States determines where to prioritize financial resources in relation to quality of care and safety issues.

REFERENCES

Alecxih, L. J., Lutzky, S., & Coria, J. (1996). *Estimated savings from the use of home and community-based alternatives to nursing facility care in three states* [brochure]. Washington, D.C.: American Association of Retired Persons.

Benjamin, A. E. (1993). An historical perspective on home care. *The Milbank Quarterly 71* (1), 129–166.

Boaz, R. F., & Muller, C. F. (1991). Why do some caregivers of the disabled and frail elderly quit? *Health Care Financing Review, 13* (2), 41–47.

Couch, K. A., Daly, M. C., & Wolf, D. A. (1999). Time? Money? Both? The allocation of resources to older parents. *Demography, 36* (2), 219–232.

Critchley, P., Jadad, A. R., Taniguchi, A., Stevens, R., Reyno, L., & Whelan, T. J. (1999). Are some palliative care delivery systems more effective and efficient than others? A systematic review of comparative studies. *Journal of Palliative Care, 15* (4), 40.

Doty, P., Liu, K., & Wiener, J. (1985). An overview of long-term care. *Health Care Finance Review, 32* (10), 6.

Doty P., & Miller, B. (1993). Care giving and productive aging. In S. Bass, F. Caro, & Y. Chen

(Eds.), *Achieving a productive aging society* (pp. 223–231). Westport, CT: Auborn House.

Evashwick, C. J. (1996). *The continuum of long-term care.* Albany, NY: Delmar Publishing Inc..

———. (1987). Definition of the continuum of care. In C. Evashwick & L. Weiss (Eds.), *Managing the continuum of care* (pp. 3–21), Rockville, MD: Aspen Publishers.

Jensen, G. A., & Morrisey, M. A. (1992). Employer sponsored post-retirement health benefits: Not your mother's Medigap plan. *Gerontologist, 32* (5), 695–703.

Jensen, G. A., Morrisey, M. A., & Marcus, J. W. (1987). Cost sharing and the changing pattern of employer-sponsored health benefits. *Milbank Memorial Fund Quarterly, 65,* 521–550.

Kasper, J. D., Steinbach, U., & Andrews, J. (1990, February). *Factors associated with ending caregiving among informal caregivers to the functionally and cognitively impaired elderly population.* Final report to the Office of the Assistant Secretary of Planning and Evaluation, Department of Health and Human Services, Grant #88 ASPE 209A.

Krothe, J. S. (1997). Giving voice to elderly people: Community-based long-term care. *Public Health Nursing, 14* (4), 217–226.

Levit, K., Cowen, C., Braden, B., Stiller, J., Sensenig, A., & Lazenby, H. (1996). Dataview: National health expenditures, 1995. *Health Care Financing Review, 18,* 175–214.

Liu K., & Manton, K. (1989). Effect of nursing home use on Medicaid eligibility. *The Gerontologist, 29,* 59–66.

Manning, W. G., Newhouse, J. P., Duan, D., Keeler, F., & Leibowitz, A. (1987). Health insurance and the demand for medical care: Evidence from a randomized experiment. *American Economics Review, 77,* 895–903.

McFall, S., & Miller, B. (1992). Caregiver burden and nursing home admission of frail elderly persons. *Journal of Gerontology, 47* (2), S73–S79.

Mechanic, D. (1999). The changing elderly population and future health care needs. *Journal of Urban Health, 76* (1), 24–38.

Melbinger, M. S., & Culver, M. W. (1992). The maintenance, funding and modification of retiree medical benefits. *Employee Benefits Journal, 17* (3), 2–10.

Miller, B. (1989). Adult children's perceptions of caregiver stress and satisfaction. *Journal of Applied Gerontology, 8* (3), 275–293.

Morrisey, M. A. (1993). Retiree health benefits. *Annual Reviews of Public Health, 14,* 271–292.

Morrisey, M. A., Jensen, G. A., & Henderlite, S. E. (1990). Employer sponsored health insurance for retired Americans. *Health Affairs, 9* (1), 57–73.

National Center for Health Statistics. (1995). Hyattsville, MD: Public Health Service, Department of Health and Human Services.

National Hospice and Palliative Care Organization. (2000). *Facts and figures on hospice in America.* Retrieved October 16, 2000, from the World Wide Web www.nhpco.org.

Pratt, J. R. (1999). *Long-term care managing across the continuum.* Gaithersburg, MD: Aspen Publications.

Preston, S. H. (1996, September 29). Children will pay. *New York Times Magazine,* 96–97.

Scheffer, R. M. (1988). An analysis of Medigap enrollment: Assessment of current status and policy initiatives. In M. V. Pauly & W. L. Kissick (Eds.), *Lessons from the first twenty-one years of Medicare* (pp. 321–337). Philadelphia: University of Pennsylvania Press.

Schneider, E. L., & Guralnik, J. M. (1990). The aging of America: Impact on health care costs. *Journal of American Medical Association, 263,* 2335–2340.

Scitovsky, A. A. (1994). The high cost of dying revisited. *Milbank Mem Fund Quarterly, 72,* 561–591.

Scott, S. J. (2000). Never underguesstimate the financial future of Medicare. *Healthcare Financial Management,* 28–29.

Short, P. F., & Vistnes, J. P. (1992). Multiple sources of Medicare supplementary insurance. *Inquiry, 29* (1), 33–43.

U.S. Department of Commerce, Bureau of the Census, Economics and Statistics Administration. (May 1995). *Statistical brief, sixty-five plus in the United States,* 2–5.

U.S. Department of Health and Human Services. (2001). The national elder abuse incidence study. Retrieved July 11, 2001, from the World Wide Web www.aoa.dhhs.gov/abuse/report.

U.S. General Accounting Office. (1994). *Medicaid and long-term care successful state efforts to expand home services while limiting costs.* Washington, D.C.: Author.

U.S. Vital and Health Statistics. (2000). Physician visits. Retrieved September 29, 2000, from the World Wide Web www.cdc.gov/nch-swww.

Weiner, J., Illston, L. H., & Hanley, R. (1994). *Sharing the burden: Strategies for public and private long-term care insurance.* Washington, D.C.:

The Brookings Institution.

Weiner J., & Stevenson, D. G. (1998). Long-term care for the elderly: Profiles for the thirteen states. Occasional paper number 12. Washington, D.C.: The Urban Institute.

Wood, E., & Sabatino, C. (1996). Medicaid estate recovery and the poor: Restitution of retribution? *Generations, 20,* 84–87.

Zalot, G. N. (1989). Planning a regional palliative care services network. *Journal of Palliative Care, 5,* 42–46.

INDEX

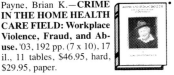
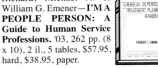

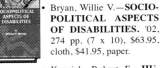